Fodor's EXPLORING

South Africa

FODOR'S TRAVEL PUBLICATIONS
NEW YORK • TORONTO • LONDON • SYDNEY • AUCKLAND

WWW.FODORS.COM

Important Note
Time inevitably brings changes, so always confirm prices, travel facts, and other perishable information when it matters. Although Fodor's cannot accept responsibility for errors, you can use this guide in the confidence that we have taken every care to ensure its accuracy.

Published in the United States by Fodor's Travel Publications.
Published in the United Kingdom by AA Publishing.

Fodor's is a registered trademark of Random House, Inc.

ISBN 0-679-00685-0
ISSN 1524-6809
Third Edition

Fodor's Exploring South Africa

Author: **Melissa Shales**
Joint Series Editor: **Josephine Perry**
Revisions Editor: **OutHouse Publishing Services**
Cartography: **The Automobile Association**
Cover Design: **Tigist Getachew, Fabrizio La Rocca**
Front Cover Silhouette: **Nik Wheeler**

Printed and bound in Italy by Printer Trento srl

How to use this book

ORGANIZATION

South Africa Is,
South Africa Was
Discusses aspects of life and culture in contemporary South Africa and explores significant periods in its history.

A–Z
Breaks down the country into regional chapters, and covers places to visit, including walks and drives. In addition, Focus On articles consider a variety of topics in greater detail.

Travel Facts
Contains the strictly practical information vital for a successful trip.

Accommodations and Restaurants
Lists recommended establishments throughout South Africa, giving a brief summary of their attractions.

Safari Guide
Rounds up South Africa's most common birds and animals and describes how to recognize them.

ADMISSION CHARGES
An indication of an establishment's admission charge is given by categorizing the standard adult rate as Expensive (over R25), Moderate (R10–R25), or Inexpensive (under R10).

ABOUT THE RATINGS
Most places described in this book have been given a rating:

► ► ►   **Do not miss**

► ►   **Highly recommended**

►   **Worth seeing**

MAP REFERENCES
To help you locate a particular place, every main entry has a map reference to the right of its name. This is made up of a number, followed by a letter, followed by another number, such as 54A2. The first number (54) refers to the page on which the map can be found. The letter (A) and the second number (2) pinpoint the square in which the place is located. The maps on the inside front cover and inside back cover are referred to as IFC and IBC, respectively.

Contents

5

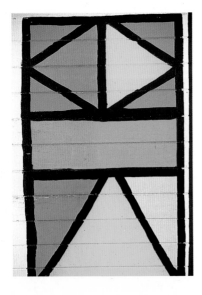

My South Africa

Melissa Shales has written guides to India, France, Spain, Kenya, Zimbabwe, and South Africa, as well as many newspaper and magazine articles. Her work currently includes broadcasts on radio and TV, photography, and editing travel guides.

As a child, living in sanctioned, war-torn Zimbabwe (then Rhodesia), I saw South Africa as a land of plenty and sophistication. Once a year, the family would pile into the car, hitch up a caravan and head south on a vacation and shopping bonanza, stocking up with a year's supply of everything from dried fruit to Marmite, theater, ballet, and beaches. I was vaguely aware that there were problems, but never saw beyond the gates of Eden. In 1977, when I returned to the U.K., my eyes were opened abruptly by the horror of the nightly news broadcasts from Sharpeville and Soweto. They seemed to come from a different universe.

I didn't return to South Africa until 1995, when Mandela was in power. Over three months and 10,000 miles, I traveled by boat, plane, car, bus, and helicopter. I stayed in guesthouses, game lodges, historic homes, business hotels, and tents. I watched whales tumbling in Hermanus Bay, sat breathlessly still as an overly playful elephant tickled the back of my neck, and ate crocodile and ostrich, washed down with ambrosial wines. I played tourist under indigo skies and a blazing sun, in sandstorms and heaven-splitting thunderstorms, gossiped to kindly Afrikaner landladies, saw Cape Dutch mansions, Zulu huts, and elegant Victorian town houses. Everywhere I went, I was overwhelmed by kindness and generous hospitality; it seemed an almost perfect holiday destination.

Yet I found myself still in a segregated, almost schizophrenic society. The black people I talked to were welcoming, but even they agreed that it was unsafe to wander the townships or villages. There is the inevitable, inexorable rise of reverse discrimination. I grew tired of hearing how much better things were in the old days, angry at the unnecessary violence and anarchy rampaging through the cities, and despairing at the vastness of the task facing the government. In the end, my emotions and impressions were still scrambled. I'd seen the beautiful but fragile mask and caught glimpses of a tortured soul. The real face of the new South Africa has yet to be revealed.
Melissa Shales

South Africa

Dismayed by horrific films of squatter camps and township violence, of police brutality and children lying dead in the dust, many tourists stayed away from South Africa until the 1994 elections. Now they are arriving in droves in search of the New South Africa; by 1999, visitor numbers had risen to nearly 6 million (1.8 million from outside Africa).

THE EUROPEAN IMAGE At first glance, South Africa looks like an affluent suburb superimposed on the African bush—exactly the impression its former rulers, middle-class urban whites, tried so hard to create. If it seems a little old-fashioned in some ways, it is also superficially comfortable, familiar, well tended, and nonthreatening.

South Africans used to pride themselves on clinging to the old virtues by which everyone went to church on Sunday, women stayed at home to look after their families, and the niceties of afternoon tea were strictly observed. It was a squeaky clean image based on the biggest conjuring trick in history—nearly 40 million people were made to vanish. The

*Above: sprawling Soweto shanties
Below: the Dutch Reformed church is the social center of most small Afrikaner communities (see page 16)*

harsh laws of apartheid kept Africa and poverty out of sight in huge settlements of corrugated iron and cardboard that appeared on no map or signpost. Black people were allowed into view only if they were smiling and subservient. Most towns were— and are—as European as possible, filled with chintz and antiques, trendy boutiques and coffee shops.

Tourism, designed largely for the South African home market, traditionally concentrated on the coast, whites-only game parks, and cool, green uplands where golf courses stretch amid the pine plantations.

THE NEW SOUTH AFRICA Of course, this image of rich white/poor black, good black/bad white is as simplistic and unrealistic as any other cultural stereotype. The truth is far more complicated. South Africa has a population of about 41 million, with 11 official languages and cultural

10

traditions from across Europe, Asia, and Africa. There has been violence and oppression, the nonwhites have been shamefully used, and the townships are a sin against humanity, but today luxury dwellings and run-down shanties stand side by side on the same street. Tribal chiefs and traditional healers live and work alongside pinstriped politicians and orthodox medical professionals. There are black millionaires and professors, white taxi drivers, waiters, and beggars, and even, astonishingly, black people who mourn the passing of apartheid.

The New South Africa is a mind-bending paradox: a sunny land of apparent peace and harmony with a boiling undercurrent of violent crime in its centers. Voices of doom mutter about chaos and corruption or talk of

Below: fruit stalls are affordable and accessible. Right: middle-class suburbia lives behind tight security

betrayal. A surprisingly large number of people embraced the Government of National Unity's call for "Masakhane" ("Working together for a better future"). Most people, of whatever color, are still waiting to see what will happen.

It may seem as if little has changed so far, but these are still early days

11

for the New South Africa. It will take time for people to be rehoused, for economic as well as political power to shift, for the richness of African culture to emerge from the townships and villages, for the history books and museums to be revised, and for a people used to being invisible to take possession of their true heritage. Meanwhile, tourists still live largely in a luxurious and almost totally white world, with only a quick tour of black South Africa. The difference is that they can now wander the lush gardens, swim in limpid pools, and quaff fine wines without the slightest twinge of conscience.

Most world maps, with their Eurocentric projection, give little idea of how large South Africa actually is. With an area of 474,276 square miles, it is five times the size of the U.K. and one-eighth the area of the U.S. Kruger National Park alone is as big as Texas, and the distance between Johannesburg and Cape Town is the same as from London to Rome. The country has 1,835 miles of coastline bordering the Atlantic and Indian oceans.

BOUNDARIES South Africa has land borders with Mozambique, Swaziland, Zimbabwe, Botswana, and Namibia, and totally surrounds the enclave of Lesotho. Since the 1994 elections, the country has been re-divided into nine provinces, along roughly tribal lines—Western Cape, Eastern Cape, Northern Cape, North-West Province, Gauteng, Northern Province, Mpumalanga, the Free State, and KwaZulu-Natal. At the time of writing, it still has three capitals, a legacy from the Second Anglo-Boer War. The legislature is in Cape Town (the former British capital); the administration is in Pretoria (capital of the old Transvaal); and the judiciary is in Bloemfontein (capital of the Orange Free State). Pretoria is currently the favorite to become sole capital should it be decided to consolidate them into one.

GEOGRAPHY The terrain ranges in altitude from sea level to South Africa's highest peak, Injasuti (11,178 feet), in the Drakensberg, near the Lesotho border, and covers ecosystems from tropical forest to desert dunes. Almost every crop known to humanity can find a natural home somewhere in the country.

The Western Cape, cut off from the hinterland by the mountains of the Cederberg, Hex River, and Swartberg, has a distinct Mediterranean climate with cool, gray, wet, and windy winters and warmer, sunny summers. It is ideal for wine and deciduous fruits. The more northerly KwaZulu-Natal coast, also cut off by the vast wall of the Drakensberg, is subtropical, hot, and humid, clipped by the southwest monsoon. Here, the main crops are tropical fruits, such as bananas (the country's most profitable product), pineapples, and sugarcane.

Beyond the mountains is the Karoo, a dramatic semidesert capable of supporting only sheep, ostriches and, increasingly, antelope, while in the west blow the barren red sands of the Kalahari. In the center, the land climbs on to the high, flat central plateau, to the cattle and corn prairies of the Free State and, most importantly, the gold and diamond deposits of Kimberley and the Witwatersrand (see pages 137 and 160–161).

Finally, in the northeast, the highveld drops off a dramatic escarpment in a flurry of mountains where tea and avocados, cherries and bananas, eucalyptus and pine all flourish cheek by jowl. Below, the lowveld provides a hot, dry habitat for baobabs and acacias, elephant and lion.

WATER South Africa is a land of plenty, rich in agriculture, industry, and minerals, but there are only two

❏ Cape Town is at about the same latitude as Sydney in Australia and Rio de Janeiro in Brazil. If folded into the northern hemisphere, it would be level with Cyprus or Los Angeles, while the Kalahari Desert would fit neatly into the Sahara. ❏

From the roads across the Free State to the Kalahari and the fruit farms of the Cape, distances are vast and the horizons endless

major rivers, the Vaal and the Orange. The whole subcontinent is regularly gripped by drought, the population is rising steadily, and with the change in government came long-overdue schemes for creating proper water supplies, plumbing, and drains in all the black towns and villages. The demands on the water supply continue to increase sharply and, in spite of careful water management and the occasional season of magnificent rains, the water table is dropping below the level of the bore-holes, and the desert is expanding. In some areas, people have already been forced off the land, while the government is trying to implement massive projects to bring water down from the mountains of Lesotho and even from as far north as the Zambezi (despite the fact that Zimbabwe has its own serious water problems to contend with).

South Africa is wealthy, ranking at 29 among the world's top trading nations and one of its largest producers of many minerals, notably gold. It accounts on its own for 27 percent of the GNP of the African continent, but it also has Third-World slums, horrendous unemployment, homelessness, and increasing crime levels. Vast problems must be overcome if the country's two societies are ever to merge without the entire economic structure collapsing.

14

SANCTIONS During the last years of apartheid, sanctions were enforced officially by the U.N. However, South Africa was situated across the Cape sea route and was a major supplier of vital minerals such as uranium and chrome. Most developed countries continued to trade under the counter, while neighboring black countries were totally reliant on South Africa's ports for survival. The economy was battered but it survived and, turning inward, became broadbased and self-sufficient.

THE NEW WORLD Since the 1994 elections, when South Africa was welcomed back into the global fold, the economy has been pulled in many conflicting directions. Exports have risen rapidly; the wine industry has doubled production; and there are now five times as many foreign tourists, with numbers still rising. The government policy of affirmative

❏ South Africa is the world's leading supplier of gold (19.9 percent), aluminosilicates (61.1 percent), chromium (45.6 percent), platinum (47.1 percent), vermiculite (43.9 percent), and vanadium (56.9 percent). It ranks second for titanium and zirconium; third for fluorspar and manganese; fourth for antimony; and fifth for diamonds and coal. It also has significant iron, uranium, lead, silver, zinc, nickel, and copper deposits. ❏

action is providing fast track promotion for black managerial candidates. Multinational companies are lining up and the government welcomes anyone prepared to invest.

On the downside, new imports have damaged the balance of trade, while union demands for improvements for black wages to meet those of white workers, for a shorter working week, better conditions and housing, has exacted a heavy toll on profits; the gold price dropped and the worldwide recession of the late 1990s hit hard. Nervous white workers left in droves, creating a brain drain, before there were enough well-qualified and experienced black workers to take their place. Strikes, lockouts, and other industrial actions crippled some industries, while wage demands pushed prices sharply upward.

The move from the land to the cities has been less a drift than a deluge; the black market or "informal sector" runs most small businesses in the townships; and, as a final complication, an estimated 4 million illegal immigrants from elsewhere in Africa have flooded the job market.

REDEVELOPMENT The main economic focus of the government is the implementation of the Reconstruction and Development Programme (RDP), a nationwide scheme to provide a proper infrastructure, including housing, water, drainage, electricity, schools, and clinics for all black townships and villages. Large amounts of money are needed, with global aid being poured into the void alongside

every available scrap of tax revenue. The fledgling welfare system is stretched beyond its limits; inessentials and luxuries are being stripped away. Disgruntled whites, who still form the vast majority of taxpayers, seem unable to understand why they are paying more and receiving less and, with the honeymoon over, the black community is waiting impatiently for its slice of the cake.

So far, the government has steered a skillful route along this narrow, potentially treacherous divide, preaching a gospel of self-help, patience and understanding, sustainable and environmentally friendly development, the expansion of legal business and equal opportunities, and capital investment for the common good. If they can convince their electorate and the international business community to back them with hard cash, South Africa has the potential to become an economic Utopia. As of now, the government debt stands at over 55 percent of the GDP and unemployment is about 22 percent, but the economy is on the mend and the immediate prospects look exciting.

Top: downtown Johannesburg
Below: the Rand Club, still a focus for Gauteng's financiers

*"Let us be channels of love, of peace, of recon-
ciliation. Let us declare that we have been
made for togetherness, we have been made for
family, that, yes, now we are free, all of us,
black and white together, we, the Rainbow
People of God!" Archbishop Desmond Tutu.*

The New South Africa has adopted
Archbishop Desmond Tutu's catchy
phrase as the slogan of its quest for
racial harmony. It is singularly apt,
given the country's complicated
population mix. Of its estimated
41 million people, 4.4 million are
white, 3.6 million of mixed race,
1 million Indian, 31.5 million black.

The black population is subdivided
into nine main tribal groupings based
on language. Zulu (23 percent of the
population) and Xhosa (18 percent) are
the largest groups. Ndebele, Northern
Sotho, Southern Sotho, Swati, Tsonga,
Tswana, and Venda are all first languages for more than 1 million people,
and each is further divided into local
tribal groups. Minorities include the
all-but-extinct San (Bushmen) and
Khoikhoi (Hottentots), the aboriginal
inhabitants of the country, and the
Cape Malays, whose ancestors came as
slaves from the Dutch East Indies in
the 18th century.

The "coloreds" are mixed-race people, the result of early black-white or
Khoi-San-Malay contact, although
since the 19th century they have
largely married among themselves,
creating a distinct cultural group.The
Indians, brought in to work the Natal

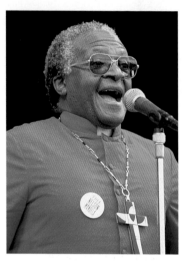

*Desmond Tutu, archbishop of Cape
Town during the years of struggle*

cane fields and lumped together ethni-
cally under apartheid, came mainly
from the south, but most of India's 65
main "tribes" are represented.

Most whites are Afrikaner (of Dutch
extraction) or English. However, the
17th century saw significant
immigration of Germans and French
Huguenots fleeing religious persecution. Later additions include Greeks,
Italians, and Portuguese, as well as
immigrants from every other nation
in Africa and Europe. Finally, there is
a substantial Jewish community.

LANGUAGE Afrikaans is the first
language of around 15 percent of the
population, including many of the
coloreds, and English of 9 percent.
These and the nine main black

*South Africa's "colored" community has
its own distinctive and vibrant culture*

□ The Zulu, Xhosa, and Ndebele all belong to a related racial group, the Nguni. Though similar in language and culture, they have been responsible for some of South Africa's most persistent conflicts: 19th-century frontier wars between the Zulus and Xhosa; traditional conflicts between the Xhosa and their off-shoot tribe, the Mfengu; the Zulus' attempted slaughter of the renegade Ndebele in the early 19th century; and the vicious township wars of the late 20th century between the largely Xhosa-run ANC and the mainly Zulu Inkatha Freedom Party (IFP). □

survived even the darkest years of apartheid. The nearest thing to a state church has been the sternly Protestant Dutch Reformed Church, the most influential of the myriad Christian churches.

Other important Christian denominations include the Church of England, the Roman Catholics, the Methodists, and the thriving Church of Zion. There are significant numbers of Hindus, Muslims, and Jewish people, while many people still follow traditional African religions—often in tandem with Christianity.

Whatever their faith, South Africans are a fairly religious people, many of them deeply shocked by so-called Western liberalism and the upsurge in pornography since censorship was abolished. Most are also conservative (with a small "c") when it comes to women's rights in the home or workplace. Though more women work today, few so far have risen higher than junior management.

languages are now all official languages of the country. English is used as the main language of government and business, and each province uses English, Afrikaans, and whichever African language predominates. Most people speak fluent English and Afrikaans as well as their home tongue. The television news is presented in different languages on different evenings, and many programs are multilingual.

THE CONSERVATIVE MAJORITY
South Africa has always been a secular state that allowed freedom of religion—a liberal policy that

Right: Ndebele woman
Top: traditional bead work

From the time in 1652 when Jan van Riebeeck laid out his kitchen garden in the settlement that was to become Cape Town, to the emergence of Johannesburg's dramatic skyline from the squalor of a mining camp, South Africa's towns and cities have been carefully planned.

GRACIOUS LIVING Most towns were built on a grid layout, with Dutch-style squares and English-style parks to give a feeling of space, and broad streets lined with ornamental trees. Official buildings became ever larger and grander, culminating in Sir Herbert Baker's (see page 166) superb Union Buildings in Pretoria. Until the early 20th century, the towns were relatively multiracial, with areas like Cape Town's District Six and Johannesburg's Sophiatown as vibrant cultural melting pots. They produced innovative art, music, and dance and created pockets of bohemian life beneath the stern noses of the Dutch Reformed pastors.

From the turn of the 20th century onward, South Africa experienced an explosion of immigration from Europe. While suburbs of mock-Tudor houses cocooned in cool green

Above: jacarandas shade many of Pretoria's streets. Below: some of Soweto's better housing

gardens sprouted across the hills, the urban centers became crowded. The whites were increasingly anxious to enjoy their idyll untroubled by signs of poverty or race. A series of forced "slum clearances" began as distraught nonwhites were dumped far out of town. As soon as they were gone, their properties were bulldozed and the land redeveloped.

TOWNSHIPS Satellite townships grew up rapidly around every city. Few were marked on the maps or street signs, even though many were soon larger than their white neighbors. Some had family dwellings, serried rows of tiny tin-roofed houses. Others consisted of squalid, barrack-style hostel accommodations for male workers living three to a room and sharing a basic kitchen and bathroom among 12. Wives and families remained in the villages, seeing their men only once or twice a year. A very few of the larger townships like Soweto—already the size of a

major city—developed small middle-class areas with good houses and suitable facilities. On the whole, however, there were few real stores, the only food available sold from tiny market stalls. Clinics and schools were scarce and many of the latter were boycotted by children refusing to learn in Afrikaans. A boycott of the white alcohol trade led to the growth of shebeens, illegal drinking haunts. By the 1980s, shanty towns began to grow up around the official townships, vast seas of plastic, corrugated iron, and cardboard. With the repeal of the Pass Laws in 1986, the situation became even worse as families flocked to the city to join their men, where they lived three families to a room or built new shanties.

DEVELOPMENT The government now has to sort out the mess. Most of the townships have been incorporated within the municipal boundaries of the white towns and money is being poured into development. The first phase alone of the Reconstruction and Development Program aims to build 1 million new houses by 2003. In some areas, the authorities are simply building streets, drains, and lavatories. Families are allocated a plot with a lavatory and it is up to them to build their house around it. As black stall-holders take their wares to the streets of the white cities, specially built

❏ Official figures show that 60 percent of the population live in towns. Today, however, the figure is probably closer to 80 percent as women and children leave the villages to join their menfolk. ❏

Market stalls in Peddie—a lively and essentially African, small town

markets offer them new opportunities. Outside Johannesburg, few black families have moved into the white suburbs.

Levels of violent crime have finally leveled out, but are still high and tourists should be cautious in cities, especially Johannesburg. White people visiting any black township are strongly recommended to take a black friend or guide to escort them.

Most of South Africa's large population is clustered in a few key cities. Much of the rest of the country seems almost empty. Large tracts of the Kalahari are virtually uninhabitable, with settlements spread sparsely along the few watercourses, while farms in the Free State and Karoo stretch over vast areas.

20

THE REMOTE LIFE The farmers are almost all white, many the descendants of trekboers who set out into the unknown in order to shake off the constraints of civilization. Today they pride themselves on being rugged individualists, living self-contained lives, mixing only with their families and a small handful of neighbors within driving distance. Water comes from boreholes run by windmills; many have their own electricity generators, although the national electricity grid is spreading. The arrival of TV satellite dishes, video recorders, and fax machines has given them their first access to daily news and entertainment. All shopping is done by mail or on infrequent sorties into the nearest market town. Even these can be remote. Upington in the Northern Cape is 275 miles from its nearest city, Kimberley. Those who can afford it run small planes and plan their rare shopping trips to the city like a military campaign.

FROM SHEEP TO ANTELOPE The huge farms of the Free State and Karoo run half-wild cattle across virgin bush, or grow vast prairies of wheat and corn. In the Karoo, ostrich farming is making a triumphant return and many farmers are restocking the land with game shot out by their ancestors. Some are breeding antelope for the table, but more deal in live animals to sell to other farmers; others hope to set up lucrative private game reserves. Many are creating hunting concessions for the foreign market.

THE GOOD LIFE Near the coast, the landscape changes. In KwaZulu-Natal, there are still huge plantations of pineapple,

Top: picking onions in Ceres
Above left: Venda village
Left: farming in the Transkei

sugarcane, and bananas, but most are within a few hours' drive of Durban and the resort towns on the coast. People here have far more contact with the outside world, while in the Western Cape, farmers are wealthy. The area specializes in intensive farming of high-yield fruit crops and, above all, wine. The valleys are patterned by small, neatly combed vineyards, and life is far more sociable, with everyone within easy reach. Because of the international nature of the wine trade, the strong French Huguenot influence, and the proximity of Cape Town, the winelands are a remarkably sophisticated area with some of the finest hotels and restaurants in the country. They also have some of the finest architecture—the white Cape Dutch houses built by the early settlers.

BLACK LIFE Outside those areas once designated as tribal homelands, there is virtually no independent black rural life. All nonwhites were removed from any usable land. Some remained on the white farms, each of which has a thriving village housing the farm workers and their

Grapes are one of South Africa's most important crops

families. The work is hard and the pay poor, but in other ways life is not all bad. Apartheid was always prepared to be paternal to those who toed the line and asked for little. Workers' houses are very basic, too small but hygienic; rudimentary medical care and schooling are provided; the pay often includes a ration of basic foodstuffs; and the farmer's wife usually runs a general store selling everything from canned foods to medicines, pens to beer. Some even provide staff and retirees with small plots to grow produce for themselves.

The traditional villages have all but disintegrated. The men have long worked away from home while the women brought up the children and took what work they could find locally. Some of the villages have grown into towns in all but name; others have been left to the old while the youngsters flock to the city. Hardly anywhere do you see the tiny patches and tethered goats of traditional rural life in Africa.

South Africa's constitution is one of the most liberal ever written, with a bill of rights guaranteeing equality for men and women of all races, creeds, and color, with freedom of speech and expression.

South Africa is now a republic within the Commonwealth, with two houses of parliament, the National Assembly, and a National Council of Provinces. Until 1996, under a temporary power-sharing constitution, which allowed any party with over 5 percent of the vote to elect a

Thabo Mbeki, who succeeded to the presidency after Nelson Mandela stepped down in 1999

vice president, Vice Presidents Thabo Mbeki from the ANC (African National Congress) and former President F. W. de Klerk from the National Party acted as deputies to Nelson Mandela as president.

In 1996, shortly before the new permanent constitution came into effect, de Klerk resigned and the National Party withdrew from the Government of National Unity to become the main parliamentary opposition. In 1999, Nelson Mandela stepped down as president amidst global celebrations of his achievement and Thabo Mbeki became executive president, with Jacob Zuma as vice president.

The nine provinces all have a high degree of regional autonomy. Only in KwaZulu-Natal is the IFP (Inkatha Freedom Party), led by Chief Mangosuthu Buthelezi, still campaigning for further autonomy as a Zulu kingdom. Thankfully, within recent years, sufficient headway has been made to stamp out the worst of the violence between the ANC and Inkatha that characterized much of the 1980s and 1990s, with battles now fought in parliament and court instead of the township streets. The small but persistent demand for an all-white Afrikaaner Volkstaat, led by Vryheidsfront (Freedom Front), the largely discredited AWB, and several other small ultra-right wing parties, can be ignored.

Today, the main problems facing the government are the all too familiar global ones of housing, health, education, and crime as the government battles to maintain white confidence and economic stability against the urgent needs of the rural villages, townships, and squatter camps.

22

South Africa Was

One of the great debates of all time hovers over a single question: what are the origins of humankind? Charles Darwin was convinced that Africa held the clue, though his contemporaries ridiculed that idea. Man, they thought, was too grand for the dark continent.

It seems that Darwin may have been right after all. With each new find, it becomes more certain that Africa was the cradle of mankind. Research in the 20th century seems to have established that the emergence of the forerunner of modern man from ape-like prehuman forms took place in East Africa about 6 million years ago. More recent attention has been focused on the Leakey family's discoveries in the Rift Valley, at such sites as Olduvai Gorge and Koobi Fora, but some of the earliest discoveries that helped create the timetable of evolution were made in South Africa.

THE BIRTH OF HUMANITY The earliest of the protohumans were the australopithecines (literally "southern apes"). The first discovery came in 1924 when a fossilized skull of an infant *Australopithecus africanus* (the "Taung baby") was found at Taung in the Northern Cape by a workman digging in a limestone quarry. Its canine teeth, like those of man, were small, and from the shape of the skull its brain showed humanoid features. The discovery was of immense importance and led to the hunt for an adult specimen. In 1936, Dr. Robert Broom found the first adult cranium in the Sterkfontein Caves, near Johannesburg. Exposed after an internment of 2.5 million years, the species was triumphantly hailed as the "missing link" between ape and man. In 1945 came definitive proof that the species walked on two legs.

Australopithecus africanus lived between 1 and 3 million years ago.

Top: reconstruction of Australopithecus africanus. *Right: fossil bones give clues to early man*

Further discoveries have since identified several other species (or possibly subspecies) in Africa: *Australopithecus robustus*, and the even earlier *Australopithecus boisei* and *Australopithecus afarensis*, thought to date back around 5.5 million years.

From about 2 million years ago, a new species emerges. *Homo habilis* ("handy man") walked upright with an awkward gait and dramatically outsplayed feet, and probably lived partially in trees. He had a brain with less than half the capacity of that of a modern human, but his hands were flexible and capable of fashioning crude stone tools for hunting.

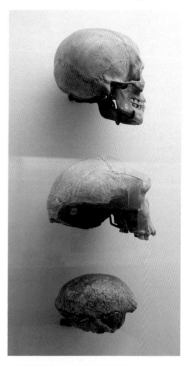

An artist's impression of
Australopithecus africanus

UPRIGHT MAN *Homo erectus*, the first of the protohumans to be fully adapted to standing and walking upright, with leg bones barely distinguishable from those of modern man, lived 1.5 million to 250,000 years ago. His brain was smaller than ours, but it is thought that he could speak, and his hands were free to develop the most crucial of human skills: the ability to make and to use tools. He was also the first to kindle a fire, and the first to have wandered beyond the African continent—*Homo erectus* bones have been found in China and Java. Some of the earliest remains were excavated in 1948 at Swartkrans, near Krugersdorp.

HOMO SAPIENS Modern man is still a babe in arms in this time frame.

The earliest *Homo sapiens* and Neanderthal subspecies are believed to have emerged about 100,000 years ago. By about 40,000 BC, *Homo sapiens sapiens* (modern man) was dominant and spreading fast, with a varied array of cultures. Southern Africa was inhabited by the San (Bushmen) whose lives as nomadic hunters remained unvaried until the arrival of black tribes from the north and white tribes from the sea.

The story has not ended, however. Each new find adds another piece to the puzzle. In 1995, some foot bones from Sterkfontein, lying forgotten in a museum, were reexamined. They belong to an australopithecine nicknamed "Littlefoot," have a slightly divergent big toe and weight-bearing arch, are extraordinarily early (dating from 3.3 million years ago, and have overturned all existing theories on how man came to walk upright.

The history of the Cape of Good Hope is inextricably linked with the search for and defense of a sea route to India. It is a history of rivalry between the Portuguese, the Dutch, the English and, to a lesser degree, the French.

26

PORTUGUESE EXPLORERS The earliest recorded voyage around the Cape was made in 1488 by the Portuguese navigator Bartolomeu Dias. Dias failed to discover the long-searched-for route to India, but a decade later one of his countrymen, Vasco da Gama, succeeded. Da Gama triumphantly rounded the Cape in 1488, then went on to reach the Indian subcontinent before returning to Europe in 1499. At last the route to the Indies had been found, and the trade potential was enormous. The Portuguese moved quickly to consolidate and protect the route, claiming the right to overlordship of the Indian Ocean and domination of its trade.

Early expeditions all called into southern Africa as they passed, to collect water or barter with the Khoikhoi for fresh meat, but no efforts were made to set up a permanent outpost. Table Bay itself was not explored until 1503, when Admiral Antonio de Saldanha climbed Table Mountain and visited Robben Island. Later that century, the Portuguese lost their dominant trading position to the Netherlands and England, who both set about finding routes to the East.

DUTCH SETTLEMENT In 1580, Sir Francis Drake rounded the Cape, and by 1591 the first English expedition bound for the Indies had left Plymouth. By 1594 the Dutch, too, were on their way. Early in the 17th century, national efforts were controlled by the British East India Company and the Dutch East India Company respectively. It was the Netherlands, with its larger merchant fleet, that dominated trade. The Dutch East India Company established a victualing station at the Cape, and in 1652 Jan van Riebeeck was dispatched to run it. His job was to provide fresh water, vegetables, and meat for passing Company mariners—who suffered all kinds of deprivation on the long voyage from Europe—as well as repair their vessels.

A STRATEGIC BASE Dutch rule came to an end with the first British invasion in 1795 as part of the military strategy of the Napoleonic

Top: Table Mountain
Left: a 16th-century view of Africa

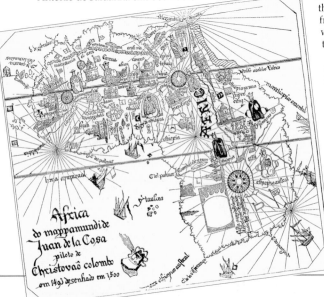

Wars. The colony was handed back in 1803, only to be invaded in 1806 when Napoleon again became a danger. This time, the Congress of Vienna (1815) confirmed the British occupation and the Cape colony was ceded to the British Crown. The aim was strategic: by then, the Cape had become a naval base on the sea route to India and the Far East.

The Cape became an important focus of

merchant shipping that might otherwise have used the Suez Canal was diverted south. After the war, the route was no longer profitable and trade dwindled until the fresh outbreak of war in 1939, when history repeated itself.

DECLINE AND RECOVERY The Egypt–Israeli war of 1967, which closed the Suez Canal, again focused attention on the Cape. In the 1980s, trade sanctions were imposed on South Africa and traffic tailed off until the Cape's most frequent visitors were bulky supertankers simply too big to pass through the Suez Canal. Regular passenger transportation declined; the last mail-ship voyage took place in October 1977. Today, with South Africa back at the helm of the continent's economy, freighters and cruise ships are lining up to get into its ports, and the future looks hopeful.

27

Left: Jan van Riebeeck
Below: Cape Town in the 17th century

communication—a vital link between the motherland and far-flung territories. The Royal Navy set up its local headquarters in Simon's Town, and many thousands of eager white immigrants landed here, ready to make their fortunes in the diamond and gold fields. The 1890s was a decade of almost unparalleled growth as South Africa's economy boomed. During World War I the route became strategically important, as

The arrival of the first Dutch settlers in the Cape in the 1650s was to have far-reaching consequences, not only for the locals, but for the very survival of stable African societies throughout the entire subcontinent.

EARLY LINKS The Khoikhoi (called Hottentots by the early Dutch colonists) were mainly gentle pastoralists who were happy to barter sheep and cattle for iron and other metals. It was a trade that became vitally important to the survival of European mariners on their months-long voyage to the East.

For centuries, the sailors came, looked, traded, and went away again. A few stayed awhile on dry land. The Portuguese, who pioneered the route to India, were sometimes shipwrecked, having to stay on the shores of Table Bay until rescued by the next passing fleet. In 1615, the British left a small party of convicts, but they retreated to Robben Island until rescued. Then, in 1647, the crew of a wrecked Dutch East Indiaman, the *Haerlem*, built a fort during their year-long stay.

FOUNDING OF THE CAPE COLONY
It was only in 1652, when the Dutch East India Company established the

❏ In 1602, the Dutch East India Company received a charter to conduct all Dutch trade between the Cape of Good Hope and the Strait of Magellan. With its head-quarters in Batavia (Jakarta), it acted more like a nation than a trading company, conquering and ruling huge territories and fighting off all competition. The profits were enormous in the 17th century, but trailed off over the next hundred years until, by 1799, with corrupt officials, it was nearly bankrupt. The company was dissolved and its possessions and debts were taken over by the Dutch state. ❏

Cape refreshment station for the scurvy-ridden crews of passing ships (see page 26), that a settled white community came into existence, with a set policy and continuity of command. The local Khoikhoi welcomed the Dutch settlers at first, conducting trade as usual. Jan van Riebeeck, the first commander of the new Cape Colony, successfully gained their trust, all the while claiming the Cape Peninsula and adjacent land for the VOC (Verenigde Oost-Indische Compagnie—Dutch East India Company, see box below). Contact with the Khoikhoi was at first restricted by the Company. As a result, a small number of Company employees—particularly those free burghers the Company had released from its service, and to whom it had granted land—were unable to find local labor, and imported slaves from the East Indies.

By the 1680s, the settlers were moving out from the embryonic Cape Town and were successfully raising their own cattle. The Khoikhoi lost not only their barter livelihood, but also, gradually, their grazing land and water rights as the Europeans annexed the lush, well-watered valleys. The Khoikhoi society began to disintegrate. In 1713, smallpox decimated the people of the south-western Cape, and by the 1740s the remaining few were working as laborers for the colonists, many of them in conditions of dreadful servitude.

EXPANSION In the early years settler numbers increased slowly. The majority were Dutch, members of the Dutch Reformed Church, but their numbers were augmented by Germans and French Huguenots escaping from persecution in their homelands. Many of these settlers

28

An ox wagon, a major form of transport, approaching a Boer farm

brought to Africa a tradition of dissent and a legacy of resentment against Europe.

As the settlement expanded, borders were extended: when the burghers sought to beat the Company's often draconian rules by quitting areas under their control, the authorities simply extended their influence into the newly formed districts.

By the 1770s many settlers had drifted well beyond the confines of van Riebeeck's original territory, heading northward as far as the Orange River and eastward toward the Great Fish River. The more determined were farmers driven by a ruthless quest for land, larger herds, and, above all, total independence. They drew European control far into the hinterland, eventually coming into conflict with more warlike indigenous people—such as the Xhosa on the Eastern Frontier—who found themselves having to defend their territory against the gun.

Governor Willem van der Stel at his farm, Vergelegen

Mfecane (*literally "crushing"*) *is a word used by the Zulus to describe the ripple effect of early 19th-century Zulu expansion and empire-building in what is now KwaZulu-Natal. The keys to these events were a need for land and the vengeful bloodlust of Shaka.*

Among the often warlike Nguni societies of the 18th century (see page 17), chiefdoms expanded, spilling over into ever more virgin territory. Consequently, by the beginning of the 19th century there was a land shortage, aggravated by a devastating drought, overgrazing, serious soil erosion, and the ever closer presence of the white Voortrekkers (see pages 32–33). A scramble for power and influence ensued, forcing many smaller chiefdoms into defensive alliances against land-hungry foes. This led to larger groupings, such as the southern Mthethwa. Their ruler (from about 1809) was Dingiswayo, normally considered to be the first of the great Zulu kings. Another such group included the northern Ngwane who, under Sobhuza, were to flee inland, defeating smaller Sotho and Nguni clans they met on the way and eventually amalgamating them into what became the Swazi nation.

SHAKA In 1815, Dingiswayo was murdered by a rival clan, the Ndwandwe. Shaka emerged as the new king. Born in 1787, the son of a minor Zulu chief, he grew up in Dingiswayo's court and became a military commander. One of his first acts was to change the name of the ruling tribe and all the conquered clans to that of his clan, the Zulus. Shaka was a military genius and totally ruthless. From the moment he took power, he set about expanding his army, turning it into one of the deadliest fighting forces in Africa. He invented the hugely effective, short stabbing *assegai* to replace the traditional javelin-style throwing spear, allowing the army to reuse their weapons. He also developed brutally efficient new tactics, such as the terrifying *impi* with the warriors attacking in a curved "bull-and-horns" formation. In this, the main army advanced on the enemy from the front, while units of the fastest runners created diversions down the opposition's flanks, and troops from the rear moved around outside the horns to close the circle. By the end of his reign, Shaka had subjugated most of the smaller, weaker clans and controlled a vast area of land, left vacant by the flight of those who refused to submit to his authority. Murdered in 1828 by his half

British Lieutenant Farewell negotiates with Shaka

❏ A second word, *Difaqane*, also describes this period of black South African history. A Sotho word, it is used for the intertribal wars west of the Drakensberg that followed invasions of peoples fleeing the Mfecane wars farther east. Of all the conquered and dispossessed tribes, the Sotho were the most affected, and their word has connotations of defeat and loss. ❏

brothers, Dingane and Mhlangane, he remains one of the greatest heroes of the Zulu nation.

THE BATTLE FOR LAND It was the ripple effect caused by the refugees from Zulu might that created such widespread upheaval. As terrified peoples moved north, they collided and clashed with other inhabitants who had settled in a wide arc that spread from what is now Swaziland to the highveld and Lesotho. In turn, the new arrivals displaced the former settlers as they secured land on which they could graze their cattle and grow their crops.

The events of this period gave rise to an enduring myth: that the land into which the Voortrekkers and other early pioneers stepped in the 19th century was empty country, depopulated by the Mfecane. The reality was quite different. In fact, this was a land where people had gathered in places of safety and were desperately endeavoring to reestablish order in their shattered societies. The presence of the settlers—with their guns, wagons, and horses—only exacerbated an already unpleasant situation, eventually leading to appalling violence and some of the most tragic episodes in South Africa's history, among them the horrifying Battle of Blood River (see page 204).

Boers charge Dingane's army

31

The Great Trek signaled the determination of Dutch-speaking farmers (Boers) to find a "Promised Land" where they would be beyond the limits of British control. This led briefly to the establishment of several independent Boer republics. The Great Trek is a landmark in the history of South Africa, heralding an era of expansionism, bloodshed, and land seizure.

INTO THE INTERIOR The Trek began in 1835, when the first of many groups of bitter Voortrekkers left Grahamstown, Uitenhage, and Graaff-Reinet and headed for the largely unknown interior. The Eastern Cape was a particularly tense region, being the frontier between Xhosa territory and the Cape Colony and a focus for refugees who had fled the rise of the Zulu state. The Boers were unhappy about having to fight the Xhosa for land or submit to British rule. They felt that the colonial government had failed to provide them with sufficient protection against the Xhosa, while the abolition of slavery in 1834 had robbed them of valued possessions. That year,

reconnaissance expeditions claimed that Natal was fertile and largely uninhabited. In fact, the Africans had only moved away temporarily in the wake of the Mfecane and were soon to return, only to find themselves ousted by Boer intruders (see page 31).

During the following decade, thousands more Boers migrated, many of them the so-called "trekboers," semi-nomadic pastoral farmers; others were cattle ranchers or sheep farmers. Each group of Voortrekkers had its own leader but they all followed much the same route through "Transorangia" (the highveld), only splitting when some went into Natal while others continued north.

VOORTREKKER LIFE A family might have more than one wagon carrying all its worldly goods. Drawn by oxen, the wagons could hold a surprising amount—household effects, furniture, bedding, clothes, food, agricultural implements, weapons and shot, even fruit trees. They were narrow and designed to put as little weight as possible onto the oxen. In the evenings the wagons were drawn into a protective circle (*laager*), the gaps and space under the wheels filled with thorn branches. The *laager* became an instant fort for the Voortrekkers, who would hide behind the wagons and shoot at any attackers. The cattle and other livestock were herded into a *kraal* (corral) in the center. People would gather around a fire to sing, pray, chat—and even dance.

Top: tapestry homage to the Voortrekkers, Pretoria. Left: statue of Piet Retief, Pietermaritzburg

THE BOER REPUBLICS The varied terrain the Voortrekkers covered, at a rate of about 6 miles a day, was treacherous. Not only was the topography often difficult, but they ran the risk of encounters with wild animals, the tsetse fly, and the malarial mosquito. The courage they displayed is still a key feature of Afrikaner folklore. They also ran into strong local resistance. Small parties of trekboers, missionaries, and adventurers had preceded them, so the Africans were not completely unused to the white man, but this was the largest group they had ever seen. In 1838, a party led by Piet Retief was massacred by Dingane.

Desire for revenge led to the Battle of Blood River (see page 204) and eventually to Dingane's death and the creation of the Boer Republic of Natalia (1838), which was promptly annexed by Britain. The Boers then trekked north, and in 1860 formed the South African Republic (ZAR) in Transvaal. Another party proclaimed the Orange Free State (1854) beyond the Vaal and Orange rivers. Others headed for Delagoa Bay and were annihilated by the Tsonga, while a party led by Louis Trichardt ended up in Lourenço Marques, where most died of tropical diseases.

Voortrekkers crossing the Transvaal

The British ruled this corner of Africa for most of the 19th century. Their initial occupation of the Cape in 1795 had little impact, and it was only from 1814 onward, eight years after they had wrested the Cape Colony from the Dutch for the second time, that they started to develop the Cape's potential for settlement and trade. This African subcontinent, Britain finally realized, would be an excellent source of labor and raw materials and a market for manufactured goods.

34

British rule in the 19th century was characterized by certain key events now regarded as milestones in South Africa's history. It started with the mass immigration in 1820 of settlers from Britain. This resulted in exhausting conflict with the Xhosa on the eastern frontier, and the gradual settling by whites of what is now called KwaZulu-Natal following the Great Trek. In 1843, Natal was annexed by Britain as a second colony. Subsequent bloody clashes between Zulu, Boer, and Briton punctuated the following decades.

BOERS VERSUS BRITAIN In 1852 and 1854, Britain recognized the independence of two new Boer republics, the fledgling South African Republic (ZAR) in the Transvaal and the Orange Free State. Then, in 1877, it annexed the Transvaal in the first attempt to create a federation in southern Africa. In 1880, the Boers under Paul Kruger revolted against their new government. Within a few weeks they had won the first Anglo-Boer War, enjoying a crushing victory at the Battle of Majuba (1881). Kruger became president of the ZAR, while William Gladstone's government agreed to withdraw the British force and restore self-government to the Boers. Kruger grudgingly accepted this arrangement, which

Top: a model soldier in Talana Museum, Dundee
Left: the Battle of Majuba— a crushing defeat for the British

(see page 37). The raid was a disaster, but it indicated British intentions to Kruger. The Second Anglo-Boer War was not long in coming (see pages 38–39). The victorious British granted limited self-government to former Boer republics, but from then on, they effectively controlled the whole of modern South Africa and all its mineral wealth.

Above: Cape Prime Minister Cecil Rhodes. Right: ZAR President Paul Kruger

was formalized by the Convention of Pretoria in 1881.

The empire-builders were far from content. They had visions of controlling territories in Africa from the Cape in the south to Cairo in the north, and although Britain still claimed status as the paramount power in South Africa and reserved ultimate control over the Transvaal's foreign affairs, it could not now claim the republic as a colony. Many resented this, among them the multimillionaire diamond magnate, Cecil John Rhodes (prime minister of the Cape in the 1890s).

The discovery of gold in 1886 made the Transvaal the richest and most powerful nation in southern Africa— and that made Britain nervous. It also made millionaires Cecil Rhodes and Alfred Beit a second fortune, and brought Boer and *uitlander* (foreigner) into conflict. The wealth of the Witwatersrand proved too alluring a prize. In 1895, Rhodes and others conspired to take over the Transvaal and install a British administration by means of the ill-fated Jameson Raid

UNION After the war, the colonial government began the process of reconstruction. The mines were put back into operation and, by 1907, the former republics were given representative government. In 1910, the Cape, Natal, the Orange Free State, and the ZAR were bound into a single national entity, the Union of South Africa. The local black Africans were not consulted. Voter franchise —or the lack of it—was the single most negative outcome. Only whites could be elected to parliament, and English and Dutch became the official languages. By excluding blacks, the Act of Union sowed the seeds of discontent resolved only with the freeing of Nelson Mandela in 1990.

In the last quarter of the 19th century, the discovery of diamonds in Kimberley, followed by the first gold diggings on the Witwatersrand, transformed the landscape, population, and history of South Africa. Almost overnight, what had been a poor and little-known country became rich, famous, and powerful.

Fortune hunters rushed to the arid zones of discovery from every corner of the globe. They included some two dozen men, most of them immigrants from England, Holland, and Germany, who staked claims but also started auxiliary services. They opened hotels, set up dealerships, and even ran the elevators that gave the men access to their diggings. They also built alliances, fed feuds and appetites and, in the 1870s and 1880s, went on to take control of the diamond fields. From 1886 onward, they moved north to finance and run the gold mines. Nicknamed the Randlords by the British press, they acquired immense wealth, power, and influence.

WEALTH AND POWER Supreme among the Randlords was Cecil John Rhodes—diamond magnate, gold mine owner, politician, and empire-builder extraordinaire. His chief rival for control of the diamond fields was showman Barney Barnato, who combined financial wizardry and cabaret. Other high fliers in this mixed bunch were Lionel Phillips, Alfred Beit, Joseph Robinson, Julius Wernher, Solly Joel, and Samuel Marks. Later, Ernest Oppenheimer founded the dynasty that still controls the world's diamond market.

The Randlords' lives were colorful and controversial. Their ostentatious wealth contrasted dramatically with the increasing poverty of the rural poor, both white and black. Only the feather barons in Oudtshoorn (see page 80) came anywhere near matching their flamboyant lifestyle. They built large, showy mansions in and around fledgling Johannesburg as well as in fashionable parts of London. They collected art, much of which forms the

Top: the diamond diggings at Kimberley
Above left: the powerful Oppenheimer family in 1933
Left: showman millionaire Barney Barnato

Prospectors used simple methods to find gold in 1900

Photo: Mr. G. T. Ferneyhough
PROSPECTING FOR GOLD ON THE RAND.

37

core of major national galleries in Cape Town and Johannesburg, sponsored foundations, and set up scholarships. But this immense wealth brought with it a lust for power—those who controlled the gold controlled the country.

THE SHAPING OF MODERN SOUTH AFRICA

The Randlords' most enduring legacy is to the economy of South Africa. The discovery of gold and of diamonds contributed hugely to South Africa's regional power base and gave it a crucial standing in the world economy. Mining has affected the lives of every one of the social and ethnic groups in the country. One of the first pieces of discriminatory legislation to be passed on the way to apartheid was designed to oust black miners from their diamond claims, make sure that claim ownership was white, and reduce the blacks on the diamond fields to a cheap, compliant labor pool. Gold was vital to the subcontinent and cheap labor was vital to gold if profit margins were to be kept high on international sales. The Randlords were easily persuaded to ally themselves with many of the worst racial excesses of the republican and, later, the South African government.

THE JAMESON RAID

The struggle for control finally toppled into intrigue and war. Rhodes, as prime minister of the Cape Colony, wanted to oust Paul Kruger, leader of the Transvaal Boers, and set up a British-ruled Federation of South Africa. With his sights on yet another personal fortune, he was convinced that only Britain possessed the know-how to exploit the region's immeasurable riches. The deeply religious Kruger not only regarded the discovery of gold as a mixed blessing, but was hostile to the presence of the British and other *uitlanders*. In 1895, Dr. Leander Jameson, a close associate of Rhodes, led a raiding party into the Transvaal aiming to cause an insurrection and remove Kruger. The Jameson Raid not only ended in ignominious defeat and finished Rhodes' political career in South Africa, it also sowed the seeds for the Second Anglo-Boer War.

In 1870, the British annexed a small hill on the Orange Free State border, which turned out to be the Kimberley diamond pipe; then gold was discovered, and in 1877 they annexed the South African Republic (ZAR). The furious Boers fought for their independence and won, at the Battle of Majuba in 1881.

38

THE PATH TO WAR The ZAR was officially given its independence again in 1884, but by then its gold was attracting great interest from scores of foreign prospectors. British imperialists, goaded on by the huge wealth being engendered, instigated the Jameson Raid in 1895 (see page 37), hoping to ignite an uprising that would lead to the installation of a British administration in the ZAR. It was a disaster, and subsequent events led President Kruger to demand that Britain withdraw the troops massed on his border. Ignored, he invaded Natal in 1899, and so began the Second Anglo-Boer War.

Kruger's commandos were in essence a "people's army," wearing civilian clothes. But they had a distinct advantage over the regular British troops because they knew the countryside and climate and were excellent horsemen. Before the war was over, Britain had committed 448,715 troops—outnumbering the Boers by nearly five to one.

THE SIEGE OF LADYSMITH The Boers started out well: they beat the British at Talana Hill and routed them at Nicholson's Nek. But their four-month siege of Ladysmith in northwest Natal was ill-timed and ended in disaster. The Boers' original aim was to advance into Natal and the Cape to stem the influx of British troops, but the siege lasted too long. Even though it tied up four-fifths of the British army, the road to Durban was left virtually open, and the Boers—aside from attacks at Weenen, Estcourt, and Mooi River—remained far too cautious. The British had time to bring up fresh troops via Durban, the Boers lost their advantage—and ultimately lost the war.

Various unsuccessful attempts were made to relieve Ladysmith, such as the disastrous Battle of Colenso, but it was not until after such famous battles as Spienkop and Paardeberg that the siege was lifted.

Top: the Battle of Majuba, 1881. Left: Jameson captured by the Boers in 1895

CONCENTRATION CAMPS In 1900, Pretoria and then Johannesburg surrendered, but the war was not yet over. A rural guerilla war began as Boer commandos split up, continuing the fight in smaller, more mobile bands in an effort to deny the British control of the countryside. Retribution was swift and terrible. For every belligerent act, every sabotage of railroad lines, the British reacted with twice the force. They burned farmhouses, instituting a devastating scorched-earth policy. Anything that might sustain the guerillas was flushed out of the countryside, and that included horses, cattle, sheep, women, and children. Boer women and children—so-called refugees—were dumped into huge camps, located near the railways and run along military lines—the world's first concentration camps. Neglect of elementary precautions led to epidemics of typhoid and dysentery. By the end of the war, 136,000 Afrikaners were imprisoned in 50 camps; over 26,000 women and children · had died of disease and neglect. The horror of the camps was brought to light by an English philanthropist, Emily Hobhouse, and these revelations helped bring about the Peace of Vereeniging (1902). There is a memorial to the Afrikaner dead in Bloemfontein (see page 127).

❏ Whites were not the only inmates of the concentration camps. Entire populations of black locations or mission stations were uprooted and transferred to sites adjoining the Boer camps. It is believed that by the end of the war, there were some 115,700 Africans living in 66 camps. Unlike the whites, they were used as a labor force for the British army, and were not fed, as they were expected to be self-sufficient. More than 14,000 deaths are recorded; there were undoubtedly many others. There is no memorial to the African dead. ❏

Boers hold their position against the Grenadier Guards, 1900

"Apartheid" means the segregation and separate development of the races. Though its roots go back to the slave-owning colonists and to economic and political developments in the 19th century, much of the legislation that made up the core of apartheid policy was, in fact, born of 20th-century British policies.

40

FIRST STEPS Basing their thinking on the teachings of John Ruskin, the British colonial administrators came up with an ideal of separate development, by which the "superior" (i.e. white) race assisted the other races toward an eventual goal of equality and reintegration. Meanwhile, they would be given tasks suitable to their abilities and progress (i.e. menial). It was, of course, in the interests of the dominant whites to insure that progress was not too swift. The ultra-right-wing Afrikaner Broederbond (Brotherhood), founded in 1918, took the notion much further.

It was Jan Smuts's Native Affairs Act of 1920 that took the first step toward real political segregation, establishing the principle that African political activity should be divorced from "white" South Africa. It ushered in a period of intense debate on "native policy," during which state ideology was refined and clarified.

APARTHEID LEGISLATION Nearly 30 years later, in 1948, the Afrikaner National Party under Hendrik Verwoerd and D. F. Malan coined the word "apartheid," and fought and won the election on a ticket of oppression. It immediately adopted apartheid as a national political program, bringing in many new laws. What is called "petty" apartheid was instituted: separate public benches, building entrances, and public lavatories. These regula-

tions were united under the Separate Amenities Act. Sex outside marriage between races was already banned, but the 1949 Mixed Marriages Act and the Immorality Act of the following year banned any sex between the races. The Population Registration Act of 1950 legislated for a national register according to racial classification, with every citizen to be issued with documents stating their racial group. Race was identified by physical attributes, "measurable" in ways that defy belief: for example, if an official stuck a pencil in your hair and it stayed fast, you were black, not colored (mixed race).

Laws allowing Africans into urban areas were redefined; Africans had to carry a pass with them at all times. Failure to do so was a criminal offense. This effectively made Africans aliens in their own land. "Group Areas" defined as White, Black, Indian, or Colored made physical separation absolute. You lived where the state told you to. If you tried to resist, you were forcibly removed. On the crucial issue of land, the Prevention of Illegal Squatting Act (1951) gave the government power to move African tenants from privately or publicly owned land.

Top: apartheid even led to separate beaches
Left: Hendrik Verwoerd, architect of apartheid

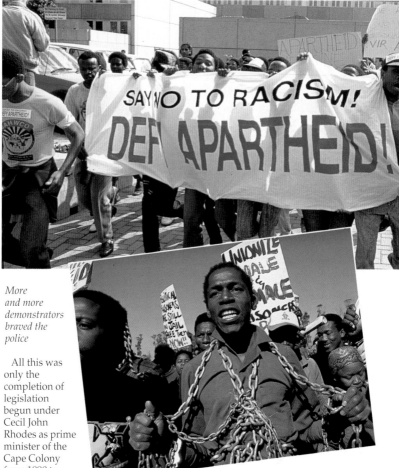

More and more demonstrators braved the police

All this was only the completion of legislation begun under Cecil John Rhodes as prime minister of the Cape Colony from 1890 to 1895. The exclusively Afrikaner Nationalist politicians justified the ruthless apartheid system as the only alternative to segregation and the end of white South Africa.

THE DEATH OF APARTHEID For 30 years the National Party government wrestled with the implementation of apartheid, an unwieldy, contradictory and deeply unsavory policy. There was heavy media censorship, a total lack of freedom of speech, and increasing violence, with torture, poorly explained deaths, disappearances, and attendant horrors. But the level of protest, at home and abroad, grew steadily and bravely until white South Africa was an international pariah.

Under the force and effect of economic sanctions and diplomatic pressure, President F. W. de Klerk announced that he would repeal discriminatory laws. Seizing the political initiative, he surprised his supporters by unbanning the African National Congress (ANC), the Pan African Congress (PAC), and the Communist Party—and releasing from jail the popular hero Nelson Mandela. The government, bowing to the inevitable, finally abandoned the indefensible apartheid policy, explaining it away as an experiment that foundered and did not work.

The roots of the Struggle are nearly as deep as those of the oppression. By the end of the 19th century, a feeling of African nationality was emerging among the Christian-educated blacks. At first this was centered on religion, with the foundation of many African churches, but political movements were not far behind.

42

FIRST STIRRINGS In 1912, a handful of mission-educated black men in the Eastern Cape and Natal founded the South African Native National Congress (SANNC), the country's first black political party. Four years later, the University of Fort Hare opened, giving blacks a first chance at higher education. Around the same time, a young Indian lawyer, Mohindas Karamchand Gandhi, began the first of his many non-violent protests on behalf of the Natal Indians. In the 1920s, the mainly Zulu Inkatha Movement was founded, also in Natal. Any small political successes were met with a massive right-wing backlash.

In 1923, the SANNC became the African National Congress (ANC),

which in 1928 began to work with the Communist Party. The war years saw the creation of the African Miners' Union and the ANC Youth League, the first mass protests in the townships, bus boycotts, squatter camps, and black-run strikes in the mines. All were crushed violently by the police. The outcome was the Nationalist victory in the 1948 elections, and the official implementation of apartheid.

Below and opposite: violence and death dogged the fight for freedom
Right: Steve Biko

PROTEST AND SUPPRESSION In 1959, the more militant Pan African Congress (PAC) was formed by breakaway members of the ANC, led by Robert Sobukwe. In 1960, Sobukwe persuaded thousands to burn their pass books (see page 40). In Sharpeville, south of Johannesburg, the police panicked and fired on a crowd, killing over 200 people. The government declared a state of emergency, arrested Sobukwe, and banned the PAC and ANC. Both organizations went underground and formed military wings, the PAC's *Poqo* and the ANC's *Umkhonto we Sizwe*.

Oliver Tambo and several other key leaders fled into exile. In 1962, many remaining ANC leaders, including Nelson Mandela and Walter Sisulu, were charged with treason and sabotage in the Rivonia Treason Trial, and sentenced to life imprisonment—most on Robben Island. Effective protest was over for nearly a decade.

TOWNSHIP VIOLENCE By the early 1970s, a new generation of young, bright, and committed activists was ready to take up the Struggle. The most charismatic and famous was Steve Biko, leader of the Black Consciousness movement. Speaking to black and white students, he aimed to raise black awareness and pride. Biko was to die under dubious circumstances in a police cell in 1977.

Meanwhile, the schoolchildren of Soweto took to the streets. The police responded brutally and many hundreds were killed, injured, or arrested while others fled to ANC camps outside the country. By 1980, violence on the township streets was commonplace. The media was heavily censored, but pictures of singing children facing armed police and attack dogs were being daily flashed onto TV sets across the globe. There was a permanent state of emergency, with tens of thousands detained without trial to face torture, police brutality, and inexplicable deaths in custody. Zulu Chief Mangostho Buthelezi, who had revitalized Inkatha, was not prepared to play second fiddle to the ANC. Horrific factional violence broke out in the townships and workers' hostels between supporters of the various political parties and tribal groups. So-called traitors were burned

alive, with a car tire filled with gas hung around their necks.

In 1986, international sanctions were imposed and the first cracks were seen in the apartheid armor. The pass laws were repealed, the Indians and coloreds were given a limited franchise, and many of the petty rules of apartheid were abolished. The real drama was still to come.

The road to freedom was finally opened in 1990, when President F. W. de Klerk made a momentous speech in parliament, repudiating apartheid, repealing the laws that upheld discrimination, and unbanning organizations such as the ANC. He withdrew the South African army from Angola, gave Namibia its independence, and pledged to work toward a truly democratic society.

But the greatest indication that freedom was here to stay came with the release of Nelson Mandela from his 27-year imprisonment on Robben Island. He would accept his own freedom only when all South Africans had theirs. Over 100,000 people waited for hours on the old Parade Ground in the heart of Cape Town before Mandela stepped out onto the balcony of City Hall to give his first public address.

massacres at Boipatong south of Johannesburg and Bisho in former Ciskei, and has still not died away completely, with sporadic trouble in the townships. In 1994, however, the country held its first truly democratic elections, and Nelson Mandela and F. W. de Klerk jointly accepted the Nobel Peace Prize. On May 10, with the eyes of the world watching, Nelson Mandela took office as President of the New South Africa.

❏ "We have, at last, achieved our political emancipation. We pledge ourselves to liberate all our people from the continuing bondage of poverty, deprivation, suffering, gender, and other discrimination.

Never, never, and never again shall it be that this beautiful land will again experience the oppression of one by another... The sun shall never set on so glorious a human achievement.

Let freedom reign. God bless Africa!"

Nelson Mandela, Presidential Inaugural Address, quoted in *The Long Walk to Freedom*, 1994 ❏

Talks now began in earnest between the government and the various opposition parties. To the astonishment of the world, a referendum held in 1992 among white South Africans resulted in an overwhelming vote to end apartheid. The violence continued unabated until the last moment, with

Top: Nelson Mandela and F. W. de Klerk Below: ANC election poster

'N BETER LEWE:

KOM ONS LAAT DIT HIER GEBEUR

Stem ANC ANC

 ▶▶▶ REGION HIGHLIGHTS

Western Cape

FIRST INTENTIONS
"It is apt to be forgotten
that the Cape was not
occupied with the view to
the establishment of a
European colony in our
present sense of the
word. The Dutch took it
that they might plant a
cabbage garden: the
English took it that they
might have a naval station
and half-way house to
India."
James Bryce, *Impressions
of South Africa*, 1897

PATCHWORK LAND The Western Cape's plump, roughly
L-shaped body borders the Indian and Atlantic oceans. At
its heart, where the two oceans meet, is Cape Town, a life-
line to sailors and a magnet to tourists. The city is the
single biggest tourist attraction in South Africa, with
around 800,000 foreign visitors a year. Yet the authorities
are aiming for many more, with new hotels under construction and a convention center in the pipeline. Century
City, a whole new district, will have a major theme park,
Ratanga Junction (see page 63), and Africa's largest shopping center and entertainment complex.

The founding fathers chose well when they colonized
the coastal strip. The climate is moderate and pleasant,
the land fertile and well watered, and the scenery superb.
As might be expected when a colony is founded by a
gardener, the first farms were up and running within a
very few years. With the planting of the first vines only
three years after Jan van Riebeeck's arrival in 1652, the
Cape had found its true vocation. The area surrounding
Cape Town is as steeped in wine as Bordeaux—and has
its roots in the same place. It was the arrival of the French
Huguenots from 1685 that spurred the industry into
something more than the occasional flagon of cheap wine,
while the German contingent provided the fruity tones,
redolent of the Mosel, that characterize so much of the
best South African white wine. Today, the industry is up
there with the best, and for the connoisseur or the tippler,

a dozen local wine routes offer an extraordinary range of tasting opportunities.

Beyond these tidy, whitewashed valleys lies a jagged line of craggy mountains—the Cederberg, the Hex River Mountains, and the Swartberg. The south faces, slapped by ocean clouds, are thick with forest or powerfully scented by the Cape's unique herbal *fynbos* (see page 74). On the dry far side, the picture is very different. People either love or hate the Karoo. It is rocky, dry, and dusty, twisted at times into fantastic rock formations. From a distance its scrubby vegetation looks unimpressive, but if you look closely and carefully it is magnificent, and when the spring flowers are in bloom it is an artwork worthy of Jackson Pollock. The inhabitants of this tough land are as rugged as their surroundings. Their ancestors headed into the unknown with nothing more than a flimsy wagon and a few cooking pots to escape the ordered urban life with all its rules and regulations. These communities are hospitable, but introverted. Most are more concerned with physical survival than metaphysics, but the desert has sometimes borne extraordinary blooms in powerful writers or artists such as Laurens van der Post, Olive Schreiner, and Helen Martins (see page 113).

Then there is the coast itself, a delightful playground of rocky headlands and golden beaches, where whales and surfers alike frolic in the crashing waves. A major road, the N2, runs along the coast, linking the numerous small

Above: the lush Breede Valley is perfect for growing fruit

Below: weird rock formations, including the "Sewing Machine," crown the Cederberg

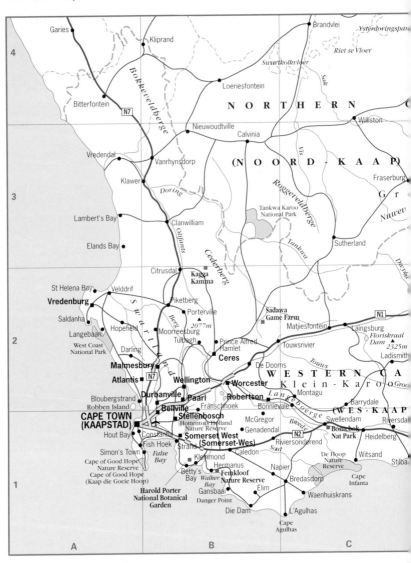

towns of the Garden Route, so called because of its rampantly green forests. A favorite vacation destination with white South Africans, the area has inevitably become crowded, with bungalows and vacation homes stretching along the dunes to link many of the towns in a continuous ribbon development. At the same time, the forest has been pushed a little farther away and the coast has lost a little of its beauty, but at least there are now facilities and entertainment for the many thousands who flock here each year. And there are still plenty of isolated coves and deserted dunes for those who care to seek them out.

This is a patchwork land, the ideal vacation destination with something for everyone, and all within a reasonable distance. It may not be "real" Africa, but the Western Cape has a magic all its own.

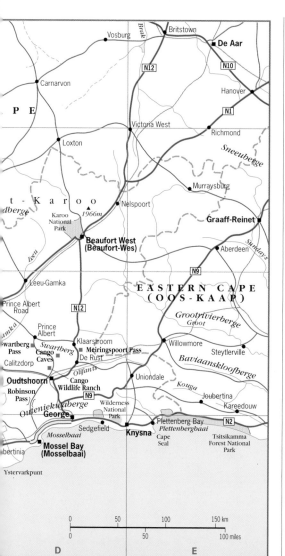

TOURIST INFORMATION
Western Cape Tourism
Board, The Pinnacle,
corner of Burg and Castle
streets, Cape Town 8000
(tel: 021-426 5639 or
021-426 5647,
fax: 021-426 5640,
www.wcapetourism.co.za).

Vosburg   Britstown   ■ De Aar

N12   N10

Carnarvon   Hanover

P E   N1

Victoria West   Richmond

Loxton   Sneeuberge

Murraysburg

t - K a r o o   Nelspoort   Graaff-Reinet ■

dberge   Karoo   1966m
National
Park

Leeu   Beaufort West   Aberdeen   Sundays
(Beaufort-Wes)

Leeu-Gamka   N9

Prince Albert   E A S T E R N   C A P E
Road   N12   (O O S - K A A P)

Prince   Grootrivierberge
Albert   Groot
Swartberg Klaarstroom   Willowmore
Pass   Cango Meiringspoort Pass   Steytlerville
Caves   De Rust   Baviaanskloofberge
Calitzdorp   Olifants   Uniondale   Kouga
Oudtshoorn   Cango
Robinson   Wildlife Ranch   Joubertina
Pass   N9   Kareedouw
Outeniekwaberge   George   Wilderness
Sedgefield   National   Plettenberg Bay   N2
Mosselbaai   Park   Plettenbergbaai
bertinia   Knysna   Cape   Tsitsikamma
Mossel Bay   Seal   Forest National
(Mosselbaai)   Park

Ystervarkpunt

0   50   100   150 km
0   50   100 miles

D   E

49

*Brightly colored beach
huts stand sentinel at
Muizenberg*

Cape Town

Even before Vasco da Gama first rounded the Cape in 1498, sailors kept a lookout for Table Mountain, visible from 90 miles out to sea. The Phoenicians and Arabs thought it was filled with magnetism that could draw a ship in to its doom, while the massive mythical bird, the roc, nested on the slopes, and a race of dwarves called the Wac-wac lived in the bay area. When later sailors actually stepped ashore, they discovered good fresh water and the cattle-farming Khoikhoi, who were willing to trade fresh meat and milk. Table Bay became a regular revictualing stop, but it was 150 years before any Europeans came to stay, although several nationalities made abortive and short-lived attempts.

FOUNDATIONS In 1652 the Dutch East India Company sent a small fleet of three ships to the bay, commanded by Jan van Riebeeck. Their mission was to provide fresh produce for passing ships. Van Riebeeck laid out the 45-acre Company's Garden as a market garden, built a fort in which to live, founded a small hospital, and made a safe area for ship repairs: the foundations of modern Cape Town had been laid. Since then the much-loved city has grown from strength to strength, acquiring numerous nicknames, ranging from the "Mother City" to the "Tavern of the Seas."

Today, this is one of the world's prettiest cities, cocooned in a shallow bay by the looming bulk of Table Mountain, its tiny center neat and elegant. If it can be compared to anywhere else, Cape Town is most akin to San Francisco. Like that city, it owes its existence to a

Windsurfers enjoy spectacular views in Table Bay

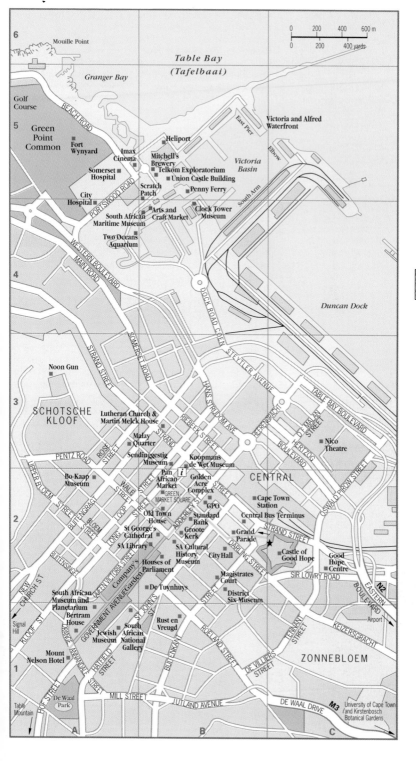

Table Bay
(Tafelbaai)

Mouille Point

Granger Bay

Golf
Course

Green
Point
Common

Fort Wynyard

Heliport

Imax
Cinema

Mitchell's
Brewery

Telkom Exploratorium

Union Castle Building

Somerset
Hospital

Scratch
Patch

Penny Ferry

City
Hospital

Arts and
Craft Market

Clock Tower
Museum

South African
Maritime Museum

Two Oceans
Aquarium

Victoria
Basin

Victoria and Alfred
Waterfront

East Pier

Elbow

South Arm

Duncan Dock

Noon Gun

SCHOTSCHE
KLOOF

Lutheran Church &
Martin Melck House

Malay
Quarter

Sendinggestig
Museum

Bo-Kaap
Museum

Pan
African
Market

GREEN
MARKET SQUARE

Old Town
House

St George's
Cathedral

SA Library

Houses of
Parliament

De Tuynhuys

Koopmans
de Wet Museum

CENTRAL

Nico
Theatre

Golden
Acre
Complex

Cape Town
Station

GPO

Central Bus Terminus

Standard
Bank

Groote
Kerk

SA Cultural
History
Museum

City Hall

Grand
Parade

Castle of
Good Hope

Good
Hope
Centre

Magistrates
Court

District
Six Museum

South African
Museum and
Planetarium

Bertram
House

Jewish
Museum

South
African
National
Gallery

Rust en
Vreugd

Signal
Hill

Mount
Nelson Hotel

Table
Mountain

De Waal
Park

ZONNEBLOEM

Airport

University of Cape Town
and Kirstenbosch
Botanical Gardens

51

THE PERFECT GARDEN

When Jan van Riebeeck laid out his market garden in 1652, the first things he planted were Turkish and broad beans, peanuts, aniseed, fennel, medlar, quince, Spanish oranges, cucumber, pumpkin, onions, watermelon, endives, and beets. The following year, the gardens were enlarged, adding parsnips, chives, artichokes, pimpernel, rosemary, gooseberries, blackberries, apricots, and plums. The 45-acre garden was tended by 300 slaves. Mr. and Mrs. van Riebeeck picked the first oranges in 1661.

52

sweeping bay and natural harbor. It lives on the edge of the Winelands, has the same mix of old, pretty buildings, a lively waterfront, and serious business, in this case as the legislative capital of South Africa and one of the country's most important business centers. Publishing, the arts, and the gay community all flourish, and the city prides itself on being liberal, although until recently this approach extended only as far as the boundaries of the white community.

Kirstenbosch National Botanical Gardens

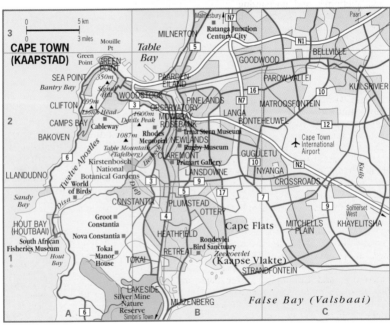

EUROPEAN STYLE Cape Town does not seem like part of Africa. The climate is Mediterranean, the buildings European, and many of the faces you see around you are light skinned. Nevertheless, it has real magic and charm, providing plenty of mellow history, fascinating museums, good shopping, and enchanting gardens such as the superb Kirstenbosch National Botanical Gardens. You can take gentle strolls around town or embark on more serious hikes on the mountain, where you also find some of the world's most dramatic views and spectacular sunsets. There are great beaches and countryside, and wineries and wine cellars, where wine tasting is all part of the experience. In season, whale-watching is within easy day-trip distance. At night, there is superb food and drink from haute cuisine to sumptuous seafood, live music (particularly jazz), theater, and dancing. For the moment, it is even relatively safe, although you should be careful after dark. The only blot on the landscape is the city's sometimes changeable and bad-tempered weather. When good, it is superb, but it can blanket the city in gray cloud on a whim, send bitter winds whistling through the winter streets, and drop dank rain for days on end.

Around the gentle urban center, Greater Cape Town is vast. Leafy white suburbs stretch up the slopes, around the mountain, and along the coast to merge almost imperceptibly into the commuter towns of the peninsula. To the east, on the Cape Flats, the black townships and squatter camps spread as far as the eye can see, an ocean of corrugated iron and cardboard, plastic bags and wooden boxes. Local population estimates range at anything from 2.5 to 3.5 million. Even the census takers have no clear idea. For tours, see page 238.

*Suburban Cape Town
under the Lion's Head*

NOT SO LIBERAL
Cape Town has always prided itself on being sophisticated, liberal, and cosmopolitan—the one place in South Africa where the races could mingle freely. Yet it is the site of the very first forced clearance. This took place in 1901, long before the official start of apartheid and while the colony was still under British rule. Whole communities have been forced from their homes no fewer than 46 times in the city's history.

Cape Town

ANTON ANREITH

The sculptor Anton Anreith (1754–1821) was, together with Louis Thibault, responsible for revitalizing Cape architecture. Born in southwest Germany, he served his apprenticeship under a rococo sculptor—which led to what has been called his "high baroque" style—then came to the Cape where, first a carpenter, he went on to become a master sculptor. His best work can be seen in the Groote Kerk, the Lutheran Church (see page 57), the Castle's Kat Balcony, and on the pediment of Groot Constantia's Wine Cellar (see page 68).

54

▶ Bertram House   51A1

Company's Gardens, top of Government Avenue
(tel: 021-424 9381)
Open: Tue–Sat 9:30–4:30. Admission: inexpensive
This beautifully proportioned red-brick house was built in 1830 for an English lawyer, John Barker, and is now a rare example of early 19th-century Cape British domestic architecture. Its Regency-style rooms are rich with furniture, ceramics, and silver illustrating the lifestyle of a well-to-do English family in the Cape.

▶▶ Bo-Kaap   51A2

Bounded by Rose, Wale, Chiappini, and Shortmarket streets
For walking tours of the area, contact Tana Baru Tours
(tel: 021-424 0719)
Built in the late 18th and early 19th centuries for European artisans, the little cube houses of Bo-Kaap were taken over by the Muslim Cape Malays (see pages 64–65), whose community survived as the only nonwhites in central Cape Town. These days the steep streets are once more bright with color and life.

The **Bo-Kaap Museum** (71 Wale Street, tel: 021-424 3846. *Open* Mon–Sat 9:30–4:30. *Admission: inexpensive*), in one of the finest surviving houses, offers a fascinating glimpse into late 19th-century Muslim life and the contribution of Islam to South African history, culture, food, and the Afrikaans language.

▶▶ Castle of Good Hope   51C2

Castle Street (tel: 021-469 1249)
Open: daily 9–4. Conducted tours 11, noon, 2
Changing of the Guard, noon; no unaccompanied sightseeing
Admission: moderate
Founded by Simon van der Stel as the headquarters of the VOC (Dutch East India Company), this solid pentagonal fort is the oldest European building in South Africa (1666–1679). Five bastions surround utilitarian structures from dingy, graffiti-covered cells to armories. From 1691, several officers' houses were built onto a massive defensive wall, the Kat. The Secunde's House, home of the deputy-governor (1695), has rooms furnished in 17th-, 18th-, and early 19th-century style. The Governor's Residence, best known for Anton

Anton Anreith's Kat Balcony in the Castle of Good Hope

Anreith's magnificent baroque Kat Balcony (ca1785), is furnished in grand style with military and maritime artifacts and part of the William Fehr Collection of furniture, paintings, china, and glass with an African theme. Look for the many paintings of Cape Town through the ages, and paintings by Thomas Baines.

► **City Hall and the Grand Parade** see pages 66–67

►►► **Company's Garden and Government Avenue** see pages 66–67

► **District Six**   *51B2*
District Six began life as a cosmopolitan port area where some 60,000 people of a dozen races and every color mingled to create a vibrant community. In 1966, it was declared whites-only and all other races were shipped off to townships; in 1979, the area was bulldozed and the rubble used to build the new harbor. Since then, protests

Former residents re-create their bulldozed homes in the District Six Museum

have been so vociferous that the land has remained empty. Today, a fascinating **Museum** (Buitenkant Methodist Church, 25a Buitenkant Street, tel: 021-461 8745. *Open* Mon–Sat 10–4:30; Sun by appointment. *Admission: moderate*) displays photos and recollections of the district and its street signs, saved from the bulldozers. Past inhabitants all sign a cloth (now over 225 feet long) and write down memories on a huge floor map.

► **Greenmarket Square**   *51B2*
The second-oldest square in Cape Town, built in 1710 as a market, is still home to one of the city's liveliest and most popular flea markets. It also contains the city's first civic building—the Old Town House (see page 58).

► **Groote Kerk**   *51B2*
Adderley Street, entrance in Church Square, off Parliament Street (tel: 021-461 7044)
Open: Mon–Fri 10–2. Admission free
Until a wood and thatch church was commissioned by Governor Willem Adriaan van der Stel in 1678 and consecrated in 1704, services were held on Van Riebeeck's ship, the *Dromedaris*. The original church was replaced by this rather drab, but much larger building in 1841. Only the pretty clock tower belongs to the first edifice.

Inside, the huge room has sturdy box pews and a magnificent wooden pulpit, carved by Anton Anreith in 1788. The organ is the largest in the southern hemisphere, with 6,000 pipes and 32 foot pedals. This is the Mother Church of the Dutch Reformed Faith.

A VENERABLE PEAR
The oldest tree in Company's Garden is a saffron pear that stands near the café. It is believed to have been imported from Holland in the time of Jan van Riebeeck and to have provided fruit for 17th-century sailors. The tree needs careful treatment but still produces edible fruit each year, most of which is pickled.

COMMERCIAL ART GALLERIES

Over the last few years, the art scene has exploded in Cape Town, with new galleries opening every month. The quality, of course, varies hugely, but a number have exciting, constantly changing exhibits that showcase the best in South African art. Among the best are: the Association for Visual Arts (AVA), 35 Church Street (tel: 021-424 7436); Bang the Gallery, 92 Breede Street (tel: 021-422 1477); and Le Bon Ton... & Art, 209 Breede Street (tel: 021-423 3631). The tourist office publishes an excellent arts and crafts map with listings of many other galleries.

Powerful studies still crowd the walls of Irma Stern's studio

▶ Houses of Parliament 51B2

Parliament Street and Government Avenue (tel: 021-403 2460/1)
Enter via Parliament Street gate. Tickets available for parliamentary sessions (Jan–Jun) on presentation of passport at Room V12, Old Assembly Wing. Guided tours Jul–Dec, Mon–Thu 11 AM and 2:30 PM, Fri 11 AM. Jacket and tie required during parliamentary sessions
Admission free

Cape Town's imposing brick and stucco Houses of Parliament (1884) are the seat of the country's legislative government. Inside, the enthusiasm and jazzy African dress of the new multiracial parliamentarians is breathing new life into the gloomy old building.

Next door, De Tuynhuys (1700) is the office of the state president (see page 67).

▶ Irma Stern Museum 52B2

The Firs, Cecil Road, Rosebank (tel: 021-686 9340)
Open: Tue–Sat 10–5. Admission: inexpensive

Once the home of South Africa's best-known painter, Irma Stern (1894–1966), this little museum houses an excellent collection of the artist's own work and the souvenirs of her travels, from Zairi masks to oriental ceramics and old furniture. A follower of the German Expressionist movement, Irma Stern painted South African people and landscapes.

▶ Jewish Museum 51A1

84 Hatfield Street, Company's Garden (tel: 021-465 1546)
Open: Mar–Nov, Tue and Thu 1:30–5; Wed and Sun 10:30–12:30; Mar–Nov, Tue and Thu 2–5, Sun 10:30–5
Admission free

The first service in South Africa's oldest synagogue took place on Yom Kippur in 1841. The ornate Egyptian Revival building contains a museum of the Jewish communities in the Cape.

Nearby, the recently opened **Holocaust Centre**, 1st floor, Albow Centre, 88 Hatfield Street (tel: 021-462 5553. *Open* Sun–Thu 10–5, Fri 10–1. *Admission free*) uses photographs, exhibits, survivors' testimonies, and audio-visuals in a moving tribute to the victims of Nazi genocide.

▶▶ Koopmans de Wet House 51B3

35 Strand Street (tel: 021-424 2473)
Open: Tue–Sat 9:30–4:30. Admission: inexpensive

This charming Georgian town house (now a museum) was built in 1701, and much altered by later owners. The pink and white pilastered facade has been attributed (without proof) to Louis Thibault and Anton Anreith. Its name comes from its most famous inhabitant, Maria Koopmans de Wet (1834–1906) who, as well as being a noted hostess and art collector, was an enthusiastic advocate of the Afrikaans language.

The spacious rooms, decorated in European style with *trompe l'oeil* pilasters, swags, and friezes, are elaborately furnished in the late 18th-century manner. Behind the courtyard, in contrast, are the slave quarters.

▶ Long Street   51A2

Laid out in the 18th century, Long Street runs right through the center of town, from sea to mountain. Wander through the place slowly, craning upward at the delightful architectural details or peering under the shadowed balconies at the extraordinary stores. There are churches, mosques, banks, offices, apartment buildings, cafés, restaurants and clubs, art-deco storefronts, curly cast iron, double-tiered verandas on elaborate Victorian houses, and exuberant neoclassical buildings awash with brightly painted decorative plasterwork; the roofline is a profusion of turrets, gables, and minarets.

The oldest inhabitants could pack a theater on tales of former residents: retired pirates, drag queens, exotic dancers... Tamer, but still lively, it now offers anything from Zulu beads to 1970s nostalgia clothes, secondhand books, vintage wine, plumbers' fittings, or 18th-century Cape Dutch furniture. Explore the back shelves of the **Junk Shop**, deck yourself out with a Madiba shirt at the **Pan African Market** (76 Long Street, tel: 021-424 2957. *Open* Mon–Fri 9–5, Sat 9–3), or have a sauna at the **Turkish Baths** (*Open* Mon–Fri 7 AM–8 PM, Sat 7–7, Sun 8–6; women—Mon, Thu, Sat; men—Tue, Wed, Fri, Sun).

▶ Lutheran Church and Martin Melck House   51B3

96 Strand Street
(tel: 021-421 5854)
Open: Wed 9 AM and noon,
Sun 10:15 AM. Admission
free

Until 1771, Lutherans and other denominations were forced to worship in the Dutch Reformed church. This, the country's first Lutheran church, was built in 1774 by a wealthy merchant, Martin Melck. Anton Anreith carved its magnificent wooden pulpit, and it so impressed the council of the Dutch Reformed church that they wanted one, too (see page 55). Next door, the old parsonage, Martin Melck House, is a rare surviving example of a building with a *dakkamer*—a room in the roof with windows looking toward the sea. It now houses an art gallery and restaurant.

LONE SURVIVOR
Although many 18th-century houses on Long Street are undoubtedly entombed within later shells, only one (No. 185, now the Palm Tree Mosque) survives intact. It was converted into a mosque in 1805 by a freed Malay slave, Jan van Boughies, who planted the two palms that gave the building its name.

57

Office buildings dwarf Koopman de Wet House, a delicate relic

TOURING CAPE TOWN

Topless Tours (tel: 021-418 5888) operates two-hour guided tours of the city on an open-topped bus, as well as daytrips to the peninsula. **Legend Tours** (tel: 021-697 4056/7) operates full-day tours of "ethnic" Cape Town, visiting Bo-Kaap, District Six, the townships, Cape Flats, and Robben Island. They also run tours of the peninsula and Winelands. Cultural tours are offered by **Grassroute Tours**, 90b Heritage Street, Breede Street (tel: 021-424 8480) and **Amava Tours**, 221 Blaauwberg Road, Table View (tel: 021-557 5429). For extreme sports tours in the Cape Town area, including rappelling, shark diving, sky diving, and other options, contact **Adventure Village**, 229 Long Street (tel: 021-424 1580). For helicopter flights over the city, try **Court Helicopters** (tel: 021-425 2966/7). **Waterfront Charters** (tel: 021-418 6436) runs harbor cruises and sailing excursions from the V&A Waterfront.

The grandiose Rhodes Memorial

▶▶ Old Town House 51B2

Greenmarket Square (tel: 021-424 6367)
Open: Mon–Fri 10–5, Sat 10–4. Admission free
By the 18th century, the Burgher Watch, responsible both for law and order and fighting fires, was making nightly patrols of the city. Its base was in Old Town House (1755). Citizens were summoned by the bell in the tower to listen to proclamations read from the balcony. The building later became the town hall, superseded in 1905 by the present City Hall. Today it is an art gallery, containing the magnificent Michaelis Collection of 17th-century Dutch and Flemish paintings.

▶ Rhodes Memorial 52B2

Off Rhodes Drive, Rondenbosch (tel: 021-689 9151)
Open access (tea garden closed Mon)
Cecil Rhodes (1853–1902) became a multimillionaire businessman, scholar, founder of several British colonies, and builder of most of southern Africa's railroads. In between, he found time to be prime minister of the Cape Colony. This memorial stands near the University of Cape Town campus and Rhodes' former home, Groot Schuur, a 17th-century barn sumptuously converted for him by Sir Herbert Baker in the 1890s. It is now the main residence of the president. There are fine views across the city from the memorial and a pleasant tearoom nearby.

▶ Rugby Museum 52B2

Boundary Road, Newlands (tel: 021-685 3038)
Open: Mon–Fri 9:30–4. Admission free
Occupying the first floor of Josephine's Water Mill (1840), the world's largest rugby museum is also a shrine to South African greats of the game. Its collection of mementos dates back to 1891.

▶▶ Rust en Vreugd 51B1

78 Buitenkant Street (tel: 021-465 3628)
Open: Mon–Fri 9–4. Admission free
The name of this double-storied 18th-century house means "rest and joy." One of the finest domestic buildings

in the Cape, it was once the home of the state prosecutor and had a splendid view of the bay. Now it is tucked away inland behind the ugly foreshore. Inside is part of the William Fehr Collection of Africana (see also Castle of Good Hope, page 54), with fine watercolors by Thomas Baines, lithographs, engravings, and paintings of the early Cape, plus extraordinary cartoons by George Cruickshank.

Rust en Vreugd, built for the Cape state prosecutor

▶ St. George's Cathedral   51B2

Wale Street
Open: daylight hours. Admission free
Consecrated in 1834, the first Anglican Cathedral of St. George the Martyr was thought to look like an average English parish church, not nearly grand enough for the Mother City. In 1901, architect Sir Herbert Baker was let loose, adding considerably to the length and grandeur of the building and replacing the neoclassical entrance with his favorite gray stone neo-Gothic design. The cathedral is much bigger now, but still looks like a large, welcoming parish church. The vaulted interior is more imposing than the outside. The highlights are a series of modern stained-glass windows by Gabriel Loire. The eight along the nave depict the Creation; the Christ in Majesty above the transept is dedicated to Lord Louis Mountbatten. This was the seat of Cape Town's flamboyant archbishop, Desmond Tutu, and it also hosted events such as the memorial service for Joe Slovo, the communist, atheist, ex-Jewish Minister of Housing in the Government of National Unity, who died in December 1994.

▶ Sendinggestig Museum   51B3

40 Long Street (tel: 021-423 6755)
Open: Mon–Fri 9–4. Admission free
This charmingly decorative apricot-and-white mission church was built by the South African Missionary Society in 1804, and used both for worship and the education of slaves and non-Christians. It now houses a museum of mission work in South Africa.

ARCHBISHOP DESMOND TUTU
Archbishop Desmond Mpilo Tutu was born on October 7, 1931. Ordained in 1961, he became Anglican Dean of Johannesburg (1975–1976), Bishop of Lesotho (1976–1978), and the first black secretary-general of the South African Council of Churches (1979), representing around 12 million Christians. In 1984, he became the first black bishop of Johannesburg and was awarded the Nobel Peace Prize. In 1986, he was elected the first black Anglican archbishop of Cape Town. An outspoken advocate of nonviolent reform and black nationalism, he nevertheless avoided imprisonment and won the hearts of South Africans of all colors. He resigned as archbishop in 1996, but continues to play an active role in the rebuilding of South Africa.

BIG BANG
Just below Signal Hill, the Noonday Gun shatters the air on the dot of noon every day except Sunday. It was instituted to help ships in the bay correct their chronometers and, after 1918, to mark a two-minute pause in honor of South Africa's war dead.

▶ **Signal Hill**   *52A2*

Off Kloof's Nek, or reached on foot via Bo-Kaap and Longmarket Street

Forming one arm of Table Bay, Signal Hill is far smaller than Table Mountain but has easy access, no lines, and superb views across the bay and city, particularly dramatic at sunset and at night, when a vast field of lights spreads below. At the summit are picnic tables and short, pleasant (if windy) strolls. Nearby is the tomb of the Saudi saint, Tuan Sayeed Alawie, incarcerated on Robben Island for 11 years.

▶▶ **South African Cultural**   *51B2*
     History Museum

49 Adderley Street (tel: 021-461 8280)
Open: Mon–Sat 9:30–4:30. Admission: inexpensive

For 130 years, this long, low house (built in 1685) was used to house slaves working in Company's Garden. After the second British occupation in 1811, Louis Thibault converted it into government offices. Today it is one of the finest museums in the country, with beautifully displayed exhibits from Greek and Roman amphorae to ferocious throwing knives of the Sudan. The second half of the museum is dedicated to South Africa, with coins, weapons, ceramics, stamps, and textiles, excellent collections of furniture and *objets d'art* (particularly silver) from white South Africa, and tribal art and utensils from the black community. Notice the roughly engraved postal stones found in Table Bay near the Versse River (see panel opposite).

The National Gallery graces the end of Government Avenue

▶ **South African**   *51B2*
     Library

Queen Victoria Street (tel: 021-424 6320)
Open: Mon–Fri 9–6, Sat 9–1. Admission free

Founded in 1818, this national copyright and preservation library is the oldest cultural institution in South Africa and one of the world's first free libraries. Regular exhibitions include the 5,000-volume private collection of former governor Sir George Grey, which has more than 100 medieval illuminated manuscripts. Among them are the oldest book in South Africa, a gospel dating to AD 900, and a First Folio Shakespeare.

▶ **South African Maritime Museum**   *51B4*

Dock Road, V&A Waterfront (tel: 021-419 2505/6)
Open: daily 10–5. Admission: moderate. Children under 12 must be accompanied by an adult to visit the ships

The Cape of Good Hope has produced some fascinating maritime history. Here you can learn about it *in situ*: the frequent shipwrecks, Table Bay Harbour, shipping lines, and maritime archeology, with models, a shipwright's workshop, SAS *Somerset* (the world's only surviving boom defense vessel), and the *Alwyn Vincent*, built in 1959 and the only steam tug still in use in the southern hemisphere.

▶ South African Museum and Planetarium

51A1

25 Queen Victoria Street (tel: 021-424 3330)
Open: daily 10–5
Admission: inexpensive; museum free on Wed

This stately building is South Africa's oldest museum, dating from 1825. The anthropology hall specializes in southern African tribal culture and includes rock paintings and several dioramas of San and Khoikhoi life. Other sections include white South African furniture, silver and *objets d'art*, geology (with replica dinosaurs), and marine life in the Southern Ocean, with a 67-foot skeleton of a blue whale. The Planetarium gives a delightful explanation of the southern hemisphere's night sky and shows audiovisual programs about Robben Island.

▶▶ South African National Gallery

51A1

Government Avenue, Company's Garden (tel: 021-465 1628)
Open: Tue–Sun 10–5
Admission free

Although the gallery began life exhibiting mainstream European art with a number of fine oils and a collection of sporting pictures by such painters as Stubbs and Munnings, sanctions and the collapse of the rand forced the curators to buy locally. It now has a good collection of contemporary South African art, an increasing amount of traditional tribal art, from decorated knobkerries to beadwork, and exciting work by modern black artists in both traditional and ultramodern styles. Traveling exhibitions include foreign work, photography, and experimental and ethnic art.

POSTAL STONES
In the early days of the Cape Sea Route, sailors could be away for years on end. To send news home and make contact with other ships in their fleet, they would leave letters under a rock engraved clearly with the name of the ship from which it had come and for whom it was intended. The stones were also sometimes used to pass on personal letters, delivered by ships newly arrived from Europe or on their last leg home.

61

View from Signal Hill; the hill was once used to watch for the arrival of ships to Table Bay

▶▶▶ Table Mountain and Cableway   52A2

Lower Cable Station, Tafelberg Road, off Kloof's Nek
(tel: 021-424 8181)
The cableway operates daily, weather permitting (not in cloud
or high wind), mid-Apr–mid-Sep daily 8:30–5, mid-Sep–end
Nov daily 8–6:30, Dec–Apr daily 7:30 AM–9 PM
Admission: expensive

Guarded by Lion's Head and Signal Hill (right) and Devil's Peak (left), Table Mountain towers 3,565 feet above Cape Town. Its sloping pedestal, covered with *fynbos* (see page 74) and forest, leads to a 1,640-foot-high sheer-sided slab of bare sandstone marking the northern end of a ridge stretching 30 miles to Cape Point.

The mountain started to form some 700 million years ago when mud and sand deposits were laid deep on the seabed; 600 million years ago, they were pushed upward and molten granite poured in around them. After 200 million years of erosion, a shallow sea returned, leaving mud, ripple marks, and marine fossils, before the whole of southern Gondwanaland (a huge ancient continent) was covered in heavy sheet ice. Some 160–300 million years ago, shifting tectonic plates lifted the mountains clear of the water and Gondwanaland began to break up into the modern continents. About 70 million years ago, further upward movement reexposed Table Mountain to the winds and rain.

A spectacular revolving cable car affords easy access to the viewing platforms and restaurant. The weather can be treacherous, so get a guide if you're planning to walk up the steep but easy path or to go any distance on the top. During peak season, reserve in advance for the cable car and check ahead if uncertain about wind or visibility. Tickets are available from Waterfront Information Centre (tel: 021-418 2369) and Lower Cable Station. For walking tours, contact Walk Up Table Mountain (tel: 021-424 2503). To see the mountain from inside, try Adventure Village (tel: 021-424 1580). To abseil (rappel) down the mountain, contact Abseil Africa (tel: 021-425 4332).

THE TABLECLOTH
Table Mountain is all too frequently covered by a swirling layer of white cloud that fits comfortably over the top like a cloth. Some say that each summer the retired pirate, Van Hunks, has a pipe-smoking contest with the Devil (the rheumatic old man cannot climb in winter, so the mountain remains clear). In reality, the Cape's summer south-easterly prevailing wind (known as the Cape Doctor) sweeps into the bay, gets trapped, and deposits its moisture neatly over the mountain.

Table Mountain is South Africa's top tourist attraction

▶▶ Two Oceans Aquarium   51A4

Dock Road, V&A Waterfront (tel: 021-418 3823)
Open: daily 9:30–6:30 (last entry 5)
Admission: expensive

This beautiful aquarium concentrates on the species found in and around the Cape Peninsula, from both the Indian and Atlantic oceans and from the mountain lakes and streams inland. There are 4,000 fish of 300 species in several large set pieces, including a kelp forest, an open ocean pool, a tropical tank and seal and penguin pools, a tidal tank showing life above and below the watermark, and an ecosystem following the progress of river life from mountain stream to estuary. Smaller tanks show sections of reef and water management, and children can examine creatures such as anemones and starfish in the touch pool. Experienced divers may dive in the shark tanks.

▶▶▶ Victoria and Alfred Waterfront   51C5

Victoria and Alfred Basins, Table Bay Harbour
(tel: 021-418 2369)
Open: all hours. Admission free. There is a satellite tourist information office at the entrance and a regular shuttle bus to Adderley Street

In 1860, Queen Victoria's second son, Alfred, tipped the first rock for the construction of the Victoria Basin. A century later, Cape Town's old harbor was left virtually derelict by the advent of the container port. Given a new lease of life in one of the world's most successful urban reclamation projects, it now hums as the heartland of the city. Working fishing boats, yachts, and harbor cruise boats skim the water, while wooden walkways hold brightly lit shopping malls, the largest crafts market in South Africa, restaurants, and a fascinating maritime museum (see page 60) and aquarium (see above). Other attractions include an **Imax Cinema** (tel: 021-419 7364) with a five-story screen, the **Telkom Exploratorium** (tel: 021-419 5957. *Open* Tue–Sun 9–6), a hands-on science exhibit; and harbor cruises (see page 58), which leave from Quays 4 and 5. Boards throughout the development identify old buildings and explain the area's history.

The Victoria and Alfred Waterfront is a favorite evening playground

RATANGA JUNCTION
Take the Sable Road exit off the N1, 6 miles from Cape Town, tel: 0861-200 300. Open: daily 11–7. Admission: expensive (entry includes all rides).
Africa's first full-scale theme park provides an entertaining day out with rides for all, from toddler-friendly trains to squeal-making waterslides and a gruesome rollercoaster. The theme is Africa, from some nonspecific souks (marketplaces) to the mines and bushveld safaris.

This is the first leg of a massive development project, **Century City**, which is creating a whole new suburb around the largest shopping mall in Africa. Still under construction at the time of writing, it is destined to have a series of canalside restaurants, an exploratorium, and a variety of entertainment centers, including theaters, cinemas, and cabaret.

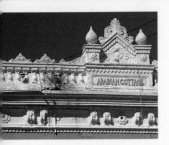

Under the old regime, there was a distinct hier-archy. First came the northern European whites, then the Latins, followed by the Japanese, Chinese, Cape Malays, Indians, Cape coloreds and blacks. Each had a different level of housing, education, and social status. The communities, particularly those imported from the East, retained their own cultural traditions.

64

THE SACRED CIRCLE
In 1693, Sheikh Yusuf, who claimed descent from Mohammed, was banished to the Cape, where he and his follow-ers continued to live and worship much as before. On his death in 1699, his tomb became a center of pilgrimage, while the 25 holy men who followed him were buried in Constantia, Oudekraal, on Signal Hill, on the slopes of Table Mountain, or on Robben Island. Their tombs (or *karamats*) form a "sacred circle" around Cape Town, and are said to provide the city with spiritual protection against natural disasters.

SAFE JOURNEY
The most famous of Sheikh Yusuf's disciples was Paay Schaapie, a freed slave responsible for the establishment of Islam in South Africa. He was recognized as a saint while still living, and after his death it became the practice among his follow-ers to take soil from his tomb when going on a journey. It is said he loved the Tana Baru, the burial ground at the top of the Bo-Kaap, so intensely that he would not allow the soil to remain away too long, and thus a safe journey was ensured.

"Coloreds" There are about 1.4 million "coloreds" of mixed race. Some originate from the offspring of black servants and their white masters, some from the integra-tion of the San and Khoikhoi (see page 132) to form the KhoiSan. Some of these women then had children by white men, some intermarried with black tribes from farther north and east. Historically, in Europe and America, anyone with any black ancestry is considered part of the black culture. This is not the case in South Africa; the coloreds were isolated, accepted socially by neither black nor white communities, while their only true heritage, the San culture, was destroyed by urban living.

By the late 19th century, there were sufficient numbers for them to form a distinct cultural group. They were mainly Christian, Afrikaans-speaking, and worked as skilled manual laborers, particularly on the railroads.

Cape Malays There is a large Islamic presence in the Cape region, drawn from Indian, Far Eastern, black, and colored communities. The Cape Malays are a much smaller group of about 12,000 people, largely confined to the tiny Bo-Kaap district of Cape Town (see page 54). Virtually none has Malay ancestry, most having been imported as slaves from Singapore, Sri Lanka, Madagascar and, above all, Indonesia by early Dutch settlers. The name comes from the Malayal language used as a lingua franca among traders across the Dutch East Indies. The community calls itself either Cape Muslim or Indo-African.

Unlike most people from slave nations, these were highly educated and skilled people, prized as builders and carpenters as well as household servants. They brought with them Sufism (the mystical branch of the Islamic faith), holy men and teachers, and a strong cultural iden-tity. Relatively few have intermarried with other ethnic groups and they are proud to have kept their nationhood and traditions, many of which have died out elsewhere.

Their language and history were officially banned during centuries of repression, but were kept alive by under-ground classes and texts written in Arabic script, known to all good Muslims but totally indecipherable to the Afrikaners. People do still speak Malayal today, but most commonly use Afrikaans. In fact, the first book in Afrikaans is said to have been written in Bo-Kaap, and the language was taught formally for the first time at the Auwal Mosque in Dorp Street, one of the oldest mosques

in Cape Town (1804).

The holy men did their best to buy up the slaves and free them, but it was not until slavery was banned throughout the British Empire in 1834 that the newly freed Muslims moved into Bo-Kaap. There are now 11 mosques scattered among the small, square, vividly painted houses that crawl up the side of Signal Hill. In 1966, the area was declared a slum and the Muslims were ordered out. Some went, but many more remained and eventually the authorities lost interest and left them alone, the only nonwhite community to survive in central Cape Town. Many of the houses were even rebuilt to the original design. Today, the area is a unique, fascinating testament to the old city, vibrant with noisy street life, as women in traditional *burkhas* (headscarves) and men in *kufias* (robes) gather on the corners to chat.

Yet the community is under threat once more, a victim of its success. Young, trendy Capetonians have recognized the charm of the district and the fascination of the archi-tecture and are snapping up houses, driv-ing prices way out of the reach of locals.

The houses in Bo-Kaap are rapidly becoming some of Cape Town's most sought-after real estate

CARNIVAL TIME
For two days a year (January 1 and 2) the colored community erupts onto the streets of Cape Town in a blaze of color and noise. Their exuberant Carnival began as a thanksgiving for the abolition of slavery and, almost incidentally, welcomes in the new year. Preparations are intense and often competitive as district troops are formed. They spend several months creating spectacular orig-inal costumes, music, and dance.

Walk

Historic Cape Town
(see map, page 51)

The old center of Cape Town is surprisingly small; much of it is built on reclaimed land and the harbor water used to lap the castle walls. This gentle stroll takes in most of the main attractions. Allow one to two hours, or a full day if you plan to visit the many sights en route. Start beside the **Castle of Good Hope** (see page 54).

Walk across into the **Grand Parade**, usually less than grand with a noisy mix of cars parking, taxis cruising for business, and a colorful flea market full of buckets of flowers and bolts of cloth. Carefully positioned in front of Table Mountain, the positively imperial **City Hall** (Darling Street, tel: 021-400 2230. *Open* during business hours and for concerts. *Admission free*) was built in 1905 in a blend of Italian Renaissance and British colonial styles. It has been carefully restored and is now the home of the Cape Town Symphony Orchestra, which holds regular concerts there. After Nelson Mandela's release from jail in February 1990, a crowd of 100,000 people waited for up to seven hours to hear his first speech from the balcony. It began: *"Amandla! Iafrika! Mayibuye!"* (Power to the people!).

Walk along Darling Street until you come to Adderley Street. To your right is the **Heerengracht**, a dull area of 1960s concrete apartment houses. One of the few mixed-race areas of Cape Town was demolished to create this monstrosity. Turn left up **Adderley Street**, the city's main shopping street. It has several charming small arcades and grand colonial and art-deco buildings. The **Standard Bank** is on the left; peer inside at the magnificent 19th-century banking hall used by Cecil Rhodes and other luminaries of the time.

Also on the left, toward the top of the street, are the somber, plain gray **Groote Kerk** (see page 55) and the Cape Dutch **South African Cultural History Museum** (see page 60), in front of which stands a statue of Jan Smuts in battle dress. To the right, by Government Avenue, is **St. George's Cathedral** (see page 59). From here, walk up leafy, pedestrian **Government Avenue►►►**, where squirrels play under the trees. A little way up on the left are the red-brick and white stucco **Houses of Parliament** (see page 56). To the right is the **South African Library** (see page 60).

Just beyond is the entrance to **Company's Garden►►►** (top of Adderley Street. *Open*

Well-shaded Government Avenue is the historic heart of Cape Town

Above: Company's Garden began as a market garden
Right: De Tuynhuys is now home to the office of the state president

daily 7–dusk. *Admission free*). In 1652, Jan van Riebeeck and the Dutch East India Company laid out a 45-acre vegetable garden to supply merchant ships heading east with fresh fruit and vegetables. Only 8 acres of South Africa's first market garden survive, transformed by Sir Herbert Baker into a lush English park with lawns, shady trees, elegant walkways, and manicured flower beds. Opposite the entrance, **De Tuynhuys** was built in 1700 as a Company Guest House to accommodate any overflow of dignitaries from the castle. Altered over the centuries, it has been restored to its 1795 Regency appearance and is now the office of the state president.

At the top of the garden is an open plaza. On your left are the **South African National Gallery** (see page 61) and the **Jewish Museum** (see page 56). Directly ahead is the **South African Museum and Planetarium** (see page 61). Continue to the top of Government Avenue, where you will see **Bertram House** (see page 54) on your right. Cross the street and walk under the pillars up Hof Street to reach the strawberry pink **Mount Nelson Hotel**. This is the oldest and plushest hotel in central Cape Town (see page 258), where you can indulge in tea with smoked salmon sandwiches while resting your aching feet.

If you wish to continue, return along **Long Street** (see page 57), stopping for a traditional African meal at the Pan African Market before getting down to some serious haggling at the crafts market in **Greenmarket Square** (see page 55).

Cape Town environs

▶ Cape Flats

For township tours contact One City Tours
(tel: 021-426 4644); Legend Tours (tel: 021-697 4056/7);
Grassroute Tours (tel: 021-424 8480);
Western Cape Action Tours (tel: 021-461 1371)
Admission: expensive

The wide, marshy plain of the Cape Flats—site of Cape Town's townships—lies inland from Table Mountain. The first township in South Africa was founded 3 miles from Cape Town in 1901. It was later moved because it was considered to be too close to the center of town, and the people were resettled in **Langa**, which survives today. The infamous **Crossroads** now has regular streets and drains, but for many years it was a massive squatter camp where residents lived under the daily threat of the bulldozers. The most astounding of the three main townships in the area is **Khayelitsha**, which sprang from nothing to become a shanty city of over 1 million people in the space of a very few years. Serious efforts are being made to provide better conditions, but steady urban drift ensures that as soon as one area is sorted out, another squatter camp springs up to replace it.

Shanties on the Cape Flats show a very different view of Cape Town

▶ Groot Constantia

About 9 miles south of the city center. Take the M3 to the Constantia exit and follow the signs (the turnoff is on the left)
Museum (tel: 021-794 5067). Open: daily. Cellar tours on the hour every hour until 4; tastings 10–4:30. Admission: moderate

One of the oldest estates in South Africa, founded in 1685, this was the home of Governor Simon van der Stel, who planted the first vines. A century later, it was taken over by the Cloete family, who created a range of world-famous dessert wines, Constantia Frontignac, Pontac, and Steen. Sadly, the grand age ended with the phylloxera outbreak in the 1860s and the estate was sold to the nation in 1885 by a near-bankrupt family. Since then, it has been used as an experimental station and museum. However, from 1975 onward, there has been significant replanting and Constantia wine is regaining both quality and reputation.

At the entrance a small museum shows the history of the manor. The elegant Cape Dutch house itself, designed by Louis Thibault, was destroyed by fire in 1925, but has

DIVINE WINE
Napoleon is said to have demanded nothing but Constantia wine during his exile on St. Helena; Bismarck was a patron; Jane Austen recommends its "healing powers on a disappointed heart"; and King Louis Philippe of France liked it so much that he bought the whole vintage in 1833.

been carefully restored to the original plans, with high walls, flagged floor, heavy wooden ceilings, and dark green shutters. It is beautifully furnished in sturdy, late 18th-century style. Behind it, the old cellars, with their magnificent pediment by Anton Anreith (1791), contain a fascinating small museum of wine. The modern cellars include a cellar tour, wine tasting, and a shop, while the Jonkershuis (old stables) houses an excellent restaurant (see page 264).

▶▶▶ Kirstenbosch National   52A2 Botanical Gardens

Rhodes Drive, Newlands
(tel: 021-762 9120/761 4916 – weekends)
about 6 miles from the city center
Open: Apr–Aug daily 8–6, Sep–Mar daily 8–7
Admission: moderate. Guided walks Tue and Sat 11 AM

In 1895, Cecil John Rhodes bought this estate and bequeathed it to the nation. In 1913, Henry Harold Welch Pearson, Professor of Botany at the University of South Africa, founded the National Botanical Gardens. They grew rapidly to become one of the world's most important botanical collections. Most of the 1,310-acre estate, stretching up the eastern flank of Table Mountain, is local *fynbos* and coastal forest, but there are 89 acres of delightful formal gardens. These have rich collections of flowers and trees, a fragrance garden and Braille trail for the blind, a pond, a herb garden, and specialist collections of pelargoniums, restios, proteas, cycads, and ericas. Concentrating on the indigenous flora of southern Africa, the gardens contain some 6,000 of South Africa's 22,000 plant species, while a further 900 grow in the wild areas. Several walking trails, lasting from 45 minutes to six hours, lead into the woods and up the mountain. A strong educational and scientific program concentrates on the conservation of many rare and endangered species. The restaurant serves tea, coffee, and lunches and a garden shop sells plants, souvenirs, and books. Concerts are held in the gardens every Sunday during the summer. Allow at least half a day to explore.

GREEN HISTORY

The Kirstenbosch Gardens contain a living history of the Cape region, starting with the remains of a wild almond hedge planted by Jan van Riebeeck in 1660 to protect the cattle from marauding Khoikhoi. There is an avenue of fig and camphor trees (from China and Japan) planted by Rhodes during his tenure, and Professor Pearson, founder of the gardens, is buried among his first collection, in the Cycad Amphitheatre.

Anton Anreith's magnificent carving adorns the old cellars at Groot Constantia

▶▶▶ Robben Island 48A2

6 miles off the Green Point coast
Robben Island Cruises (tel: 021-419 2875)
Departures on the hour every hour between 10 and 3, from
Pier 1, by the Clock Tower, V&A Waterfront. The tour lasts
3½ hours and includes a bus tour of the island and a prison
tour led by a former inmate. Admission: expensive

Measuring only 1¼ by 2 miles, Robben Island takes its name from "robbe," the Dutch word for seals. It still has colonies of Cape fur seals and penguins, but the island is far more infamous for its past inhabitants: high-ranking exiles, Islamic holy men, political dissidents, robbers, pirates, and murderers. In the 19th century, it held black leaders captured during the Frontier Wars; from the 1960s inmates included high-profile political detainees such as Nelson Mandela, who spent 27 years here. The last prisoners left in May 1991, leaving the island a wildlife sanctuary and place of pilgrimage for South African nationalism.

▶▶ Simon's Town 48A1

25 miles south of Cape Town
Tourist Information, Main Road (tel: 021-786 2436)
Named after Simon van der Stel, governor of the Cape from 1691 to 1699, this little port became the Royal Navy headquarters in 1814 and was taken over by the S. A. Navy in 1957. Today it is a rather quaint seaside town with charming Victorian houses. The governor's residence (built 1777), later a court and prison, is now the delightful **Simon's Town Museum** (Court Road, tel: 021-786 3046. *Open* Mon–Fri 9–4, Sat 10–4. *Admission: inexpensive*). Other places to visit are the **South African Naval Museum** (Masthouse, West Dockyard, tel: 021-787 4686. *Open* daily 10–4); and the **Warrior Toy Museum** (St. George's Street, tel: 021-786 1395. *Open* daily 10–4. *Admission: inexpensive*) with a collection of dolls, toy soldiers, model cars, boats, and trains. At **The Boulders**, outside town, is a colony of African penguins, one of only two on the African mainland.

CONVICT ISLAND
The first-ever European attempt to colonize the Cape Peninsula was in 1615, when eight British convicts were left on the shore. They crossed to Robben Island and remained there until rescued by a passing ship some months later. With the arrival of the Dutch 40 years later, Robben Island became a high-security prison, which it remained for nearly 350 years.

70

Below: splendid Victoriana along the main road in Simon's Town. Bottom: African penguins strut for the tourists at The Boulders

Drive

The Cape of Good Hope

A spiny ridge of mountains tails south along the Cape Peninsula to tumble into the sea in a riotous confusion of rocks at Cape Point. The scenery is spectacular, the beaches idyllic, and many of the charming small towns offer an enticing blend of good food, interesting shops, and plentiful history. Allow at least one full day.

Cape Town to Muizenberg From the city center, take the M3 (De Waal Road) to Muizenberg. There are turnoffs en route for **Kirstenbosch** and **Groot Constantia** (see pages 68–69).

Herbert Baker once wielded his architect's pencil in trendy **Muizenberg** (Tourism Information, Municipal Building, Atlantic Road, tel: 021-788 6193, fax: 021-788 6208, e-mail: peninsulatourism@yebo.co.za), the favorite resort of the Randlords. Numerous fine houses include the cottage in which Cecil Rhodes died in 1902, kept as a museum/shrine (Main Road, tel: 021-788 1816. *Open* Tue–Sun 10–1, 2–5). Now the town is a bit tired and shabby, but nothing can spoil its lovely, safe, shallow beach,

Kalk Bay, one of many small towns with delightful beaches along the Cape Peninsula

lined by rows of colorful changing booths. The Venetian-style **Natale Labia Museum** (192 Main Road, tel: 021-788 4106. *Open* Tue–Sun 10–5, closed Aug) is a pleasant art gallery; also visit the **South Africa Police Museum** (186 Main Road, tel: 021-788 7035. *Open* Mon–Fri 8–3:30, Sat 9–1, Sun 2–5) and the **Toy Museum** (8 Beach Road, tel: 021-788 1569. *Open* Tue–Sun 10–5).

Kalk Bay to Cape Point A little farther down the coast, **Kalk Bay** ("lime bay") was named after the kilns in which shells were burned to produce lime. It is a busy fishing port. The main road has antiques and junk stores, crafts shops, and eateries. Soak up the atmosphere, climb up to the deep caves pitting the mountain slopes, or try surfing on **Danger Beach**.

Continue south along the coast-hugging M4 to **Fish Hoek**, a resort that has the distinction of being the only teetotal town in the country—a stipulation laid down by Lord Charles Somerset in 1818. He also declared free fishing rights for all. **Peers Cave**, a rock shelter nearby, is named after the man who discovered the 15,000-year-old skeleton called "Fish Hoek Man." This is the best place on the peninsula to see whales.

Cape Point divides two oceans

Continue through **Simon's Town** (see page 70) to the farthest tip of the peninsula and the bleak, beautiful 19,150-acre **Cape of Good Hope Nature Reserve** (tel: 021-780 9100. *Open* daily 7–6. *Admission: moderate*). The accepted meeting place of the Atlantic and Indian oceans is **Cape Point**, which is also the psychological if not physical end of Africa (the most southerly point is actually Cape Agulhas, see page 94). There are drives, places to picnic, walk, and swim, plus magnificent flora and small game. The east coast cliffs sheer abruptly into the warm waters of the Indian Ocean's **False Bay**; to the west the land slopes downward more gently to the Atlantic. The visitors' center has a funicular up to the viewing point and a good restaurant. For walks, contact the Senior Nature Conservation Officer (tel: 021-780 1100).

Chapman's Peak Drive
Heading north, take the N65 along the Atlantic coast to **Kommetjie**, a quiet seaside village with a good surfing beach. The water, famously, is freezing, but a shallow, warmer tidal pool provides safe swimming for children. From here, the beautiful 4-mile **Long Beach**, unsafe for swimming but popular with horse riders, leads up to **Noordhoek** (Tourist Information, just off Main Road, tel: 021-789 2812. *Open* daily 9:30–5:30), where you join the **Chapman's Peak**

Drive to Hout Bay. Built between 1915 and 1922, this winding 6-mile drive is a magnificent feat of engineering. Along it are continuous, spectacular views with plentiful vista points, picnic areas, climbs, and mountain walks.

Hout Bay to the city Dominated by the towering peak of The Sentinel, little **Hout Bay** (Tourist Information, Andrews Road, tel: 021-790 1264. *Open* Mon–Fri 9–5, Sat–Sun 10–1) was named after the wood (*hout*) harvested for shipbuilding. Traditionally a center of crayfish and *snoek* (barracouda) fishing, it is a lively seaside town filled with vacation cottages, fishermen, a thriving marina, and several popular restaurants. The local **museum** (4 Andrews Road, tel: 021-790 3270. *Open* Tue–Sat, 10–12:30, 2–4:30. *Admission: inexpensive*) has an excellent display of *strandloper* (beachcomber) culture, while the **South African Fisheries Museum** (Hout Bay Harbour, tel: 021-790 7268. *Open* Tue–Sun 10–4) has fascinating models, audiovisuals, and other fishing displays. From the harbor, Drumboat Charters (tel: 021-438 9208) runs boat trips to the seal colony and seabird sanctuary on **Duiker Island**. In the summer you can see thousands of Cape fur seals here. Nearby, the **World of Birds Sanctuary** (Valley Road, tel: 021-790 2730. *Open* daily 9–5. *Admission: moderate*) is one of the largest bird sanctuaries in South Africa, with over 3,000 birds from around 450 varieties flying free in walk-through aviaries.

Beyond Hout Bay, the coastline becomes one long ribbon development, with houses clustering ever more thickly as you head back into the city. Lovely undeveloped **Sandy Bay** is the local nudist beach. **Bakoven**, named after a large cave shaped like a baker's oven, has two small beaches and is safe for children and popular with snorkelers. Trendy **Camps Bay**, tucked in at the base of the Twelve Apostles, has a wide beach with lawns and a good selection of affordable restaurants. The sea here is very cold with a strong undertow. Surfers use Glen Beach in the adjoining cove. **Clifton** is *the* place to be and be seen. Although the water is freezing, people flock to its four overcrowded beaches. **Sea Point** is closer to the city center and not quite so fashionable, but is lively and trendy with a slightly bohemian tinge.

73

Camps Bay and the Twelve Apostles on the Atlantic Coast

The world is divided into six "floral kingdoms," distinct botanical habitats from tropical rain forest to tundra. The smallest (35,000 square miles) and, for its size, the richest is the Cape, which stretches from the Cederberg in the Western Cape to Port Elizabeth in the east.

74

SMALL IS BEAUTIFUL
The largest of the floral kingdoms, the Boreal, stretches much of the way across the northern hemisphere and covers 42 percent of the earth's land surface. The Cape kingdom covers just 0.04 percent—a mere 35,000 square miles.

Top: proteas in bloom at Kirstenbosch
Below: quiver trees in the Karoo

Within the Cape kingdom are a staggering 8,500 species of plants (42.5 percent of the total for southern Africa), of which 6,000 are endemic. There are more indigenous plant species on Table Mountain (1,470) than in the whole of the British Isles (1,443). Many more are found in the spectacular spring displays of the Karoo and Namaqualand on the far side of the mountains.

Fynbos This magical array of Cape plants and flowers is known overall as *fynbos* (literally "fine bush"), a group of evergreen fine-leafed plants that thrive in poor, sandy soil and harsh conditions, with hot dry summers and cold wet winters. From a distance, this heathland vegetation seems less than inspiring, with low, scrubby plants rolling on across the hills, few bushes standing higher than a person's knee. It is only when you look closely that you begin to see the enormous variation in species. Three-quarters are found nowhere else and many are so specialized that they survive in only one valley.

Fynbos is made up of three main plant families—reeds, proteas, and ericas—along with several smaller groups of legumes and bulbs. The most common are the wind-

pollinated reeds (*restios*) that here replace grass as general ground cover. Hardy and unpleasant grazing, they survive the weather and wildlife, but are harvested by locals for thatching. Proteas (*proteaceae*) are the national flower of South Africa. Most familiar are the king proteas, with their heavy, furry black-and-pink heads, but there are an infinite number of species, ranging from spiky red flowers to a great mass of minute florets and even inconspicuous, low-lying pincushions. Ericas (*ericaceae*), related to the European heathers, are the only true *fynbos* plant to translate happily to the gardens of the world, although other local species, such as freesias, pelargoniums, campanulas, lobelias, and the subtropical gladioli and strelizias have become popular with gardeners and florists alike.

Orange-breasted sunbird in a blooming Protea pityphla

Spring color Mesembryanthemums and daisies (*asteraceae*) dot the mountains and coast with color, but really come into their own in Namaqualand, where spring sees magnificent sheets of vibrant pinks, oranges, and purples cloaking the landscape for miles on end. The Karoo also flowers in spring, but here there is a more subtle cover with tiny yellow and purple flowers gently tinting the soft gray of rock and shale.

Subtropical forest Until about 3 million years ago, the Cape is thought to have had a milder climate and to have been covered by lush, subtropical woodland. This survives a little farther north, along the hills of the Garden Route (Knysna Forest and Tsitsikamma National Park, see pages 100–101) and through into KwaZulu-Natal. Here, the mountains foster a totally different range of species: the most dramatic are the huge, hard yellowwoods and stinkwoods, from which most Cape Dutch furniture is made. Lurking in the undergrowth below these giants are some of the most extraordinary plants in South Africa, the cycads, said to be unchanged since the Jurassic period (150–200 million years ago), when dinosaurs roamed the earth.

FLOWER HUNTING
No one has yet attempted to produce a layman's guide to Cape flora, although there are many huge tomes on specialist aspects, such as proteas. The Kirstenbosch Gardens (see page 69) are an essential first stop, but to see the mass of flowers in all their glory, visit in winter (July/August) for *fynbos*, and spring (September/October) for the desert flowers. Most of the desert plants are heliotropic (keep their faces turned toward the sun), so are best seen in the midday heat, with your back to the light. Expect long traffic jams at the height of the season. A telephone hot line, MTN Flowerline (tel: 083-910 1028), operates between June and October.

EARTHQUAKE
On September 29, 1969, a massive earthquake measuring 6.5 on the Richter scale reduced much of Tulbagh to ruins. Many early buildings, such as Thibault's Drostdy (1806), were totally destroyed. One of the biggest restoration programs ever undertaken in South Africa swung into action. Over the years buildings had been altered and extended, windows blocked up, and gables rearranged. The earthquake-shattered plasterwork allowed the Tulbagh Restoration Committee to reconstruct the original pattern of building. In Church Street alone, 32 small whitewashed, gabled homesteads have been carefully restored. The results are remarkable.

The Oude Kerk Volksmuseum, Tulbagh, restored after a disastrous earthquake

The Breede River Valley area

▶ Ceres 48B2

80 miles northeast of Cape Town, off the N1
Tourist Information, John Steyn Library, corner Voortrekker and Owen streets (tel: 023-316 1051, fax: 023-316 1287)
Named after the Roman goddess of fertility, Ceres is all about fruit. Tour the huge **Ceres Fruit Growers and Ceres Fruit Juices Co-operative** (tel: 023-312 3121) to see fruit dried, processed, and packaged, or pick your own at the **Klondyke Cherry Farm** (tel: 023-312 2085. *Open* Nov–Jan).

In early days the town was often cut off by winter snow, but in 1848, Andrew Geddes Bain built Mitchell's Pass, after which it became an important stop en route to the diamond fields. The **Transport Riders Museum** (8 Orange Street, tel: 023-312 2045. *Open* Mon–Fri 8:30–1, 2–5, Sat 9–noon. *Admission: inexpensive*) traces the transport riders' part in local history.

About 50 miles north (gravel road), **Kagga Kamma** (P.O. Box 7143, North Paarl 7623, tel: 021-863 8334) is a private game reserve, home to some of South Africa's last traditional Bushmen (San). Nearby is the 39,536-acre **Sadawa Game Reserve** (tel: 023-312 2512).

▶ Tulbagh 48B2

About 100 miles north of Cape Town
Tourist Information, Church Street (tel: 023-230 1348)
Open: Mon–Fri 9–4:30, Sat 10–4, Sun 11–4
Parts of rural Tulbagh seem to be an almost perfect 18th-century town. Church Street is particularly charming, and the old church is the focal point of the **Oude Kerk Volksmuseum** (4 Church Street, tel: 023-230 1041. *Open* Mon–Fri 8–1, 2–5, Sat 10–1, 2–4, Sun 11–1, 2–4. *Admission: inexpensive*). This complex of four restored buildings

houses a collection of furniture and costumes, and displays on the 1969 earthquake (see panel opposite). The **Miniature Houses Museum** (4 Witzenberg Street, tel: 023-230 0651. *Open* Mon–Sat 9:30–12:30, 2:30–4:30, Sun 9:30–12:30. *Admission: inexpensive*) is dedicated to dollhouses.

The **Oude Drostdy** (2½ miles from Tulbagh, tel: 023-230 0203. *Open* Mon–Sat 10–12:50, 2–4:50, Sun 2:30–4:50. *Admission: inexpensive*) is now a museum, housing an unexpected collection of early gramophones as well as the usual Cape Dutch furniture.

▶▶ Worcester 48B2

65 miles northeast of Cape Town
Breede River Valley Tourist Information, Kleinplasie Museum Complex, Worcester 76411 (tel: 023-347 6411, fax: 023-347 1115, e-mail manager@breede rivervalley.co.za). Worcester Tourist Information, 23 Baring Street (tel: 023-347 1048, fax: 023-347 4678). Open: Mon–Fri 8–5, Sat 8:30–12:30

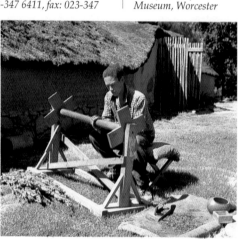

Rolling tobacco at the Kleinplasie Open Air Museum, Worcester

This sprawling, modern market town is "capital" of the biggest wine-producing district (see pages 86–87, 92–93). It is also home to the vast **KWV Brandy Cellars** (Church Street, tel: 023-342 0255. Guided tours Mon–Sat at 10 (Afrikaans) and at 2 (English). Open for sales Mon–Fri 8–5, Sat 9–4. *Admission: moderate*), where 120 copper pot kettles distill the famous KWV 10- and 20-year-old brandies.

Allow plenty of time to visit the open-air **Kleinplasie Museum▶** (off Robertson Road, tel: 023-342 2225. *Open* Mon–Sat 9–4:30, Sun 10:30–4:30. *Admission : moderate*). Reconstructed dwellings and farm buildings are accurately furnished according to dates between 1690 and 1900, and there is an explanation of the lifestyle and agricultural techniques of pioneer farmers. The area hums with traditional activities, from baking and tobacco rolling to distilling *witblitz*, the local firewater (on sale, with tastings, in the museum).

Next door to the open-air museum is the **Kleinplasie Reptile World** (off Robertson Road, tel: 023-342 6480. *Open* daily 9–5. *Admission: moderate*), with over 80 species of snakes, lizards, turtles, and crocodiles. Three further museums: the Cape Dutch **Beck House** (1841), furnished as a late 19th-century town house, and **Stofberg House** (1920s), which covers the history of Worcester, are both on Baring Street (*Open* Mon–Sat 9–1, 2–5. *Admission: donation*). The **Hugo Naudé House** (Russell Street, tel: 023-342 5802. *Open* Mon–Fri 9–4:30, Sat 9–12:30. *Admission: donation*) is the former studio of the South African pioneer painter. It now houses the municipal art collection.

The **Karoo National Botanical Garden** (Roux Street, tel: 023-347 0785. *Open* daily 8–5. *Admission: moderate*) has 356 acres of natural semidesert vegetation, 25 acres of landscaped gardens full of quiver trees, aloes, and vygies, and greenhouses filled with extraordinary stone plants.

77

OTHER STOPS
The Breede River valley is an important fruit- and wine-producing area, prolifically fertile and festooned with orchards, vineyards, and wheatlands. It has small reserves of plants and birds, and successions of pools, rapids, and waterfalls are ideal for trout anglers, canoeists, mountaineers, and nature lovers. Several other towns in the region repay a stop. They include Robertson (renowned for its Muscatel grapes and wines and a good base for climbs into the Langeberg range), McGregor, Rawsonville, Bonnievale, Ashton, and the spa towns of Montagu and Goudini. Most have a small museum and a wine route.

The vast empty plains of the Great Karoo

THE KAROO
Aptly named "the land of thirst" by the Khoikhoi, the Karoo is a vast arid wilderness peppered with flat-topped *koppies* of hard doleritic rock trapping thousands of fossils, from enormous trees to strange amphibious creatures with mammalian features. Its hardy little desert plants curl unnoticed into the grayish dust, bursting into life in spring when their magnificent blossom splashes the landscape with pure color. The desert is divided into the markedly more fertile Little Karoo, around Oudtshoorn, separated from the sea by the Langeberg and Outeniqua Mountains, and the vast expanse of the Great Karoo beyond the Swartberg to the north (see also page 112).

Groot- (Great) Karoo

▶ Beaufort West   49D3

30 miles northeast of Cape Town
Central Karoo Tourist Information, D.C. Office,
Donkin Street, Beaufort West (tel: 023-415 1160)
This is the Karoo's largest town, with streets shaded by pear trees, and three small **museums** (Donkin Street. *Open* Mon–Fri 9–12:45, 1:45–4:45. *Admission: inexpensive*). One has exhibits on Dr. Christian Barnaard, the first man to perform a heart transplant, and one is a history museum.
  Karoo National Park (off the N1, tel: 023-415 2828; reservations tel: 021-422 2810, fax: 021-424 6211, e-mail: reservations@parks-sa.co.za. *Open* daily 5 AM–10 PM, reception 7:30 AM–8 PM. *Admission: moderate*), 2½ miles south of Beaufort West, encompasses 113,965 acres of virgin Karoo veld and the Nuweveldberge. Remarkably fecund for a semidesert, it has 64 mammal species, including mountain zebra, black rhino, and springbok; 194 bird species, including black eagles; and 59 reptile species. There is a small museum (*Open* daily 8–12:30, 1:30–6), a restaurant, basic accommodations, hiking, and 4x4 trails.

▶▶ The Swartberg   49D2

High and gnarled, the Swartberg (Black Mountains), known as the Cango (Water) Mountains, formed an almost impenetrable 125-mile barrier to the interior until the arrival of the great Victorian road builders.
  Of the seven passes in the area, the most dramatic is the 15-mile **Swartberg Pass**, built by Thomas Bain using convict labor (1881–1888). It has wide panoramas on the southern slopes, but the northern face plunges into a ravine, ending in a cauldron of rock at Eerstewater, near the village of Prince Albert. At the top is a remote valley, Gamkaskloof (once called "Hell"), settled for nearly 200 years by a group of farmers who were totally isolated before the arrival of the road in 1962. Also worth driving along is the shorter **Meiringspoort Pass** on the road from De Rust to Beaufort West.

Klein- (Little) Karoo

▶▶ Cango Caves
49D2

18 miles north of Oudtshoorn on the R328 (tel: 044-272 7410)
Open: daily 9–4. Access to
caves on guided tours only,
every hour on the hour
Admission: moderate/
expensive. Reservations
advised

The San lived in the entrance to this huge limestone system under the Swartberg Mountains, but they never penetrated far inside. A local farmer, Jacobus van Zyl, led the first expedition into the heart of the caves in 1780, discovering the first of three sequences of caverns adorned with stalactites and all manner of fantastical dripstone formations. The largest of the chambers is a stunning 350 feet across and 53 feet high. The entire system remains at an even temperature of 64°F. Three levels of tours are available: easy half-hour strolls that take you through two of the caverns; more comprehensive one-hour tours into eight chambers; and full-scale adventure tours, requiring you to wriggle through narrow passages and climb steep pipes; you should be reasonably fit for this but do not need any previous experience.

Cango Caves' dramatic dripstone formations

▶ Cango Wildlife Ranch
49D2

About 6 miles north of Oudtshoorn, on the Cango Caves road, R328 (tel: 044-272 5593)
Open: daily 8–6 (restaurant open until late)
Admission: expensive

Operating mainly as a breeding center for rare species, this farm has everything: over 400 crocodiles, a snake park, lions, cheetahs (some of which are tame and you can pet), and jaguars; comical pygmy hippos and warthogs; miniature horses and goats; and a deer park. Nearby are the **Cango Ostrich Farm** (see page 81) and the **Cango Angora Rabbit Farm** (tel: 044-279 1259. *Open* daily 7–5).

▶ Matjiesfontein
48C2

About 160 miles east of Cape Town

James Logan (see panel) found the dry, crisp Karoo air good for his weak chest. In the late 19th century, he founded Matjiesfontein as a resort and health spa, attracting similarly afflicted guests including Lord Randolph Churchill and the Sultan of Zanzibar. During the Boer War, it became the headquarters of the Cape Command, then a military hospital. Not much has changed in the last 100 years. Now called the Lord Milner (see page 259), the hotel is a monument to Victoriana and is said to be haunted by armies of jolly, party-loving ghosts. The old station has a private museum of Victorian artifacts.

LOGAN'S LUCK
James Logan arrived from Scotland in 1877, eventually settling in the Karoo where he bought a farm, Tweedside, and gradually added land until he owned over 120,000 acres. A model and prosperous farmer, Logan had the first private residence in South Africa with electricity, pioneered water and sewage treatment, and made a second fortune from his hotel and restaurants. His third fortune came from selling water to the railroads: a locomotive consumed 55,000 gallons of water in crossing the Karoo and therefore any dependable supply was invaluable. He died in Matjiesfontein on July 30, 1920.

Oudtshoorn's ostrich feather millionaires built themselves fantastically palatial homes

PEAR POWER
In 1916, a Karoo farmer invented a new alternative to gas, brewed from prickly pears. To prove it worked, he invited writer Lawrence Green to accompany him on a drive from Cape Town to Bulawayo (described in Green's book, *Karoo*). Sadly, the venture failed when the farmer inhaled poisonous fumes from the fuel and died. Karoo farmers went back to turning prickly pears into a potent liqueur, which they say is particularly good poured over ice cream!

▶▶▶ Oudtshoorn   49D2
314 miles east of Cape Town
Klein Karoo and Oudtshoorn Tourist Information,
corner of Baron van Rheede and Voortrekker streets
(tel: 044-272 2241, fax: 044-279 2667,
e-mail: kkdr@pixie.co.za)
Open: Mon–Sat 9–1, 2–5

Diamonds may have been the treasure of Kimberley, but ostrich feathers were the wealth of the Little Karoo. From the 1880s, sweeping ostrich plumes and feather boas were the height of ladies' fashion. Designers could not get enough, and the arid Karoo proved to be perfect breeding territory. In 1905, the feathers plucked from just six birds fetched $2,000 (R12,000). By the time the railroad arrived in 1913, the district was awash with millionaires. Ordinary little Oudtshoorn was transformed into a boom-town filled with spectacular mansions. Oudtshoorn's "feather palaces" were large, ornate, and lavish beyond your wildest dreams. Most were swirling sandstone art nouveau, with circular turrets, iron railings, and—the colonial variation—corrugated-iron roofs. The ceilings and cornices were embossed papier-mâché, while the walls and windows were bright with stained glass and vividly glazed tiles.

With World War I the market crashed and for a time Oudtshoorn was in decline. In the late 1930s, however, ostriches again came to the rescue; the first show farm was opened and the tourists arrived. Today the trade is thriving, but this time feathers, though still valuable, are not the crucial product. International demand for low-fat, almost cholesterol-free ostrich meat is soaring. Supple ostrich leather is increasingly popular for expensive designer shoes, bags, belts, and accessories. Even the eggs fetch a good market price, both for eating and—halved or carved—as souvenirs.

The town has two excellent museums. Don't miss the **C. P. Nel Museum** (3 Baron van Rheede Street, tel: 044-272 7306. *Open* Mon–Sat 9–5. *Admission: inexpensive*), which occupies the old Boys' High School, a building designed in 1907 by leading "feather" architect Charles Bullock. The core of the compelling collection was donated in 1953 by C. P. Nel, a prominent local businessman. It tells the history of Oudtshoorn, ostriches, and the feather trade. **Le Roux Townhouse** (146 High Street, tel: 044-272 3676. *Open* Mon–Fri 9–1, 2–5. *Admission free*) is a carefully restored offshoot of the C. P. Nel Museum. Built by Charles Bullock for J. H. J. Le Roux in 1909, it is one of the finest of the "feather mansions." Lavishly appointed, it still contains most of its original furnishings.

There are several ostrich show farms in Oudtshoorn offering a full range of tours and facilities. **Highgate** (off the Mossel Bay Road, the R328, 6 miles from the town center. Tel: 044-272 7115. *Open* daily 8–5, tours last up to two hours. *Admission: expensive*) was one of the first ostrich farms in the valley (1887). It was also the first to turn ostriches into a tourist attraction in 1937, setting the agenda for all tours. There you could—and still can—investigate every aspect of the birds' life: see them being born, reared, and plucked; handle a baby, sit or ride on an adult, and watch an ostrich Derby, with "professional" jockeys on board; buy the eggs, eat the fillet, and wear the shoes. At the **Safari Ostrich Farm** (off the Mossel Bay Road, the R328, 3 miles from the town center, tel: 044-272 7311. *Open* daily 7:30–5. *Admission: moderate*) there is a restored feather baron's mansion, Welgeluk (1910), and the tour includes an explanation of how ostrich products are made, from feather dusters to handbags. The **Cango Ostrich Farm** (about 9 miles north of Oudtshoorn on the Cango Caves road, the R328. Tel: 044-272 4623. *Open* school holidays 8–5; out of season daily 8–4:30. *Admission: moderate*) is smaller and simpler than the other two but has a wine cellar and butterfly farm.

OSTRICHES
There are about 250,000 ostriches in the Oudtshoorn area, on around 300 farms. The female lays up to 15 eggs per clutch, each weighing the equivalent to 24 hen's eggs. They take six weeks to hatch. The young are fawn colored, while adult males are black and white and the females chocolate brown. They take two years to reach maturity, when they weigh about 220 pounds. The birds run in herds of 100–150 and are plucked every nine months, each bird losing over 2 pounds of feathers at a time.

81

The lap of honor in an ostrich race

WHALE AHOY!
Of the world's 80 species of cetacean (sea mammals), 39 are found around South Africa. Migrant herds of southern right whales reappear in the seas off the Overberg every winter from May/June to November. You may also see porpoises and dolphins and, occasionally, Brydes and Sei whales. The best places to see them are at Stony Point, near Betty's Bay, Kleinmond, Onrus, Walker Bay in Hermanus, and at Koppie Alleen in the De Hoop Nature Reserve. With luck and patience, you can get to within 55 yards. Whale hot line, tel: 083-910 1028.

Whales and tourists dominate daily life in Hermanus

The Overberg and South Coast

The Overberg ("over the mountain") is the end of Africa, the segment of the south coast on the far side of the Hottentots Holland Mountains from Cape Town. It was one of the first areas beyond the bay to be colonized. Cut off by the mountains, the isolated Overbergers developed their own distinctive food, language, and a strong sense of independence, heavily influenced by missionaries at **Genadendal** (which has an excellent mission museum in Herrnhut House), Elim, and Zuurbraak.

There are several pleasant resorts: **Gansbaai**, an unspoiled fishing village with safe swimming (for shark diving off the coast, contact White Shark Ecoventures, tel: 021-419 8204); **Betty's Bay**, backed by magnificent mountains and site of the superb 495-acre **Harold Porter National Botanical Garden▶** (tel: 028-272 9311. *Open* daily 8–6. *Admission: inexpensive*); and **Kleinmond**, between Hermanus and Betty's Bay, where you can find within a 3-mile radius every type of Western Cape natural habitat, from beach dunes to *fynbos*.

▶ **Cape Agulhas and environs** see pages 94–95

▶ **Hermanus**   48B1
62 miles east of Cape Town
Tourist Information, 105 Main Road (tel: 028-312 2629, fax: 028-313 0305, e-mail: infoburo@hermanus.co.za)
Open: Mon 9–5, Sat 9–3, Sun 9–1
Fashionable Hermanus was founded early in the 19th century by Hermanus Pieters, who earmarked its green cliffs and freshwater stream as excellent summer grazing. But it was fishermen who settled it in the 1850s, and since the 1900s it has been a popular summer resort.

There are several fine beaches nearby, but the real draw is the whales. Hermanus is the only town in the world with an official "whale crier" (tel: 083-212 1074) who wanders the streets with a sandwich board and kelp horn. There are good viewing points for whales from the cliffs and the Old Harbour. The harbor was the focal point of the early village; now it is the hub of a tourist town, part of a "living" **Old Harbour Museum** (Marine Drive,

tel: 028-312 1475. *Open* Mon–Sat 9–1, 2–4. *Admission: inexpensive*), with exhibitions on local fishing and whaling. A sonar buoy catches the whales' song and transmits it live into the museum hall. In the square above is a lively crafts market, while the Old School House is an annex to the museum with fascinating old photographs. There are hiking trails, including one through the mountain and coastal *fynbos* of the 3,573-acre **Fernkloof Nature Reserve**.

▶▶ Swellendam   *48C1*

134 miles from Cape Town
Tourist Information, Voortrek Street
(tel/fax: 028-514 2770, e-mail: infoswd@sdm.dorea.co.za)
Open: Mon–Fri 8–1, 2–5, Sat 9–12:30

The well-watered area around Swellendam, now rich in wheat fields, cows, and fruit trees, once attracted great quantities of game, which in turn attracted the Hessekwa Khoikhoi. The first Europeans arrived in the 1740s, carving out farms along the Breede River. Many of their original homesteads still exist. By the early 19th century, Swellendam was a gung-ho eastern frontier village on the pioneering Kaapse Wapad (Cape wagon road). Named after Governor Swellengrebel and his wife, Helena ten Damme, the town flirted briefly with independence before settling down as a charming country town with oak-lined streets, pristine Cape Dutch and Victorian houses, and a splendid Dutch Reformed church.

The **Drostdy Museum** (18 Swellengrebel Street, tel: 028-514 1138. *Open* Mon–Fri 9–4:45, Sat–Sun 10–4. *Admission: moderate*) is in the former seat of the *landdrost* (official representative of the governor). One of the finest such buildings in the country, it dates from 1747 and incorporated a residence for the *landdrost*, a courtroom and an office. It now displays a fine collection of 18th- and 19th-century Cape furniture as well as art. The museum also includes the old jail and two houses: Mayville (1853), an impeccably furnished Victorian house with a delightful cottage garden, and its neighbor, the Auld House.

The **Bontebok National Park** (entrance 4 miles south of Swellendam, tel: 028-514 2735. *Open* daily 8–7) is the home of the once rare antelope that has given it its name. To the north, the **Marloth Nature Reserve** climbs a flank of the Langeberg Mountains.

Swellendam's magnificent Dutch Reformed church

83

Try the Cederberg for wilderness walking and dramatic views

The West Coast and Cederberg

▶▶ Cederberg   48B2/B3

About 137 miles north of Cape Town
Cederberg/Olifants River Valley Publicity Association, Old Jail Building, Main Street, Clanwilliam (tel: 027-482 2024, fax: 027-482 2361). Open: Mon–Fri 8:30–5, Sat 8:30–12:30

The 62-mile-long, north–south Cederberg take their name from the endangered Clanwilliam cedar tree (*Widdringtonia cedarbergensis*), which grows uniquely in these mountains at an altitude of 3,280–4,920 feet. With a protected wilderness area of some 175,450 acres, there are numerous opportunities for hiking, walking, climbing, and riding, with magnificent views and sandstone formations such as the dramatic Wolfberg Arch. There are clear pools for swimming in the rivers and San rock paintings up to 6,000 years old. Rare and wonderful flora and fauna includes the snowball protea, the Clanwilliam yellowfish, the red-fin minnow, and a mass of colorful bird life, plus a healthy local leopard population. Pick up your hiking permits and maps, and information about the wilderness area from the Algeria Forestry Station, or write ahead to the Cederberg Publicity Association (see panel and above).

The two nearest towns are **Clanwilliam** (Tourist Information, see above) and **Citrusdal** (Tourist Information, Sandveldhuisie Country Shop, Church Street, tel: 022-921 3210, fax: 027-921 2186. *Open* Oct–Jul, Mon–Fri 9–4:30, Sat 9–12; Aug–Sep, daily 9–4:30). Clanwilliam is famous for its health-giving rooibos tea (see panel), Citrusdal for its oranges. The area between was named Olifants River valley by early explorers because of the herds of elephant roaming it. Today it is all very different, a honeycomb of neatly manicured citrus groves and well-kept vineyards.

TOURS AND HIKING
For specialist tours of the region, contact Cederberg Travel, P.O. Box 25, Clanwilliam 8135 (tel: 027-482 2444). Obtain hiking permits and information from Algeria Forestry Station; (tel: 027-482 2812. Postal address: Private Bag XI, Citrusdal 7340).

▶▶ West Coast and Swartland   48A2/A3

West Coast Publicity Association, Oorlogsvlei, Van Riebeeck Street, Saldanha 7395 (tel: 022-714 2088, fax: 022-714 4240) Open: Mon–Fri 9–5, Sat 9–noon
Greater Vredenburg Tourism Bureau, Hugo and Hugo Toyota, corner of Main and Veldrift roads, Vredenburg (tel/fax: 022-715 1142). Open: Mon–Fri 9–5

Dominated by the icy, plankton-rich Benguela Current, the Atlantic West Coast is a region of huge kelp beds and abundant seafish, crayfish, abalone, seabirds, and seals. Known as the "Lobster Coast," after the prolific Cape rock lobster (*Jasus lalandi*) found along these shores, the area was once a key whaling station. It is still a crucial commercial fishing ground, although it is struggling against rampant overfishing.

Although the water is bitterly cold, the dry climate, cool sea breeze, and easy access from Cape Town make this a popular vacation area, centered on **Langebaan** (Tourist Information, Library, tel: 022-772 1515. *Open* Mon–Fri 9:30–4:30, Sat 9–noon), where watersports on the sheltered lagoon are the main attraction. The lagoon is part of the 49,500-acre **West Coast National Park** (tel: 022-772 2144. *Open* daily 7–7), famous wetlands whose offshore islands offer predator-proof nesting sites for an estimated three-quarters of a million seabirds of 200 different species, including swift terns, Cape gannets, crowned cormorants, African black oystercatchers, migrant curlew sandpipers and other waders, and small colonies of African penguins. In spring, the whales arrive.

Saldanha Bay (Tourist Information, see above) is named after Portuguese Admiral Antonio de Saldanha, who never actually came here, although he anchored in Table Bay in 1503. The name was mistakenly moved on the map. The huge natural harbor is famous for its mussels and as a major port, processing iron ore from mines 534 miles inland.

St. Helena Bay and **Elands Bay** (Tourist Information, Church Street, tel: 022-972 1640) have world-famous surf.

A little way inland, **Darling** (Tourist Information in the museum, tel: 022-492 3361, fax: 022-492 2935. *Open* daily 9–4) marks the start of the flower lands, a blaze of color throughout the spring (see pages 74–75). The **Darling Museum** (Pastorie Street. *Open* daily 9–1, 2–4) has a wide array of butter-making utensils. This is also the home of comedian Pieter Dirk Uys' seminal character, Mrs. Evita Bezuidenhout, who holds court at Evita Se Perron (tel: 022-492 2831). The Moravians, Catholics, and Dutch Reformed Church were all active in the area in the early 19th century, and several of the local villages—Ebenhaeser, Eselbank, Goedverwacht, Mamre, Rietpoort, Vergenoeg, Wittewater, and Wupperthal—began life as missions.

ROOIBOS

Rooibos ("red bush," *Aspalanthus linearis*) is an indigenous plant of the Cederberg. The colored population were the first to drink it as a tea, but by the mid-19th century it was being drunk more widely. In 1904, Benjamin Ginsberg started trading seriously, and by 1930 full-scale cultivation was under way, centered on Clanwilliam. Now common throughout South Africa, with small quantities exported, it is brewed and presented like ordinary tea, looks a dark, reddish brown—and is terribly healthy. It is free of tannin and stimulants, rich in vitamin C, relaxing, and contains antiallergenic agents. The Rooibos Factory, Clanwilliam (tel: 027-482 2155) runs tours Mon–Fri 10, 11:30, 2, and 3:30.

85

Saldanha Bay survives largely on Atlantic deep-sea fishing

THE HUGUENOTS

Like other early Protestants, French Huguenots were persecuted by the Catholic church, their darkest moment coming on St. Bartholomew's Day, 1572, when 10,000 were massacred in Paris. Shortly afterward, Henry of Navarre took the throne. While he was forced to convert to Catholicism, he remained sympathetic and signed the Edict of Nantes allowing religious freedom. It was revoked by Louis XIV in 1685 and thousands of Huguenots fled France. Most were skilled artisans and were of real benefit to their host countries, creating a range of industries from tapestry to wine, while France went into a long period of industrial decline.

The Winelands

▶▶ Franschhoek   48B2

50 miles northeast of Cape Town
Tourist Information, Huguenot Road (tel: 021-876 3603,
fax: 021-876 2768, e-mail: info@franschhoek.org.za)
Open: winter, Mon–Fri 9–5, Sat 9:30–1:30, Sun 10–1:30;
summer, Mon–Fri 9–6, Sat 9–5, Sun 10–5

In 1688, Governor Simon van der Stel granted the valley to a small group of Huguenots (see panel). The French tradition lives on in the sea of vines, in farms with names such as La Provence, Bourgogne, and Mont Rochelle, in the French surnames of current Afrikaans-speaking residents, and in the exceptional number of good restaurants.

Today, Franschhoek is basically all about wine (see pages 92–93), but also visit the **Huguenot Museum** (Lambrecht Street, tel: 021-876 2532. *Open* Mon–Sat 9–5, Sun 2–5. *Admission: inexpensive*). Housed in the curious Saasveld, a replica of a Cape Town house built by Louis Thibault in 1791, it contains a fascinating collection of Huguenot memorabilia that ranges from family trees and bibles to estate deeds and furniture. Across the road is a small **Village Museum** (*Open* Mon–Fri 10–5, Sat 10–1).

Next door is the **Huguenot Memorial**, a large edifice by Coert Steynberg, erected in 1938 to celebrate the 250th anniversary of the Huguenots' arrival. Above the town,

Coert Steynberg's
Huguenot Memorial,
Franschhoek

the winding **Helshoogte** (Hell's Heights) **Pass** has views over a pretty valley.

▶ Paarl   48B2

34 miles north of Cape Town on the N1
Tourist Information, 216 Main Street (tel: 021-872 3829, fax: 021-872 9376, e-mail: paarl@cis.co.za)
Open: Mon–Fri 9–5, Sat 9–1, Sun 10–1

Paarl gets its name from the nearby Paarl Rocks, three huge, granite domes, 500 million years old. They are said to glisten like pearls after rain, but the mountain was known more aptly to the Khoikhoi as Skilpad (Tortoise Mountain). The surrounding area is a nature reserve with walks and scenic drives. On the hilltop is the **Taal Monument** (1975), a huge sculptural homage to the Afrikaans language by Ian van Wyk (tel: 021-863 2800. *Open daily 9–5. Admission free*).

In town, be prepared for a hike; Main Street is over 7 miles long! A more manageable 1¼-mile stretch near the tourist office includes many of the finest historic buildings. A walking guide is available. The **Paarl Museum** (303 Main Street, tel: 021-872 2651. *Open* Mon–Fri 10–5. *Admission: inexpensive*) is in a Cape Dutch house and former Dutch Reformed parsonage (1787). The rooms have embroidered Victorian fashions, silver, ceramics, and furniture. The museum has a full history of Paarl with documents and photographs, and a display on the Group Areas Act. For the **KWV Wine Cellars** and winery tours, see page 93. Displays in the **Afrikaans Language Museum** (Pastorie Lane, tel: 021-872 3441. *Open* Mon–Fri 9–5. *Admission: inexpensive*) include the printing press of the first Afrikaans newspaper, *Die Afrikaase Patriot*. **Le Bonheur Crocodile Farm** (Babylonstoren Road, 4 miles from Paarl, tel: 021-863 1142. *Open* daily 9–5. *Admission: moderate*) features crocs live, on the plate, and as fashion accessories. **Butterfly World** (Klapmuts, tel: 021-875 5628. *Open* daily 9–5, Jun–Aug 10–4. *Admission: moderate*) has more delicate pleasures.

▶▶▶ Stellenbosch see pages 90–91

▶ Wellington   48B2

5 miles north of Paarl
Tourist Information, 104 Main Road (tel: 021-873 4604, fax: 021-873 4607, e-mail: welltour@cis.co.za)
Open: Mon–Fri 9–4:30, Sat 10–noon

Originally named Wagenmakersvallei (Wagon Maker's Valley), little Wellington was the northernmost of the early Cape settlements, where people transferred their goods to wagons for the trek north. Its name was changed in 1840, in honor of the British Duke of Wellington. It has a wine route, fine historic houses, and a small **museum** (Church Street, tel: 021-873 1410. *Open* Mon–Sat 9–1, 2–5. *Admission free*) containing early Dutch tools and Egyptian artifacts.

Paarl is the uncrowned capital of the Cape Winelands

AFRIKAANS
The earliest European settlers in South Africa were Dutch. Over the years, their language evolved into Afrikaans, soaking up a number of French, German, and English words from later settlers, Malay terms from the slaves, and a little smattering of local African languages. It was recognized as an official language in its own right in 1925. Afrikaans and Dutch are still very closely related; the Dutch understand it easily but say it is comparable with an English person listening to a simple form of Shakespearean English.

As a result of sanctions South Africa may not be the best-known producer in the world, but it has the oldest wine industry outside Europe and the Mediterranean. The first grapes were planted in 1655.

The country is currently the world's seventh largest wine producer, with about 3 percent of the global market. It has some 314 million vines, producing about 1 billion bottles of wine as well as table grapes, raisins, grape juice, fortified wines, spirits, and industrial alcohol. The industry supports 300,000 jobs. Sudden international acceptance and marketing possibilities in the mid-1990s launched a frenzy of activity, with over 400 new wines hitting the shelves in 1995 alone. It also created problems, as the vineyards were unable to satisfy demand. In 1995, some sold their entire vintage within three weeks, leaving disgruntled locals to complain as favorite wines simply disappeared into more lucrative foreign markets. Since then, more vines have been planted and are beginning to be productive, and exports are rising (28½ million gallons in 1999).

The Winelands There are increasing numbers of vineyards in the Orange River valley (Northern Cape) and the Northern Province, but most are concentrated in a small area of the Western Cape, from the Swartland in the west to the Overberg in the east. There are 50 official growing regions, of which the most important include Constantia, Stellenbosch, Paarl, Worcester, and the Klein-Karoo. Together they make up the Winelands, a landscape of soaring, rugged mountains and steep-sided valleys combed with emerald-green, razor-straight lines of vines, embellished with thickets of oak and gracious, whitewashed Cape Dutch homesteads.

The grapes The whites include global favorites such as Chenin Blanc (Steen), Chardonnay, and Sauvignon Blanc, as well as the more specialist Muscatels or Moscadels (also known to local winegrowers as Hanepoot), Colombard, Gewürztraminer, and Bukettraube. Look for the two unrelated Rieslings (European Weisser Riesling and local Cape Riesling). Among the reds are Cabernet Sauvignon, Merlot, Gamay, Pinot Noir, Shiraz, Cinsault (also known as Hermitage), and a local hybrid grape called Pinotage (Pinot Noir and Cinsault).

Top: the year begins for the winegrowers with the grape harvest
Above: elegantly carved show casks displayed in the KWV cellars

The wines Much of the actual wine production is handled by a series of growers' cooperatives, all of which are, in turn, members of the giant KWV. The results include many unexceptional, pleasant table wines. There are virtually no

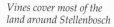

Vines cover most of the land around Stellenbosch

bad wines, although local taste tends to veer toward sweet, fruity wines. The real gems are the tiny estate-bottled vintages (known as estate or boutique wines) that are extremely difficult to find outside South Africa. Many of these are superb, with full-bodied, slightly smoky reds and lightly scented, fruity whites. For foreigners unfamiliar with the names and even in some cases the grape varietals, exploring the wine list becomes an intensely pleasurable adventure. Even French vintners are having to admit, reluctantly, that South Africa's whites are superb.

Boschendal, founded in 1685, is one of the oldest wineries in South Africa

The vineyards The larger vineyards produce at least half a dozen wines including white, red, sparkling, dessert, and fortified wines. Stellenbosch's Rustenberg estate has been producing wine for 300 years, while from the recently restored Klein Constantia vineyards, which produced some of the earliest and most famous wines in the Cape, comes exceptional Sauvignon Blanc. Meerlust, between Cape Town and Stellenbosch, has been in the Myburgh family for seven generations; it specializes in Pinot Noir and the Bordeaux-style Rubicon. Boschendal is known for Pinot Noir and Sauvignon Blanc, Backsberg for Pinotage and Chardonnay, Villiera for Merlot, and L'Ormarins for Shiraz. Most estates offer tastings, though some charge a small fee (see pages 92–93).

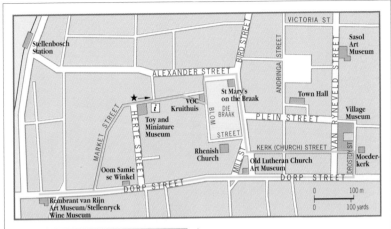

Walk

Stellenbosch

Governor Simon van der Stel was not a modest man. In November 1679, he visited the Eerste River valley and founded the Cape Colony's second town, naming it Stellenbosch after himself (he is also responsible for Simon's Town on the peninsula). Although it is now home to a major university and is one of the centers of the wine industry, Stellenbosch remains a picture-perfect town of whitewashed Cape Dutch cottages and elegant Georgian and Victorian town houses, with oak-lined avenues

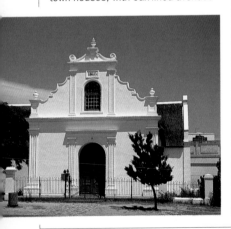

set around a village green. Some of it is an illusion: careful reconstruction and restoration has repaired the ravages of three major fires, and the suburbs contain their fair share of hideous 1950s garages and super-markets. The center is charming but full to the brim with tourists. The best way to see the town is on foot. This walk marks the high points; the tourist office publishes a walking tour guide giving details of the many old buildings you will see en route.

Start at the Tourist Office, housed in an old Cape Dutch rectory that also contains a small **Toy and Miniature Museum** (corner of Market and Herte streets. *Open* Mon–Sat 9:30–5, Sun 2–5. *Admission: inexpensive*).

Walk up Market Street. At the top, the **VOC Kruithuis**, the Dutch East India Company arsenal (1777), has a small military museum (Blom Street, tel: 021-887 2902. *Open* Mon–Fri 9:30–1, 1:30–5. *Admission: inexpensive*).

Nearby is the Rhenish church, built in 1823 (and enlarged in 1840) as a project to train local colored people and former slaves in a profession.

Straight ahead, **Die Braak** (meaning "fallow land") was once a military parade ground but is now a combination village common and parking lot. In the northeast corner is the pretty Anglican church of **St. Mary's on the Braak** (1852). A bevy of delightful

Stellenbosch has many of South Africa's finest Cape Dutch houses

Georgian and Victorian houses surrounds it. Walk across the common and turn up Church Street to reach the jewel in the crown of Stellenbosch.

A whole block has been included in the **Village Museum** (18 Van Ryneveld Street, tel: 021-887 2902. *Open* Mon–Sat 9:30–5, Sun 2–5. *Admission: moderate*), with four period houses restored and furnished to illustrate architectural development and changes in fashion between 1709, 1780, 1800–1820, and the 1850s. Future plans include a further two houses to be furnished in style up to 1929. The detail is impeccable, down to the cottage gardens, and the progression from sturdy wooden furniture and flagged floors to fustian Victoriana is fascinating.

Turn onto Drostdy Street, then right along **Dorp Street**, one of the longest streets of old houses surviving in the country. Everything is here, from Dutch gables to Georgian pediments.

Toward the bottom is **Oom Samie se Winkel** (82–84 Dorp

Shopping at Oom Samie's is a step back in time

Street, tel: 021-887 0797. *Open* daily 8–5:30). It is not often that a store becomes a tourist attraction in its own right, but the architecture, layout, and stock of this glorious Victorian shop appear not to have changed for 100 years. Some of its delights include souvenirs, African masks, toys, spices, and dried fruit. There is a dusty, atmospheric wine shop that specializes in rare vintages, and a tea garden, while an oak-beamed pub is next door.

Farther along the road, the H-shaped Cape Dutch house, Libertas Parva, contains the **Rembrandt van Rijn Art Museum** (Dorp Street and Aan-De-Wagenweg, tel: 021-886 4340). In the same courtyard is the **Stellenryck Wine Museum** (tel: 021-883 3588). Both museums: *Open* Mon–Fri 9–12:45, 2–5, Sat 10–1, 2–5. *Admission free*.

Retrace your steps and turn left onto Market Street to reach the Tourist Office.

> ❑ Stellenbosch is 30 miles east of Cape Town. Tourist Information, 36 Market Street, Stellenbosch 7600 (tel: 021-883 3584, fax: 021-883 8017, www.stellenbosch.org.za). *Open* Sep–May, Mon–Fri 8–5:30, Sat 9–5, Sun 9:30–4:30; Jun–Aug, Mon–Fri 9–5, Sat 9:30–4:30, Sun 10–4. Guided tours leave from the tourist office Mon–Fri at 10 and 3, Sat 3, Sun 10. *Admission: expensive*). For guided walking tours, contact Stellenbosch Historical Walks (tel: 021-883 9633). ❑

Touring the wineries

Fruits of the vine

No fewer than 12 districts of the Western Cape have wine routes, totaling literally hundreds of properties. These pages cannot provide a comprehensive guide, or even a coherent route. Instead, a few of the most rewarding visits have been included, whether for the quality of the wine or the tour, or for the setting and architecture of the vineyard. Every property listed offers tastings and sales; most also have restaurants, tea gardens, or picnic baskets. For organized tours, contact Vineyard Ventures (tel: 021-434 8888).

Backsberg (Klapmuts/Simondium Road, Paarl, off the R45, tel: 021-875 5141. *Open* Mon–Fri 8:30–5, Sat 8:30–1). A famous estate, owned by the Back family, specializing in classic reds; there is a small museum of early winemaking equipment and an audio-visual self-guided tour of the cellars.

Boschendal (off Hellshoogte Pass Road, between Franschhoek and Stellenbosch, tel: 021-870 4211. Tastings: Mon–Fri 8:30–4:30, Sat 8:30–12:30; Dec–Jan, also Sun

❏ **Tasting** You may be offered up to a dozen different wines at a tasting. Start with the dry whites and work through to the heavier reds, leaving fortified wines and spirits till last. Sniff the bouquet, take a small mouthful, swill it around your mouth and—if you are strong willed—spit it out. Rinse your glass and mouth with water between each wine. Appoint a nondrinking driver and pace yourself or you will be seriously lightheaded by the end of the visit. Most vineyards are happy to provide soft drinks for drivers and minors. ❏

8:30–12:30. Manor house: *Open* daily 9:30–5). This is among the area's oldest wineries (1685), and has become one of South Africa's preeminent producers of red wines. Combine a vineyard tour with a trip around the superbly restored Cape Dutch manor, which is filled with magnificent 17th- and 18th-century furniture, Ming porcelain, and Dutch East Indies Company glass.

Chamonix (Uitkyk Street, off the R45 to Cape Town, Franschhoek, tel: 021-876 3241. *Open* daily 9:30–4). There is a guesthouse for those who wish to stay . Originally part of La Cotte, one of the early Huguenot estates, this has been a separate property only since 1990, but has already produced several highly acclaimed wines. It also bottles its own spring water and breeds American pinto horses.

Fairview (Suider-Agter Road, Paarl, off the R101, tel: 021-863 2450. *Open* Mon–Fri 8–5:30, Sat 8–1). Owned by the Back family, this fine but less illustrious vineyard is a good family outing. Additional attractions are a herd of 500 Saanen goats, some of which live in a tower, and a thriving cheese-making operation. Milking is at 4 PM daily, except in kidding season (Jul–Sep).

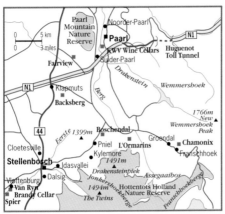

L'Ormarins (off the R45 to Cape Town, Franschhoek, tel: 021-874 1026. Tastings: Mon–Fri, 9–4:30, Sat 9–12:30. Cellar tours: by appointment). This was the very first wine estate in the Franschhoek Valley, the property of a Huguenot settler, Jean Roi. In 1969, the estate was bought by the multimillionaire philanthropist, Anton Rupert. Since then it has leapt to prominence, producing some of the country's finest wines. It has a truly magnificent Cape Dutch homestead.

KWV Wine Cellars (Kohler Street, Paarl, tel: 021-807 3007. *Open* Mon–Fri 8–4:30, Sat 8:30–4, Sun 10–2:30. Tours: Mon–Sat 9:30 (Afrikaans), 10:15 (German), 10, 10:30, and 2:15 (English), 3 (Wed only, French). This formidable cellar is not only the heart of the Cape industry but the largest winery in the world. It can store up to half a million gallons of wine and 75,000 gallons of fortified wine at any one time, and has the five largest vats in the world, fashioned from giant sequoia wood.

KWV was set up to handle South Africa's surplus wine. This vast cooperative, with nearly 4,900 members, now controls virtually all wine production and, with affiliates, the sale of about 80 percent of all alcohol (except beer) in South Africa. The KWV label is reserved almost exclusively for wine sold abroad, much of which is mass-produced from the "wine lake." KWV

Boschendal manor is home to one of the country's finest wines

admits that most wines with its labels are undistinguished. It no longer has any surplus; in fact, with other countries such as Australia buying up South African wine to bottle as their own, KWV is actually running short.

Spier (between Cape Town and Stellenbosch, on the R310, tel: 021-881 3321. *Open* daily with sections open 9:30 AM–11:30 PM. Cellar tours: Mon–Fri 10, noon, 3. *Admission: moderate*). This beautiful Cape Dutch complex is one of the Cape's oldest farms (1652). Now a thriving entertainment center, it has a winery offering tours and tastings, a shop stocking all the best Cape wines, a farm stand selling excellent foods (including picnics), a gift shop, an open-air amphitheater with a lively program of arts events, and a vintage train from the V & A Waterfront. There are also three good restaurants/cafés, a cheetah park, and an equestrian center.

Van Ryn Brandy Cellar (Vlottenburg, near Stellenbosch, tel: 021-881 3875. Tours: Mon–Fri 10, 11, 3; Sat 10, 11:30. *Admission: moderate*). Attractions are an audiovisual presentation on brandymaking, tours of the distillery, cellar, and cooperage, and of course, a tasting.

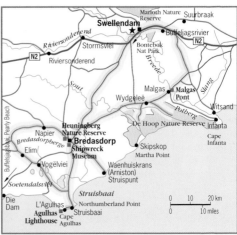

Drive

Swellendam to Cape Agulhas

Known as the Suidpunt (South Point), this area is famous for its wild flowers, calm, sandy beaches and treacherous underwater rocks, vacation homes, and historic missions. Distances are not huge, but the route involves some backtracking and gravel roads. Allow one to two days.

Leave Swellendam on the N2 toward Cape Town, then turn left for **Bredasdorp** (Suidpunt Tourism Bureau, Dr. Jansen Street, tel: 028-424 2584, fax: 028-424 2731, e-mail: suidpunt@brd.dorea.co.za). This sleepy little town, founded in 1838, is the "capital" of a region almost totally dependent on wheat and sheep farming. The **Shipwreck Museum** (Independent Street, tel: 028-424 1240. *Open* Mon–Fri 9–4:45, Sat 9–1, 2–4:45, Sun 11–12:30. *Admission: inexpensive*) catalogs the history of maritime disasters in the area, displaying figureheads, coins, and furniture salvaged from vessels wrecked off the coast. On the edge of town, the **Heuningberg Nature Reserve** produces spectacular displays of fiery Bredasdorp lilies in April and May.

The Cape Agulhas lighthouse marks the southernmost point in Africa

❏ On May 30, 1815, the *Arniston*, a British troop carrier sailing from India to England, was forced onto the rocks at Waenhuiskrans and broke up; six of its 378 passengers survived. Among the dead were four boys on their way back to school. A memorial erected by their parents stands on the clifftop, and the ship itself can sometimes be spotted at low tide. It is one of more than 400 wrecks strewn along the Cape coast. ❏

Take the road through Napier and turn left for **Elim** (Tourist Information, Churchyard, tel: 028-482 1086, fax: 028-482 1750. *Open* Mon–Fri 8–1, 2–4:30, Sat 8–noon), an almost forgotten, colored village that grew up around a 19th-century Moravian mission (1824). The architecture has been left intact, with whole streets of thatched "Karoo" cottages. The villagers' main income is from dried flowers, cut in the local *fynbos;* you can visit the drying sheds.

Leaving Elim, head for Struisbaai and L'Agulhas. Named the "Cape of Needles" after its murderous rocks, **Cape Agulhas▶**, 29 miles south of Bredasdorp, is the southernmost tip of Africa. It is marked by a small plaque, where a compass needle points due north with no magnetic variation. The real drama is out to sea, where 124 wrecks lie within a 50-mile radius, their crews drowned between 1673 and 1990 in what Rudyard Kipling called the "dread Agulhas roll." **L'Agulhas** is one of a series of beach resorts stretching from Pearly Beach in the west, through Buffelsjagsbaai and Die Dam to Struisbaai in the east. The swimming is safe and the angling excellent. **Agulhas Lighthouse**, built in 1849 and modeled on the Pharos lighthouse of Alexandria, Egypt, is the second oldest in the country and the most southerly in Africa. Its beam reaches 30 miles out to sea. It still works and houses a **museum** (Main Road, tel: 028-435 6078. *Open* Mon 1–5, Tue–Sat 9:30–4:45, Sun 11–3. *Admission: inexpensive*).

Head back to Bredasdorp, then turn back to the coast for **Arniston** (15 miles south of Bredasdorp), officially called Waenhuiskrans—"wagon house cliff"—after an enormous cave nearby, said to be large enough to turn an ox wagon around inside. You can explore the cave at low tide, and there are numerous other caves, cliffs, and rock formations in the area. The village is named after a ship that foundered here in 1815 (see box opposite). Today it is best known as an attractive resort, with vacation homes and excellent fishing, and for its handful of delightful 19th-century fishermen's cottages.

Fishing boats drawn up on the beach at Arniston

Return to Bredasdorp and head for the **De Hoop Nature Reserve** (30 miles east of Bredasdorp. Private Bag X16, 7280 Bredasdorp, tel: 028-542 1126/7. *Open* daily 7–6; overnight visitors should arrive before 4). Stretching 3 miles out to sea, this is an important 89,000-acre conservation area incorporating rare lowland *fynbos*, dunes, and wetlands. It is home to 86 species of mammal, including the Cape mountain zebra, gray rhebok, and leopard, and over 250 species of birds, among them the last breeding colony in the region of the rare Cape vulture. Basic accommodations, trails, walks, and drives.

Leaving the park, go north, crossing the Breede River on the **Malgas Pont** (a hand-operated pontoon bridge, the only one left in South Africa), through Bontebok National Park to Swellendam.

95

❏ The right whale, *Eubalaena australis*, was so named because it was thought to be the right whale to catch—large, slow-moving, and rich in oil. It is estimated that about 4,000 are still alive today. Up to 60 feet long and 88 tons in weight, they have a smooth, rounded, mainly black body, with occasional white markings on the back and belly, and no dorsal fin. The white, cauliflower-like callosities (knobbly dollops of tough skin) on the head and jaw are as distinctive as fingerprints. Right whales live on plankton and krill filtered from the water. ❏

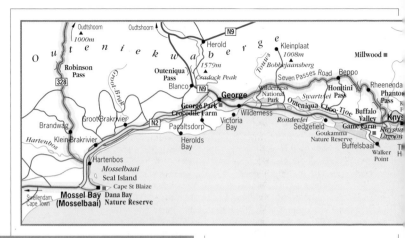

Drive

The Garden Route

One of South Africa's most popular visitor destinations is the Garden Route, named for its landscape of green forests and fertile meadows. Officially it is the strip of the south coast from Mossel Bay in the west to Plettenberg Bay in the east, ranging inland to the Outeniqua Mountains. In practice, Captour includes the whole coast from Cape Town to Port Elizabeth in its marketing campaigns. This is one of the busiest resort areas in the country and the forests and gardens are giving way to roads and golf courses, hotels, vacation homes, and campgrounds. Accommodations are plentiful, but sell out in peak season, so reserve in advance. Allow at least two days.

The route is easily followed, with the main N2 running the full length and on to Durban. Any stops are clearly signposted. If you have the time, take the more picturesque old roads, which wind through the forests and villages, often on gravel. For the Overberg coast, from Cape Town to Swellendam, see pages 82 and 94. **Swellendam to Mossel Bay.** This section runs through several small villages (see map pages 48–49). **Heidelberg** (Tourist Information, tel: 028-722 1917, fax: 028-722 1157) was the site of the southernmost battle of the Anglo-Boer War. **Riversdale** (Tourist Information, tel: 028-713 2418, fax: 028-713 3146) is home to the **Julius Gordon Africana Museum**, Langstraat (*Open* Mon–Fri 8–noon, or by arrangement), which has a fine collection of paintings by many top South African artists. Nearby, a turnoff to the right (B323) leads to **Stilbaai** (Tourist Information, Palinggat, tel: 028-754 2602, fax: 028-754 2549), a coastal resort with good fishing, boating, and swimming. Its highlights are the prehistoric (but still working) fish traps, and the town's fountain, full of tame eels. Watch them being fed at 11 AM Mon–Sat. Back on the N2, **Albertinia** (Tourist Information, Main Street, tel: 028-735 1000, fax: 028-735 2055) is a mining community producing yellow ocher, silica quartzite, and kaolin. It also has an aloe factory extracting sap for use in cosmetics and medicines, and is the world's largest producer of thatching reed. A little farther on, there is **bungee jumping** off the Gourits River Bridge every weekend; ask the tourist office for details.

The whole section runs through fairly dull farmland, with wide, rolling wheat fields. Consider taking the mountainous inland route along the R62 through the Karoo villages of Barrydale, Ladismith, and Calitzdorp to Oudtshoorn before heading south on the R328 over Robinson Pass to **Mossel Bay** (Tourist Information, Market Street, tel: 044-691 2202,

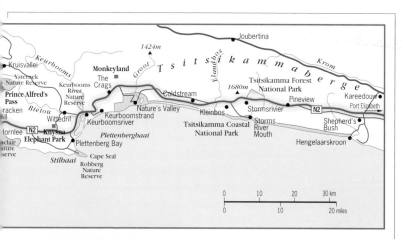

fax: 044-690 3077, www.garden route.net/mby/. *Open* Mon–Fri 9–5, Sat 9–1). This is South Africa's fifth largest port, with local industry fueled by the oil and gas fields off the coast.

The first European to show up here was Bartolomeu Dias in 1488. In 1500, a ship's captain left a letter under a local giant milkwood tree; a year later it was found by the commander of the Third East India fleet. For the next 400 years, the tree became a post office for all passing sailors, and it now forms the heart of the **Bartolomeu Dias Museum Complex** (Market Street, tel: 044-691 1067. *Open* Mon–Fri 9–4:45, Sat–Sun 9–4. *Admission: moderate*). The complex has collections of local and maritime history, with a life-size replica of Dias' caravel, a shell museum, a Malay graveyard, Khoi artifacts, and the Fountain, a spring used by Dias. A stone cross, the Padrao, donated by the Portuguese government, commemorates Vasco da Gama's visit in 1497. Other small museums nearby include the **Aquarium** (tel: 044-691 1067) and the **Model Shipyard** (Ochre Barn, Market Street, tel: 044-691 1531). Walks weave through the **Dana Bay Nature Reserve** to the St. Blaize Lighthouse and Bat Cave, used by early KhoiSan inhabitants, boat trips run to Seal Island (contact the tourist office for details), and you can try shark diving (tel: 082-455 2438).

The Portuguese explorer Bartolomeu Dias rounded the Cape in 1488 and made shore in Mossel Bay

Around the bay to Knysna Follow the old coast road around the bay to **Hartenbos,** where the **Great Trek Museum** (tel: 044-950 1111. *Open* Mon–Fri 9–4, Sat 10–12:30. *Admission: inexpensive*) covers everything from wagon building to Zulu *impis*, entertainment, and the role of women in Boer society.

Rejoin the N2 for about 20 miles, then branch left (N12) for 6 miles to **George** (Tourist Information, 124 York Street, tel: 044-801 9295, fax: 044-873 5228. *Open* Mon–Fri 8–4:30, Sat 9–noon). Founded in 1788 as a forestry outpost at the foot of the Outeniqua Mountains, George became a town in 1811. It was named after King George III of England. It grew up as an administrative center, living off the timber trade and hops. The huge **Dutch Reformed church** (corner of Meade and Courtenay streets), built in 1842, has a magnificent yellowwood ceiling and pillars and a pulpit that took two men a year to carve. By contrast, the Anglican **Cathedral of St. Mark** (York Street), built eight years later, is tiny. The former **Drostdy** was a private residence and hotel before it became the local **museum** (corner of Courtenay and York streets, tel: 044-873 5343. *Open* Mon–Fri 9–4:30, Sat 9–12:30. *Admission: donation*), with local history and art, a display on the area's indigenous woods and timber industry, mechanical musical instruments, plus a selection of gifts presented to the ex-president

The scenic Outeniqua Choo-Tjoe railroad in full steam

P. W. Botha. The massive Slave Tree, in front of the information office, has an old chain and lock embedded in the trunk. Once the site of local slave auctions, it is now said to be the biggest oak in the southern hemisphere.

Nearby are two small beach resorts, **Herolds Bay** and **Victoria Bay**; the **George Park Crocodile Farm** (York Street, tel: 044-873 4302. *Open* daily 9–5, feeding at 3. *Admission: moderate*); as well as the wonderful steam railroad (see page 235), which runs between George and Knysna through the beautiful Wilderness National Park. Head north from here on a sidetrip to Oudtshoorn and the Klein-Karoo (see pages 79–81).

Return to the N2 and continue for another 5 miles to **Wilderness** (Tourist Information, Leila's Lane, tel/fax: 044-877 0045, e-mail: info@weta.co.za). In 1877, the legend goes, a young Cape Town man, George Bennett, was allowed to marry as long as he took his bride to live in the wilderness. He bought a farm, named it Wilderness, and triumphantly brought his bride home. Today this is one of the prettiest towns on the Garden Route, tucked behind high dunes along the Touws River estuary. The swimming and beaches are excellent and you can canoe, windsurf, and fish on the lakes.

Between Wilderness and Sedge-field, the **Wilderness National Park** (tel: 044-877 1197, fax: 044-877 0111) protects a sensitive wetlands area from encroaching development. In its 6,455 acres are five rivers, four lakes, two estuaries, and 17 miles of southern Cape coastline, and it is surrounded by a further 25,000 acres of lakes. This is a good area for bird-watchers, anglers, and hikers, and home to 79 of South Africa's 95 species of waterfowl, as well as the elusive Knysna loerie and many king-fisher species.

The next stop along the N2 is cozy **Knysna** (Tourist Information, 40 Main Street, tel: 044-382 5510, fax: 044-382 1646, www.knysna-info.co.za),

the largest and most beautiful of the coastal resorts, curled around the hilly shores of a huge (5 square miles) lagoon. Its narrow access to the sea is guarded by The Heads, two large sandstone cliffs (656 feet and 380 feet high), and a coral reef. The lagoon is perfect for water sports, while several companies run boat trips, fishing charters, and diving on both wrecks and nearby coral reefs (ask the tourist office for details). In addition, the lagoon is home to 200 species of fish, including a rare seahorse, provides excellent fishing, and is a major source of oysters.

Plettenberg Bay, a gentle curve of tawny sand

**Knysna to Tsitsikamma Forest
National Park** The **Knysna Museum**
(Queen Street, tel: 044-382 1638.
Open Mon–Fri 9:30–4:30, Sat 9:30–1.
Admission: donation) is made up of
four houses: **Millwood House**
(ca1880) and **Parkes Cottage** (1890)
both have displays on the history of
Knysna, including memorabilia of its
founder, George Rex; the corrugated
iron **Parkes Shop** (1890) deals with
the Knysna timber industry; the **Old
Gaol** (1858) was the first public building. It housed convict laborers on their
way to Prince Alfred's Pass. Its bell
was used both as a fire alarm and to
signal the arrival of the mail. It now
has angling and maritime museums

and an art gallery. The **Goldmining
Museum** (Pitt and Green streets,
tel: 044-382 5066. *Open* Mon–Sat
9:30–4:30, Sun 9:30–12:30.
Admission: donation) has memorabilia
of Millwood. The **Knysna Oyster
Company** (Long Street, tel: 044-382
6941. *Open* Mon–Fri 8–5, Sat–Sun
9–3) gives farm tours and tastings of
oysters and mussels. There is a small
aquarium (*Open* daily 9–6) at Knysna
Heads, and harbor cruises from
Thesen's Jetty.

Knysna Forest South Africa's largest
expanse of indigenous high forest is
home to rare reserves of yellowwood,
ironwood, and stinkwood trees, some

up to 800 years old. It is a dark, eerie world where antelope and birds flit through the dense undergrowth and monkeys trapeze across giant hardwood trees. The late 1990s saw the tragic demise of a once-famous herd of elephants that used to roam the entire south coast. The **Knysna Elephant Park** (15 miles east of Knysna, off the N2, tel: 044-532 7732. *Open* daily 8:30–4:30. *Admission: moderate*) has three young, tame elephants for an up-close encounter. The **Buffalo Valley Game Farm** (12 miles southwest, tel: 0445-22481. *Open* off season, Mon–Sat 11–3, Sun 9–5. *Admission: moderate*) has a wide variety of plains animals,

Storms River mouth in the Tsitsikamma Forest National Park

antelope, and birds. **Millwood** (20 miles from Knysna) is a ghost town, based on the abandoned Bendigo gold mine. There are hiking trails nearby.

It is 20 miles from Knysna to **Plettenberg Bay** (Tourist Information, Kloof Street, tel: 044-533 4065, fax: 044-533 4066, www.plettenbergbay. co.za. *Open* Mon–Fri 8–5, Sat 9–1), one of South Africa's most fashionable beach resorts. Named Baia Formosa ("beautiful bay") by the 16th-century Portuguese mariner Manuel da Perestrello, this little town is set on a gently curving sandy bay backed by towering mountains. The governor of the Cape, Baron Joachim von Plettenberg, renamed it after himself in 1779. The tip of the peninsula is now the **Robberg (Cape Seal) Nature Reserve**, with walks and caves, while the cliffs provide excellent positions for whale- or dolphin-watching. Species seen along here include southern right, humpback, Brydes, minke, and killer whales. Information: 083-910 1028, www.cape-whaleroute.co.za

A little way east of "Plett" is **Monkeyland** (10 miles east, on the N2, tel: 044-534 8906. *Open* daily 8–6. *Admission: expensive*), an excellent sanctuary for all sorts of apes and monkeys, from lemurs to South American squirrel monkeys. East again is the start of the beautiful **Tsitsikamma Forest National Park►** (tel: 012-343 1991, fax: 012-343 0905, e-mail: reservations@parks. sa.co.za), whose Khoikhoi name means "place of sparkling waters." Dedicated in 1964, it stretches 40 miles along the coast and 3½ miles out to sea, covering an extraordinarily rich variety of ecosystems, flora, and fauna. Inland there is coastal forest, part of the great Knysna Forest belt, where ancient yellowwoods grow up to 165 feet high. On the coast, freshwater wetlands give way to dunes, crashing waves and shallow pools, coral reefs, and plunging deep waters. At **Storms River mouth** there are places to swim and snorkel, and a restaurant and shop. For hikers, the Otter Trail (see page 236) runs right through the park.

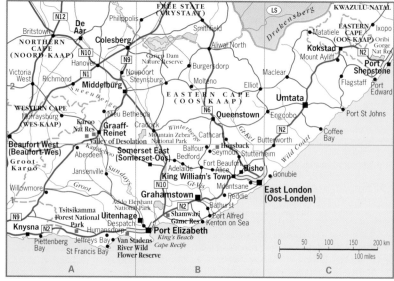

		A		B		C

FREE STATE (VRYSTAAT)

Phillippolis

De Aar

Britstown

Colesberg

Smithfield

Aliwal North

KWAZULU-NATAL

Drakensberg

EASTERN CAPE (OOS-KAAP) Ixopo

Matatiele Oribi Gorge Nat Res

Kokstad

Port Shepstone

NORTHERN CAPE (NOORD-KAAP)

Hanover

Gariep Dam Nature Reserve

Burgersdorp

Mount Ayliff

Victoria West

Richmond

Middelburg

Noupoort Steynsburg

Molteno

Elliot

Maclear

Flagstaff

Port Edward

Umtata

Engcobo

Port St Johns

WESTERN CAPE (WES-KAAP)

Murraysburg

Nieu Bethesda

Karoo Nat Res

Graaff-Reinet

Cradock

EASTERN CAPE (OOS-KAAP)

Queenstown

Cathcart

Stutterheim

Butterworth

Coffee Bay

Beaufort West (Beaufort-Wes)

Aberdeen

Valley of Desolation

Mountain Zebra National Park

Winterberg

Hogsback

Seymour

Wild Coast

Somerset East (Somerset-Oos)

Balfour

Bedford

Fort Beaufort

Groot-Karoo

Jansenville

Adelaide

Alice

King William's Town

Mdantsane

Bisho

Gonubie

Willowmore

Tsitsikamma Forest National Park

Addo Elephant National Park

Grahamstown

Reddie

East London (Oos-Londen)

Knysna

Plettenberg Bay

Jeffreys Bay

St Francis Bay

Van Stadens River Wild Flower Reserve

Uitenhage

Despatch

Humansdorp

Port Elizabeth

King's Beach

Cape Recife

Bathurst

Port Alfred

Kenton on Sea

Shamwari Game Res

0	50	100	150	200 km
0		50		100 miles

A NEW BEGINNING The Eastern Cape is made up of numerous disparate cultures and ecosystems. It came into being only when the provincial boundaries were rearranged in 1994 (see page 12). Until then, most of the area was simply an extension of the Western Cape, both geographically and politically.

In the far west, the Tsitsikamma Forest (see page 101) gives way to rolling scrub, while to the north are the eastern reaches of the Great Karoo. Around Grahamstown are lush green farmlands and montane forest. In the far east, the Wild Coast lives up to its name as one of South Africa's last undeveloped stretches of coast, the ragged cliffs and towering dunes broken by trailing river mouths and hidden coves of silver sand.

HISTORY This was a frontier land, inhabited initially by the Khoikhoi in the southwest, the Xhosa in the southeast, and the San to the north. The Great Trek took the Afrikaners along the coast to the Fish River and ever farther out into the Karoo. They dispossessed the San and Khoikhoi, but left the more warlike Xhosa alone until 1780, when the Cape government extended its authority to the river and forced the two groups into direct conflict

▶▶▶ **REGION HIGHLIGHTS**

Grahamstown
pages 108–109
Tour: The 1820 Settler Towns *pages 110–111*
Graaff-Reinet
pages 112–113
Addo Elephant Park
page 117
The Wild Coast
page 119

TOURISM INFORMATION
For information on the whole Eastern Cape, contact the state tourist board, Tourism House, Phalo Avenue (P.O. Box 186), Bisho 5605 (tel: 040-635 2115, fax: 040-636 4019, www.ectourism.org.za). In the U.K., contact the Eastern Cape Call Centre (tel: 01473-225 652, fax: 01473-226 199).

Previous pages: the marina at Port Alfred

HUMAN PAWNS
The 1820 Settlers were moved into the region (known as Albany) by the ruthless governor, Lord Charles Somerset, chiefly as a way of breaking an expensive and irritating deadlock in the Frontier Wars. The sudden influx of 5,000 people was sufficient to force the hand of the Xhosa. Each settler family was allocated only 100 acres of land, scarcely enough to survive on. The settlers had a rough time for the first 50 years and many gave up farming, retreating to the towns.

Xhosa women selling vegetables in Peddie

in the first of a series of nine bloody Frontier Wars that lasted until the mid-19th century. Meantime, in 1806, the British took control of the Cape, and in 1820, 5,000 British settlers arrived in the Grahamstown area. The Xhosa, who were already fighting not only the Boers but also the Zulus and their own offshoot tribe, the Mfengu, had to fight them, too. Inevitably, the British, with their superior firepower, won the day, and the whole area became part of the Cape Colony.

The dramas continued, however. Owing to the intensity of missionary activity in the area, the black population gained a higher level of education than was the norm elsewhere, and in 1916 the black University of Fort Hare was founded. The area became one of the most politically active in South Africa, providing the nationalist cause with many of its greatest leaders, including Nelson Mandela, Walter Sisulu, and Steve Biko of the ANC, and Robert Sobukwe, founder of the hard-line PAC. During the apartheid years, two black homelands were formed in the province's eastern section: the technically independent Xhosa territory of Transkei and the satellite Mfengu homeland of Ciskei.

A BRIGHT FUTURE Today, most of the region's towns look like charming toys. The Karoo is dotted with sparklingly clean Afrikaner villages, the coast lined with neat, Disneyesque waterfront estates. Bisho, once capital of Transkei and now state capital of the Eastern Cape, looks as though it is made of Lego, and, from a distance, even the tiny pastel-colored houses of the Xhosa hill villages appear to have just been taken out of the box. Only little Peddie, with its noisy street markets and

Above: hardwood forest still coats much of the Hogsback. Left: stone leopards guard the main square of Bisho

blaring music, battered Coca-Cola billboards and line of minibus taxis, seems like the rest of Africa.

Though much less known than the Western Cape or KwaZulu-Natal, the Eastern Cape is just as rich in possibilities for the tourist. Almost every inlet along the Wild Coast has a small hideaway resort tucked unobtrusively along its banks, but as yet there are few towns and ribbon development of vacation homes is slow, with most people being deterred by the bumpy, dusty roads that lead down to the coast. Yet the beaches here are probably the best in South Africa and the real estate agents' billboards are moving ever closer. This is the hot new area, partly because wealthy whites can now safely buy property in the former homelands.

The Garden Route extension to Port Elizabeth is being strongly marketed, with the added bonus of the only good game parks in the south. At the same time, a whole new tourism industry is dedicated to following in the footsteps of Nelson Mandela. The future for this fledgling province seems bright.

THE COELACANTH

Over 350 million years old and thought to have been extinct for 65 million years, the coelacanth (*Latimeria chalumnae*) was rediscovered in 1938 when an East London fisherman landed one in his nets and showed it to museum curator Marjorie Courtenay-Latimer. It was about 5 feet long, weighed 125 pounds, and was covered in deep-blue scales. Several other specimens have been caught since, and underwater photographs were taken in 1987.

This strange, predaceous fish has a deep, stocky body and rounded, lobe-like fins. The first spine of the dorsal fin is hollow (the name means "hollow spine" in Greek). Because of the structure of the fins it is thought to be a "missing link" in the evolution of land animals.

Below: the coelacanth
Bottom: fishing off the rocks near East London

▶ **East London**   *102B1*

Tourist Information, Old Library Building, 35 Argyle Street
(tel: 043-722 6015, fax: 043-743 5091, 24-hour info: 043-722 6034) Open: Mon–Fri 8:30–4:30, Sat 8:30–11
Eastern Cape Tourist Board, Lock Street Jail, Fleet Street
(tel: 043-743 9511, fax: 043-743 9513)

East London on the Buffalo River was founded in 1847. The city is not exciting architecturally, although there are some fine individual buildings such as the City Hall and St. Peter's church, but it is a highly popular resort with magnificent golden beaches stretching 25 miles along the coast in either direction. **Nahoon** and **Eastern Beaches** have some of the finest surf in South Africa. The old **Lock Street Gaol** (South Africa's first women's prison) is now a shopping center, while the former fishing harbor is a mini waterfront development called **Latimer's Landing** (where the coelacanth—see panel—was landed in 1938).

The **Anne Bryant Art Gallery** (St. Mark's Road, tel: 043-722 4044. *Open* Mon–Fri 9–5, Sat 9:30–noon. *Admission free*) is an imposing Edwardian mansion containing a fair collection of South African art from the 1880s onward. **Gately House Museum** (1 Park Gates Road, tel: 043-722 2141. *Open* Tue–Thu 10–1, 2–5, Fri 10–1, Sat–Sun 3–5. *Admission: inexpensive*), once home of East London's first mayor, is furnished with fine Cape furniture. The impressive **East London Museum** (Oxford Street, entrance in Dawson Road, tel: 043-743 0686. *Open* Mon–Fri 9:30–5, Sat 9:30–noon, Sun 11–4. *Admission: inexpensive*) has Xhosa culture, shells, and stuffed animals. Star attractions are the world's only dodo egg and a stuffed coelacanth. If you prefer live animals, visit the **aquarium** (Esplanade, tel: 043-705 2637. *Open* daily 9–5; fish feeding at 10:30 and 3, seal shows 11:30, 3:30. *Admission: moderate*) and the **Zoo** (Queen's Park, tel: 043-722 1171. *Open* daily 9–5. *Admission: moderate*). The **Calgary Transport Museum** (Macleantown Road, tel: 043-730 7244. *Open* daily 9–4:30. *Admission: inexpensive*), 8 miles from town, has a collection of horse-drawn vehicles.

▶ Alice   102B1

About 53 miles northeast of Grahamstown

Alice's claim to fame is **Fort Hare University**, the first black university in South Africa, founded in 1916 out of the mission-run Lovedale College. Nelson Mandela and many other nationalist leaders studied here. On campus, the **De Beer Centenary Art Gallery** (tel: 040-602 2011. *Open* Mon, Wed, Fri 9–noon, Tue, Thu 1–2. *Admission free*) has an excellent collection of contemporary black art.

▶ Bisho   102B1

33 miles northwest of East London
Tourist Information, Tourism House, Phalo Avenue
(tel: 040-635 2115)

Bisho was a satellite township to King William's Town before becoming the capital of Ciskei, then the Eastern Cape. The fledgling city consists of a sprawl of small grid housing, one vast, pink cement office and shopping building, overlooked by stern stone leopards (locals say they smile when a virgin enters the square), and a casino.

▶▶ Hogsback   102B1

90 miles northwest of East London
Tourist Information,
Stormhaven Crafts, Main Road
(tel: 045-962 1050)

In the Amatola Mountains (Amatola means calf—the hills are said to look like a row of calves), Hogsback is a hill station, set in cool green forests with planted pine and eucalyptus on the high ground and virgin hardwood forest on the lower slopes. It is perfectly designed for leisure, with tumbling waterfalls, cozy fireside bars, ideal walking and riding, and trout fishing.

▶▶ King William's Town   102B1

37 miles west of East London
Tourist Information, Library,
Ayliff Street (tel: 043-642 3391)
Open: Mon–Fri 8:30–5:30,
Sat 8:30–1

The birth- and burial place of Steve Biko, this Settler town was an important military base in the Frontier Wars. It has 19th-century churches and colonial architecture. The **Kaffrarian Museum** (3 Albert Road, tel: 043-642 4506. *Open* Mon–Fri 9–12:45, 2–5. *Admission: inexpensive*) covers natural history and Xhosa culture. The **Missionary Museum** (Berkeley Street, tel: 043-642 4506. *Open* Mon–Fri 9–1, 2–5) explains the role of the missions in the development of South Africa.

King William's Town is rich in ornate Victorian architecture

HUBERTA

In 1928 Huberta, the happy hippo from St. Lucia, decided to go for a walk. Over the next three years she became a national celebrity, with the local press charting her progress on a 620-mile journey that took her to the Eastern Cape—the first hippo there for over 50 years. Sadly, Huberta was shot by a farmer in 1931 while she was dining on his crops. Now stuffed, she lives on amid her press cuttings in King William's Town's Kaffrarian Museum.

THE GRAHAMSTOWN FESTIVAL

This unlikely town has become the venue for the second-largest arts festival in the world (topped only by Edinburgh). Each July, for ten days, artists and performers, patrons and aficionados descend on Grahamstown for a riot of music and dance, art, and literature. Separate jazz, fringe, and children's festivals run simultaneously, and with South Africa's reemergence onto the international scene, the festival will surely soon be firmly on the mainstream circuit.

For information and reservations, contact Festival Director, Standard Bank National Arts Festival, P.O. Box 304, Grahamstown 6140 (tel: 046-622 7115, fax: 046-622 4457).

▶ ▶ ▶ Grahamstown   102B1

80 miles northeast of Port Elizabeth; 36 miles from the coast
Tourist Information, 63 High Street (tel: 046-622 3241,
fax: 046-622 3266, www.grahamstown.co.za)
Open: Mon–Thu 8:30–1, 2–5, Fri 8:30–1, 2–4, Sat 9–11

Founded by Colonel John Graham in 1812, Grahamstown began as the military headquarters of the Cape Colony's eastern frontier, commanding a chain of small forts along the Fish River. After many of the 1820 Settlers had abandoned their unprofitable little farms for the security of urban life, the town took off and flourished, becoming for a time the second city of the colony. In the late 19th century, however, inhabitants were lured north by the prospect of instant wealth in the diamond and gold fields, and the city withered. Today, it is a charming country town, with many delightful old buildings and several educational establishments, notably the prestigious Rhodes University, which has about 4,000 students.

Buildings of note The broad, tree-lined streets are filled with imposing public buildings and pleasing Victorian shops and houses. The heart of the town is triangular **Church Square**, originally the military parade ground between Colonel Graham's house and the officers' mess. In the center rises the spire of the Anglican **Cathedral of St. Michael and St. George**, which was built as a parish church in 1824 and became a bishopric in 1852. The Lady Chapel was finally completed in 1952. The Gothic Revival Methodist **Commemoration Church** was dedicated in 1850 in thanks for the settlers' triumph after 25 grueling years. It has a fine organ and stained-glass windows. The **Drostdy Gate** was designed for military purposes in 1835 by Major Selwyn and built by the Royal Engineers in 1841 on the site of the old Drostdy. It now forms the pedestrian entrance to Rhodes University. There are fine restored buildings in Hill and MacDonald streets and in Artificers Square (corner of Bartholomew and Cross streets), the artisan quarter where craft workers were given plots to set up workshops.

Memorials The **Settler Memorial Tower**, now part of the City Hall, was built in 1870 to commemorate the 50th anniversary of the arrival of the 1820 Settlers. Work on the main City Hall began in 1877. Overlooking the town, the **1820 Settlers Monument** (Gunfire Hill, tel: 0461-27115) is an arts center opened in 1974, the home of the Grahamstown Festival (see panel). The **Bible Monument** (Bedford Road) marks an occasion in 1837 when some local British settlers

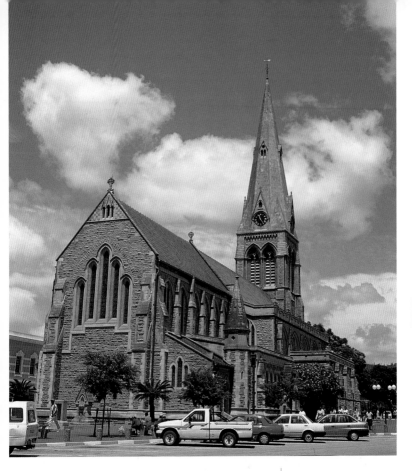

presented a bible to passing Voortrekkers as a token of friendship for the Dutch community. The **War Memorial** (Church Square) has an inscription specially composed by Rudyard Kipling.

Left: the Settler's Memorial, Grahamstown Above: Grahamstown Cathedral

Museums The **Albany Museum** (Somerset Street, tel: 046-622 2312 for all sections. *Open* Mon–Fri 9–1, 2–5, Sat–Sun 2–5. *Admission: inexpensive*), founded in 1855, has several distinct sections. The **History Museum** specializes in the history of the British settlers of 1820 and later, with a good cultural history collection of domestic utensils, furniture, and applied arts, and a large collection of 18th- and 19th-century South African art. It also has an excellent display on Xhosa lifestyles and traditions. The **Natural Sciences Museum** deals both with animals and early humans in southern Africa. The **J. L. B. Smith Institute of Ichthyology** is a fish museum, with pride of place given to the coelacanth (see page 106). Away from Somerset Street are **Fort Selwyn** (Gunfire Hill), built in 1836, which saw several battles against Xhosa forces, the **Provost Prison** (Lucas Avenue. *Open* Mon–Sat 10–5), and the **Observatory Museum** (Bathurst Street. *Open* Mon–Fri 9:30–1, 2–5, Sat 9:30–1. *Admission: inexpensive*), with displays on Victorian South Africa and the early diamond industry, and a working camera obscura on the roof.

MARIMBAS AND MBIRAS
The International Library of African Music (Prince Alfred Street, tel: 046-636 8557. *Open* Mon–Fri 8–5 by appointment. *Admission: donation*) displays more than 200 traditional, working African musical instruments, and there's a large tape library.

Tour

The 1820 Settler towns

Grahamstown is surrounded by a circle of small market towns founded by the early settlers from Britain. Together they make a very pleasant one- or two-day tour. The route forms a basic figure of eight with Grahamstown at the center. You can do a longer loop northward over the Hogsback to include Balfour, Seymour, Cathcart, Stutterheim, Bisho, and King William's Town (see page 107).

Southern loop Leave Grahamstown on the A67, heading south to Port Alfred. The first stop, after 25 miles, is **Bathurst▶**, named after the British colonial secretary in 1820. Several national monuments here include the Anglican and Wesleyan churches, Bradshaw's water-driven wool mill, and the Settler fort. There is also an

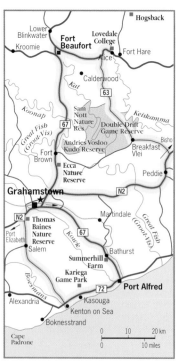

excellent **Agricultural Museum** (Trappes Street, tel: 046-625 0853. *Open* Mon–Fri 9–4, Sat 9–1, Sun 9–4. *Admission: inexpensive*).

The Bathurst pineapple is an unlikely but highly visible landmark

On the top of Baillie's Beacon, 1¼ miles from the town, a toposcope marks the spot from which the settlers staked out their farms. The most obvious attraction is the 53-foot-high pineapple on **Summerhill Farm** (tel: 046-625 0833), which you can climb. The farm gives tours with audiovisual performances about pineapples, the biggest crop in the area. The **Pig and Whistle Inn** (1831) is one of the oldest hostelries in the country.

Port Alfred (Tourist Information, The Causeway, tel: 046-624 1235, fax: 046-624 4139), 6 miles on, is a tidy little coastal resort on the Kowie River estuary with a marina, boat cruises, canoe trips, and fishing charters. The **Kowie Museum** (Pascoe Crescent, East Bank, tel: 046-624 4713. *Open* Mon–Sat 9:30–12:30. *Admission free*) has personal files on all the 1820 Settlers. Just off the coast is one of South Africa's most colorful reefs (contact Kowie Dive School, tel: 046-624 2213).

From here, take the A72 west for 13 miles to the pleasant resort of **Kenton on Sea** (Tourist Information, Municipality Building, tel: 046-648 1304, fax: 046-648 2118), with good beaches and safe swimming. The 1,631-acre **Kariega Game Park** (8 miles from Kenton on Sea, on the Grahamstown road, tel: 046-636 1904, fax: 046-636 2288, www.kariega.co.za) has birds, game, and hiking trails. Take the A72 back toward Port Alfred and turn left for Grahamstown, via the village of **Salem** and the **Thomas Baines Nature Reserve**.

Northern loop Leave Grahamstown on the N2 heading toward Bisho, and turn left after 4 miles, via the 330-acre **Ecca Nature Reserve**. **Fort Beaufort** is 43 miles farther on, beside the Kat River. It has a **local history museum** and a Martello Tower of 1847; the officers' mess now houses a small **Military History Museum** (Durban Street. *Open* Mon–Sat 9–5), with

several paintings by local hero, Thomas Baines. Nearby **Lovedale College** (1841) has educated many of South Africa's great nationalist leaders, including Nelson Mandela, Oliver Tambo, and Mangosuthu Buthelezi.

Take the A63 east for 13 miles to **Alice** and **Fort Hare** (see page 107).

The road south from here leads through the **Double Drift Game Reserve**, part of a formidable wildlife preserve on a magnificent looping gorge of the Great Fish River. At the intersection with the N2, turn right.

Peddie, named after Colonel John Peddie, was built in 1835 as an earth fort. In May 1846 the town, defended by a small white contingent and friendly Mfengu tribesmen, was attacked by an army of 9,000 Xhosa warriors. From the mid-19th century a town developed around the fort (no longer extant). It is now a lively, largely black community, with music and market stalls. Grahamstown is 36 miles west on the N2.

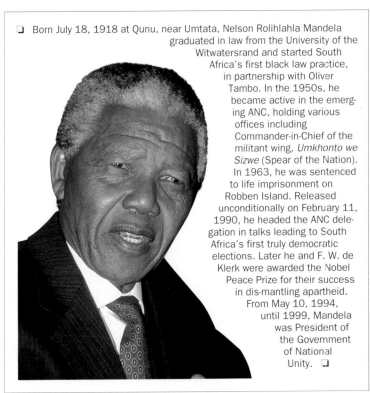

❏ Born July 18, 1918 at Qunu, near Umtata, Nelson Rolihlahla Mandela graduated in law from the University of the Witwatersrand and started South Africa's first black law practice, in partnership with Oliver Tambo. In the 1950s, he became active in the emerging ANC, holding various offices including Commander-in-Chief of the militant wing, *Umkhonto we Sizwe* (Spear of the Nation). In 1963, he was sentenced to life imprisonment on Robben Island. Released unconditionally on February 11, 1990, he headed the ANC delegation in talks leading to South Africa's first truly democratic elections. Later he and F. W. de Klerk were awarded the Nobel Peace Prize for their success in dis-mantling apartheid. From May 10, 1994, until 1999, Mandela was President of the Government of National Unity. ❏

The Karoo

► Cradock
102B2

150 miles north of Port Elizabeth
Tourist Information, Civic Centre, Market Square
(tel: 048-881 2383, fax: 048-881 1421)

This quaint Karoo town in the upper Fish River valley was founded in 1813. The incongruous 1867 **Groote Kerk** (great church) Stockenstroom Street, was modeled on London's St. Martin in the Fields. Local author Olive Schreiner (*The Story of an African Farm*, published 1883) lived here as a child; the **Schreiner House** (Cross Street, tel: 048-881 5251. *Open* Mon–Fri 8:45–12:45, 2–4:30. *Admission free*) is now a museum. The **Great Fish River Museum** (High Street, tel: 048-881 4509. *Open* Tue–Fri 8–1, 2–4, Sat 8–noon. *Admission: inexpensive*) has displays of local pioneer life. **Die Tuishuise Hotel** (see page 260) comprises nearly a whole street of impeccably restored and furnished houses.

►►► Graaff-Reinet
102A2

156 miles northeast of Port Elizabeth
Tourist Information Centre, Old Library, corner of Church
and Somerset streets (tel/fax: 049-892 4248,
www.graaffreinet.co.za)
Open: Mon–Fri 9–12:30, 2–5, Sat 9–noon

An architectural jewel, Graaff-Reinet is the fourth-oldest town in South Africa, tucked into a horseshoe bend in the Sundays River, at the foot of the Sneeuberg. Founded in 1786 and named by the governor after himself and his wife, it remained a troubled frontier town for nearly a century. Much of its superb Cape Dutch architecture has been restored and the town is now home to 200 historic monuments (walking maps available).

Beyond the Valley of Desolation stretch the Plains of Kamdeboo

Louis Thibault designed the **Drosdty Hotel** (1806), but as he lived far away in Cape Town, the local builders used their own initiative; for instance, they substituted a half-moon gable for the planned dome and bell tower. Behind the hotel, **Stretch's Court** is a complex of mid-19th-century Karoo cottages built for colored workers and emancipated slaves. They are now used as hotel rooms. **Reinet House** (1 Parsonage Street, tel: 049-892 3801 for all museums. *Open Mon–Fri 9–12:30, 2–5, Sat 9–noon, Sun 10–noon. Admission: inexpensive*), built in 1806–1812 as the Dutch Reformed parsonage, is the local history museum, while **Urquhart House**, next door (*Open Mon–Fri 9–12:30, 2–5, Sat 9–noon. Admission: inexpensive*), is furnished as a Victorian dwelling.

The Owl House, a strange concrete legacy of a tormented artist

The early 19th-century **Old Residency** (Parsonage Street, see Urquart House for opening times) houses the Jan Felix Laegan Memorial Collection of firearms, as well as the Middellandse Regimental Memorabilia.

The **Hester Rupert Art Museum** in the 1821 Dutch Reformed Mission church (Church Street, tel: 049-892 2121. *Open Mon–Fri 10–noon, 3–5, Sun 10–noon. Admission: inexpensive*) has an excellent collection of contemporary South African art, and the **Old Library** (corner of Church and Somerset streets. *Open Mon–Fri 10–2, 3–5, Sat–Sun 10–noon. Admission: inexpensive*) has Karoo fossils, San art, photography, and costumes. Other fine buildings include the Dutch Reformed church, the Town Hall, the John Rupert Little Theatre (Parsonage Street), built as the church of the London Mission Society, and the Graaff-Reinet Pharmacy (24 Caledon Street), preserved as a Victorian drugstore.

To the south, the **Karoo Nature Reserve** (tel: 049-892 3476) has walks, hiking trails, and an 8-mile drive up to the twisted rock formations of the **Valley of Desolation**, with superb views across the Plains of Kamdeboo.

Thirty miles north of Graff-Reinet, in the tiny Afrikaner village of **Nieu Bethesda**, is the **Owl House**►► (*Open daily 9–5. Admission: inexpensive*), the powerful, disturbing home of artist Helen Martins (see panel).

► Mountain Zebra National Park   102B2

12 miles west of Cradock (tel: 048-881 2427, fax: 048-881 3943, e-mail: reservations@parks-sa.co.za)
Open: daily Oct–Apr, 7–7, May–Sep, 7:30–6
Admission: moderate

This 16,150-acre sanctuary saved the distinctive Cape mountain zebra from extinction. There are over 200 zebras here, with more than 200 bird species, many antelope, and the caracal (or lynx). There are driving routes, nature trails, and day walks, while the Mountain Zebra Hiking Trail (16 miles) offers three days of hiking in the rugged Karoo landscape—the views are worth the effort.

HELEN MARTINS
Brought up in the strict, isolated Dutch Reformed village of Nieu Bethesda, Helen Elizabeth Martins left home abruptly in 1915, married briefly and disastrously twice, and returned to nurse her ailing parents in 1935. After their deaths, when she was about 50, she began to decorate the family home, the Owl House, covering every available surface (including chair seats) in boldly patterned ground glass, with huge sun motifs on the windows and ceilings. She also designed powerful naive concrete sculptures (actually made by colored helpers) of owls and camels, nativity scenes and mermaids. She spent the rest of her life alone in dire poverty. In 1977, with her sight failing, she committed suicide by drinking caustic soda.

The most characteristic architecture of the Cape is the simple yet elegant style known as Cape Dutch, which evolved over the 17th to early 19th centuries. Later, the British influence made itself felt in Georgian and Victorian buildings, some of the latter epitomizing imperial pomp.

Top: wrought-iron gingerbread balconies in Swellendam
Below: elaborate 19th-century style in Grahamstown

Most early Cape Dutch buildings were farmhouses, simple rectangular structures with a wooden frame, wattle and clay infill, a steeply pitched thatched roof, central front door, and symmetrically placed windows with heavy wooden shutters. The house often made up one side of a courtyard, with the barns, stables, and servants' quarters on the other three. Most had whitewashed walls and dark green paintwork (the only paint available to early settlers), a color scheme that became traditional. Inside, the hall led to just two rooms, one for sleeping, the other for living. Floors were of polished dung or mud inset with peach pits. Furniture was basic: a solid box bed, dining table, and chairs with woven gut seats. Few houses of this style survive in their original form outside museums such as those in Worcester (see page 77) and Pretoria (see page 164).

In time, as fortunes were made, the house began to sprout wings, becoming H-, T-, or U-shaped, and acquired

a small, raised veranda (*stoep*). The two largest rooms were in the front: the living room (*voerkammer*—front room) and the main bedroom. Behind, interconnecting at first, but later leading off a central corridor, were a second public room (the *agterkammer*—back room), sometimes a study/office, further bedrooms and, right at the back, the kitchen. There were no indoor bathrooms until the mid-19th century. Before then, the lavatory was in an outhouse and the bath movable. These grander houses had ceilings and floors of highly polished yellowwood or stinkwood. The furniture became more varied and sophisticated, mirroring European fashion; the very wealthy imported everything.

It was the arrival of the gable that signaled the coming of age of Cape Dutch design. Based on the intricate gables fashionable in 17th- and 18th-century Holland, the typical Cape house had one large gable over the front door. Embellished with curved and curled edges, space for statues, the date of construction or the arms of the family, these provided an element of chic and individuality, elevating the house from cottage to mansion. The master

architect was Louis Thibault; the master sculptor, Anton Anreith. The Cape Winelands (see pages 86–89) are littered with these beautiful houses, a number still owned by the original family and with period furnishings.

By the end of the 18th century, design was shifting away from the rectangular farm to the square, two-story town house of Georgian England, with symmetrically positioned windows, a triangular pediment, and flat roof. The facade became more intricate, with pastel colors, pilasters, and plaster garlands. Inside, traditional white walls gave way to elegantly painted *trompe l'oeil* columns and urns. Not many of these houses have survived urban progress, but there are a few outstanding examples, such as the Koopmans de Wet House (see page 56) in Cape Town. In the country towns they became the model for the tiny, square-built Karoo-style cottages, flat-roofed and with a small fanlight above the door, the interior quartered into four connecting rooms: living room, kitchen, and two bedrooms. Many fine examples survive in Karoo towns such as Graaff-Reinet (see page 112) and even in the Bo-Kaap quarter of Cape Town (see page 54).

The last great shift before the modern era came in the mid- to late 19th century with the advent of neo-Gothic churches, the large-scale work of South Africa's first major architect, Sir Herbert Baker, and the prevalence of Victorian houses with steeply pitched roofs (many pitched only in front as the stunted trees did not provide sufficiently long timbers) and corrugated-iron verandas that sported elaborate gingerbread trim.

Top: elegance in Graaff-Reinet
Above: a typical, simple rectangular house with a curved gable, in Tulbagh

Port Elizabeth and environs

OUT AND ABOUT
Numerous boat trips are on offer in Port Elizabeth, leaving from King's Beach (tel: 041-561 040) and the harbor (tel: 041-556 290). For sea-going sailing trips or deep-sea fishing (tel: 082-550 4502); for scuba diving (tel: 041-583 5316). For adventure sports, including white-water rafting, rappelling, hiking, riding, and cycling (tel: 041-585 4384, 041-721 0500 or 041-586 3460). A local steam train, the Apple Express, runs from PE to Thornhill (tel: 041-507 2333). For township and cultural tours (tel: 041-581 0091 or 043-743 0472); for city orientation tours (tel: 041-585 1801).

A few early buildings have survived the redevelopment of bustling Port Elizabeth

Port Elizabeth lies 470 miles east of Cape Town. A garrison was stationed here in 1799, but the real settlement came in 1820 with a large contingent of British immigrants. The acting governor, Sir Rufane Donkin, named the port after his wife. Port Elizabeth (or PE) is now South Africa's third-largest port and fifth-largest city. There are several excellent beaches in the area, including King's (from the harbor to Humewood) and Humewood itself.

The main **Port Elizabeth Museum** (Beach Road, Humewood, tel: 041-586 1051. *Open* daily 9–5. *Admission: moderate*) has several distinct sections. The museum itself has an interesting small collection of 18th- and 19th-century South African art, plus history, costume, and marine exhibits. Far more fun, however, are the living satellites—a **Snake Park** (shows daily Dec–Jan, Apr, 10 and 2. *Admission: expensive*), **Tropical House** (*Admission: moderate*), and **Oceanarium** (seal and dolphin shows daily 11 and 3. *Admission: expensive*). Here you see tropical vegetation with slithering snakes, exotic birds, 40 species of fish, including sharks, and—stars of the show—African penguins, bottlenose dolphins, and Cape fur seals.

Elsewhere, the **Castle Hill Historical Museum** (7 Castle Hill, tel: 041-522 515. *Open* Sun–Mon 2–5, Tue–Sat 10–1, 2–5. *Admission: inexpensive*) displays a fine collection of Cape furniture in PE's oldest surviving house, a former parsonage; the **King George VI Art Gallery** (Park Drive, tel: 041-561 030. *Open* Mon–Fri 8:30–5; closed Tue AM, Sat 8:30–4:30, Sun 2–4:30. *Admission free*) has 19th- and 20th-century British and South African fine art; and the **St. Croix Motor Museum** (Mowbray Street, Newton Park, tel: 041-392 5111/5212. Open by appointment) is a small private collection of vintage and classic cars, dating back to 1901.

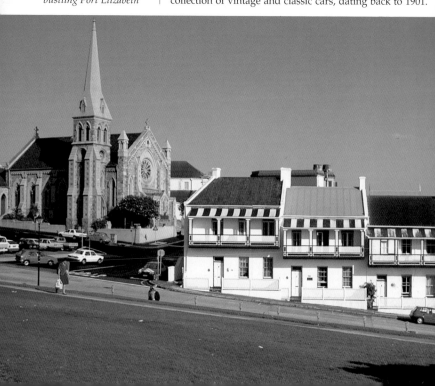

Tourist Information, Donkin Lighthouse, Donkin Reserve; tel: 041-585 8884, fax: 041-585 2564, www.pecc.gov.za. *Open* Mon–Fri 8–4:30, Sat–Sun 9–3.

▶▶ Addo Elephant National Park   *102B1*

45 miles north of Port Elizabeth (tel: 042-233 0556,
fax: 042-233 0196, e-mail: quezettevd@parks-sa.co.za)

Enormous herds of elephants once roamed across the Eastern Cape. An animal without other predators, the elephant met its match in man, as towns cut across the ancient paths, forests were felled indiscriminately, the open grassland was planted with crops, and the elephants themselves were shot—for sport and ivory, and as a pest. By 1931, the Eastern Cape was down to its last 11 elephants.

This 28,956-acre reserve—which is now linked to several surrounding private reserves, more than doubling the space available for animals to roam—was created solely to protect the tiny herd along with the last surviving Cape buffalo. Today, the population has risen to around 262 elephants, together with numerous other species including eland, kudu, red hartebeest, bushbuck, and Cape buffalo, 21 endangered Kenyan black rhino, and 185 bird species. There are two walking trails, a rest camp, a restaurant, and a store.

▶ Jeffreys Bay/St. Francis Bay   *102A1*

About 44 miles west of Port Elizabeth
Tourist Information, Shell Museum Complex, Da Gama Road,
Jeffreys Bay (tel: 042-293 2588, fax: 042-293 2227,
e-mail: jbay@ilink.nis.za)
Open: Mon–Fri 9–5, Sat 9–1

This remote corner of the coast between Port Elizabeth and the Garden Route is little known except by surfers

The Campanile

who, like the dolphins and whales, flock here to ride such magnificent waves as the 3-mile-long "Supertubes."

With a series of small, low-key vacation resorts strung along superb, white-sand beaches, it is an area best suited to doing nothing but surfing, swimming, canoeing, and beachcombing for shells (stop at the **Shell Museum**, Da Gama Road, tel: 043-293 1111, centered on one woman's 20-year obsession with shells), fishing, and taking 4x4 rides across the dunes.

St. Francis Bay is built around a series of pretty canals on the Kromme River estuary (boat trips available), while Port St. Francis is an upscale marina and resort.

MONUMENTAL GLORIES
A walking guide to historic PE is available from the tourist office. Look for the original Fort Frederick (Belmont Terrace), which was built in 1799 and never saw a shot fired in anger; the 170-foot (204-step) Campanile Clock Tower (harbor entrance) with a carillon of 23 bells, built as a memorial to the 1820 Settlers; the Horse Memorial (corner of Cape and Russell roads), erected in honor of all the horses that died in the Anglo-Boer wars; and Sir Rufane Donkin's stone pyramid, erected in memory of his beloved Elizabeth, next to the Donkin Lighthouse.

Shamwari has been completely restocked with game

RHINO HORN
The name rhinoceros comes from the Greek words *rhis* (nose) and *keras* (horn). The horns have no bony core but are made of heavily compacted fibers. They grow continuously but are restricted by wear and tear to about 2 feet (front horn) and 1 foot (rear horn). They contain no magical aphrodisiac properties, and are, in fact, made of exactly the same substance as human fingernails. This is a mild analgesic—which may be why we chew our nails in times of stress.

▶ **Shamwari Game Reserve**   *102B1*

45 miles east of Port Elizabeth, off the N2 (tel: 042-203 1111)
The park runs a special train from Johannesburg
Open: guided game drives only (see page 260)
Admission: moderate

Shamwari (the name means "friend") is a private game park covering some 34,600 acres, a mix of former farmland (20 percent) and hunting preserve (80 percent). The very landscape here was endangered; its five ecosystems include dense, low-growing valley bushveld—a mix of acacia scrub, milkwood, and succulents—destroyed by sheep and goats, but thriving under elephant and rhino. Only small animals such as mongoose remained. More than 26 species, from black and white rhino, elephant, and lion to the dung beetle and oxpecker, have been reintroduced and the reserve is carefully rebuilding an indigenous ecology. Also in the reserve is **Kaya Lendaba** (tel: 042-851 1196), a traditional African healing village.

▶ **Tsitsikamma Forest National Park** see page 101

▶ **Uitenhage**   *102B1*

24 miles north of Port Elizabeth
Tourist Information, Municipality, Market Street
(tel: 041-994 1111, fax: 041-994 1210)

Uitenhage began as a wool center but now has several automobile manufacturing factories. Among a number of fine historic buildings, the **Old Drostdy Museum** (tel: 041-992 2063) includes a Volkswagen Motor museum alongside local history and Africana collections, while the **Old Station** (tel: 041-922 8210. *Open* Tue–Thu 10–1, 2–4:30) is a perfectly preserved Victorian setting for a small railway museum. **Cuyler Manor Cultural Museum** (3 miles out of town on the Port Elizabeth road, tel: 041-922 0372. *Open* Mon–Fri 10–1, 2–4:30, Sun 2–5) has demonstrations of traditional farming, a mohair farm, and an annual prickly pear festival. The **Van Stadens Wild Flower Reserve** (tel: 041-561 000) is a 922-acre reserve and bird sanctuary on the eastern rim of the Van Stadens River gorge.

The Wild Coast

Tourist Information, P.O. Box 52791, Umtata 5100 (tel: 047-531 5290, fax: 047-531 5291, e-mail: ectbwc@icon.co.za)
Central Reservations for Wild Coast hotels (tel: 043-743 6181)
The great Kei River once marked the border of the Xhosa kingdom and later of the supposedly independent Transkei homeland. The region is markedly different from its neighbors; a few miles from the river's banks the ribbon of vacation homes comes to an abrupt halt, and the few towns are quite obviously poorer. From the 1970s, tourism here took the form of getaways on the Wild Coast and gambling weekends in the local casinos. But even this began to trail off, in the mid-1990s, as a strong antiwhite stance regularly threatened violence.

These days, with Transkei reintegrated into South Africa, the area has opened up again, but the towns, particularly the capital Umtata, are still not always friendly and you do have to be careful. With the exception of pretty little **Port St. Johns**, an increasingly popular backpackers' hangout, there are few reasons for tourists to visit the towns. Instead, glory in the virgin hardwood forests, the flower-strewn meadows and, above all, the sea.

The Transkei's very poverty and isolation have protected the local ecology from development. Here is a totally pristine stretch of magnificent coast, with gentle grasslands rolling down to wave-pounded cliffs, dunes as big as mountains, and glistening, snakelike river estuaries. Dolphins play in the surf around the rusting hulks of long-wrecked ships and kingfishers dart through the twisted mangrove swamps. Occasional roads lead down to small, remote resort hotels, where you can catch your own dinner, or enjoy mounds of fresh oysters, lobster, crab, periwinkle, yellowtail, and kingfish.

A hiking trail runs the full length of the Wild Coast. It takes about 14 days to walk the whole route, but you can do a shorter segment (for information and permits, contact the Environmental Conservation Office, Private Bag X5002, Umtata 5100, or visit Room 3–117, Botha Sigcau Building, Owen Street, Umtata, tel: 047-531 2711).

PROPHECY OF DOOM
In 1856, a young Xhosa medium named Nongqawuse had a prophetic vision while staring into a pool at the Qolora River mouth. In the vision the ancestors promised that if the Xhosa would destroy all their cattle and crops they would drive away the white men and provide the Xhosa with new and better animals and grain. The elders gathered, believed her, and the order went out. The cattle were driven into the sea and the granaries and fields set alight. The gleeful British forcibly shut the mission-aries' aid stations, and some 25,000 people are thought to have died in the ensuing famine.

119

The Wild Coast car ferry across Kei River mouth

The Xhosa, Zulu, and Ndebele—the latter are actually a breakaway Zulu clan—are all Nguni, a closely related cultural group whose languages are sufficiently similar for people to understand each other. They are spread across the Eastern Cape, KwaZulu-Natal, the borders of Northern Province, and Mpumalanga.

The three cultures have a great deal in common. By tradition, all are pastoralist, the older boys herding cattle (which count as wealth), the younger boys looking after the goats, and the women growing maize, vegetables, and some fruit on small farms. In their youth, the men were warriors; as elders they form the local council. These days, however, the old structure has all but vanished. Most men work away in the mines or factories, while the women rear the children, either separately in the villages or—increasingly—in the townships.

People The Xhosa come from the hills and coast of the Eastern Cape, around the area separated off under apartheid as the Transkei and Ciskei (see page 104). The many clans of the Zulu nation, unified under Shaka in the early 19th century (see page 30), live mainly in KwaZulu-Natal. The Ndebele, who fled north away from Shaka, live on the borders of the Northern Province and Mpumalanga, although a large number went farther still, crossing the Limpopo River into what is now Zimbabwe.

Religion The traditional religion is monotheistic: one all-important god looks after the big things in life, leaving smaller tasks to an army of ancestors. Because of this, people revere and pray to their ancestors in much the way Catholics pray to the saints. Few Nguni see any real conflict with Christianity and many happily

120

A young Zulu dancer dressed for a performance

Three Ndebele women

practice both religions simultaneously. They still consult the *sangomas* (diviners), who act as mediums, interpreting the wishes of the ancestors, and the *nyangas* (traditional herbal doctors)—although they may try the better-safe-than-sorry approach by visiting a Western hospital, too. There is still a belief in the evil influence of witchcraft. The only real difference made by the church has been in cutting down to some extent the number of wives each man takes in a polygamous culture.

Traditional life The life cycle is carefully marked as people progress from childhood to youth, marriage, and so on. Traditionally, female dress changes at each stage, while teenage boys are circumcised before they start training for adulthood. A boy must pay *lobolo* to the family of the girl he wishes to marry; this used to be in cattle, but today is more usually cash. Her parents must provide a dowry of useful household objects and clothes. For weddings, on the eve of battle, or just for a night out with the boys, every opportunity is taken to dance—energetically and competitively, with harmonizing song and rhythmic drums.

Decoration Western dress is becoming the norm, so that almost the only time you see the often magnificent traditional costume is during rituals and tourist pageants. Most people are very fond of personal adornment and bright color. All the Nguni used animal skins and beads of ostrich shell, seashells, and seeds until multicolored glass beads were introduced by the early 19th-century missionaries. These have now become an integral part of the culture, used not only for decoration, but as a clearly understood language. Illiterate Zulu girls write love letters to their boyfriends in beads, and a woman's exact status, clan, and home village can be told from the patterning of her headband and necklaces. The Ndebele took the love of adornment one stage further, the women creating jazzy geometric patterns on both inner and outer walls of their houses, at first in natural earth colors, but later, after they were introduced to acrylics, in a dazzling array of blues and greens, pinks and purples. Sadly, these adornments are increasingly rare, although Ndebele designs are very popular on plant pots and souvenirs.

BEER
Beer, which is brewed by the women, has ritual and social connotations. Maize and sorghum are wrapped in wet sacks until they sprout, dried in the sun, ground into flour, boiled to a thin porridge, then strained through a woven grass tube and left to ferment, a process that takes up to ten days. The sediment is given to the ancestors. Traditionally the beer is drunk from a communal clay or woven pot. A bowl placed facedown as a lid shows there is beer available; if it is faceup, visitors know that drinks are off.

121

Xhosa people still sometimes whiten their faces in the traditional way

*Blesbok silhouetted
against the desert sunset*

SEA OF SAND In the center of South Africa, on the high plains of the Free State, mile upon mile of maize and wheat coat the endless prairies, punctuated by nothing but an occasional windmill or isolated farmhouse. To the north and west is an enormous expanse of almost empty semidesert, stretching from the Karoo through the rust-red dunes of the Kalahari to merge with the even more terrible Namib Desert, one of the thirstiest places on earth. Together, they make up a truly massive area of wind-blown sand extending from the Northern Cape to southern Zaire—the largest continuous stretch of sand in the world. Like the Sahara, the desert is expanding.

It is a harsh, bleak, wonderful environment of strange, wind-carved rock, red-gold sand, and weird succulents and stone plants. Thousands of shallow round or oval pans, ranging in size from a few hundred yards to several square miles, trap tiny amounts of rain and dew in their hard, gray clay. These lifesaving water holes support a surprising

Free State, Northern Cape, and North-West Province

variety of life, from small reptiles to dramatically beautiful, drought-hardened antelope such as gemsbok and springbok. Where rivers or underground water feed the grass, there are some of Africa's largest remaining wildlife sanctuaries, including the remote Kgalagadi Transfrontier Park. Even people manage to survive here, from the last few desert-wise San (see page 132) to hardy Afrikaner farmers who bleed water drop by drop from deep boreholes to support scattered herds of cattle and game.

Game farming is increasingly popular in such difficult terrain. Live game is shown off to tourists and sold at auction; the surplus is hunted. Staggering numbers of people in all three provinces are eager to help hunters shoot the animal of their choice; many private reserves are stocked specifically for hunting, and quite a few small towns are proud of the local taxidermist. As a result, the animals are far too wary of humans to get close, limiting your chances of decent photographs. The good news is

Free State, Northern Cape, and North-West Province

TOURIST INFORMATION
Free State Tourism, P.O. Box 4041, Welkom 9460 (tel: 057-352 4820, fax: 057-352 4828, www.fstourism.co.za). Northern Cape Tourism Board, Private Bag X5017, Kimberley 8300 (tel: 053-832 2657, fax: 052-831 2937, www.tourismnorthern cape.org.za). North-West Parks and Tourism Board, P.O. Box 4488, Mmabatho 2735 (tel: 018-384 3040, fax: 018-384 2524, www.tourismnorthwest. co.za).

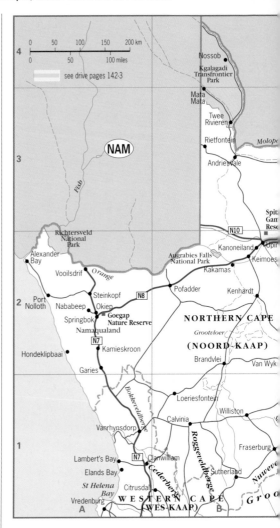

THE GRIQUA
The Griqua (the name is a simplification of "Xurikwa") originated in the Piketberg area—Khoikhoi people who were enslaved and became a subcaste of mixed-blood people. In the early 19th century, some of them sought freedom, wandering north as herders and cattle raiders and calling themselves Bastaards. A freed slave, Adam Kok, former cook to the governors of the Cape, was their leader. They settled around Klaarwater, where they drew in other displaced people of all races, from fragmented Tswana clans to army deserters. The surrounding area (now Griqualand West in the Northern Cape) succeeded in remaining independent until the 1860s, when diamonds were discovered in the area.

Right: the flowers of
Crassula marnierana
bloom in the desert

that hunting is expensive, controlled, and carried out under strict supervision. Licenses for big-game hunting are handed out only when culling is strictly necessary.

The thread that binds—and feeds—the region is South Africa's largest river, the Orange River. It rises at Maluti in the Lesotho Drakensberg, flowing northwest for 1,400 miles to meet the Atlantic coast at Alexander Bay. The river basin covers 234,247 square miles (47 percent of South Africa) and drains 22 percent of all water in South Africa. The country's second-largest river, the Vaal, is a tributary. The Orange River Development Project, founded in 1963 to provide hydroelectric power and irrigation, includes long tunnels and canals and two massive dams, the Gariep (Hendrik Verwoerd) and the Vanderkloof (P. K. Le Roux). From the central prairies, the river flows through the desert in a narrow strip of emerald green. The Orange River valley is one of the major wine areas of South Africa, and also produces table grapes, raisins, and other fruit.

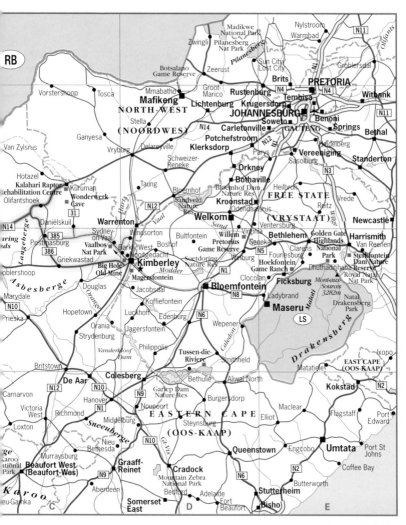

The real money, however, comes from underground. Diamonds were discovered here in 1869, and vast fortunes were made in the Kimberley area. There are still many working diamond mines in the region as well as increasing undersea harvesting of old river gravel. In April 1938, a borehole sunk on St. Helena Farm, near Welkom, drove through the lava walls of a vast underground treasure trove. Gold was found in quantities that staggered the world. By 1946, following the discovery of fabulous deposits on a farm named Geduld, at Odendaalsrus, it seemed that the Free State was the new El Dorado.

The Free State goldfields currently produce more than a third of the country's output; the names of its mines daily echo around international stock exchanges, and its goldfields rival those of the Witwatersrand as the richest in the world.

Local resources also include many other valuable minerals, from manganese and copper to uranium.

BY APPOINTMENT
Several of the most magnificent buildings in the President Brand Conservation Area may be visited by appointment only. They include the City Hall (tel: 051-405 8911), designed in 1934 by Sir Gordon Leith; the twin-spired 1880 Tweetoringkerk (Charles Street, tel: 051-430 4274); the Supreme Court (corner of President Brand and Fontein streets, tel: 051-447 8837); the 1929 Appeal Court (corner of President Brand and Charles streets, tel: 051-447 2631); and the Fourth Raadsaal (corner of President Brand and Charles streets, tel: 051-447 8898), built in 1893, with a magnificent Greek Revival council chamber.

The First Raadsaal museum has done duty as a council chamber, school, and community hall

Free State

▶ **Bloemfontein**   *125D2*

247 miles south of Johannesburg
City Tourist Information, 60 Park Road, Willow (tel: 051-405 8489/90, fax: 051-447 3859, e-mail: bloem@internext.co.za)
Open: Mon–Fri 8–4:15, Sat 8–noon

Some say Bloemfontein (Fountain of Flowers) was named after a local Griqua leader (see page 124), Jan Bloem, others that it came from the flower garden planted around the perennial spring by the first settler, Johannes Brits. The city itself was founded by Major H. D. Warden, British resident of the area between the Orange and Vaal rivers. In 1854, it became capital of the new Boer Republic, the Orange Free State. Following the Union in 1910, Bloemfontein became—and remains—the judicial capital of South Africa, an oddly provincial town with imposing public buildings and museums.

Conservation Area museums Many of the most impressive buildings, clustered around President Brand Street (walking tour maps available), now house museums. The thatched-roofed, dung-floored **First Raadsaal** (95 St. George Street, tel: 051-447 9610. *Open* Mon–Fri 10:15–3, Sat–Sun 2–5. *Admission free*) was built in 1848 as the first council chamber and school. It contains a small museum of the Republic, with a collection of carriages and wagons. Highlights of the **National Museum** (corner of Charles and Aliwal streets, tel: 051-447 9609. *Open* Mon–Sat 8–5, Sun noon–6. *Admission: inexpensive*) are a re-created 19th-century street and an extensive archeological and fossil collection, including the Florisbad skull, South Africa's earliest example of *Homo sapiens*. The Old Government Building (1908) is now home to the **National Afrikaans Literary (Letterkundige) Museum** (corner of President Brand and Maitland streets, tel: 051-405 4711. *Open* Mon–Fri 8–12:15, 1–3:45, Sat 9–noon. *Admission free*). The opulent, Scottish baronial **Old Presidency** (corner of President Brand and St. George streets, tel: 051-448 0949. *Open* Tue–Fri 10–noon, 1–4, Sat–Sun 2–5. *Admission free*) was built in 1885 on the site of the original Bloem Fonteyn farm as official residence of the presidents of the Free State Republic.

EMILY HOBHOUSE
A staunch supporter of Afrikaner independence, Emily Hobhouse spent much of her life trying to mediate between the British and Boers. In 1900, she began to raise money to alleviate the suffering in Boer concentration camps, eventually whipping up enough support to help improve conditions and force a settlement. Notably, she never visited any black camps. After the war, she established a series of 26 spinning and weaving schools for Boer girls. Regarded as a local heroine, she is buried at the foot of the National Women's Memorial.

Left: painted tiles depict the Battle of Colenso. Below: memorial to Boer victims of the concentration camps. Both are in the War Museum, Bloemfontein

Other museums Colonial **Freshford House** (31 Kellner Street, tel: 051-447 9609. *Open Mon–Fri 10–1, Sat–Sun 2–5. Admission: inexpensive*) is full of brass, stained glass, and Victoriana. The **Oliewenhuis Art Gallery** (Harry Smith Street, tel: 051-447 9609. *Open Mon–Fri 8–5, Sat 10–5, Sun 1–5. Admission free*) was a neo-Cape Dutch homestead. **Queen's Fort** (Church Street, tel: 051-447 5478. *Open Mon–Fri 8–4. Admission free*), built in 1848, houses a small military museum.

The excellent **National Women's Memorial and War Museum**►► (Monument Road, tel: 051-447 3447. *Open Mon–Sat 9–4:30, Sun 2–5. Guided tours by appointment. Admission: inexpensive*) gives a compelling (if one-sided) account of the Anglo-Boer War, with horrific details of prisoner-of-war and concentration camps (see page 39). In the grounds is a memorial to the 26,370 Afrikaner women and children who died in them.

Gardens The finest of Bloemfontein's gardens are the lush 112-acre **National Botanical Garden**► (Rayton Road, tel: 051-431 3530. *Open daily 8–6. Admission: inexpensive*) and rose-filled **King's Park**. The **Zoo** (King's Way, tel: 051-405 8483. *Open daily 8–6 in summer, 8–5 in winter. Admission: moderate*) is famous for its "liger" (a lion-tiger cross) and primates.

Naval Hill includes the 476-acre **Franklin Game Reserve** (Union Avenue, tel: 051-405 8124. *Open daily 8–5. Admission free*). Nearby, in Hamilton Park, is the **Orchid House**► (Union Avenue, tel: 051-405 8124. *Open Mon–Fri 10–4, Sat–Sun 10–5. Admission free*).

SIR HARRY SMITH

A renowned and charismatic hothead, Harry Smith began his career as an aide to the Duke of Wellington during the Spanish Peninsular Wars. During this time he married a young Spanish noblewoman, Juana Maria de los Dolores de Leon. Smith served for a time in America and fought at Waterloo. In later life, he became governor of the Cape Colony, where he managed to stir up trouble along most of the borders, fighting bloody wars against the Xhosa and Sotho. Harrismith is named after him, while both Ladysmith in KwaZulu-Natal and Ladismith in the Western Cape are named after his wife.

Eastern Highlands

The Eastern Highlands are an area of great natural beauty and drama, where cold winters frequently blanket the higher reaches of the Maloti Mountains and the Drakensberg in snow. Traces remain of the various peoples who have lived here—in the San rock paintings, the scattered Sotho, Bakwena, and Balokwa villages, and the tidy sandstone towns and churches of the Boers and British.

For tourists, however, this area is all about the great outdoors, with a whirl of activities from bird-watching and game viewing to horseback riding, mountain biking, hiking and climbing, water sports, and golf.

Several charming small towns with fine Victorian buildings of local sandstone make up the Highlands Route. Prosperous **Harrismith** (Tourist Information, Andries Pretorius Street, tel: 058-622 3525, fax: 058-623 0923) was founded in 1849. Nearby are the 2,471-acre **Mount Everest Game Reserve** and the 44,480-acre **Sterkfontein Dam Nature Reserve** (tel: 058-622 3520, fax: 058-622 1772. *Open* daily 6–10. *Admission: inexpensive*) surrounding a lake. Stunningly situated beneath the Titanic, a huge ship-shaped wedge of rock, **Clarens** (Tourist Information, 171 Main Street, tel/fax: 058-256 1542) is a delightful village, founded in 1912 and named after the Swiss town where President Kruger died. The great local attraction is **Cinderella's Castle** (Naauport Street), a full-size fantasy lovingly constructed out of 55,000 empty beer bottles. It has various fairy-tale tableaus and, inevitably, a curio shop.

Bethlehem (Tourist Information, Municipality, Muller Street, tel: 058-303 5732, fax: 058-323 5876) has a local history museum, a particularly fine collection of Victorian buildings, and several lakes nearby. **Fouriesburg** (Tourist Information, tel: 058-223 0552, fax: 058-223 0166) was founded in 1892. Surrounded by flat-topped sandstone hillocks, many of them pierced by caves, it was a Boer stronghold during the Anglo-Boer War. An Asparagus Festival takes place here in September.

Ficksburg, on the Caledon River border with Lesotho, was founded in 1867 as a bulwark between disputed Boer and Sotho territory. The **General J. J. Fick Museum** (Town Square) sheds light on local history and the customs and life of the Sotho people.

San rock art adorns the caves of the Imperani Mountains nearby, and the **Hoekfontein Game Ranch** (8 miles from town, off the R26 to Fouriesburg, tel: 05192-3915) is home to white rhino and hippo and has ox-wagon rides.

The district around the town produces 90 percent of the cherries grown in South Africa. It celebrates this with a Cherry Festival each November.

Sotho women chatting in Ficksburg

▶ Gariep Dam   125D1

About 100 miles south of Bloemfontein (tel: 051-754 0026)
The biggest stretch of inland water in South Africa lies
behind this vast dam on the Orange and Caledon rivers.
The reservoir covers an area of 144 square miles when full
and provides water for irrigation and hydroelectric
power. The dam wall (1972) is 2,175 feet long and 297 feet
high. Around the shores are huge expanses of grassland
and Karoo vegetation dotted with rocky outcrops and
massive boulders, most of it protected by the 27,768-acre
Gariep Nature Reserve (tel: 051-754 0026) and the
54,364-acre **Tussen-die-Riviere** (tel: 051-763 1114), which is
a normal sanctuary in winter and hunting preserve
in summer. Aasvoelkop, near the eastern boundary,
preserves some San rock paintings. Both reserves offer
accommodations, sailing, fishing, and swimming.

The **Pellissier House Museum** (tel: 051-763 0103) in
nearby **Bethulie** (Tourist Information, tel/fax: 051-763
0002) is thought to be the oldest settler structure north of
the Orange River.

▶▶ Golden Gate Highlands National Park   125E2

*Approximately 224 miles south of Johannesburg and 186 miles
northeast of Bloemfontein*
(tel: 012-343 1991, fax: 012-343 0905, www.parks-sa.co.za)
In the upper valley of the Little Caledon River and the
foothills of the spectacular Maloti Mountains of Lesotho,
this 28,665-acre reserve preserves a strange landscape of
brilliant yellow, orange, and red sandstone cliffs, and
high outcrops and caves, pummeled into bizarre shapes
by water. Early hunters were driven out of this area by the
Sotho, who settled on the secure heights of the sandstone
outcrop "fortresses." The reserve has a variety of animals
and birds, including black wildebeest, black eagles, and
blue cranes. There is hiking, trout fishing, and riding.

*Highly colored sandstone
cliffs in the Golden Gate
Highlands National Park*

THE BERG MARATHON
During the Anglo-Boer
War, a British major, John
Belcher, insulted the
citizens of Harrismith by
referring to "their" mountain, Platberg (5,700
feet), as "that little hill of
yours." They bet that he
would not be able to reach
the summit in 60
minutes. He took them
on, won easily, and then
donated a trophy for an
annual race. The course
consists of a 3-mile run,
climbing 1,440 feet to the
top, followed by a run
along the summit and
down an old bridle path
back to the town.

FREE STATE BATTLEFIELDS
There are 22 battlefield sites in the Free State. The three earliest mark the Battle of Vegkop between the Afrikaners and the Matabele, led by Mzilikaze, in 1836; the Afrikaner uprising against the Griqua in 1845, put down by the British at Swartkoppies; and the 1848 Battle of Boomplas, when Sir Harry Smith tried to annex the Orange River Sovereignty. The other 19 belong to the Second Anglo-Boer War. Most are well signposted. Some—including Paardeberg (1900), near Jacobsdal, Sannaspos (1900), east of Bloemfontein, and Magersfontein (1899)—have small museums.

► **Jagersfontein**   125D2

68 miles southwest of Bloemfontein
Tourist Information, Municipality, Market Square
(tel: 051-724 0003, fax: 051-724 0447)
A Victorian mining town, Jagersfontein has a number of attractive buildings, including four designed by Herbert Baker. The main reason to come here is the **Mining Village** (*Open* Mon–Fri 8–1, 2–5. *Admission: inexpensive*), an open-air museum on the rim of the local "Big Hole," nearly 1,640 feet in diameter and 1,640 feet deep. The 971-carat Excelsior diamond was discovered here in 1883.

► **Philippolis**   125D2

Tourist Information, Transgariep Museum, 25 Kok Street
(tel: 051-773 0157/0209)
Philippolis is an oasis of white stucco and deep-green trees in the immense, dry plain. Dating from 1823, it is the oldest town in the Free State, founded as a mission station for the Griqua people (see page 124). It has some interesting Karoo architecture, including a splendid Dutch Reformed church, Adam Kok's home on Voortrekker Street, his *kraal* on Justisie Street, and his *kruithuis* (arsenal) on a hill west of town. Emily Hobhouse (see page 127) established her first spinning and weaving schools here. The **Transgariep Museum** (tel: 051-773 0216. *Open* Mon–Fri 10–12. *Admission free*) covers all the town's fascinating history, and each April brings out its distilling kettle for a *witblitz* (moonshine) festival.

► **Phuthaditjhaba**   125E2

Previously known as Witsieshoek, **Phuthaditjhaba** was the capital of Qwa Qwa, the former homeland of the Bakwena and Balokwa tribes. The **Balokwa Museum** covers local tribal history.
   Within **Qwa Qwa National Park** (tel: 058-721 0300), a magnificent area of 52,000 acres crossed by rich green valleys and sparkling streams interspersed with gnarled sandstone cliffs, is the **Basotho Cultural Village** (tel: 058-721 0300. *Open* Mon–Fri 9–4:30, Sat–Sun 9–5. *Admission: expensive*). Though a little like a theme park, the village is fascinating, with a display of Sotho huts, from beehive-style thatch to bright, geometric clay. You can see demonstrations of southern Sotho ways of life, too.

► **Sandveld Nature Reserve**   125D3

6 miles northwest of Bloemfontein; 6 miles from Bloemhof on the R34 (tel: 053-433 1701/2)
Stretching down to the horseshoe-shaped Bloemhof Dam, this is a 98,844-acre wonderland of Kalahari thornveld. It has a 148-mile shoreline, softened by sandy beaches and shaded by giant camelthorn trees. White-backed vultures build huge, unruly nests in the high branches; below scuttle small mammals like aardwolf and antbears, porcupines and springhare. Gemsbok, wildebeest, white rhino, giraffe, and kudu also thrive here.

► **Welkom**   125D3

Tourist Information, Stateway (tel: 057-352 9244,
fax: 057-352 9501)
Planned as a garden city, this industrial giant is a mine-scape of machinery, dumps, reduction works, and

belching factories. Water pumped from the mines has formed shallow pans that attract prolific bird life, including flamingos. There is a museum (Tulbagh Street), but it is worth coming here only if you want an underground tour of a gold mine (ask at the tourist office).

▶ Willem Pretorius Game Reserve 125D2

93 miles northeast of Bloemfontein off the N1; the turnoff is between Winburg and Ventersdorp (tel: 057-651 4003)
Open: daily 7 AM–10:30 PM. Admission: inexpensive

The Sand River and Allemanskraal Dam divide this 29,653-acre park into a densely covered, hilly northern section, which provides a perfect habitat for baboons, bushbuck, kudu, and duiker, and open grasslands to the south, teeming with springbok, wildebeest, blesbok, eland, impala, and zebra. White rhino and buffalo move freely through the park. On the summit of Beckersberg are a restored prehistoric settlement of dry-stone-walled huts and *kraals* belonging to the now-vanished Leghoya people, and a small site museum.

At nearby **Senekal** (Tourist Information, tel: 014-331 2142) are the remains of a 250,000-year-old petrified forest. **Winburg** (Tourist Information, tel/fax: 051-881 0003) is a Voortrekker town with a local history museum.

Zebra, springbok, and wildebeest drinking

The San were dubbed "Bushmen" by the Dutch because of their knowledge of and affinity with nature. Nomadic hunter-gatherers, they are thought to be the earliest aboriginal inhabitants of southern Africa. Their lifestyle has changed relatively little over some 40,000 years.

132

Top: San paintings are a powerful affirmation of the natural world Below: a dwindling number of San still hunt for their food

The San roamed the animal-rich central plains and left archeological evidence of their passing—paintings and engravings—in lush, mountainous areas with plentiful water, such as the Drakensberg. Some of the most recent paintings depict soldiers on horseback wearing red and blue tunics, proving that the last of the San did not leave the Drakensberg area until after the arrival of the Europeans in the mid-19th century.

End of an era Most were long gone by then, however, pushed into the harsher fringes of the continent by the Nguni, who began to arrive around AD 500. When the Voortrekkers began to compete—often violently—for the same water sources, many of the remaining San were killed, while some were taken prisoner and turned into servants and farm laborers. Yet others died of epidemic European diseases such as smallpox and even flu, to which they had no immunity. Most mingled with the Khoikhoi, Malays, and incoming Nguni, and have slowly been absorbed into the general "colored" population. By the early 19th century, their independent lifestyle and tribal identity had all but disappeared. Today, the last few surviving groups skillfully scratch out a meager existence from the Kalahari sands. There are claimed to be some 60,000 San left across South Africa, Namibia, and Botswana, but relatively few are pure blood and living a traditional life.

Traditional life San huts consist of a domed framework of branches, covered in grass and reeds; in the dry season, when shade is more important than a waterproof covering, partly open shelters are made from reed mats bent over a frame. Always on the move, the San have few material possessions. Both men and women traditionally wear only a small "skirt" with front and back aprons of animal skin, hung from a beaded belt; these days it is as likely to be a loincloth or a pair of swimming trunks, while the women

San villagers at Kagga Kamma, near Ceres

133

often feel more comfortable in Western dress when strangers are around. Both sexes wear elaborate, beaded headdresses, necklaces, bracelets, and anklets. Until the arrival of beads, these decorations would have been made of ostrich eggshell and seeds.

Tortoise shells are used as dishes; with one end filled in and the other corked, they also serve as containers and snuffboxes. Ostrich eggshells and dried springbok pouches are used as water containers, both for rations when on the move and for storage in the long dry season. The San have perfected a technique of skinning the animal without splitting the skin, then simply tying knots in the legs and head hole to make a watertight container.

The men hunt in groups, with bows and poison-tipped arrows, wooden clubs, and spears. They also set snares, and track bee eaters in search of their favorite luxury— honey. The gathering, which accounts for most daily food, is done by the women, who search the veld for roots and tubers, berries and fruit. In the dry season, fruit such as melons are a vital source of liquid. Cooking was traditionally done in clay pots, but today the pan may well be an old tin can.

San art Above all, the San are known for their art, which adorns many caves, overhangs, or even particularly smooth slabs of rock, depicting local animals, the thrill of the hunt, or a dance. The painters used natural dyes such as carbon, iron oxide, or yellow ocher mixed with blood or animal fat; other pictures are engraved into the surface of the stone. The shapes are alive with movement and obviously executed with love.

Northern Cape

▶▶ Augrabies Falls 124B2

75 miles west of Upington (tel: 054-451 0050)
Open: Apr–Sep, 6:30 AM–10 PM; Oct–Mar, 6 AM–10 PM

The Khoikhoi called it *Aukoerebi* ("Place of Great Noise") after the thunder of the Orange River as it crashes foaming down five flights of granite falls (totaling 184 feet) into a magnificent 11-mile canyon. The Augrabies Falls are the fifth largest in the world, made all the more dramatic by the massive surrounding boulders and parched desert landscape. The three-day Klipspringer Hiking Trail runs along the canyon through the 38,092-acre **Augrabies Falls National Park**, full of weird rock formations and desert vegetation such as the quiver trees, whose branches were hollowed by the San to hold their arrows. There are spectacular views along the rim and some game, including rhino, as well as sports activities. Many roads are gravel; drive slowly, and reduce tire pressure. Augrabies is a malaria area, so take precautions.

The Augrabies Falls are a spectacular torrent of water splitting the barren desert rock

▶ Colesberg 125D1

Tourist Information tel: 051-753 0678, fax: 051-753 0574

This classic Karoo town halfway between Cape Town and Johannesburg grew up around a water hole at the foot of the conical Coleskop, a landmark for many early travelers. Its first settlement, a mission, was forced to close when local farmers decided its San and Griqua followers were a security threat. A white town (named after Sir Lowry Cole, Cape governor in 1828–1833), Colesberg was founded in 1830. Whole streets of small Karoo block houses survive, as well as grander Victorian buildings, **Kemper Museum** (Murray Street) is one of the best small-town collections , with a fascinating photographic exhibition on the Karoo nomads. Walking tours are offered by the tourist office.

▶▶ Kgalagadi Transfrontier Park 124B4

222 miles north of Upington (tel: 054-561 0021)
Open: daily 6 AM–7:30 PM in midsummer, 7:30 AM–6 PM in midwinter

This is a vast park up in the northwest on the borders of Namibia and Botswana, in the harsh Kalahari Desert. The whole area, more than 8.9 million acres, is one of the world's largest unspoiled ecosystems, set up during the 1930s to protect the magnificent gemsbok from poachers. Much of the park is in Botswana but about a quarter, 2.4 million acres, is in South Africa. Access and facilities, including accommodations and fuel, are easily available only from the South African side.

There are just three roads in the whole area, two of them following the river-beds, where the animals tend to cluster around the small amounts of water. The game includes wildebeest, harte-beest, and springbok, more than 215 bird species, and a spectacular range of flora, from the creeping desert melons on the Kalahari dunes to fertile woodland and savannah, only where there is water enough to sustain life.

There are few or no gas stations or stores on the road north from Upington. Bring supplies.

►►► **Kimberley** see pages 137–139

► **Kuruman**   *125C3*

148 miles northwest of Kimberley
Tourist Information, Main Street (tel: 053-712 1095/6/7,
fax: 053-712 3581)

Known locally as **Gasegonyana** ("Place of the Little Calabash"), Kuruman is a lush oasis in the dusty Kalahari, built around the Eye of God, a huge spring. Four million gallons of water a day gush from the dolomitic rock, never weakening even during the most severe drought. In 1821, Robert Moffat of the London Missionary Society set up a base here, and the little settlement was tagged the Fountain of Christianity. Moffat made only eight converts locally, but his daughter married David Livingstone, who used Kuruman as a base from which to explore the hinterland and spread the gospel. Meanwhile, Moffat translated the Bible into Tswana, printing it on his own press. The mission is now a museum, and the church (1838) is still in use.

The **Kalahari Raptor Rehabilitation Centre** (Tsineng Road, tel: 053-712 3576), is a good place to see some of Africa's fiercest birds, and there is a **bird sanctuary** on Hotazel Road. The **Wonderwerk Cave** (25 miles from Kuruman, on the Daniëlskuil Road, tel: 053-384 0680) was a San home until 1914, and it contains their etchings.

The Eye of God in Kuruman is a real desert oasis

TOO HOT FOR COMFORT
Hotazel (38 miles north-west of Kuruman) was named by two young prospectors who stopped here on their travels in 1917. They proclaimed the farm was "hot as hell" and were so busy recuperating that they failed to notice that the land underneath was almost solid manganese. It turned out to be the richest deposit in the world.

BIGGEST AND BEST
Upington collects statistics. It has the world's longest avenue of date palms (half a mile), needed in the intense desert heat, and the longest runway in the southern hemisphere (3 miles), used for land speed trials and as a possible emergency landing strip for the space shuttle. The winery is the second largest in the southern hemisphere.

In spring, the whole of Namaqualand bursts into bloom

▶▶▶ Namaqualand   *124A2*

Springbok is 347 miles north of Cape Town
Tourist Information, P.O. Box 96, Springbok (tel: 027-712 2011, fax: 027-712 1421, e-mail: namakwaland@interkom.co.za)

The northwest Cape is semidesert—harsh and dry for most of the year. With an economy based almost entirely on a few scattered copper and diamond mines, it is sparsely populated. The only reasonably sized town is the region's capital, **Springbok**. In spring (mid-Aug to mid-Sep) the area is transformed by millions of bright, colorful daisies, aloes, and lilies. The **Goegap Nature Reserve** (9 miles southeast of Springbok, tel: 027-712 1880. *Open* daily 8–4) is one of the easiest places to see them, with 581 plant species, 45 species of mammal, and 94 bird species.

In the far north, the 2-million-acre **Richtersveld National Park** (58 miles east of Alexander Bay, tel: 0256-831 1506. For guided 4x4 tours, contact Richtersveld Challenge, tel: 027-712 1905, fax: 027-718 1460, e-mail: richtersvel challen@kingsley.co.za) is a lunar landscape slashed by deep gorges, and fascinating for botanists—half the plants here are rarities.

▶ Upington   *124B2*

497 miles west of Kimberley
Tourist Information, The Library Building, Mutual Street (tel: 054-332 6911, fax: 054-332 7064)
Open: Mon–Fri 9–6, Sat 9–noon

By local standards Upington is a metropolis, with two interesting monuments. One, at the police station, is to the early Camel Corps; the other, commemorating the donkeys used to open up the area, is by the **museum** (Schroeder Street. *Open* Mon–Fri 8–12:30, 1:30–5). Tour the **Orange River Winery** (tel: 054-332 4651. Tastings: Mon–Fri 8–noon, 2–5) or visit **Spitskop Game Reserve** (tel: 054-332 1336), or visit **Kanoneiland** (Cannon Island) in the Orange River, with its vineyards and catfish farm (tel: 054-491 1223). Many Koranna (mixed-race Griqua and Tswana) retained their land against all the odds and still farm in **Keimoes** (Tourist Information, Main Road, tel: 054-461 1230). **Kakamas** (Tourist Information, 19 Voortrekker Road, tel: 054-431 0838) has a complex network of waterwheels, canals, and irrigation tunnels (1898–1901).

Kimberley

The famous diamond town lies 608 miles northeast of Cape Town and 301 miles southwest of Johannesburg. In 1871, the first diamond was discovered at Colesberg Kopje. Prospectors rushed to the area and a tented town sprang up. Originally called New Rush, the village was renamed Kimberley in 1873, in honor of the British secretary of state for the colonies. During the Anglo-Boer War, the town was besieged by the Boers for 124 days. Over 3,000 women and children took shelter in the mine tunnels, while the mine workshops were converted to make ammunition and a huge gun, Long Cecil. The **Honoured Dead Memorial** (Memorial Road), commissioned by Rhodes, has an inscription by Rudyard Kipling and commemorates those who died during the siege. At the base stands Long Cecil. Kimberley is now a city of around 200,000 people with several museums, although diamonds are the biggest draw. The mines still produce about 4,000 carats a day.

Kimberley's wealth paid for some beautiful buildings, such as the rococo **City Hall** (1899, Market Square), the **Dutch Reformed church** (1885, Hertzog Square), and the **Kimberley Club** (1882, Du Toitspan Road). Equally imposing are the mansions built by the diamond magnates, such as **Dunluce** (1897, 10 Lodge Road), the **Rudd House** (5–7 Loch Road), and the **Oppenheimer House** (7 Lodge Road). The **Diggers' Fountain** by Herman Wald, in the Oppenheimer Memorial Gardens, shows five miners holding a diamond sieve.

After John Weston made a nonstop flight of 8 minutes, 30 seconds in 1911, the country's first flight school opened in Kimberley. The **Memorial to the Pioneers of Aviation** (Oliver Road, 2 miles from the airport; tel: 053-842 0099. *Open* Mon–Sat 9–4:30, Sun 2–5:30. *Admission: inexpensive*) consists of a monument, a reconstruction hangar, and a replica Compton Paterson biplane.

An extraordinarily dainty town hall graces the center of rough, tough Kimberley

BASICS
Tourist Information:
Diamantveld Visitor Center,
121 Bultfontein Road,
P.O. Box 1976, Kimberley
(tel: 053-832 7298,
fax: 053-832 7211,
www.kimberley-africa.com).
Open Mon–Fri 8–5, Sat
8:30–11:30. For guided
half- or full-day tours
featuring Cecil John
Rhodes, historical
Kimberley, diamonds,
S.A. Battlefields,
townships, and local
ghosts, contact Steve's
Tours, P.O. Box 3017,
Kimberley 8300 (tel/fax:
053-831 4006,
e-mail: stevestours@
kimberley.co.za).

CECIL JOHN RHODES

Rhodes (1853–1902) came to South Africa in 1870 for his health. In 1871, he headed for the Kimberley diamond fields. By 1888, he had formed the De Beers Mining Company and controlled 90 percent of the world's diamond production. He made a second fortune from the Transvaal gold-fields and, in 1889, founded the British South Africa Company (BSAC). In 1890, he became prime minister of Cape Colony, while the BSAC colonized Rhodesia (now Zimbabwe and Zambia). He died in Muizenberg, near Cape Town, but is buried in the Matobo Hills, Zimbabwe. Part of his fortune still funds the Rhodes Scholarships to Oxford University.

138

The Star of the West is one of the oldest pubs in South Africa

▶▶▶ The Big Hole and Kimberley Mine Museum 125C2

Tucker Street (tel: 053-833 1557)
Open: daily 8–6. Admission: moderate

The hole really is big, the largest manmade excavation in the world, with a circumference of 1 mile and a surface area of 33 acres. It is now part of an open-air museum that vividly re-creates old Kimberley, with over 40 carefully restored buildings, from homes and dealers' offices to stores, a church, and Barnato's Boxing Gym. All are furnished in period style, with photos and plentiful explanation. A diamond exhibition hall has replicas of some of the world's most famous diamonds, plus about 2,000 gleaming carats of the real thing, including the cut and polished Eureka diamond (see page 140).

A trolley runs from the town to the museum, the last vestiges of a route that began as a mule-drawn service in 1887. Near the main entrance, the **Jewel Box** has demonstrations of diamond polishing and goldsmithing, while the atmospheric, 19th-century-themed **Star of the West** pub (see page 265) is one of the busiest drinking spots in the city.

▶▶ Bultfontein Mine 125D2

Molyneux Road, Kimberley (tel: 053-842 1321)
Surface tours: Mon–Fri, 9 and 11 (no children under 8 years); underground tours: Mon–Fri by appointment, minimum age 16 years. Advance reservations essential
Admission: moderate

The first diamonds discovered here in 1869 were actually in the mud walls of the Bultfontein farmhouse, which was destroyed in the attempt to find more. Today there is a large hole where the house once stood. Bultfontein Mine, owned by De Beers, is still operational. To see high-tech diamond mining, take the daily surface and underground tours.

▶ The Duggan-Cronin Gallery 125D2

Egerton Road, Kimberley (tel: 053-842 0099)
Open: Mon–Sat 9–4. Admission: moderate

A. M. Duggan-Cronin was an avid photographer and recorder of "native" life in South Africa at the turn of the 20th century, and the collection includes many photos that are fascinating, if rather dubious—it is rumored that he traveled with a leopard skin for people to wear when posing.

▶ The McGregor Museum 125D2

Atlas and Chapel streets, Kimberley (tel: 053-842 0099)
Open: Mon–Sat 9–5, Sun 2–5, public holidays 10–5
Admission: moderate

Built as a sanatorium, this became a luxury hotel, and Cecil Rhodes lived and worked here during the Boer siege. Today it is a museum of Kimberley history and the ecology of the Northern Cape, with a fine collection of 19th-century furniture. The **Alexander McGregor Memorial Museum** (Chapel Street, tel: 053-842 0099. *Open Mon–Sat 9–5, Sun 2–5. Admission: inexpensive*), a satellite of the main McGregor Museum, contains displays about geology worldwide and the history of the Northern Cape, as well as a small costume collection.

► **Magersfontein Battlefield**   *125D2*

20 miles from Kimberley, on the Modder River road
(tel: 053-831 6711)
Open: daily 8–5. Admission: moderate
On December 11, 1899, in an effort to break the siege of Kimberley, a troop of 12,500 British soldiers led by Lord Methuen attacked a well-entrenched Boer force of 8,200 under General Cronje. The battle lasted ten days, leaving 239 Britons and 87 Boers dead. It was one of the worst British defeats in the Anglo-Boer War. A small museum at the battlefield contains uniforms, weapons, documents, and photos.

► **The William Humphreys Art Gallery**   *125D2*

Jan Smuts Boulevard (tel: 053-831 1724/5)
Open: Mon–Sat 10–1, 2–5, Sun 2–5
Admission: inexpensive
Founded around a personal collection of 16th- and 17th-century Dutch and Flemish masters and British and French paintings belonging to former Member of Parliament William Benbow Humphreys (1889–1965), this gallery is one of the best in South Africa. In addition to the international collection, it has an innovative selection of South African art by both black and white artists.

THE BIG HOLE
Diamonds produced: 14,504,566 carats (5,988 pounds).
Ground excavated: 24,800 tons.
Depth of hole: 705 feet.
Depth from surface to water: 571 feet.
Depth of water: 135 feet.
Original depth of open cast working: 787 feet.
Original depth of underground working: 3,598 feet.

The aptly named Big Hole in Kimberley was one of the world's richest sources of diamonds

139

The story goes that in 1866 young Erasmus Jacobs was playing on his father's farm, near Hopetown, when he picked up a pretty pebble. A neighbor, Schalk van Niekerk, offered to buy the stone; thinking it worthless, the family gave it to him. Erasmus' plaything turned out to be the 21.25-carat "Eureka" diamond, the trigger for the Kimberley diamond rush.

"Of course I thought when once on the field,
Every load of stone would yield,
But, I owned, after many a weary day,
That gravel is gravel, and clay is clay."
Longlands, 1908

140

Early days In 1869, Schalk van Niekerk bartered with a Griqua shepherd for a second, larger stone, later named the "Star of South Africa," weighing 83.5 carats. Diamonds were also found on two other farms, Bultfontein and Dorstfontein (now known as Du Toitspan), about 25 miles south of the Vaal River. By 1871, diggings had also been opened up on the De Beers farm, Vooruitzicht, and Colesberg Kopje. It was this small, rocky hill that was eventually to turn into the Kimberley Big Hole. Some 50,000 people streamed into the area from across the globe, living in tents and flimsy houses of wood and galvanized iron. There were not even the most basic facilities such as drains, disease was rife in the hot summer months, and the diggers had to pay up to 2.5 cents for one bucket of muddy water or 10 cents for a loaf of bread.

By the mid-1880s, the hills were flattened and the diggings began to hollow out the land. At 50–60 feet down, the last of the yellow oxidized earth began to run out. Disappointed diggers were preparing to move out when, to their astonished delight, someone discovered that the harder blue rock beneath (now named kimberlite) was even richer in gems. They had tapped into the volcanic pipe in which the diamonds had been born, in the center of the earth.

Above top: production line in the De Beers diamond sorting sheds (1900)
Above: aerial ropeways at Kimberley

Seeking a fortune The biggest problem was the owner-ship of the diamond fields. The whole area was known as Griqualand West and claimed by the Khoikhoi Griqua people, who had lived there for 70 years. It was also on the frontier, and the governments of the Orange Free State, the South African Republic, and the Cape Colony all claimed so rich a prize. In 1880, the British simply annexed it and dared the others to complain.

There was also the problem of individual claims. Each new rumor led to a frantic rush to stake claims and obtain licenses. Early maps are a patchwork of tiny squares of land—eventually there were some 1,600 individual properties, each only 30 feet by 30 feet, in the Big Hole alone. As they dug farther into the earth, the dividing walls collapsed. There were often brutal fights over who owned the resulting heap of earth—and it became ever harder for prospectors to reach their workings or get the gravel out of the pits. Enterprising businessmen set up pulley systems that covered the diggings like a cobweb. The used the fortunes they made to buy up small claims. Kimberley came to be dominated by a handful of key players such as Cecil Rhodes, Charles Rudd, and Barney Barnato, who worked together in an increasingly powerful cartel, eventually merging to become De Beers Consolidated Mines. Today, under the Oppenheimers, De Beers still controls much of the world's diamond market, although South Africa's ranking has slipped to fifth.

❏ **Sparklers** There are six common shapes for cut and polished diamonds. The round brilliant, oval marquise, emerald cut, and pear-shaped each have 58 facets; the oblong baguette has 25; and the square cut 30. The normal color range is from white to dark yellow, but defects in the crystal lattice can produce unusual colors. Known as "fancies," these are more expensive still. ❏

THE BIG ONE
The largest uncut diamond in the world, and the largest ever found at Kimberley, is the 616, found in 1974 at Du Toitspan Mine by Abel Maratela. It was named after its carat weight, which happened to coincide with the De Beers' box number.

Below: the Cullinan diamond—530.2 carats

Left: rough diamonds in many shapes and colors
Below: De Beers' newest mine—Venetia, Transvaal

Tour

Diamond drive
(see map pages 124–125)

Kimberley is the heart of South Africa's diamond trade, but many other places in the neighborhood have commercial mines, and diggers else-where still scratch at the riverbanks under a blazing sun amid ocher sands and camelthorn trees. Allow one to two days for this tour.

Leave Kimberley on the R31 toward Barkly West. After 15 miles, turn right

There are many small diamond-digging operations, such as these near Barkly West, northwest of Kimberley

to Nooitgedacht and follow the dirt road for 5 miles. Here extraordinary pavements of 2,500-million-year-old Ventersdorp lava were polished by glaciers 250 million years ago, then covered in engravings by the San.

Return to the main road and continue for 5 miles to **Barkly West** (Tourist Information, tel: 053-531 0673). Once known as Klipdrift, this is the site of the Northern Cape's first diamond rush to Canteen Kopje in 1869. A cairn marks the spot. In 1870, the Klipdrift diggers declared independence from the Transvaal, only to be annexed by Britain in 1871. Two years later the name was changed in honor of the governor, Sir Henry Barkly. There are mementos of the Diamond Rush in St. Mary's church (1871). Numerous small diggings line the Vaal River in nearby Windsorton (take the R374 north for 20 miles). Return to Barkly West and

continue west along the R31 through the old diamond diggings at Sydney-on-Vaal (17 miles farther on). Nearby is the 64,250-acre **Vaalbos National Park** (tel: 053-561 0088, www.parks-sa.co.za. *Open* daily dawn–dusk. *Admission: moderate*), with buffalo and both black and white rhino. From here, keep going along the R31 for 60 miles to **Daniëlskuil**—literally "Daniel's Den" (Tourist Information, Barker Street, tel: 053-384 0013). Mining began here in 1960, when a group of hopefuls found 26 diamonds in the first two hours.

Take the R31 south for 6 miles, then turn west on the R385 for 30 miles to **Postmasburg** (Tourist Information, Springbok Street, tel: 053-313 0343). Founded in 1892 as a trading center, Postmasburg discovered wealth in a meerkat burrow in 1918. The huge kimberlite pipe turned into a Big Hole (surface area of nearly 1 mile and depth of about 148 feet) that was worked until 1935. It is now filled with water and stocked with fish. You can still visit the West End Diamond Mine and ancient mine workings in the Gatkoppies (by appointment only). Around AD 700, the Khoikhoi were mining a glittering black iron oxide called specularite here, which they used for personal adornment.

Head north to **Olifantshoek** (Tourist Information, Lanham Street, tel: 053-331 0002/311 0103) on the R385 (33 miles) or via the N14 and the R386 (44 miles, but a better road). The little town is named after the elephant whose tusks paid for the ground on which it stands. This is the gateway to the **Roaring Sands**. When disturbed air rushes through these 328-foot-high sand dunes, it produces curiously human moans. Below the surface is pure, sweet water.

From Olifantshoek, you can take the N14 west for 104 miles to Upington (see page 136), set amid near desert, or east for 62 miles to Kuruman (see page 135), where you can stay at the marvelous **Tswalu Private Desert Reserve** (see page 260). Alternatively, return to Postmasburg and head south to **Griekwastad (Griquatown)** on the R386 (60 miles; Tourist Information, tel: 053-343 0019).

Once "capital" of Griqualand (see page 124), this small settlement under the Asbesberge (Asbestos Mountains) was a mission station, founded by the London Missionary Society. The old mission house, birthplace of David Livingstone's wife, Mary Moffat, is now the **Mary Moffat Museum** (Voortrekker Street, tel: 053-343 0180. *Open* Mon–Fri 8–4:30), where curator Hetta Hager knows all there is to know, and will happily tell. Griquatown is also famous for gemstones, including jasper and tiger's eye, a semiprecious stone so common here that the British Stone Fort on Prieska Koppie (50 miles south)

Mary Moffat, missionary and wife of David Livingstone

is built of it. For a full range, visit the interesting **Earth Treasures** (6 Moffat Street, tel: 053-343 0121. *Open* Mon–Fri 8–4).

Take the R64 back for 98 miles to return to Kimberley.

North-West Province

▶ **Mafikeng and Mmabatho** *125D3*

Baden-Powell refusing to surrender Mafeking

Tourist Information, Lichtenburg Road, Mafikeng (tel: 018-381 3155) Open: Mon–Fri 8–4:30

The African town now called Mafikeng ("Place of Stones") was known as Mafeking under the British protectorate in Victorian times. A small town much lauded as an example of British courage at its best, Mafikeng was besieged by the Boers in 1899, a few days after the outbreak of the Anglo-Boer War. The British commander, Colonel Robert Baden-Powell (who went on to found the Boy Scout movement), held out for 271 days before relief finally arrived, an event rapturously celebrated in the streets of London. The fort on Cannon Koppie has been restored, and the **Mafikeng Museum** (Old Town Hall, tel: 018-381 6102. *Open* Mon–Fri 8–4, Sat 10–12:30. *Admission free*) outlines the history of the area and all its people and arranges tours to nearby historic sites.

In 1977, Mmabatho, which was built on the outskirts of Mafikeng, became capital of the Tswana homeland of Bophuthatswana, a fragmented "state" with no fewer than 17 different parcels of land scattered through white South Africa. Mafikeng was incorporated into its former satellite in 1980. The 14,332-acre **Botsalano Game Reserve** (18 miles north of Mmabatho, tel: 018-384 3040) has a wide variety of game, with a successful white rhino-breeding program, amid acacia plains and dramatic outcrops of volcanic lavas.

▶▶ **Pilanesberg National Park** *125D4*

14 miles from Sun City (tel: 014-555 5351, fax: 014-555 5535) Open: daily Sep–Apr 5:30 AM–7 PM, May–Aug 6 AM–6:30 PM Admission: expensive

Pilanesberg, South Africa's third-largest park, sprawls over 338,540 acres around an extinct volcanic crater. The terrain is dry bushveld and Kalahari thornveld, with wooded ravines and grassy plains. Several farms were taken over in the 1970s. Operation Genesis, the largest animal translocation program in the world, then restocked the park with over 7,000 animals, including the "big five." There are also more than 300 bird species, as well as walk-in aviaries, a self-guided walking trail around Manyane Camp (which is also the information center), hides near several dams, over 125 miles of gravel roads for game viewing, and regular hot-air balloon flights over the park. Farther north, the huge **Madikwe National Park** (56 miles north of Zeerust on the R505, tel 014-565 5960, fax: 014-565 5964, www.tourismnorthwest.co.za) covers 185,325 acres along the Botswana border. Established in 1991, it is already South Africa's fourth-largest reserve, has "big five" game viewing, including large herds of elephant, and rare species such as cheetah, brown hyena, and wild dog.

RELIEF
The overembellished stories of the siege of Mafeking tapped a vein of heroic imperialism but had little to do with reality. Baden-Powell loved every minute, exaggerating the number of Boers from 5,000 in 1899, to 12,000 in 1937. Throughout the siege he made a marked distinction, in all matters, between white and black: healthy rations for the 2,000 whites were denied to the 5,000 Africans. Baden-Powell advised that "the toe of the boot" be applied to disapproving "grousers."

▶▶▶ Sun City 125D4

*About 115 miles northwest of
Johannesburg, 25 miles from Rustenburg
(tel: Sun City, 011-780 7800; The Palace,
014-557 3133)*

*Open: daily 24 hours, day permits
available at the gate*

Admission: expensive

This is a place to spend money—you
could easily lose the shirt off your back
in the 24-hour casino. To do it in style,
stay at the Palace of the Lost City, a
magnificently kitsch rich man's
fantasy that is the nearest thing in
South Africa to Las Vegas. Re-creating
Rider Haggard's turn-of-the-century novel *King Solomon's
Mines*, Sun City is like a film set; attractions include the
Valley of the Waves, an inland sea complete with wave
machine, beach, and waterslides; the "volcanic" Bridge of
Time, which erupts every hour; and a Vegas-style extrav-
aganza of showgirls in feathers. The owners, Sun
International, are trying to transform the whole complex
into a family destination with gambling, as Las Vegas has
tried to do, by incorporating a kids' club, amusement
park, petting zoo, and a host of sports, including two of
the best golf courses in Africa (with live crocodiles in the
water hazard at the 13th hole), and a lake offering water
sports from windsurfing to parasailing. It could be
ghastly, but isn't. The Palace is splendid, the other hotels
comfortable, the gardens superb, the food delectable, the
water warm, and the weather (usually) sunny. Sun
International answers critics' condemnation of this
island of wealth amid an ocean of desperate poverty by
financing local schools, clinics, and housing projects.

*Inland seas and brand
new ancient ruins are
just some of Sun City's
attractions*

BUILDING TO EXCESS

The Palace of the Lost
City complex cost R800
million ($114 million) and
took 5,000 workers 19
months to build. Experts
handcrafted the finishing
touches, including the
massive painted dome.
The mosaic in the Crystal
Court is made from 30
different semiprecious
stones, such as jasper,
malachite, and amethyst.

Gauteng

Johannesburg from the Carlton Panorama

TOURIST INFORMATION
Gauteng Tourism Centre,
The Rosebank Mall,
Rosebank 2196
(tel: 011-327 2000/340
9000, fax: 011-327 7000,
www.gauteng.net).
Open Mon–Fri 8:30–5.
Tourism Johannesburg,
Village Walk Shopping
Centre, corner of Rivonia
and Maude streets,
Sandton (tel: 011-884
4033, fax: 011-883 4035,
www.tourismjohannesburg.
co.za). *Open* Mon–Fri
10–6, Sat 9–1.
Pretoria Tourism, Old
Nederlandsche Bank
Building, Church Square
West (tel: 012-337 4337,
fax: 012-308 8891,
www.visitpretoria.co.za).
Open Mon–Fri 7:30–3:45.

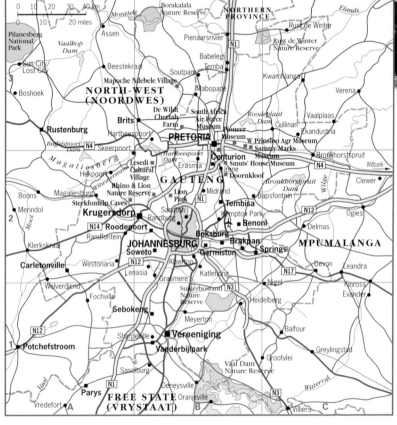

BUILT ON GOLD Gauteng means "place of gold" in Sotho, and so does Egoli, the Zulu name for Johannesburg. A theme begins to emerge—for this is a region built, quite literally, on gold. Gauteng is a small region in central South Africa, once known as the PWV (Pretoria Witwatersrand Vereeniging). Pretoria is the administrative capital of South Africa, populated almost entirely by civil servants. Vereeniging and the surrounding area, which includes the notorious township of Sharpeville (see page 43) is predominantly industrial, with very little to recommend it to visitors. Between these areas is the Witwatersrand (Ridge of White Water), one of the country's main watersheds, under which lie unimaginably large reserves of gold, carbon, uranium, green diamonds, iron pyrites (fool's gold), chromite, silver, and platinum. Above these reserves tower the skyscrapers of Johannesburg, the social and economic powerhouse of the whole African continent. And beside that is Soweto, the political heart of black South Africa and now one of the largest cities in the country. The province, geographically the smallest in South Africa, has 43 percent of South Africa's urban population; generates 36.9 percent of the country's gross domestic product; accounts for 60 percent of its fiscal revenue; contains about 30 percent of the world's known gold reserves, and accounts for a staggering 28 percent of the GDP of sub-Saharan Africa.

Johannesburg

In 1886, an Australian prospector named George Harrison found the first gold on the Witwatersrand at Langlaagte Farm, Roodepoort; Johannes Joubert was sent north to investigate. Hot on his heels came the surveyor-general, Johannes Rissik, who had the responsibility of choosing a site for the new mining village that would inevitably appear. The fledgling town of Johannesburg, now known irreverently to locals as "the Big Naartjie" (tangerine), derived its name from these two men.

Gold has always been the pulse of this boomtown. From the air, the headgear of working mines and the tell-tale yellow mounds are clearly visible. In fact, with modern techniques to help, original dumps are being remined to extract the many trace minerals left behind by the early prospectors. The city center, built over exhausted tunnels, is steadily expanding upward and outward. In little over a century, it has grown into a massive conurbation covering 200 square miles, with more than 600 parks and 260,000 trees lining its streets. There are now fewer than 25 miles between northern Johannesburg and southern Pretoria, and with several smaller settlements in between, it seems likely that Gauteng is destined to become one giant city.

Greater Johannesburg is expanding rapidly as the rich move into closely guarded northern suburbs and more and more rural families flock toward Soweto

Johannesburg is exciting, restless, and energetic, with bubbling street life and plenty of excellent restaurants, theaters, and other entertainment. To date, this is one of only a few cities in South Africa where the black Africans have moved into the center; the whites have moved out en masse to wealthy northern suburbs such as Sandton.

In addition, there is a considerable crime problem, with literally millions of serious offenses including frightening numbers of armed robberies, rapes, and car-jackings, and a murder rate per capita five times that in the United States. The good news is that in 1999, the level of violent crime leveled out while petty crime actually dropped by 26 percent. Locals are confident that the police are finally getting things under control. However, you must still be extremely careful, take local advice, and do not walk around the streets on your own, particularly at night.

▶ **Bernberg Museum of Costume**   *150B4*

Corner of Jan Smuts and Duncombe avenues, Forest Town (tel: 011-646 0716)
Open: Tue–Sat 9–5. Admission free
This Victorian house, still containing most of its original furniture and decor, makes an ideal setting for a museum of fashion. Most of the dresses are 19th century, but there are also displays showing the development of style from the hooped skirts of the 1750s to Dior's "New Look" of the 1950s.

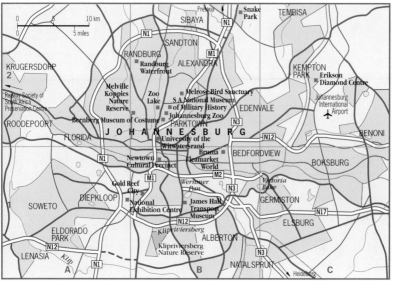

▶ Bruma Fleamarket World 149B1

Ernest Oppenheimer Drive, off Marcia and Allum roads,
near Eastgate Shopping Centre (tel: 011-622 9648)
Open: Tue–Fri 9:30–6, Sat 8:30–6, Sun 9–6
Admission free

Billed as the world's only flea-market theme park, Bruma is the single largest tourist attraction in Gauteng, with 2.5 million visitors a year. It has over 300 stalls during the week, more than 600 on weekends, and 15 restaurants. There are plenty of excellent souvenirs and around-the-clock entertainment, from South African tribal dancers to Tanzanian acrobats.

Sandton shopping mall has some of the most exclusive and expensive stores in Africa

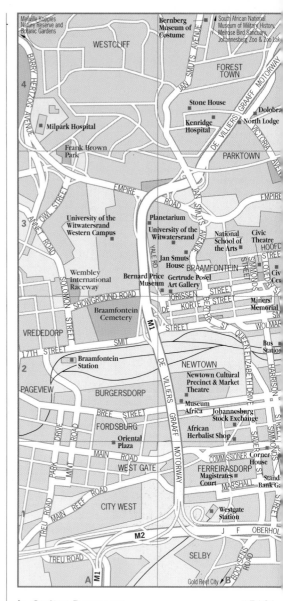

TOURING GAUTENG
For organized tours of Johannesburg and Pretoria, contact **Springbok Atlas** (tel: 011-396 1053) or Welcome Tours (tel: 011-328 8050). For a personal guide, contact **Gold Reef Guiding Services** (tel: 011-496 1400), who can offer tours in 29 different languages, locally and throughout South Africa. To tour a working gold mine, contact **Gold Mine Tours** (tel: 011-498 7100; reservations essential). For tours of Soweto, contact **Jimmy's Face to Face Tours** (tel: 011-331 6109) or **Imbizo Tours** (tel: 011-838 2667).

▶ **Carlton Panorama**   *151C1*

Commissioner Street, entrance at upper level of Carlton
Shopping Centre (tel: 011-331 1088)
Open: daily 9 AM–11:30 PM

The hideous, 663-foot-high Carlton Centre was once the heart of downtown Johannesburg, with a luxurious hotel, huge shopping mall, several movie theaters, and an array of eateries. Sadly, at present, the hotel is closed and the surrounding area is extremely rough, but up on the 50th floor, the Top of Africa Panorama still offers superb views of the city and beyond. On a clear day you can see as far as the Magaliesburg.

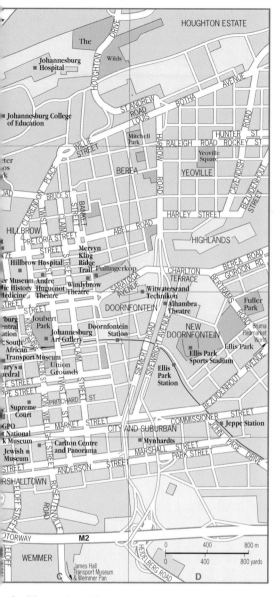

"An extended brickfield
is the first impression:
a prosperous powder-
factory is the last …"
—John Buchan on
Johannesburg, *The African
Colony* (1903)

*A mini Manhattan—
Johannesburg at night*

▶ Diamond cutting

*Mynhardts, Suite 233, 240 Commissioner Street
(tel: 011-334 8897)*
Although the diamond mines are elsewhere,
Johannesburg is South Africa's major market and polishing center. On a tour of a diamond cutting and polishing
workshop you can learn how to turn a dull pebble into a
real gem—how to pick out the quality, decide on the cut,
polish, and even set the stones. There are also, inevitably,
stores. **Diamond Supply Co**., 27 Ridge Road, Parktown (tel:
011-484 3524) and **Erikson Diamond Centre**, Monument
Road, Kempton Park (tel: 011-970 1355).

Gauteng

EARLY JOHANNESBURG
A few key historic buildings have survived the rush to build shiny modern skyscrapers. The 1907 Standard Bank (5 Simmonds Street) is part stone, part brick, steel-framed with a Renaissance exterior. There are visits to the old store and art gallery. The Corner House (corner of Commissioner and Simmonds streets), South Africa's original skyscraper (1903), is a curious blend of classical and art nouveau styles. Other notable buildings include the General Post Office; City Hall (corner of Market, Rissik, President, and Harrison streets), which is now the Gauteng provincial parliament; the 1930s Johannesburg Public Library (Market Square); and the 1904 Rand Club (corner of Loveday, Commissioner, and Fox streets; visits by arrangement).

The Gold Reef City dancers are a top attraction

▶▶▶ Gold Reef City   *149B1*
Off Xavier Road (off M1), 5 miles south of the city
(tel: 011-496 1600)
Open: Tue–Sun 9:30–5. Dance shows 11:30, 3
Admission: expensive

A combination of open-air museum and theme park with a bewildering but jolly mix of ersatz and real entertainments, Gold Reef City is built around a famous gold mine (No. 14 Shaft of the Crown Mines), and reconstructs the pioneering days of Johannesburg during the gold-rush era. You can watch demonstrations of pouring liquid gold into bullion, or take the elevator 720 feet down the shaft into what was once the richest gold mine in the world. Thirty thousand men toiled in unbearable conditions below the earth's surface to produce about 3 million pounds of gold during its working life. Above ground are several reconstructed Victorian streets with pubs, a hotel, restaurants, old-fashioned apothecary's shop, Chinese laundry, tailor, newspaper office, bank, brewery, and early stock exchange. There are many live demonstrations, a number of fairly tame fairground rides and a Victorian amusement park, souvenir shops, and plenty of places to eat and drink; you can also ride a miniature railroad around the edge of the park.

Can-can dancers and the Gold Reef City International Dancers perform both traditional and gumboot dances (developed because of the miners' heavy protective footwear). Additional attractions include several white-knuckle rides and a massive casino and entertainment complex.

▶ Jewish Museum   *151C1*
2 Elray Road, Raedene (tel: 011-485 1020)
Open: Mon–Thu 8:30–5, Fri 8:30–3. Admission: inexpensive

South Africa has a large Jewish population. Some Jewish settlers came to the country in the late 19th century; many arrived from Eastern Europe in the 1920s. This museum covers the history of South African Judaism from the 1920s to the present, and displays several beautiful religious artifacts.

▶▶ Johannesburg Art Gallery   *151C2*
Joubert Park (tel: 011-725 3130)
Open: Tue–Sun 10–5. Admission free

In 1904, Lady Phillips, wife of Randlord Sir Lionel Phillips, went to London and sold a 21½ carat diamond ring, returning home with three paintings by Wilson Steer. She spent the next five years wringing sufficient money out of wealthy friends such as Max Michaelis, Otto Beit, Abe Bailey, Julius Wernher, and Frederick Eckstein to found an art gallery. Sir Edwin Lutyens (1869–1944) was commissioned to design the imposing classical gallery, opened in 1915. Further sections were added in 1940 and 1984.

The gallery has three distinct collections. The first is European, with works by masters such as El Greco, Picasso, and Rodin alongside the inevitable minor Flemish portraits. The second includes works by many of South Africa's finest artists, such as Jackson Hlungwane, J. H. Pierneef, Irma Stern, and William Kentridge. Finally, the gallery now houses the somewhat eccentric

Brenthurst Collection of African Art, which comprises curios originally taken back to Europe by 19th-century missionaries, explorers, travelers, and scientists; most exhibits are of Nguni, Sotho, or East African origin. The complex has excellent gift and coffee shops.

▶ Johannesburg Stock Exchange 150B2

Corner of Diagonal and Pritchard streets
(tel: 011-377 2200)
Open: tours of trading floor
Mon–Fri 11, Tue–Thu 4
Booking essential

This was the second stock exchange in South Africa, founded in 1887. The first was simply unable to cope with the sudden surge in business following the gold strikes. Consequently, the authorities chained off an open area between Commissioner and Market streets and the trading floor went *al fresco*. This led to the expression "between the chains," still used in common parlance for stock trading. Guided tours paint a vivid picture of gold-rush Johannesburg and the fevered trading that made and lost fortunes. Today, trading takes place in slightly more restrained fashion in the modern Stock Exchange on Diagonal Street, but dealing is to move to a new building in Maude Street, Sandton, at the end of 2001.

The Stock Exchange (above) and the Art Gallery (below)—key facets of city life

GREEN SPACES

Johannesburg is one of the greenest cities in the world, with huge, shady trees lining every suburban street. It also has some magnificent parks.
Among the finest are the **Johannesburg Botanical Garden**, Thomas Bowler Street, Roosevelt Park (tel: 011-782 0517), which has the largest rose garden in the world; and the **National Botanical Gardens**, Malcolm Street, Poortview, Roodepoort (tel: 011-958 1750). *Open* daily 8–5:50. Guided tours leave from the Interpretation Centre Mon–Sat 2:30, 3:30, Sun 3.

Museum Africa is a magnificent celebration of Johannesburg, past and present

▶ Johannesburg Zoo and Zoo Lake   *149B2*

Hermann Eckstein Park, Jan Smuts Avenue, Parktown (tel: 011-646 2000)
Open: daily 8:30–5:30. Admission: moderate

It may be nothing like seeing animals in the wild, but Johannesburg Zoo is a good second-best. Surrounded by impeccable gardens, the 136-acre zoo is home to around 300 animal species, most of which are in danger of extinction. It is also a center for conservation, scientific research, and education. Across the street, Zoo Lake is popular for picnics. Once a month, it hosts an open-air art exhibition, "Art in the Park."

Minor museums

The **Standard Bank Gallery** (5 Simmonds Street, tel: 011-636 4231) has excellent, constantly changing exhibitions featuring the best of modern South African art and photography. The **James Hall Transport Museum** (Rosettenville Road, La Rochelle, tel: 011-435 9718. *Open* Tue–Sun 9–5. *Admission: inexpensive*) displays the history of land transportation in South Africa. The **African Herbalist Shop** (14 Diagonal Street, Newtown, tel: 011-420 2862. *Open* Mon–Sat 7:30–5) is a working shop, dispensing traditional African remedies, but it has become such a tourist curiosity that it also runs guided tours.

▶▶ Museum Africa   *150B2*

121 Breë Street (tel: 011-833 5624)
Open: Tue–Sun 9–5
Admission: moderate

Several older, smaller museums scattered across the city have been closed, and their collections gathered under one roof to create one of the finest and most imaginative museums in South Africa. Museum Africa is housed in an old market warehouse in the recently revived Newtown Cultural Precinct. The aim is to tell the true, multicultural story of South Africa, from Big Bang to the present.

The **Museum of South African Rock Art** contains not only a magnificent collection of original San paintings, but some of the clearest explanations on record of how these powerful works were created. The **Johannesburg Transformations** section concentrates on a few key aspects of the city's history, from local prehistoric settlements onward. There is a special exhibition on gold, but more powerful are three interlinked sections describing township music, the growth of the townships and squatter camps, and South African politics over the last 40 to 50 years.

Beyond these are two traditional displays. The original **Africana Museum** collection, founded in 1934, includes a huge array of paintings, documents, photographs, prints, traditional African art, and costumes, from the Cape to the Zambezi. The **Bensusan Museum of Photography** contains hundreds of cameras spanning the period from the magic lantern to digital imaging and CD-

ROM. Photographs include everything from pioneering classics by Englishman William Henry Fox Talbot to a powerful local exhibition of South African life. Finally, the **Geological Museum** has fabulous crystals and rocks in a rainbow of vivid colors. There are also constantly changing special exhibitions, workshops, and activities from music and dance to storytelling.

▶ Newtown Cultural Precinct   *150B2*
Breede Street (tel: 011-838 4563)

The old fruit and spice market buildings of Newtown have been given a new lease on life as the city's bohemian quarter, centered on the Museum Africa complex and the **Market Theatre**, itself once a market hall, built in 1911 and ennobled with an impressive beaux-arts facade. The theater became renowned internationally for its courageous stand during the apartheid era; many of its powerful dramas, both black and white, were openly critical of the government. The surrounding precinct has a total of four theaters, an art gallery, fascinating stores, places to eat, drink, and listen to music, and a buzzing Saturday market.

The **South African Breweries' Centenary Centre** (corner of President and Bezuidenhout streets, tel: 011-836 4900. *Open* Tue–Sat 10–6. *Admission: moderate*) explores the history of brewing from ancient Egypt to modern South Africa via Europe and Mesopotamia. There is a reconstructed 1960s shebeen (unlicensed bar), an exhibit on the science of brewing, and several opportunities to sample the product. Nearby is a **Workers Museum** with a photographic record of industrial South Africa. On Saturdays, the square has an excellent market.

REBIRTH
Newtown was once a multicultural district of slum housing, known as Farm Bloemfontein (1853), Brookfields (1887), and Burgersdorp (1896). In 1904, the inhabitants were evacuated and the area burned, supposedly in response to an outbreak of plague. Afterward, it was renamed Newtown. During the 1970s, in line with the Group Areas Act, much of neighboring Fordsburg was demolished, and its Indian community moved out to Lenasia township. Now it has been reclaimed as a thriving multicultural center for the arts and entertainment.

155

The Market Theatre, once a market hall

*Sir Herbert Baker's
Stone House*

▶ Parktown   *150B3*

*For guided walks, contact the Parktown and Westcliff Heritage
Trust (tel: 011-482 3349)*
Open: Mon–Fri 9–1. Admission: expensive
Johannesburg took three years to become the largest city
in southern Africa; originally a typical miners' town, it
was rife with crime, alcohol, and prostitution. Parktown
was one of the first "respectable" leafy suburbs created by
the mining magnates as a suitable environment for their
wives and daughters. There are still some fine mansions,
including Sir Herbert Baker's home, Stone House, and
Lord Alfred Milner's "kindergarten," Moot Cottage.

▶ Sibaya Traditional Zulu Boma   *149B2*

*Main Road, Kyalami (northwest of Sandton), P.O. Box 545,
Rivonia 2128 (tel: 011-468 1196)*
*Performances by arrangement. Admission: expensive (inclusive
of food, drink and entertainment)*
The name "sibaya" is a Zulu word for a *boma*, the sheltered area used to keep cattle safe and for all meetings and
celebrations. This entertaining venue, set in a traditionally built Zulu village, gives visitors a chance to explore
Zulu culture through dance, fighting techniques, beadwork and other crafts, storytelling, food, and drink.

▶ South African National Museum of   *149B2*
Military History

*Hermann Eckstein Park, Erlswold Way, Saxonwold
(tel: 011-646 5513). Open: daily 9–4:30. Admission: moderate*
This is one of Johannesburg's most popular museums. It
has fighter aircraft from both world wars, tanks and
artillery, uniforms and medals, displays on the Namibian
and Angolan wars, and a German one-man submarine.

▶ South African Transport Museum   *151C2*

*Old Concourse, Johannesburg Station Complex,
De Villiers Street (tel: 011-773 9118)*
Open: Mon–Fri 7:30–3:45
Admission: inexpensive

BIRD'S EYE
Several companies offer
flights with a bird's-eye
view of the skyscrapers
and Soweto. Court
Helicopters (tel: 011-827
8907) operates daily from
Rand International Airport;
Gold Reef City Helicopters
(tel: 011-496 1600) fly on
weekends only. Air
Champagne (tel: 011-788
8957) operates trips by
night or day. Bill Harrops
Original Balloon Safaris
(tel: 011-705 3201/3) fly
hot-air balloons over
nearby countryside, but
not over the city itself.

This small museum houses a unique collection of model trains, as well as displays on South Africa's railroads, highways, harbors, and airlines. It also has a number of landscape paintings by the notable South African artist, J. H. Pierneef. The museum runs regular steam safaris to raise the funds that pay for its preservation program (see pages 234–235).

Train enthusiasts should also stop at the **Railway Society of South Africa Preservation Centre** (Randfontein Road, Krugersdorp, off the R28, tel: 011-888 1154. *Open* first Sun of every month), which has a number of historic locomotives and other rolling stock, all of which are in full working order.

▶ **University of the Witwatersrand**   *150B3*
museums

Founded in 1896 as a training institute for the diamond industry, "Wits" is now one of the largest and most highly regarded universities in South Africa, with numerous small museums. The **Bernard Price Museum of Palaeontology** (Jorrison Street, Braamfontein, tel: 011-716 2726; guided tours on request) is dedicated to the study of fossils. It contains a mass of tools and bones, such as those of *Australopithecus africanus* and *Homo erectus*, found at various sites in South Africa including the Sterkfontein Caves (see page 159).

The **Planetarium** (Yale Road, Milner Park, tel: 011-716 3199. Presentations: Fri 8 PM, Sat 3, 8, Sun 4, Sun 10:30 for small children. *Admission: expensive*, reservations essential) offers a wonderful way to identify the Southern Cross and explore the unfamiliar southern skies, where the crescent moon hangs upside down. Then you can head out into the bush and see the real thing as you have never seen it before. With no artificial light to dim the eyes, the sky seems to have twice the number of stars. The Planetarium bookshop sells all the maps and charts you need.

A range of exhibits at the **Adler Museum of the History of Medicine** (in the grounds of the South African Institute for Medical Research, Hospital Hill, Hillbrow, tel: 011-489 9482. *Open* Mon–Fri 9–4) includes a dental museum, a hospital optometry, a video room, a coach house, and reconstructions of a 19th-century pharmacy, surgery, and African herbalist's shop.

The **Zoology Museum** (tel: 011-716 2307) has butterflies, moths, and shells; the **Adler Museum of the History of Music** (tel: 011-716 1111) has valuable and historical musical instruments and scores; the **Gertrude Posel Art Gallery** (Senate House, Jorissen Street, tel: 011-716 3632. *Open* Mon–Sat 10–4. *Admission free*) presents changing exhibitions of African art.

RANDBERG WATERFRONT
Tel: 011-789 5052.
Illuminated fountains
nightly at 7:30 and 8:30.
Built as a safe haven for middle-class Johannesburg and rapidly becoming one of the city's top tourist attractions, this development has a large number of stores, a flea market with over 300 stalls, 30 eateries from pizzerias to steakhouses, cinemas, a bowling alley and arcade games, all built around a small lake with a 1,000-nozzle, 55-foot-high musical fountain.

157

Randberg Waterfront, family fun and shopping

TOWNSHIP MUSIC

Marabi began in the shebeens, or illegal drinking dens, of the 1920s. Fast and furious, it was played on any available instrument, from an organ to a can of stones, with anyone and everyone joining in the jam sessions. Never written or recorded, it ended when the slums were bulldozed in the late 1930s. In multicultural Sophiatown, however, it fathered other forms of music, including township jazz (heavily influenced by American big bands and swing), *kwela*, and *mbaqanga* (the earliest protest songs). From the mid-1970s, anticonscription white musicians also began to use music as a form of protest.

BUILDING A CITY

From 1923, the Native Urban Areas Act tried to stop any more black people migrating to the cities and set up segregated "locations," away from the city centers. In the 1930s, the Johannesburg council bought Klipspruit farm and built the first black township for 80,000 people, inconveniently distant from facilities such as stores and transportation. Since then, Soweto (which stands for South Western Townships) has grown to incorporate 50 districts, with a population of around 4.5 million. It is now the largest city in sub-Saharan Africa.

Johannesburg environs

▶ Heidelberg 146B1

18 miles southeast of Johannesburg on the N3
Tourist Information, Library, corner of Verwoerd and
Ueckermann streets (tel: 016-976 0765)
This small Victorian town, founded in 1861 by a general dealer, Heinrich Ueckermann, stands on part of Langlaagte Farm, site of the first Rand gold strike. It has a number of attractive old houses and several small museums, including the **Diepkloof Farm Museum** (AECI, Modderfontein, tel: 011-904 3964), a restored 1850s farmhouse in the **Suikersbosrand Nature Reserve**, and the **Transport Museum** (tel: 016-341 6303), with a fine collection of veteran bicycles, motorcycles, and cars.

Nature reserves 146B2 and 149B2

Several game and nature reserves lie in the Gauteng area surrounding Johannesburg, of which the most interesting is the 495-acre **Johannesburg Lion Park** (18 miles north of Johannesburg, tel: 011-460 1814. *Open* daily 8–4:30. *Admission: expensive*); where 60 lions are fed daily between 9 and 9:30 AM. There are also gemsbok, impala, wildebeest, and ostrich, an Ndebele village, and a small-animals area for children. The **Snake Park** (Halfway House, tel: 011-805 3116. *Open* daily 9–4; demonstrations Mon–Fri 11, 3; Sat 11, 2, 3, 4; Sun 2:30, 3:30, 4:30. *Admission: expensive*) has a collection of mainly African snakes. The **Rhino and Lion Nature Reserve** (Kromdraai Conservancy Area, tel: 011-957 0109. *Open* daily 8–5. Reservations essential for game drives and accommodations) also has a variety of big and small game including lion, cheetah, rhino, and wild dog, at close quarters.

▶▶▶ Soweto 146B2

About 12 miles southwest of Johannesburg (tel: 011-331 2041,
fax: 011-331 2015, www.sowetosa.co.za)
For tours, contact Jimmy's Face to Face Tours (tel: 011-331
6109) or Imbizo Tours, P.O. Box 25031, Fereirasdorp 2048
(tel: 011-838 2667). It is advisable to visit only with a tour guide
Most people have an image of Soweto, based on decades of horrific news footage, as a place of ghastly deprivation dogged by unspeakable violence. Both are obviously present, but the overwhelming impression left by a tour is not of the horrors, but the enormous strides that have been made into creating a thriving city. There are areas of shanty settlement and many of the houses are simple two-room buildings with an outside toilet and standpipe, but the streets are orderly and there are basics such as electricity, mains plumbing, and trash collection. There are also shopping malls and markets, movie theaters, a bowling alley and golf course, schools, a university, and the biggest (if not most sophisticated) hospital in the world. There are even grand mansions and Mercedes alongside cardboard shanties. Sowetans are proud of their city, and actively welcome tourists to visit their markets, shebeens (now legal), and historic sights.

Soweto was at the forefront of the revolution. Among other sights, the usual tour takes in such landmarks as **Freedom Square**, used for many mass rallies; the poignant **Hector Peterson Memorial**, dedicated to the first child to die in the uprisings; the **Regina Mundi church**, home of the unofficial black parliament; and the **Mandela Museum** (tel: 011-982 5552), the simple home shared by Nelson and Winnie before his arrest. Winnie Mandela's new mansion is a stark contrast.

► **Sterkfontein Caves**   *146A2*
Take the R563, Hekpoort Kromdraai Road, Krugersdorp North (tel: 011-956 6342). Open: Tue–Sun 9–4; guided tours on the half-hour. Admission: inexpensive
These caves are southern Africa's treasure trove of fossils, and one of the world's most important prehistoric sites. An Italian gold prospector discovered them in 1896 on Sterkfontein Farm, near Krugersdorp. In 1936, Dr. Robert Broom discovered the first known adult cranium of the 2.5-million-year-old ape-man, *Australopithecus africanus* (a relative of the Taung baby, an infant skull found 12 years earlier). Known to locals as "Mrs. Ples", she has become a crucial pointer to man's origins, and one of many "missing links" between ape and man.

The caves contain six cathedral-like chambers, a deep underground lake (said by locals to have magic powers that cure all ailments, blindness in particular), an audio-visual display, and the **Robert Broom Museum** of fossils. Nearby, the 2.2 billion-year-old **Wonder Caves** (tel: 011-957 0106. *Open* Mon–Fri 9–4, Sat–Sun 9–5. *Admission: expensive*) have magnificent limestone formations.

Soweto is now a thriving city, and one that welcomes visitors

Gold has been admired for its beauty since about 9000 BC, but its use as currency is more recent. Even when 16th-century Spaniards were plundering Aztec hoards, gold coins were rare. In 1821, when gold became the yardstick for all currencies in the British Empire, nations had to build up bullion reserves.

For hundreds of years, people had known that there was gold in southern Africa—Arab traders were dealing with the inland tribes even in the 7th century. In 1853, prospectors found the first significant reserves in South Africa at Pilgrim's Rest, Mpumalanga (see page 183). It proved to be a thin seam, but it did generate a minor gold rush. By the time George Harrison struck it lucky in 1886 and discovered the Main Reef on the Witwatersrand, there were a lot of people to hand with a great deal of optimism, ready to start digging. Farms along the line of the reef were declared public property, ready for licensed claims, and a new city (Johannesburg) was laid out nearby. The God-fearing Boers, who had trekked north to get away from the crowds, were bemused by the onslaught of the rough-and-ready miners and the wave of sin. The British, led by Cecil Rhodes, started eyeing the area for a takeover—which they eventually achieved in 1902 at the end of the Anglo-Boer War.

"I tell you today that every ounce of gold taken from the bowels of our soil will yet have to be weighed up with rivers of tears ..."
—Paul Kruger, ZAR president (quoted in *The Randlords*, by Geoffrey Wheatcroft)

The Transvaal Gold Rush lasted for 30 years until the discovery of far richer seams on the Witwatersrand in 1886

Pockets of wealth As with the diamond fields, the real wealth soon ended up in the hands of a privileged few, such as Cecil Rhodes and Barney Barnato, J. B. Robinson, Hermann Eckstein, and Lionel Phillips. But the prospect of riches attracted countless others, including black workers, who still travel literally thousands of miles from home to work underground. South Africa's mines employ 466,400 men from ten southern African countries at any given time (258,800 of them in the gold mines). They come from a multitude of tribes, so a common "pidgin," *Fanakalo*, was developed for communication. It is still used, but is no longer considered politically correct.

Lower yields Today, the mines stretch in a 310-mile arc from Evander in Mpumalanga, through the Witwatersrand and Johannesburg to Klerksdorp, and south to Welkom in the Free State. Johannesburg is still the focus of the industry, but the Free State goldfields currently produce more than one third of the country's output.

In 1998 (the last year for which there were full statistics), South Africa's mines accounted for 6.6 percent of the GDP and 34.1 percent of export earnings. Of this,

about a third came from gold. Yet things haven't all been rosy. In 1985, the country produced 661 tons of gold (43 percent of global production) and was the world's cheapest producer; by 1998, production was down to 457 tons (18 percent of the global total) and costs were soaring. Only favorable exchange rates and a reorganization of the industry, which led to the closure of many marginal mines and the loss of around 200,000 jobs, helped shore up profits. There are numerous reasons for the fall. One is economics. After years of blatant exploitation, workers have demanded—and got—better wages, housing, conditions, and safety. It is also technical. South Africa has the deepest mines in the world, with tunnels descending 3,500 feet, making costs high. The sale of massive gold reserves by various Western governments has depressed international prices. Nevertheless, South Africa still owns 39 percent of the world's known gold deposits (30 percent of them in Gauteng). It will be a long time before the country need look for an alternative source of income.

PURE GOLD

Gold is pure, malleable, does not tarnish or corrode, is almost indestructible, and can be finely molded and remolded without alteration. It is heavy, dense, and an excellent conductor of heat and electricity. The simplest version of placer mining is panning, which uses a large sieve to collect easily separated deposits from river gravel; sluicing, hydraulic mining, and dredging are similar processes on a larger scale. In underground lode mining of quartz seams, an average 100,000 ounces of ore is required to produce 1 ounce of gold. Gold is also recovered as a by-product of copper.

161

Liquid gold being poured into an ingot at Gold Reef City

Pretoria

Born in a leisurely fashion in 1855 as a farming settlement on the Apies (Little Monkeys) River, Pretoria was roughly in the center of the newly colonized Transvaal region, so was chosen as the capital of the South African Republic. The president, Marthinus Pretorius, named it after his father, Andries Pretorius, leader of the Boer forces at the Battle of Blood River and a great Afrikaner hero. At the Union in 1910, the city became the administrative capital of the republic, and is likely to become the single capital of South Africa should the legislature, administration, and judiciary ever be merged into one city.

The city takes its role seriously, with many fine statues, 35 museums, and four universities, including Pretoria University (the largest in the country), and the University of South Africa (UNISA), the world's largest correspondence university.

Jacaranda in bloom carpets the city streets in purple

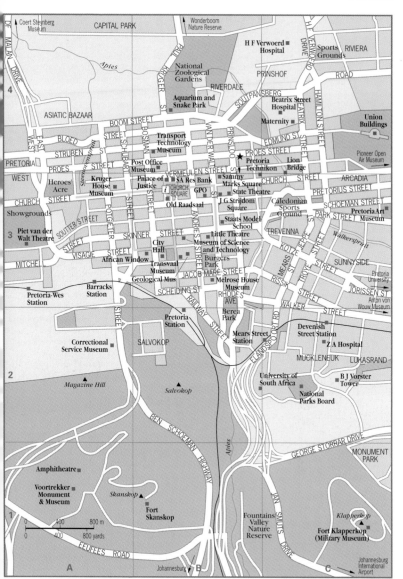

Almost totally white-collar, Pretoria was, until very recently, the only major city in South Africa where the majority of the population (estimated at 2 million) was white. Because of this fact it escaped most of the violence during the years of unrest, and is at present one of the few major cities without a significant crime problem. As a city, it is totally unlike its neighbor Johannesburg, and is mostly quiet, dignified, and conservative. It could be dull, but as befits anywhere with a large diplomatic contingent, it has some of the best nightlife around, from theaters to clubs and restaurants. Until Johannesburg begins to deal with its problems, you may find this a far more pleasant place to stay.

THE JACARANDA CITY

The first two jacarandas were planted in Pretoria in 1888. Today, some 80,000 mature trees line the streets of the city, providing much-needed shade and greenery. Every October, they burst into flower, coating the city in purple blossom. Pretoria celebrates with a jacaranda festival.

Gauteng

164

PRETORIA'S FORTS

In 1896, following the abortive Jameson Raid (see page 37), the Transvaal government built four forts to defend Pretoria. Beautifully constructed of stone with meticulously executed brickwork, they were guarded by stout armor-plated doors, fitted with bomb-resistant casements, and armed with heavy artillery. Revolving artillery pieces could be mounted on the ramparts when required, but they were never needed, and the forts were used only to accommodate Lord Roberts' troops after the British occupation in 1900. Fort Klapperkop and Fort Skanskop are still intact (both are off Nelson Mandela Road, just south of the city); Forts Wonderboom and Daspoort are in ruins.

President Kruger as a lion, in the Coert Steynberg Museum

►► African Window

163B3

Visagie Street, between Bosman and Schubart streets
(tel: 012-324 6082)
Open: daily 9–4. Admission: inexpensive

With some 4 million potential exhibits to choose from, and a fine custom-built home to put them in, this showcase of South African culture should be spectacular. However, the money ran out before the exhibits were complete and while the few galleries that are open use an interesting thematic approach, such as a display of hats, from the headdress of a traditional healer to a Boer bonnet, the overall impression is of underused space. There are some interesting temporary exhibitions and events.

Art museums

The **Pretoria Art Museum►** (corner of Schoeman and Wessel streets, Arcadia Park, tel: 012-344 1807. *Open* Tue–Sat 10–5, Sun 10–6, Wed 10–8. *Admission: inexpensive*) has works by a number of Dutch and Flemish painters, including Frans Hals and Van Dyck, as well as one of the most important collections of South African artists, such as Irma Stern, and local residents Anton van Wouw and J. H. Pierneef. Several museums occupy the artists' former homes and studios. **Coert Steynberg Museum►** (465 Berg Avenue, Pretoria North, tel: 012-546 0404. *Open* Tue–Fri 10–1, Sun 11–5. *Admission: inexpensive*); **Anton von Wouw Museum** (299 Clark Street, Brooklyn, tel: 012-467 422. *Open* Tue–Fri 10–4, Sat 10–noon. *Admission free*).

►► Church Square see Walk, page 168

► Kruger House Museum

163A3

Church Street West (tel: 012-326 9172)
Open: Mon–Sat 8:30–4, Sun 11–4
Admission: inexpensive

Paul Kruger, president of the Transvaal (1883–1899), is to the Boers what George Washington is to Americans. He was a stubborn but deeply pious man who really believed that the Voortrekkers were the elect of God and had been led out of bondage to the Transvaal. He lived in this simple home, with its tin roof and broad veranda, from 1883 until 1900, and would sit on the doorstep and chat to passersby. When Pretoria surrendered to the British in 1900, he went into exile and died in Switzerland, in 1904. His home is now a shrine to one of the country's most remarkable figures. The carved lions beside the entrance were given to Kruger by Barney Barnato. Inside you can see the state coach, presidential train, the knife he used to cut off his thumb following a gunshot wound, and many gifts and tributes. He worshiped and preached in the Dutch Reformed church opposite the house.

► Melrose House

163B3

275 Jacob Mare Street, entrance in Scheiding Street
(tel: 012-322 2805)
Open: Tue–Sun 10–5. Admission: moderate

George Heys made a fortune out of operating stage-coaches and other vehicles in the Transvaal and, like all good capitalists, aspired to the life of a gentleman. The result was Melrose House, built in 1886, a delicate confection of gables and turrets, curlicues, wrought iron, marshmallow-pink walls, and white stucco, set amid perfectly manicured gardens. Heys' new home lacked nothing, and many of its original furnishings are still *in situ*, including a fine collection of English-influenced 19th-century furniture.

In 1902, the house was requisitioned by the British and occupied by Lord Roberts, and later by Lord Kitchener. The Treaty of Vereeniging, which ended the Anglo-Boer War, was signed on the dining-room table on May 31, 1902.

Minor museums

The **Correctional Service Museum** (Central Prison, Potgieter Street, tel: 012-314 1766. *Open* Tue–Fri 9–3. *Admission free*) describes the development of South Africa's penal system with fascinating displays of homemade weapons, forged keys, and homemade tattoo machines.

The **Transport Technology Museum** (Forum Building, Bosman and Streuben streets, tel: 012-290 2016. *Open* Mon–Fri 8–4. *Admission free*) has exhibitions on meteorology and Antarctic expeditions.

The **South African Air Force Museum** (Swartkops Air Force Base, Centurion, off the M1, tel: 012-351 2153. *Open* Mon–Fri 9–3:30, Sat–Sun 10–4. *Admission free*) has exhibits on aircraft and missiles, uniforms, medals, and paintings. Flights in historic aircraft are available.

The Kruger House Museum is furnished much as it was when the president lived here

165

*Sir Herbert Baker's
Union Buildings are
among the greatest high-
lights of British imperial
architecture*

SIR HERBERT BAKER
Born in Kent, England,
Sir Herbert Baker
(1862–1946) was one of
the most influential of the
colonial architects,
scattering buildings from
suburban England and
small neo-Gothic churches
across the world. He flourished when faced with the
glory of the Empire, and
undoubtedly his two greatest works are the Union
Buildings, Pretoria, and
the Rashtrapati Bhavan
(Secretariat Buildings) in
New Delhi (over which he
had a feud with the other
great colonial architect of
the period, Sir Edwin
Lutyens). Other
particularly fine buildings
by Herbert Baker include
Rhodes' house in Cape
Town, and South Africa
House in London.

▶▶ National Zoological Garden 163B4
*Corner of Boom and Paul Kruger streets (tel: 012-328 3265,
fax: 012-323 4540, e-mail: zoologic@cis.co.za)*
*Open: daily 8–5:30 (6 in summer). Seals are fed at 11 and 3,
vultures on Wed and Sun, 2 PM. Night tours (Wed, Fri,
Sat 6 PM); advance booking essential. Admission: moderate*
Pretoria Zoo is wonderful. It has over 3,500 animals of 118
species, both indigenous and foreign, some of which, like
the pygmy hippo, are extremely rare; more than 190 bird
species; an aquarium with 300 species of freshwater and
saltwater fish; and a reptile park. The pens are semi-
natural, the surrounding gardens green and shady, and a
cable car gives a bird's-eye view.

▶ Transvaal Museum 163B3
Paul Kruger Street (tel: 012-322 7632)
Open: Mon–Sat 9–5, Sun 11–5. Admission: inexpensive
Founded in 1893, this museum is dedicated to natural
history and ethnography. The Austin Roberts Bird Hall
contains the most comprehensive collection of birds south
of the equator—each of them stuffed and in glass cases,
with a recording of their song (there is a small Austin
Roberts bird sanctuary, with the live version, in the
suburbs of Pretoria). Roberts compiled the standard
work, *Birds of South Africa*. The museum also has a large
collection of mammals, reptiles, and shells, and a skeleton
of the extinct dodo, while the **Geological Survey Museum**
(Paul Kruger Street, tel: 012-322 7632. *Open Mon–Sat 9–5,
Sun 11–5. Admission: inexpensive*) covers dinosaurs, fossils,
and the geology and mineralogy of the world (with
special emphasis on South Africa) and has fascinating
displays of precious and semiprecious stones.

▶▶ Union Buildings 163C4
Eastern end of Church Street (tel: 012-325 2000)
Open: office hours. No tours; visit the exterior and gardens only
In 1910, following the Act of Union, Sir Herbert Baker (see
panel) was commissioned by Jan Smuts to build a fitting
administration office. Never one to stint on imperial

grandeur, he created a superb sandstone eagle of a building, swooping with outstretched wings over the city.

The site, Meintjieskop, once belonged to President Pretorius and reminded Baker of the acropolises of Greece. Two great office buildings with domed towers, representing the British and Afrikaner peoples, are linked in reconciliation by the curved colonnade of the amphitheater. Columned loggias were intended to lure ministers out to "lift up their eyes to the high veld." No room was made for South Africa's black population, save a planned "small partly open Council Place for Native Indabas (meetings), where, without coming into the Building, Natives may feel the majesty of Government." It was never built.

Since 1913, this has been the headquarters of the South African government and the president's office. In 1994 Nelson Mandela was sworn in here as the country's first black president.

► Voortrekker Monument and Museum   163A1

Monument Hill, 4 miles from the center of town
(tel: 012-326 6770) Open: daily 9–4:45. Admission: inexpensive
Completed in 1949, this 130-foot-high granite block is intended to be uniquely African, symbolizing the indomitable spirit of the Voortrekkers, and harmonizing with the vastness, solitude, and mystery of the African landscape. Designed by Gerhard Moerdyk and apparently inspired by Great Zimbabwe, it looks more like a nuclear power plant. Outside, a symbolic *laager* (ring of wagons) protects the monument, while *assegais* (spears) at the gate represent the power of Zulu King Dingane. A statue of the mother and child represents the spread of civilization, surrounded by the figures of Piet Retief, Andries Pretorius, Hendrik Potgieter, and an Unknown Voortrekker. This is hallowed ground for the Afrikaners, and the marble relief frieze of Voortrekker history surrounding the lower hall is poignant—if one can ignore the many references to "barbaric" blacks and the "shining light" of Afrikaner civilization. At noon on December 16—the Day of the Covenant (see panel)—a shaft of sunlight falls on the central inscription "Ons vir jou, Suid Afrika" ("We for thee, South Africa").

The Voortrekker Museum has maps of the trek, a tapestry version of the frieze, Voortrekker weapons, clothing, and other memorabilia.

THE COVENANT
On December 9, 1838, following the massacre of Piet Retief and his companions (see page 33), a group of Voortrekkers led by Andries Pretorius took a solemn vow at Danskraal: that if God would deliver their enemies and allow them victory and vengeance, they would mark the anniversary as a holiday of thanksgiving every year forever more. On December 16, they fought the Battle of Blood River (see page 204), and won without a single fatality; the date remains a holiday in the new South Africa, a memorial perhaps to the 4,000 Zulus who lost their lives.

167

Below: a laager *of bas relief wagons*
Bottom: tapestry depiction of a Voortrekker camp in the Voortrekker Museum

Walk

Central Pretoria

This gentle walk covers many of the finest buildings in the city center. Start from Sammy Marks Square. Allow three hours. This route is best done on foot in daylight hours during the week. On weekends go by car, except for the Church Street pedestrian section. *See map on page 163.*

Take the first right onto Church Street, between **Sammy Marks Square**, named after the Randlord (see page 171), and **J. G. Strijdom Square**, dominated by a vast memorial to the former prime minister by sculptors Coert Steynberg and Danie de Jager. To one side is the **State Theatre** (tel: 012-

Melrose House, one of Pretoria's few surviving Victorian mansions

322 1665), one of the finest theaters in South Africa, with five auditoriums. The new liberal climate has fostered a broad range of quality entertainment here, including plays by Athol Fuyard, concerts from black jazz musician Hugh Masakela, and visiting overseas artists. **Church Street** runs right across Pretoria from east to west, a distance of 16 miles, and is one of the longest streets in the world. This city center section is now a busy pedestrianized mall, lined with fun craft stalls.

Continue west along Church Street for three blocks to **Church Square**▶▶ (for guided tours, tel: 012-463 226). In 1857, the Transvaal Republic's Vierkleur flag was hoisted here for the first time—and taken down for the last in 1902. The square housed the market and the city's first stores, with parking for ox wagons. Today, the wagons have been replaced by a central garden and Anton van Wouw's statue of Paul Kruger (paid for by Sammy Marks but set up only in 1954).

Many magnificent, early 20th-century sandstone buildings line the edge of the square. The facades, at least, have survived the developers. They include the **Tudor Buildings**, built by George Heys (who also built Melrose House); both the old and the new headquarters of the **South African Reserve Bank**; the **Old Mint**; the **Palace of Justice**, which was used as a military hospital during the Anglo-Boer War and later became the Transvaal division of the Supreme Court; and the Italian-Renaissance style **Old Raadsaal**, seat of President Kruger's republican government. The last two buildings both have lavishly decorated interiors, with cut stone, brass, stained glass, and elaborate tiles. Church Square is also now the home of the Pretoria Tourist Office.

Continue west along Church Street. Three blocks on is the **Kruger House Museum** (see page 164), and two blocks beyond that is **Heroes' Acre**, the pantheon of Afrikaner greats. Those who lie buried in this cemetery include presidents Kruger and Verwoerd, Andries Pretorius, and, movingly, "Breaker" Morant—the Australian soldier and poet who was executed by the British in 1902 for supposedly murdering a Boer prisoner and a British missionary.

Retrace your steps along Church Street for three blocks, then turn right onto Schubart Street. After three blocks, turn left onto Visagie Street to visit the **African Window** (see page 164). Continue along Visagie Street and you will see the **City Hall** on your right, with a frieze by Coert Steynberg and statues of Andries and Marthinus Pretorius. Turn left onto Paul Kruger Street, then right after one block for the hands-on **Museum of Science and Technology** (Didacta Building, Skinner Street, tel: 012-322 6404. *Open* Mon–Fri 8–4, Sun 2–5. *Admission: inexpensive*). Retrace your steps to the City Hall. On the opposite side of the road is the **Transvaal Museum** (see page 166). Straight ahead is Herbert Baker's magnificently over-done and impractical **Railway Station** (1910), designed like an Italian Renaissance palace. It is the home of the luxurious Blue Train. Opposite is the elegantly restored 19th-century colonial **Victoria Hotel**. The surrounding area is the central focus of the minibus taxis, and offers a fascinating glimpse of township life. Do not walk around this area at night.

From the station, turn right along Scheiding Street and left onto Jacob Mare Street for **Melrose House** (see page 164). Behind the museum, the road leads into **Burgers Park** (*Open* daily 8–6). Turn right to leave the park and left onto Van Der Walt Street, which leads north past the **Staats Model School**. Preserved as a typical Boer school, it is famous for being the place where Winston Churchill was imprisoned during the Anglo-Boer War. Continue down the street and back to the Tourist Office.

169

Opulent Church Square was the focus of historic Pretoria

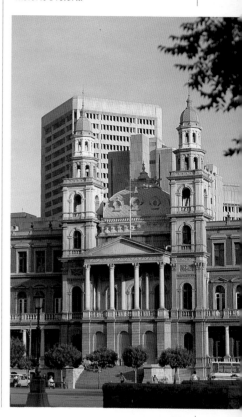

THE CULLINAN
Found in 1905 and named after Sir Thomas Cullinan, the Cullinan was the world's largest rough diamond, weighing 3,106 carats. It is thought to have been part of an even larger diamond broken up by weathering. The Transvaal government presented it to King Edward VII, who had it cut into nine major jewels. The 530-carat Great Star of Africa (the largest cut diamond in the world) is set in the Royal Sceptre; the 317-carat Lesser Star of Africa is in the Imperial State Crown. The other seven are the property of the British royal family.

Zwartkoppies Hall, the former home of Sammy Marks and his family

Pretoria environs

▶ Cullinan
146C3

Premier Diamond Tours, 99 Oak Avenue, Cullinan, 25 miles east of Pretoria (tel: 012-734 0081)
Open: Mon–Sat 8–4, by arrangement for guided surface tours; reservations essential. No children under ten
Admission: moderate

The Premier Mine is one of the richest in the world. It has yielded an average of 2 million carats a year since 1902, including some of the world's most famous diamonds—the Cullinan (see page 141, and panel), the Centenary Diamond, and the Premier Rose. Mine tours include the Big Hole (8 acres in area and 1,250 feet deep), the 2,000-foot-deep mine shaft, displays of uncut diamonds, and replicas of the most famous sparklers.

▶ De Wildt Cheetah Farm
146B3

Brits, 30 miles west of Pretoria on the R513 (tel/fax: 012-504 1921)
Open: Tue, Thu, Sat, Sun 8:30, 1:30
Reservations essential. No children under six
Admission: expensive

Wild dog, brown hyena, and cheetah, including the rare king cheetah, are bred and researched here.

▶ Hartbeespoort Dam
146B3

About 22 miles west of Pretoria

The 75-mile-long, low ridge of the Magaliesberg is an attractive area, but its history is one of conflict. Early white hunters were followed by Voortrekker pastoralists, leading to savage encounters with the Ndebele in the late 1830s. Men began hunting for gold here long before the Witwatersrand deposits were discovered—and you can still see old diggings, stamp mills, and machinery. Anglo-Boer War forts dot the hills. In the foothills, the 4,000-acre Hartbeespoort Dam has boating, angling, walking, swimming, and bird-watching. A cableway takes visitors to a

viewing site over the dam wall, built in a narrow gorge on the Crocodile River in 1923. Nearby, **Lesedi Cultural Village** (R512; tel: 012-205 1394. *Open* daily. Reservations essential) runs imaginative cultural programs depicting the traditional life of the Pedi, Sotho, Xhorsa, and Zulu peoples.

▶ **Jan Smuts' House**   *146B2*

Take the M1 south to Irene (tel: 012-667 1176)
Open: Mon–Fri 9:30–4:30; Sat–Sun 9:30–5
Admission: inexpensive

Jan Christian Smuts (1870–1950) was one of the great Afrikaner heroes and statesmen, commander-in-chief of the British forces in what was then German East Africa during World War I, and later prime minister of the Union. Doornkloof, a modest, prefabricated farmhouse of galvanized iron and wood, was his home until his death, and still contains many of the original furnishings, two of his cars, and other memorabilia.

▶ **Pioneer Museum**   *146B3*

Take exit 3 off the N4 to Witbank (tel: 012-803 6086)
Open: Mon–Fri 8:30–4, Sat–Sun 9–4. Admission: inexpensive

This delightfully imaginative museum, based around a restored Voortrekker cottage (built 1848), with several other early buildings and a carefully reconstructed farmyard, has plenty of hands-on demonstrations including candle-making, baking, and cracking a bullwhip.

▶ **Sammy Marks Museum**   *146B3*

11 miles from the city center off the R104, Old
Bronkhorstspruit Road (tel: 012-803 6158)
Open: Tue–Fri 9–4, Sat–Sun 10–4. Admission: moderate

Randlord Sammy Marks (see panel) designed his own house, Zwartkoppies Hall (completed in 1886). The somewhat eccentric and richly decorated mansion includes an imposing library, even though Marks was illiterate, and contains most of its original furnishings. There is an excellent tearoom in the rose garden.

▶ **Tswaing (Soutpan)**   *146B3*

25 miles northwest of Pretoria on the R80 (tel: 012-790 2302)
Open: daily 7:30–3. Admission: inexpensive

A 200,000-year-old meteor crater (almost 1 mile across and 1,600 feet deep), surrounding a soda lake, is the site of South Africa's first environmental museum, with walking trails and archeological sites (the area has been inhabited for 120,000 years). Nearby is the traditional **Mapoch Ndebele Village** (tel: 012-341 1320. *Open* daily 10–4. *Admission: moderate*).

▶▶ **Willem Prinsloo**
       Agricultural Museum   *146B3*

8 miles from the city center; take exit 27 off the N4 to Witbank, or follow the R104 (tel: 012-734 4171)
Open: daily 8–4. Admission: inexpensive

This is as much interactive theater as museum, with people in costume demonstrating a wide range of farm activities, from plucking geese to working in a blacksmith's shop. The museum also features an Ndebele house, a fully furnished farmhouse, and the largest collection of agricultural implements in the country.

Traditional Ndebele home in the Willem Prinsloo Museum

171

South Africa has a long tradition of white, and mainly Afrikaner, art. There have been magnificent sculptors, from Anton Anreith to Coert Steynberg, and some fine painters, from the watercolorist Thomas Baines to the expressionist Irma Stern. They have taken as their themes the landscape and people of South Africa, but their works are rooted in Europe.

Top: jazzy masks have become a favorite tourist souvenir

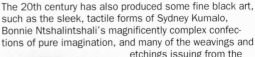

The 20th century has also produced some fine black art, such as the sleek, tactile forms of Sydney Kumalo, Bonnie Ntshalintshali's magnificently complex confections of pure imagination, and many of the weavings and etchings issuing from the Rorke's Drift school. On the whole though, most of the black art that achieved public viewing was derivative, somewhat staid, and generally unsuccessful in its attempts to emulate European media and styles.

172

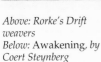

Ethnic arts Exciting things were happening elsewhere, however. Since the first San artist picked up a flint and scratched the outline of an eland on a rock, Africa has had its own superb artistic traditions. From glass-beaded Zulu bridal veils and carved tribal fighting sticks, burnished clay cooking pots to intricately patterned Sotho baskets, South Africa was filled with art. But it wasn't something to collect and hang on a wall. Art imbued every aspect of traditional culture, but because it was black and "tribal," even the most creative works were dismissed as handicrafts or curios, and their artists condemned to oblivion and penury.

Above: Rorke's Drift weavers
Below: Awakening, *by Coert Steynberg*

All that is now changing. Like the art of the Australian aborigines or Native Americans, the ethnic arts of Africa are finally trickling into view in galleries and stores across the globe. For the first time, people are being invited to take a serious look at these creations of amazing beauty, and to gain some knowledge and understanding of their creators' identity.

Township images The townships spawned a different and very vibrant art, as vivid as jazz, its feet planted in a sense of black rather than tribal identity. Some of it is born of necessity. Penniless youngsters, too poor to afford toys, patiently squat on the street corners, constructing ingenious bicycles, cars, and airplanes (complete with moving parts) from tangles of old wire.

Bored security guards while away the long night hours by weaving *imbenge* (shallow baskets) from psychedelic telephone cable wires. Others have been more ambitious, creating innovative and exciting fine art that uses exclusively urban themes, progressing with the struggle from the day-to-day street scenes of "township art" to the brutal battering of "protest art," howling with the pain of oppression. More exciting is Durban's jazzy, multi-artist Peace Wall, painted to commemorate the history of the struggle. The movement has become known as "transitional art," and there, for the moment, it stays, searching out a new identity in these days of multicultural harmony.

Repression repressed South Africa is fertile ground for creativity, for cultural sanctions cut it off from the mainstream and its talents were tempered by repression. The galleries of the world are now expecting great things. There are still two separate traditions of art-making in the country: the European, in love with the land, and the African, searching for spirituality. Both still hark back to colonialism and apartheid, and it will be a long time before their scars fade and are forgotten. Meanwhile, like everything else South African, art is in great demand across the world, and artists with real talent are likely to be successful.

Among those who have arrived are Robert Hodgins, a painter and graphic artist of figures and urban life; Jackson Hlungwani, a self-taught sculptor in wood of both religious works and symbolic animals; the Ndou brothers (Goldwin and Owen); sculptor Noria Mabasa; and painter and sculptor Malcolm Payne. Also be on the lookout for works by Willie Bester, David Koloane (co-founder of the first black art gallery in South Africa), Penny Siopis, and William Kentridge.

Olive Pickers, by Irma Stern

173

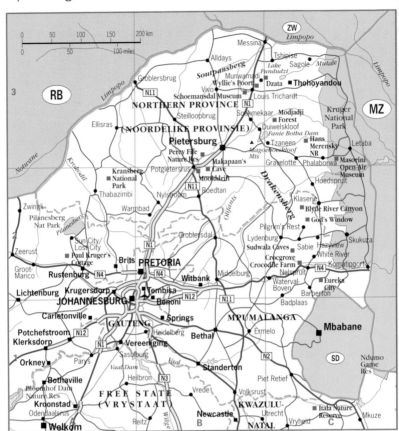

Giant baobabs dwarf the scrublands of the northern lowveld

FORESTED MOUNTAINS Much of Mpumalanga ("the place of the rising sun") lies in the northernmost section of the Drakensberg, which run from the Swaziland border and taper off as they near the Limpopo River. Considerably lower than the Natal section (see pages 208–209), the peaks nevertheless rear up to form a 7,544-foot rim around the central plateau before the land plunges down over the edge of the escarpment to the true lowveld. The Limpopo, Olifants, and Crocodile rivers, together with a host of smaller streams, flow eastward to water the rocky plains beneath.

The area is spectacularly beautiful, with several hiking trails (tel: 013-764 1058 for information). Agriculturally, it supports everything from tea to bananas, tobacco and nuts, lemons and lettuces. Above all, however, it grows trees, mainly pine and eucalyptus, and is home to the world's largest manmade forest, covering 618,000 acres. When the early underground mines were first opened, the local indigenous forests were decimated for building materials, mine props, and firewood. By 1876, a farsighted local timber merchant, Joseph Brook Shires, was replanting with fast-growing trees; about half of this timber is now used for pulp and paper, one-fifth for the mines, and the rest for telegraph poles and furniture. The eucalyptus has proved very (continued on page 176)

Mpumalanga & Northern Province

▶▶▶ REGION HIGHLIGHTS

THE BAOBAB

The baobab, *Adansonia digitata*, is one of the largest trees in the world, not because of its height, which rarely exceeds 65 feet, but because of its enormous and slightly fleshy trunk. The tree favors a hot, dry climate and can live for at least 1,000 years. It has large white, waxy flowers in October to November and furry, gourd-shaped fruit in April to May. Numerous local legends abound: one says that the baobab once offended God, was uprooted and replanted upside down; another that the flowers are inhabited by spirits and that anyone picking them will be eaten by lions.

damaging; each tree soaks up an enormous quantity of water, which drains the watershed and leads to severe drought on the plains below. Efforts are being made to change to more eco-friendly species, such as hardy Californian pine and mahogany.

The hot, arid area to the north and west feels like a different country. It used to be one. This was once the Boer Zuid Afrikanische Republiek (ZAR), known since the Union as the Transvaal. Most of it was not colonized until the mid- to late 19th century, so the hunters and farmers failed to kill off all the wildlife before it came under legal protection. The black tribes in the region are a mix of refugees from the Zulu Mfecane (such as the Ndebele and Shangaan) and people like the Venda, who are most closely related to the Zimbabwean Karanga-Rozwi group. Even the white "Vaalies" are considered a breed apart by the rest of South Africa. The descendants of the hardiest of pioneers, they are large, tough, rugby-playing, beer-drinking, hard-line conservatives, with a broad sentimental streak. The population is scattered widely, with few towns of any great size and huge farms roamed by wild horned cattle. The Northern Province survives almost entirely on farming, but has been hit severely by protracted drought at various times. In common with many other parts of the world, it sees tourism as its salvation.

Both the Northern Province and Mpumalanga have a number of thermal spring and spa resorts. The most popular are **Badplaas** in the highveld, where the hot sulfur spring emerges from the ground at a rate of 6,600 gallons per hour; **Warmbad**, in the bushveld, **Tshipise** (said to be beneficial for diabetes) and **Sagole**, in Venda territory bordering the Limpopo River. Badplaas, once known as *Emanzana* ("the healing waters"), and Warmbad, known in Tswana as *Biela bela* ("the water that boils on its own") are the most highly developed, and both have accommodations. Warmbad has a variety of

Huge, hardy, horned cattle in the Venda bush

Kruger National Park

treatment facilities. Its springs have been in use since the Iron Age—and were long popular with wild animals who, like the settlers of the 19th century, liked to wallow in the warm, mineralized mud.

However, the single real focus of the entire region is **Kruger National Park**, a vast stretch of protected land, quite literally the size of a country, stretching north along the Mozambique border. Around it cluster countless smaller reserves, infinite numbers of hotels, and tour companies offering every permutation from training as a game ranger to whitewater rafting.

Currently, most of the activity is concentrated at the southern end of the park in Mpumalanga, but everyone has a vested interest in spreading the honey farther north. The Northern Province needs its share of tourist dollars and the park needs to control the number of tourists in any one area if it is to avoid overstressing the animals and refute the accusation of being a large zoo. As Nelspruit built its airport, tiny Pietersburg was converting its old airforce base into an international airport; the road north was being dramatically improved, and even little Hoedspruit has converted the local airforce base into what it hopes will be an international airport.

Meanwhile, the authorities are currently negotiating to create a massive new transfrontier "peace" park linking up with the northern end of the Kruger and running along the line of the Limpopo River, to include territory in Mozambique, Zimbabwe, and Botswana. Since the droughts of the 1980s and early 1990s, the territory is totally unsuitable for farming, and many farms in the area have been abandoned. Villagers are being evacuated from most of the area, but a 112-mile strip around Messina will be fenced off and remain inhabited.

GEOLOGICAL SAUCER
Millions of years ago, the whole Transvaal area was completely flat. As the volcanoes settled down it became an inland sea, and a layer of mud and sand solidified and was turned into shale and quartz. A later eruption poured lava across the center, pushing it down and forcing up the sides to create a vast saucer. Since then, much of the soft shale has weathered away, leaving the hard granite outcrops exposed. The gold-bearing reefs discovered in the cliffs of Mpumalanga are the same geological strata as those found deep underground in Gauteng.

Northern Province

▶▶▶ **Kruger National Park**, see pages 186–187

▶ **Letaba District**   *174C3*

Tzaneen (from *dzana*, a Karanga word meaning "to dance") is an attractive settlement on the Letaba River (Tourist Information, 25 Danie Street, tel: 015-307 1294). Nearby, the spectacular **Magoeboeskloof Mountains** climb 2,000 feet up the escarpment, through primeval forest and banana and tea plantations. Tours are available around the **Sapekoe tea plantations** (tel: 083-627 1494. *Open* daily 10–5). The Tlou people once sacrificed to the spirits at **Debengeni Falls**, on the Ramadipa River, now a popular picnic site. Both the **Fanie Botha Dam** and **Ebenezer Dam** have nature reserves, bird-watching, water sports, and angling. In the **Hans Merensky Nature Reserve** is the **Tsonga Kraal Museum** (tel: 015-386 8727. *Open* for tours Mon–Fri 10–3, Sat 10), dedicated to the Tsonga and Shangaan peoples. **Moria** is the headquarters of the Zion Christian church, whose Easter service attracts up to 2 million pilgrims.

The **Modjadji Forest** (17 miles northeast of Duiwelskloof) has the world's largest concentration of cycads (*Encephalartar transvenosus*), the 50-million-year-old "Modjaji palm." This is also the home of the rain queens (see panel), who have protected the forest for many generations. A huge baobab in the forest has a bar inside (tel: 015-309 9039).

In Modjadji, the rain queen guards cycads as old as dinosaurs

▶ **Phalaborwa**   *174C3*

70 miles east of Tzaneen Tourist Information, next to the Kruger Park Gate (tel: 015-781 1155) Open: Mon–Fri 9–5, Sat 9–1

Phalaborwa's name derives from the Tsonga term *pala borwa*, which means "to smooth the bow," after the sandpaper-like leaves of the *Ficus capreifolia*, which grows commonly in the area. Millions of years ago, massive geological explosions forced millions of tons of magma up from the depths of the earth, bestowing the area with rich deposits of phosphate, copper, and iron ore. The **Masorini Open-Air Museum** (in the Kruger National Park) is a reconstruction of an Iron Age village; archeological findings reveal that the area was first mined in about AD 800. Tours are available around the **Phalaborwa Copper Mine** (tel: 015-780 2911), one of the world's five largest opencast mines. The **Foskor Museum** (Tambotie Street, tel: 015-789 2024. *Open* Mon–Fri 10–12:30, 2–4) charts the area's archeological, mining, and ethnographic history.

At nearby **Hoedspruit** (Tourist Information, Library, tel/fax: 015-793 1678) you can see wildlife close up in the **Moholoholo Wildlife Rehabilitation Centre** (tel: 015-795 5236. Tours daily 9:30; reservations essential), with an ever-changing array of sick and orphaned animals; the **Cheetah Project**▶ (tel: 015-793 1633. *Open* daily 8–4.

Admission: expensive), a breeding and research center for cheetah, king cheetah, and Cape wild dog; and the **Swadini Reptile Park** (tel: 015-795 5203. *Open* daily 8–5).

ROVING AUTHOR
John Buchan (1875–1940), author of *The Thirty-Nine Steps*, lived and traveled in the Tzaneen area between 1901 and 1903. He set the novel *Prester John* in the region, and later expressed a desire to return and be buried here. There is a small memorial to him on the Georges Valley Road (R538) overlooking the Ebenezer Dam.

▶ Pietersburg   *174B3*

Tourist Information, Civic Centre, corner of Landros Maré and Bodenstein streets (tel: 015-290 2010, also for all city museums). Open: Mon–Fri 8:30–4

Capital of the Northern Province, Pietersburg is a rather dull town that tries hard to be something more. There are four museums: the Victorian **Irish House Museum** (corner of Mark and Vorster streets); the **Hugh Exton Photographic Museum** (on Civic Square); the **Art Museum** (Library Gardens, Jorissen Street); and the **Bakone Malapa Ethnic Museum** (5½ miles south on Chuniespoort road (R37) ,tel: 015-295 2867), which exhibits the history and culture of the Northern Sotho people. There is also a 7,900-acre **bird sanctuary** and **game reserve** (on the R521. *Open* daily 7–6, no cars), with 280 bird species and 20 mammal species.

▶ Potgietersrus and environs   *174B2*

Tourist Information, Voortrekker Street (tel: 015-419 2244)

This attractive town was established in 1852 and eventually named after Piet Potgieter, who was shot in 1854 during the 30-day Makapansgat Siege, a retaliatory strike for the massacre of 28 Voortrekkers at **Mooiddrift** (marked by a monument). Nearly 2,000 Tlou tribesmen died of thirst and starvation in the huge **Makapaan's Caves**. Archeological digs in the caves have found plant fossils and remains of *Australopithecus africanus*. The **Arend Dieperink Museum** (Voortrekker Street, tel: 015-419 2244. *Open* Mon–Fri 8–4:30. *Admission: inexpensive*) follows local culture from prehistory to the pioneers. The **Potgietersrus Nature Reserve and Game Breeding Centre** (tel: 015-491 4314) specializes in rare African species such as *tsessebe* (antelope) and pygmy hippopotamus.

One of the shining velvet tea plantations that carpet the Magoeboeskloof Mountains

Many Venda homes still use traditional thatch

SACRIFICE
Lake Fundudzi is said to be the home of strange water sprites (each with only one eye, one arm, and one leg) and the huge, white python god who once required an annual human (female) sacrifice. The ceremony is less bloodthirsty today, but it survives in the Domba dance, part of the puberty rites of young women. Local girls line up to mimic the movements of the snake, to the echoing beat of the domba drum.

▶ **Venda**   *174B3/C3*

In the southern foothills of the **Soutpansberge** (Salt Pan Mountains—named after a powerful brine spring on their western edge), the small town of **Louis Trichardt** (Tourist Information, on the N1, at northern edge of town, tel: 015-516 0040. *Open* Mon–Fri 8–5, Sat 8–1) is named after the Voortrekker leader who opened up the area on the Mozambique coast in 1836, before dying of fever, along with most of his party. **Schoemansdal Museum** (10 miles west of the town, tel: 015-516 2082. *Open* Tue–Sun 8–4) is a vivid reconstruction of early pioneer life.

Wyllies Poort, a narrow gorge of lichen-covered cliffs, leads to an intensely hot area of wide plains and high plateaus, pitted by deep valleys. It was settled in the 18th century by the baVenda, a breakaway group of Karanga-Rozwi people from Zimbabwe, who survived the impenetrable mountains, harsh climate, and cattle-hostile tsetse fly. In 1979, it was designated the Venda tribal homeland, with its capital at **Thohoyandou**.

It is a land of ancient indigenous forests and lakes, magic and legend. Near **Lake Fundudzi** (see panel), on the Mutali River, is the sacred **Thathe Vondo Forest**, burial ground of the chiefs of the Thathe clan and forbidden to visitors. At **Dzata** is a ruined stone city similar to those of Zimbabwean culture; the heads of Venda chiefs are turned to face the city after they die. There are **museums** of Venda history at Dzata and Thohoyandou. The many magnificent forests, waterfalls, and hot springs at **Munwamadi** and **Sagole** are well worth visiting; the sandstone caves at Sagole feature San paintings and the largest known baobab tree in southern Africa.

Messina, near the Limpopo River and close to the Zimbabwean border, is South Africa's northernmost town and an important copper-mining center. Nearby are a baobab tree park with some exceptionally large specimens and a nature reserve with many species of antelope and over 200 bird species.

Mpumalanga

▶ Barberton   174C2

27 miles south of Nelspruit
Tourist Information, Market Square, Crown Street
(tel: 013-712 2121)
Open: Mon–Fri 8–1, 2–4:30, Sat 8:30–noon

On June 21, 1884, Graham, Fred, and Henry Barber found a rich gold reef in Rimer's Creek. A few days later, the mining commissioner, David Wilson, visited their camp to verify the find and, after breaking a ceremonial bottle of gin over the rocks, named the area Barberton. Over 1,400 fortune hunters rushed into the area and Barberton turned into a town of music halls, gambling dens, tin shanties, stores, and canteens. At the height of its importance in 1886, the town had a saloon for every 15 inhabitants, while the most famous of the many local prostitutes, Cockney Liz, danced on a billiard table every midnight, auctioning herself to the highest bidder.

There was plenty of gold; but when the town received news of the gold strike on the Witwatersrand, an exodus ensued that left Barberton almost uninhabited. Many of the original buildings are still intact, and you can visit several, including the 1886 **Stopforth House** (Bowness Street), the 1904 **Belhaven House**, and 1890s **Fernlea House** (both on Lee Road), while the **museum** (in the Library) covers gold-rush history and local geology. Other buildings of note in Barberton include the Kaap Gold Fields Stock Exchange (the Transvaal's first stock exchange), the 1887 Globe Tavern, and the Lewis and Marks Building (all on Pilgrim Street), the Anglo-Boer War Blockhouse, and the 1884 Masonic Temple (on opposite corners of Lee and Judge streets).

Today, the town is most noted for the Barberton daisy, first exported to Kew Gardens in London in 1884, and now a staple of many gardens across the world.

Several small gold mines are still in operation in the surrounding De Kaap valley, and it is possible to try your hand at panning for gold in the mountain streams. The **Fortuna Mine Trail** is a 1¼-mile walk through Barberton's indigenous tree park and the 1,968-foot tunnel of an old gold mine. High in the hills, 9 miles to the northeast of Barberton, is **Eureka City**, a ghost town that was originally built to house workers of the Golden Quarry Mine on the Sheba Reef, once the richest and most famous gold mine in the world.

TOURISM INFORMATION
Mpumalanga Tourism Authority, Promenade Shopping Centre, corner of Louis Trichardt and Henshall streets, P.O. Box 679, Nelspruit 1200 (tel: 013-759 5300/5438, fax: 013-759 5441, www.Mpumalanga.com).

Statue of Jock of the Bushveld

JOCK OF THE BUSHVELD
Percy FitzPatrick arrived from England at the age of 22, and became a transport rider, accompanied always by his faithful dog, Jock. In 1907, he published the story of their adventures together and the book became an instant best-seller and local classic. It has never been out of print. A statue to the canine hero stands in front of the Town Hall in Barberton.

One of Africa's most dramatic views, the Three Rondavels in the Blyde River Canyon

RIVER OF HAPPINESS
In 1844, a party of Voortrekker men went ahead to look for a route to the coast, leaving their women and children camped on the top of the escarpment. After one month, they had not returned, and the grief-stricken women assumed that they were dead. The women turned back, naming the river beside their campsite the Treur (River of Sorrow). A couple of days later, as they reached another small river, the overdue men returned. Amid the celebrations, the new river was named the Blyde (River of Happiness).

▶▶▶ **Blyde River Canyon**   174C2

About 37 miles north of Graskop on the R532
Tourism Information, Monsoon Gallery, R527, near Dublin, (tel: 013-769 6019)
Protected by a 64,248-acre nature reserve, this spectacular canyon (16 miles long and 1,150–2,624 feet deep) was gouged from the earth's crust by the humble Blyde River over 60 million years. There are superb views at regular points, the finest of them overlooking the **Three Rondavels**, three conical minimountains that look like traditional thatched huts. The canyon floor is a true wilderness, accessible only on foot on a two-day, 24-mile hike along the river. Human remains dating to the early Stone Age have been discovered here, and San cave art is abundant. Surrounding highlights include **Marieskop**, the highest peak in the district at 6,442 feet, a 656-foot waterfall, and **Bourke's Luck Potholes** (see page 184).

▶ **Echo Caves** see page 184

▶ **Hazyview**   174C2

262 miles east of Johannesburg
Tourist Information, Blue Haze Centre (tel/fax: 013-737 7414)
This is one of the most convenient places to stay in Mpumalanga, with every hilltop crowned by a delightful hotel. The town itself has little to offer, aside from lively roadside market stalls. The **Tsakani Silk Enterprise** (40 miles north, off the R40, tel: 083-379 5033. Tours: every hour Mon–Fri 9:30–2:30, Sat 9:30–noon. *Admission: expensive*) is a silk farm, with tours of the production and weaving facilities. About 5½ miles north of Hazyview on the R535, the **Shangana Cultural Village** (tel: 013-737 7000. Tours: 9, 10, 11, 3, 4 and 6 PM (with dinner). *Admission: expensive*) is an entertaining cultural village with dancing, a traditional sangoma, and mopane worms to eat.

▶▶▶**Kruger National Park** see pages 186–187

▶ **Nelspruit**   *174C2*

205 miles east of Johannesburg
Tourist Information, Shops Promenade Centre,
Louis Trichardt Street (tel: 013-755 1988, fax: 013-755 1350)
Open: Mon–Fri 8–5, Sat–Sun 9–4
Capital of Mpumalanga, Nelspruit is an attractive small
town garlanded with bougainvillea and surrounded by
citrus groves. Named after the Nel brothers, who used
the area as winter grazing for their cattle in the 1870s, the
town developed around the railroad but is now a trading
center for local farmers. Nearby are **Lowveld Botanical
Gardens** (on the R40/R37 junction, 3.7 miles from town,
tel: 013-752 4201. *Open* daily Oct–Apr, 8–4; May–Sep,
8–5:15. *Admission : inexpensive*) and **Crocgrove Crocodile
Farm** (about 15 miles west on the R539, tel: 013-752 5531).

▶▶ **Pilgrim's Rest**   *174C2*

Tourist Information, opposite Royal Hotel,
Main Street (tel: 013-768 1060). Open: daily 9–4
After Alec Patterson found the first commercial gold at
Pilgrim's Creek in 1873, Pilgrim's Rest grew up as the
adjacent miners' village. It is said to have been named by
the first group of diggers, who called themselves "The
Pilgrims" because they were always in search of spirits
(reputedly they arrived complete with a wagonload of
whisky). There were rich pickings; the largest nugget
found here weighed about 25 pounds. The miners did not
stay for long, but the little town, with its houses of
galvanized iron, has survived almost intact. A walking
map leads visitors around the cemetery, shops, and old
houses, many of which are vacation cottages. There are
several small museums, including the **Diggings Site**, the
Drezden Shop and House, and the typical wood and
corrugated-iron **House Museum**. (A single ticket, valid for
all the museums, is available from the tourist office.)

▶ **Sabie** see page 185

▶ **Sudwala Caves**   *174C2*

About 22 miles northwest of Nelspruit, off the R539
(tel: 013-733 4152). Open: daily 8:30–4:30. Tours last 1½
hours. Admission: moderate
The Sudwala Caves snake back for over 18 miles through
the dolomitic Mankelekele in the northern Drakensberg.
Tourists normally go no farther than 1,968 feet underground, yet even this section is spectacular, with giant
chambers and twisted rocks. Strange fossil algae such as
stromatolites—the earliest identifiable forms of life—date
the rocks to 2,000 million years, nearly half the age of
Earth. Below the entrance is the **P. R. Owen Dinosaur
Park**, with life-size replicas of prehistoric creatures.

▶ **White River**   *174C2*

Tourist Information, corner of Peter Graham and
Kruger Park streets (tel/fax: 013-750 1599)
This small farming town grew up as a resettlement area
for British soldiers after the Anglo-Boer War. Just outside
town, **Rottcher Wineries** (Nutcracker valley, tel: 013-751
3884) specializes in orange and ginger wines.

SHOPPING
The Kraal Kraft (9 miles
north of White River on the
White River road, tel: 013-
758 1228) is basically a
superior souvenir shop
and restaurant, but it also
has a small museum and
a living African village. The
White River Artists'
Trading Post (Christie's
Village Mall, Theo
Kleynhans Street, White
River, tel: 0131-750
1053) represents the work
of around 60 local artists
and craft workers.

REFUGE
In the 19th century,
Somquba, son of the
Swazi king Sobhuza I,
stole a number of royal
cattle, then fled. He and
his followers hid in the
Sudwala Caves while his
brother, Mswati, laid siege
outside. On several occa-
sions, Mswati tried to
smoke out the fugitives,
but the caves have a
natural ventilation system
and they survived.
Somquba was finally killed
by Mswati's troops but
survivors stayed on, led
by Sudwala (Somquba's
officer), for whom the
caves are named.

183

*The beautiful Sudwala
Caves, onetime refuge for
a royal thief*

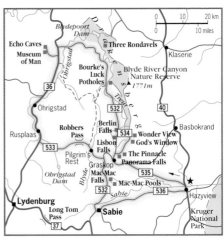

Drive

Rim of the escarpment

The scenery is stunning and the air cool and crisp, laden with the scent of a million wildflowers. Allow at least one long day. Start at Hazyview, take the R40 north, then turn left on the R535 to the pretty market town of **Graskop**.

Leave Graskop on the R532 heading north, then turn right onto the R534, a 9-mile panoramic loop with tumbling views off the escarpment and across the lowveld to the Mozambique coast. There are four main viewing points, at **Panorama Falls**, **The Pinnacle**, **God's Window▶▶**, and **Wonder View**. God's Window has the most breathtaking views, and featured as the edge of the world in the film *The Gods Must Be Crazy*. As the road rejoins the R532, paths lead to two fine waterfalls, the 300-foot **Lisbon Falls** and 492-foot **Berlin Falls**.

The R532 continues north for about 31 miles to **Bourke's Luck Potholes▶** (tel: 013-768 1215. *Open* daily 7–5. Visitors' Center 7:30–4:45. *Admission: inexpensive*), which mark one end of the **Blyde River Canyon** (see page 182). This is the confluence

of the Treur and Blyde rivers, a dramatic landscape of strange pools and cauldrons of rock, carved over the millennia by tempestuous water. The 100-foot potholes are named after a 19th-century surveyor, Thomas Bourke, who found a great deal of gold here. Unfortunately, he worked for a big mining conglomerate and never reaped any of the rewards. The Visitors' Center has a small museum, and walking trails for visitors with visual or physical disabilities. A little farther along the road you reach the first and most dramatic of several panoramas, with a magnificent view of the **Three Rondavels** (see page 182) and **Blydepoort Dam**.

The road wriggles along the rim of the canyon before looping south to join the R36. After about 6 miles, a turnoff to the right leads to **Echo Caves▶**, a huge dolomitic complex of tunnels and caverns (the largest is 328 feet long and 148 feet wide) in the Molapong valley. Tap the stalactites and they echo. The eastern end is open to the public, while the western end is home to millions of bats. A neighboring San rock shelter now houses the small **Museum of Man**, displaying archeological finds from the caves. Return to the R36 and continue south for 23 miles. A turnoff to the left, onto the R533, leads over Robbers Pass to **Pilgrim's Rest** (see page 183).

Continue along the R533 toward Graskop for 10 miles, then turn right onto the R532 in the direction of Sabie. After about 7 miles, you come to the **Mac-Mac Falls** and, 1¼ miles farther on, the **Mac-Mac Pools** on the Sabie River. Site of an alluvial gold strike in 1872, these delightful pools and falls were named by President Burgers, who looked at the 1,000-odd miners scratching for gold and was astonished to find that most of them were Scots. The water originally fell in a single stream, but was split by a dynamite blast in an attempt to reach the gold-bearing quartz on the bank.

Eight miles on, the town of **Sabie▶** (Tourist Information, Main Street, tel: 013-767 3492, fax: 013-764 2422. *Open* Mon–Fri 8–5, Sat–Sun 8–1) was founded in 1871, when someone fired a stray bullet during a shooting party,

chipped off a piece of rock, and revealed a rich gold reef. Today, wood provides the lifeblood of the town: local forests supply half of all South Africa's needs. The **Forest Museum** (Fort Street, tel: 013-764 1058. *Open* Mon–Fri 9–4; Sat 9–1. *Admission: inexpensive*) has a varied display on the timber industry, from chain saws to a model church made of matches. Little, gray-stone **St. Peter's church** was designed by Herbert Baker in 1913. The surrounding area has many stunningly beautiful waterfalls, while **Long Tom Pass**, on the R37 to Lydenburg, is one of the most spectacular mountain roads in South Africa. A disabled Long Tom field gun stands at the top as an Anglo-Boer War memorial.

Take the R536, which runs along the Sabie River valley for 28 miles, back to Hazyview.

Left: the Mac-Mac Falls
Below: Bourke's Luck Potholes

THE SABIE RIVER
There are several opinions on how this river got its name. One option derives from the Shangaan name Ulusaba ("River of Fear"). Some say it is haunted by black soldiers killed during tribal wars, whose bodies were thrown into the river without being ripped open to release the spirits. Others, more prosaically, suggest a healthy respect for the river's strong currents and large crocodile population. A more credible option comes from the Karanga word save, meaning "sand": this is the name of one of the major tributaries and of the main river farther downstream in Mozambique.

186

Termite hills feature among the scrubland of Kruger National Park

▶ ▶ ▶ **Kruger National Park** *174C2/C3*

Descend the precipitous heights of the ruggedly beautiful escarpment, and the transition from the highveld to the subtropical lowveld, with its well-watered acacia and mopane woodland, is complete. The rolling plain seldom rises above 1,150 feet as it stretches eastward toward the Mozambique coast. It is a habitat perfectly designed for antelope and lion, elephant, giraffe, and hippo. Intensely hot and dry in summer, and a natural home to diseases such as malaria and sleeping sickness, the plain is less accessible for man. Ironically, the fever allowed a small corner of wild country to survive South Africa's farmers. Today, a substantial part of this area is the home of Kruger National Park. Founded in 1903, the park is 217 miles long, up to 37 miles wide, and covers an area of 4,815,008 acres—the size of Wales or Israel. Kruger has five major rivers, 300 species of tree, 114 species of reptile, 507 species of bird, and 147 species of mammal. At any given moment, there are thought to be around 8,000 elephant, 1,500 lion, 1,900 white rhino, 220 black rhino, 15,000 buffalo, and up to 900 leopard in the park.

With fences taken down between the park and the surrounding private reserves in 1993, there are plans afoot to double the core size of the park by creating another one in Mozambique. This, eventually, would link with the new Dongola reserve (see page 177) and the parks of northern Natal, and reopen traditional elephant migration routes.

In general, the farther north you go, the drier and hotter the climate, the more desolate the vegetation, the fewer the tarred roads, and the more rudimentary the camps. Most visitors huddle in the southern half of the park, within a day's drive of Skukuza, the main camp and park administration center, which has room for 3,000 visitors on any one night. Keep away from here if you want solitude.

Practicalities From north to south, the gates are: Pafuri, Punda Maria, Phalaborwa, and Orpen in the Northern Province; Paul Kruger, Numbi, Crocodile Bridge, and Malelane in Mpumalanga. The busiest is Paul Kruger, which is the nearest entry point for Skukuza Camp (310 miles from Johannesburg; reception tel: 013-735 5611. *Open* Nov–Feb 5:30 AM–6:30 PM; Mar and Oct 5:30 AM–6 PM; Apr 6 AM–5:30 PM; May–Sep 6–6. *Admission: expensive*). Scheduled air services operate to Skukuza within the park and to nearby Nelspruit and Phalaborwa. There are about 20 camps (reservations tel: 012-343 1991, fax: 012-343 0905, e-mail: reservations@parks-sa.co.za), ranging from small remote camping areas to the main camps, which all have a store, restaurant and cafeteria, picnic facilities, toilets, gas and diesel, telephones, first aid, and accommodations. The Kruger is a malarial area, so take precautions. Do not leave your vehicle, drive off the road, or feed the animals. Speed limits are 30 mph on tarred roads, 25 mph on dirt roads. Park authorities also run three-day wilderness hikes, camping rough.

Private game parks Along the western edge of the park are several private game reserves, built up by rich, ardent conservationists to contain luxury lodges and hunting grounds. The five major blocks, from south to north, are

Sabie Sand, **Manyeleti**, **Timbavati**, **Klaserie**, and **Umbabat**, of which the 148,266-acre Sabie Sand is by far the most important for tourism and home to a dozen different luxury game lodges such as Sabi Sabi, Exeter, and Inyati (see page 262). Here you can stay in quiet luxury, with game coming to you at the waterhole or river below the terrace. Most lodges are unfenced, and you could find a buffalo or herd of kudu peering through your bedroom window; and while your ranger may not be allowed to track an elephant onto someone else's land, the animals roam freely across all boundaries. You are more likely to see the "Big Five" at the lodges than in the main park, as you will be in an open Land Rover with qualified rangers and trackers, who are able to leave the road and take you on night drives or on foot, activities usually curtailed.

Massive, graceful, and spellbinding, elephants and giraffes are highlights of any visit to Kruger

The map shows KwaZulu-Natal with locations including:

MPUMALANGA, Vaal, Grootdraai Dam, Standerton, Amersfoort, Piet Retief, SD, MZ, Ndumo Game Res, Tembe Elephant Park, Kosi Bay Nature Reserve, N2, Makatini, Flats, Lake Sibayi, Volksrust, Vrede, Charlestown, Batelesberg, Paulpietersburg, Pongola, Jozini Dam, N3, Utrecht, Louwsburg, Itala Game Reserve, Mkuze, Mkuzi Game Reserve, Sodwana Bay National Park, Warden, Newcastle, N11, Buffels, Vryheid, Nieuwe Republiek Museum, Bloedrivier, Nongoma, Phinda Resource Reserve, St Lucia Marine Reserve, FREE STATE (VRYSTAAT), Glencoe, Dundee, Nqutu, Mahlabatini, False Bay Park, Lake St Lucia, Biggarsberg, Harrismith, Biggarsberg, Wasbank, Ulundi, Babanango, Hluhluwe-Umfolozi National Park, Dumazulu, Kaap Vidal, Greater St Lucia Wetland Park, St Lucia, Sterkfontein Dam, Oliviershoek, Elandslaagte, Ladysmith, Elandskraal, Mgungundlovu, Mtubatuba, Royal Natal Nat Park, Pass, Spioenkop Dam, Melmoth, Mfolozi, Bergville, Colenso, Weenen, Nkandla Forest Reserve, Simunye, N2, Empangeni, 3282m Amphitheatre, Winterton, KWAZULU-, Mont-aux-Sources, Drakensberg Park, Armoured Train Memorial, Shakaland, Kwabulawayo, Richards Bay, NATAL, Dhlinza, Eshowe, Champagne Castle 3377m, Estcourt, Dhlinza Forest, Gingindlovu, Giant's Castle Game Res, Mooirivier, Greytown, Tugela, 3459m, Infasuti, Midmar Nat Res, Valley of a Thousand Hills, Stanger, Harold Johnson Nature Reserve, Kamber Nat Res, Howick, Paradise Valley, Salt Rock, Shaka's Rock, Sani Pass, Hilton, Mgeni, Nature Reserve, Ballito Beach, PIETERMARITZBURG, Msunduze, Tongaat, Himeville, Botha's Hill, Mount Edgecombe, Underberg, Westville, Umhlanga Rocks, Bushman's Nek, DURBAN, Drakensberg, Mbomazi, Umlazi, Amanzimtoti, Ixopo, EASTERN CAPE (OOS-KAAP), Umkomaas, Scottburgh, Matatiele, N2, Umzimkulu, Hibberdene, Oribi Gorge Nat Res, Kokstad, Mount Ayliff, Bizana, Port Shepstone, Shelly Beach, Margate, EASTERN CAPE (OOS-KAAP), Port Edward, LS, 188

Scale: 0 50 100 150 km / 0 50 100 miles

A   B   C

BITTER BEGINNINGS On Christmas Eve, 1497, the Portuguese navigator Vasco da Gama dropped anchor off a lush, green, subtropical coast. In honor of the day, he named the land Natalia. Oblivious to this fact, its inhabitants continued to raise and rustle cattle, the numerous small tribes squabbling constantly and violently. Nothing disturbed this existence until about 1809, when a formidable Mthethwa ruler, Dingiswayo, began to conquer and absorb many small groups and clans. His successor, the great Shaka, continued the task from 1815 onward. The Mfecane (see pages 30–31) marked the true birth of the Zulu nation.

At much the same time as this, the early Voortrekkers were beginning to look covetously at the fertile valleys, while the British were keeping a beady eye on any territory that the Boers might open up. In 1838, the inevitable happened. The Zulus massacred a party of Boer settlers (see page 33) and the territorial disputes dissolved into bitter bloodshed. The Boers then annexed much of the Zulu territory and broke away from the Cape Colony, creating the Republic of Natalia.

▶▶▶ **REGION HIGHLIGHTS**

KwaZulu-Natal

INDIAN DURBAN
With a huge Indian population to add to the architectural whimsy of the Raj, parts of Durban seem a continent apart. Start at the Victoria Street Market (corner of Queen and Russell streets, tel: 031-306 4021. *Open* Mon–Fri 6–6, Sat 6–2, Sun 10–2) and surrounding Grey Street trading area, a district clouded with spices and billowing gilt-embroidered silk. Other stops should include the beautiful Muslim Juma Mosque (155 Queen Street, tel: 031-306 0026), the Hindu Ganesha Temple (Mount Edgecombe, tel: 031-593 409), the Shree Ambalvanar Alayam Second River Temple (Bellair Road, tel: 031-593 409), and the Hari Krishna Temple of Understanding (Umgeni, tel: 031-312 5069).

Durban's Golden Mile, the perfect place for a suntan

The British took it all back in 1843, naming the new colony Natal. In 1877, they tried and failed to annex the Boer territory in northern Natal, and then focused on the Zulu heartland, deposing King Cetshwayo and absorbing his kingdom into the Empire. By 1902, with the final defeat of the Boers, the British had conquered the whole area.

INDIAN IMMIGRANTS Natal was immensely fertile, with sugarcane and cotton in abundance, but there was a severe shortage of labor to work the fields. Slavery had been abolished in 1834 and the Zulus showed no interest in working for the white farmers. On November 16, 1860, a paddle steamer from Madras, the SS *Truro*, docked in Durban. On board were 342 indentured Indian workers (including 75 women, and 83 children under the age of 14): it was the first of many shipments. Thousands of poverty-stricken Indians were persuaded to sign five-year contracts that forced them to work under appalling conditions. They included Hindus, Muslims, and a few Christians, and came from all areas of the Indian subcontinent, although most were from the south and west. Other wealthier, free Indians also arrived to set up as traders. In 1913, the Natal government, alarmed by the competition from these hard-working merchants, banned general Indian immigration, and in 1920 the system of indentured labor was finally ended, under pressure from Mahatma Gandhi. Today, South Africa has an Indian population of about 1.25 million, 928,000 of them living in and around Durban. The community is renowned for its success in business, while a number of Indians hold high office in government. About 70 percent are Hindu, 20 percent Muslim, and the remainder Christian. There are several fine temples and mosques across the province, fascinating Indian markets, and some of the best curries in the world. The remains of Gandhi's first *ashram* still stand at Durban's Phoenix Settlement.

ஸ்ரீ அம்பிகா சமேத அம்பலவாணர்
SRI AMBIKA   AMBALAVANAR

A MODERN KINGDOM Modern KwaZulu-Natal covers 35,321 square miles on South Africa's eastern seaboard. It is administered jointly from the old white capital Pietermaritzburg, and Ulundi, the traditional royal seat of the Zulu kings. The monarchy was restored in 1951, although it has no actual power. Nevertheless, the current king, Goodwill Zwelithini, is revered by his people and is a significant force in national affairs.

Of all nine provinces in South Africa, KwaZulu-Natal is the only one that did not submit happily and peaceably to the new constitution. However, things have now quietened down with the Inkatha Freedom Party—led by the prime minister of KwaZulu, Mangosotho Buthelezi (himself the grandson of King Dinizulu)—preferring to agitate for further autonomy from the floor of the Houses of Parliament. There is still some friction, but the violence that marred the mid-1990s and hopes of a peaceful transition is for now all in the past.

KwaZulu-Natal has the largest population (about 8.6 million) of any state in South Africa, with rich resources, including plentiful water, coal, minerals, and agricultural land (Natal produces 75 percent of South Africa's sugar, along with timber, beef, dairy products, maize, poultry, and fruit). Durban is the largest port in Africa (and ninth largest in the world), while the bulk export harbor at Richards Bay is one of the world's largest coal export terminals. The province also has the most comprehensive tourist infrastructure in the country (with around 3.2 million visitors every year), even though only about 10 percent of foreign visitors come here. The rest of them are missing a treat.

Natal has truly magnificent scenery, from the soaring peaks of the Drakensberg to the forest-covered dunes and lagoons of St. Lucia. Superb Indian Ocean beaches and remote, dramatic game parks equal or surpass even the Kruger, but with a fraction of the number of visitors. And it has history. It is a land for storytellers, with tales of confrontation and conflict, bloody treachery and glorious heroism. It is indeed a land fit for kings.

The Hindu Shree Ambalvanar Temple in Bellair Road, Durban

NATAL PARKS
Most reserves in KwaZulu-Natal come under the jurisdiction of the KZN Nature Conservation Service, Head Office, P.O. Box 13069, Cascades 3202 (tel: 033-845 1000, fax: 033-845 1299), the successor to the old Natal Parks Board. *Open* Oct–Mar, 5 AM–7 PM; Apr–Sep, 6–6. *Admission: expensive.* A Golden Rhino Passport offers free entry to all Board properties, but you need a special permit to take vehicles onto the beaches. Most Zululand reserves are malarial. Accommodations range from self-catering A-frame chalets to three-bedroom cottages. Some provide a cook, but only Itala and Hluhluwe have fully catered lodges.

Tourist Junction, Station Building, 160 Pine Street, Durban (tel: 031-304 7144, fax: 031-305 6693, www.tourism-kzn.org.za. *Open* Mon–Fri 8–4:30, Sat–Sun 9–2) is a one-stop shop for tourist information on KwaZulu Natal. This excellent center also has desks for Durban Unlimited (tel: 031-304 4934, fax: 031-304 6196, www.Durban.org.za) for information on the Greater Durban area and to organize walking tours of the city; several local tour operators, car rental, travel and accommodations agencies; and the KZN Nature Conservation Service.

Durban

This thriving metropolis is known as Durban to the British, eThegwini to the Zulus, Banana City to the irreverent, and the "city where the fun never sets" to its marketing department. Its population is approaching 3 million and it is growing faster than any other city in the world except Mexico City. It also has a multiple personality, with the normal sprawl of poverty-stricken townships around the edge, tight enclaves of white suburbia, and a decidedly Asian flavor in the middle. Indians make up nearly one-third of the city's population, and many, particularly the more confident and better educated,

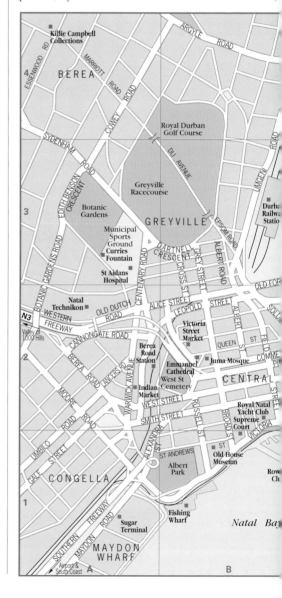

have moved out of the shadows of apartheid and into the city center. The city is famous for its curries and for the fascinating spice market that perfumes the air.

Durban is really about water. It has a port so busy that ships sometimes have to line up for days before berthing, and a long fringe of sand so perfect that it could have been custom-crafted for the thousands of sun-worshippers who flock to the sun-parched waterfront. Although it can be very humid in summer, when the tip of the southwest monsoon brushes the coast, the normally pleasant subtropical climate provides 320 days of sunshine a year, and promotes a laid-back outdoor lifestyle with year-round swimming and water sports.

Today, towering office buildings dwarf the Victorian City Hall

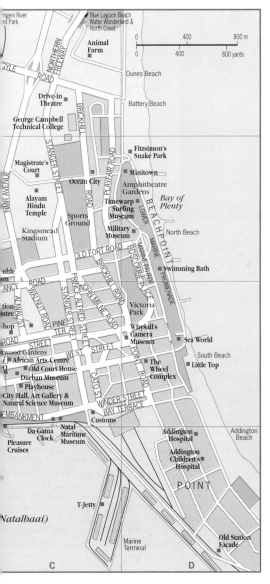

*Dick King, one of
Durban's local heroes*

▶ **African Arts Centre**   *193C2*

*1st floor, Tourist Junction, 160 Pine Street, Durban (tel: 031-
304 7915)*
Open: Mon–Fri 8:30–5; Sat 9–1
This nonprofit gallery is one of South Africa's finest
platforms for traditional African art. Browse among the
best of the best, from imaginative
township crafts to traditional
Hlabisa baskets, Rorke's Drift
weaving, wood carvings from
Empangeni, and Tugela River
beadwork. You should even find
plenty of affordable souvenirs.

▶ **City Hall and
   museums**   *193C2*

City Hall, Smith Street
Francis Farewell Square has been
the site of the local market since
Durban's first European settlers,
Henry Fynn and Francis Farewell,
set up a trading post here in 1824. It
is now dwarfed by Durban's
overblown City Hall (1910), a
replica of the city hall in Belfast,
Northern Ireland.
   Inside, the **Natural Science
Museum** (tel: 031-309 7559; *Open*
Mon–Sat 8:30–4, Sun 11–4.
Admission free) has hundreds of
stuffed animals, birds, reptiles, and
fish, a life-size model dinosaur, a
virtually complete dodo skeleton,
and South Africa's only Egyptian
mummy. The Insect Arcade is like a
chamber of horrors and includes
some mammoth cockroaches.
   On the second floor, **Durban Art
Gallery** (tel: 031-300 6238. *Open* Mon–Sat 8:30–4; Sun 11–4.
Admission free) has fine collections of Victorian paintings,
Chinese ceramics, and French Lalique glass, as well as a
powerful range of contemporary South African art,
including magnificent Hlabisa basketware.

▶▶ **Golden Mile**   *193D3*

Durban's Golden Mile stretches for 4 miles from
Addington Beach along snazzy, fun-filled Marine Parade
to Blue Lagoon Beach. Its sand gleams silver and gold,
the water is clearest sapphire, and the foam-topped
waves were designed for surfers. It is also so jam-packed
with hot, happy bodies that you can hardly pick your way
between their legs. For the more adventurous, there are
surfboards, bikes, and paragliders (Addington Beach),
and opportunities to sail, fish, snorkel, and scuba dive.
Lifeguards are on duty daily 7 AM–10 PM. Be sure to leave
valuables at home; pickpockets do good business on
these crowded sands.
   The buzzing promenade is filled with souvenir and ice-
cream sellers. **Fitzsimon's Snake Park** (24A Snell Parade,
tel: 031-337 6456. *Open* Mon–Fri 9–4:30, Sat–Sun 9–5.
Admission: moderate) wriggles with snakes, crocodiles, and

iguanas. **Funworld** (Marine Parade, tel: 031-332 9776. *Admission: moderate*) has roller coasters, swings, and bumper cars.

The **Amphitheatre** park has a busy Sunday flea market. Nearby is the rickshaw stand. The **Timewarp Surfing Museum** (Ocean Sports Centre, 190 Lower Marine Parade, tel: 082-452 1637. *Open* Tue–Sun 10–4. *Admission: moderate*) has boards and memorabilia dating back to the 1930s.

Nearby is the dour, camouflaged **Military Museum** (corner of Old Fort and Marine Parade, tel: 031-332 5305. *Open* daily 9–5). **Minitown** (114 Snell Parade, North Beach. *Open* Tue–Sat 9–6, Sun 9:30–4:45. *Admission: moderate*) displays scale replicas of Durban's best-known buildings. Across the road, the seafront hotels host a wide array of bars and restaurants.

At **North Beach**, you can also visit **Waterworld** (Snell Parade, tel: 031-337 6336. *Open* Mon–Fri 9–5, Sat–Sun 8:15–5. *Admission: expensive*) for pulsating and looping water-propelled slides, and the **Umgeni River Bird Park** (Riverside Road, off the N2 , tel: 031-579 4600. *Open* daily 9–5; flight displays at 11 and 2. *Admission: moderate*), where 100-foot cliffs with tumbling waterfalls and lush gardens of palms and cycads are home to over 3,000 birds of 400 species.

RICKSHAW RUNNERS
Since 1893, public transportation in Durban has included two-wheeled rickshaws. By 1904 there were over 2,000 clattering through the streets, laden with people and packages. The last commercial venture folded in the 1970s, but around 15 now offer rides for tourists. The runners wear colorful costumes and, when posing for photographs, add towering headdresses. There are also a few auto-rickshaws (tuk-tuks), familiar to anyone who has been to India or the Far East.

The rickshaw runners are one of the city's most colorful sights

195

The Killie Campbell Collection houses a fascinating account of traditional ethnic dress in South Africa

TOURS
There are several different ways to see Durban. The Ricksha Bus (tel: 083-289 0509, 082-809 3530) runs sightseeing tours of the city on an open-topped bus, as well as shuttle services between the city center and beaches. Aussies African Safaris (tel: 031-309 6005) do day-trips to outlying tourist sights, such as the Valley of a Thousand Hills, and longer trips around KwaZulu-Natal. Tours of Remembrance (tel: 031-337 7879) run fascinating tours of multi-ethnic Durban, from the townships to Gandhi's *ashram* at Phoenix, via the Indian Market, the Peace Wall and a history of the local Struggle against apartheid. For guided cycle tours, tel: 031-564 0730.

SHOPPING
Durban may well be the country's finest source of souvenirs. There are several market areas, including the predominantly Indian Grey Street area; the Victoria Street Market, with an enticing mix of Asian and African goods, from witch doctors' potions to great heaps of spices; the Zulu Dalton Road Market; the huge Sunday flea market in the Amphitheatre; and the Church Street Arts and Crafts Market.
Add in several particularly good shopping malls, including the Wheel and the Workshop and the Bat Centre in the city center, and the Westville Pavillion and the Heritage Market on the road up to the Valley of a Thousand Hills.

▶▶ Killie Campbell Collection   192A4
Corner of Marriott and Essenwood roads, Berea (tel: 031-207 3711)
Open: Tue, Thu 8–1. Guided tours by appointment
Sugar baron Sir Marshall Campbell built himself a magnificent neo-Cape Dutch mansion, Muckleneuk, overlooking Durban. Now swallowed up by the suburbs, it is replete with suitably imposing furnishings collected by his son, William Campbell. His daughter, Dr. Margaret Roach Campbell, was a keen anthropologist and created one of South Africa's finest private libraries of Africana. She also collected superb examples of African material culture, including musical instruments, beadwork, pottery, weapons, and costumes. A set of 250 meticulous paintings of tribal dress by local artist Barbara Tyrell complete the **Mashu Museum of Ethnology**.

▶ KwaMuhle Museum   193C3
130 Ordnance Road (tel: 031-300 6313)
Open: daily 8–4. Admission free
KwaMuhle means the "place of the good one." This thought-provoking museum, housed in the 1930s offices of the Bantu Administration Board, honors J. S. Marwick, a civil servant during the Anglo-Boer War, who—with his *iduna* Prince Pika Zulu—helped 7,000 migrant workers to escape from the Transvaal to Natal and Zululand. The museum covers the 20th-century history of Durban and South Africa as seen through the nonwhite communities.

▶ Natal Maritime Museum   *193C2*

Bayside end of Aliwal Street, use Victoria Embankment
entrance (tel: 031-300 6323)
Open: Mon–Sat 8:30–4, Sun 11–4
Admission: inexpensive
Durban is all about boats, as proved by this harborfront museum. Its many smaller maritime exhibits are collected around three old workhorses: a 1927 coal-fired steam tug, the *Ulundi;* a 1961 diesel steam tug, the *J R More;* and SAS *Durban,* a World War II minesweeper. Sea View Cottage is a re-created early settler's home. There are excellent views of the docks from the deck of the **Harbour Terminal** (Stanger Street).

▶ Old Court House   *193C2*

Corner of Aliwal and Smith streets (tel: 031-300 6240)
Open: Mon–Sat 8:30–4, Sun 11–4. Admission free
Built in 1863, Durban's first public building now houses a fascinating museum of local history. The exhibits comprise an eclectic mix of architecture, fashion, sugar, shipping, stamps, maps, documents, and fine art relating to the city's history. The museum also organizes a wide range of constantly changing and always interesting special exhibitions.

▶ Old House Museum   *192B1*

31 St. Andrews Street (tel: 031-300 6520)
Open: Mon–Sat 8:30–4, Sun 11–4. Admission: donation
This is an exact replica of a settler homestead, built by John Goodricke in 1894. It remains fully furnished and equipped with domestic items dating from 1850 to 1900.

Parks

Botanic Gardens▶ (Sydenham Road, Berea, tel: 031-211 303. *Open* daily Apr–Sep, 7:30–5:15; Oct–Mar, 7:30–5:45. *Admission free*) These botanic gardens are the oldest and most beautiful in Durban, with delightful woodlands, ancient cycads, a sunken garden, a scented garden for the blind, and a superb **Orchid House** (*Open* daily 9:30–12:30, 2–5) with over 3,000 specimens. There are also enchanting **Japanese Gardens▶** for those in search of Peace (Tinsley Road, Durban North, tel: 031-831 333. *Open* daily 7:30–4).

▶▶ Sea World   *193D2*

Lower Marine Parade (tel: 031-337 3536)
Open: daily 9–9. Admission: moderate
This is the home of the best aquarium in the country. It has cruising sharks (which are fed on Tue, Thu, and Sat at 9:30 PM), turtles, reef fish, dolphins, seals, and penguins.

▶ Whysalls Camera Museum   *93D2*

33 Brickhill Road (tel: 031-337 1431)
Open: daily 8:30–12:30. Admission free
This little museum above a camera store is a treasure trove of photographic memorabilia, from 1841 to the present day.

197

Hand-feeding the sharks in Durban's Sea World

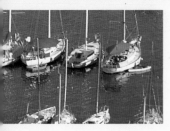

If South Africa has one obsession, it is sports. Top rugby and cricket players rank with film stars, and everyone watches compulsively, both indigenous competitions and foreign fixtures such as the English soccer league. During the 1980s sanctions, the loss of international sporting links caused real heartache.

Since 1994, South Africa has leapt back into the international arena with impressive prowess. In 1995, Nelson Mandela wore a rugby jersey to watch the Springboks win the Rugby World Cup on home ground. Subsequently, South Africa has taken on the cricketing fraternity, and hosted—and won—soccer's 1996 African Nations Cup. The country already has some of the finest golf courses in the world. A new racing circuit is planned near the coast in an attempt to put the country back on the Formula 1 tour. And, though Cape Town lost its bid to host the 2004 Olympic Games, it plans to try again.

Sports, except for soccer, still represent primarily a white man's world. The 1995 winning rugby team had only one black player, and few black townships or schools have the money for more than a dusty square of open ground where children can kick a ball around. For those with the money, anything you care to mention is on offer, from a full range of competitive sports to riding, hiking, climbing, water sports, ballooning and hanggliding, canoeing, fishing, tennis, and golf. Facilities are universally excellent.

Triumph for South Africa in the 1995 Rugby World Cup

Spectator sports Cricket, rugby, and soccer are the three top spectator sports, with keenly contested local and national leagues as well as the revitalized, headline-grabbing international competitions. For information contact **Union Cricket Board of South Africa** (tel: 011-880 2810); **South African Rugby Football Union** (tel: 021-685 3038); **South African Football Association** (tel: 011-634 0430); **Premier Soccer League** (tel: 011-643 3341).

Golf Golf is immensely popular in South Africa, with multiple courses in major cities and tourist areas such as the Garden Route, Mpumalanga, and Sun City (home of the

Million Dollar Golf Challenge, the biggest cash prize on the international circuit). Up in the Northern Cape, there is an all-sand desert course close to Upington. Visitors are welcome at most clubs during the week by prior arrangement (South African Golf Association, tel: 011-442 3723). Equipment is available to rent at hotels with their own courses. Costs (inclusive of greens fees, caddy fees, and tips) vary, but are not too high.

Fishing There are excellent opportunities for deep-sea and coastal fishing, spear fishing, and freshwater trout and coarse fishing. The deep-sea fishing season is November to April (marlin and sailfish) in the north, and September to April (long-fin and yellowfin tuna) in the south. Boat charters include equipment, bait, and rods. Permission is not needed to fish in public freshwater, but you may need a license. This is compulsory for fishing in proclaimed trout angling waters. Anglers Corner (tel: 011-832 1188) is a Johannesburg fishing emporium that can supply gear and answer all questions.

Casting from the beach, East London

Watersports Surfing conditions are excellent, with the Eastern Cape coast, around Jeffrey's Bay and Cape St. Francis, drawing top surfers from around the world. The Gunston 500 International Surfing Championship is held each July. Waterskiing can be arranged on both inland lakes and offshore (South African Waterski Federation; tel: 011-634 0430). There is windsurfing year round on inland lakes and seaside lagoons, but most offshore locations are too rough. To rent equipment, try Windsurfing Africa (tel: 011-726 7076). Boats available for rent range from rowing boats and dinghies to power boats and racing yachts (South African Charter Boats Association, tel: 031-301 1115).

199

MORE INFO
www.ananzi.co.za/
catalogue/sports is an
excellent travel website
that provides links to
hundreds of sporting
websites in or about
South Africa, covering
every possible option from
archery to wakeboarding.
Adventure Safaris and
Sports, P.O. Box 32176,
Camps Bay 8040, Cape
Town (tel: 021-438 5201)
is a specialist sports tour
operator offering
everything from golf to
shark diving.

SHARKS

The Natal Sharks Board operates the electronic shark barriers on 42 beaches between Port Edward and Richards Bay. There are 16 species of shark in the Natal waters, including the great white (Jaws), a hunter of large mammals. In the 25 years before the first shark nets were erected in the 1950s, 22 attacks on people were recorded. Since 1964 there have been none. The nets have now been replaced by hightech electronic screens. Swimmers should still beware of strong tides and waves, and stay within depth. Most public beaches have lifeguards in season and operate a red-flag warning system for safe areas.

Even crocodiles have charm in the baby stage

Durban environs

▶ North Coast   *188B2*

Sugar Coast Tourist Information, Umhlanga Rocks (tel: 031-561 4257), Dolphin Coast Publicity, Ballito (tel/fax: 032-946 1997, www.dolphincoast.co.za)

This is an attractive, although increasingly built-up area, with an abundance of places of historical or natural interest.

At **Umhlanga Rocks** (11 miles north of Durban), the Natal Sharks Board (off the M12, tel: 031-561 1001) offers audiovisual presentations and dissections of sharks (*Open* Mon noon–3, Tue–Fri 9–3, 1st Sun every month at 2; talks Tue, Wed, Thu 9, 2, Sun 2. Boats out to the shark nets, Tue, Wed, Thu 6:15 AM. Reservations essential. *Admission: moderate/expensive*). From **Ballito Beach** (Tourist Information, Ballito Drive, tel/fax: 032-946 1997) onward, the area is tagged the "Dolphin Coast" after the bottlenose dolphins that ride the local surf.

At **Shaka's Rock**, Zulu warriors proved their manhood by leaping into the sea, and the women collected salt from tidal pools at **Salt Rock. Tongaat** is the oldest Indian community in South Africa, and features the **Vishwaroop Temple** and the **Juggernath Puri Temple** (1901), and a crocodile farm at **Crocodile Creek** (D809, Greylands, tel: 032-944 3845. *Open* Sun–Fri 9:30–5; feeding times 11, 3. *Admission: expensive*). **Hulett's Maidstone Mill** (tel: 0322-24551. *Open* Tue–Thu 9, 11, 2; reservations essential) has an audiovisual presentation on sugar production and tours in the crushing season.

The **King Shaka Museum** (23 King Shaka Road, Stanger, tel: 032-552 7210. *Open* Mon noon–4:30, Tue 8 AM–10:30 AM, Wed noon–4, Thu 8 AM–1 PM, Fri noon–4) has a sugar mill, farming implements, Zulu art and weapons, and a depiction of Indian life on the plantations. At the Tugela River mouth, the **Harold Johnson Nature Reserve** surrounds **Fort Pearson** (1878) and the **Ultimatum Tree**, where, in 1878, the British demanded that Cetshwayo yield his sovereignty and army to imperial rule.

▶ South Coast   *188B1*

Scottburgh Publicity, 130 Scott Street, Scottburgh (tel: 039-976 1364); South Coast Publicity, Main Beach, Margate (tel/fax: 039-312 2322, www.sunnymargate.co.za)

The "Hibiscus Coast," as it is known, should be a paradise of golden sand, limpid waters, and tangled coastal forests. Unfortunately, its popularity has engendered a continuous strip of small resorts that have spoiled the look.

Amanzimtoti (Tourist Information, Beach Road, tel: 031-903 7498), known affectionately as "Toti," is a booming family resort with great beaches and entertainment from beauty contests to lifesaving competitions. **Scottburgh** has a miniature railroad and **Croc World** (Old South Coast Road, tel: 039-976 1103. *Open* daily 9–5. Feeding times 11, 3), with 10,000 crocodiles, an aquarium, and Zulu dancing. **Port Shepstone** (tel: 039-682 2455) is home to the narrow-gauge **Banana Express** railroad (see page 235), and has a small **museum** (near the beach. *Open* Wed, Thu noon–4) covering local history, coastal shipping, and early trade and industry. Nearby is the spectacular **Oribi Gorge** (15 miles long, 3 miles wide, 1,200 feet deep), carved out by the Umzimkulwana River. Offshore, a 1¼-mile fossilized sand dune, the **Aliwal Shoal**, and the nearby **Protea Banks** provide some of Africa's best dive sites (see page 214).

Shelly Beach, of course, has a fine **Shell Museum** (995 Marine Drive, tel: 039-315 5723. *Open* in season daily 9–5; out of season Mon–Sat 9:30–4:30, Sun 10–3. *Admission: moderate*). **Margate** is popular with the young and very young, with freshwater and tidal pools, beach entertainment, an amusement park, and an **Art Museum** (Viking Street, tel: 039-377 7525. *Open* Tue–Fri 9–5; Sat 10–1).

▶ Valley of a Thousand Hills   188B2

The uplands surrounding the huge Umgeni River valley have quintessentially English villages, cool breezes, and dramatic views. **Bergtheil Museum** (16 Queens Avenue, Westville, tel: 031-861 331. *Open* Mon–Fri 8–5. *Admission free*) is an 1850s settler cottage, with displays about the German community. The **Paradise Valley Nature Reserve** (tel: 031-723 443. *Open* daily 7–5. *Admission: inexpensive*) has 124 acres of coastal bush with waterfalls and walking trails. **Phezulu** (Botha's Hill, Durban, tel: 031-777 1405. *Open* daily 9–4; 10, 11:30, 1:30, 3:30 for dance displays. *Admission: expensive*) is a Zulu village spectacular. The ticket also allows entry to the **Assagay Safari Park** (5 Old Main Road; same tel: and opening hours as Phezulu), home to crocodiles, snakes, and a children's animal farm.

The extravagantly named Valley of a Thousand Hills

REGAL FRATRICIDE
In 1825, Shaka built a royal *kraal* of some 2,000 beehive huts at Stanger, known as KwaDukuza ("place of the lost person") because of its labyrinthine layout. He conducted meetings under an old *mkuhla* (Natal mahogany) tree, which still survives in Roodt Street. On September 22, 1828, he was murdered by his half-brothers, Dingane and Mhlangane, who then burned the entire town. A memorial in Stanger marks Shaka's grave.

SARDINE RUN
In July each year, vast schools of pilchards (*Sardinops ocellata*) migrate north from the Cape coast, coming inshore to avoid the fast-flowing Mozambique current. Driven ashore by rampaging predators, they beach themselves in great flopping heaps. Locals pour down to the beach and simply pick them up.

Battlefields

► Colenso 188A2

Tourist Information, 36 Sir George Street (tel: 036-422 2111)
Colenso, on the Tugela River, was founded in 1855 and named after the controversial John Colenso, Bishop of Natal (1853–1883). Notable historic buildings include the **R. E. Stevenson Museum** (*Open* Mon–Fri 8–6; keys available from the police station next door) in the Old Toll House (1879) next to Bulwer Bridge, which houses relics of the Anglo-Boer War's Battle of Colenso. On December 15, 1899, Sir Redvers Buller made his first serious attempt to relieve the siege of Ladysmith (see pages 206–207). Fought along the river to the east and west of Colenso, the battle was a triumph for the Boer commander, General Louis Botha, and resulted in the deaths of 1,500 British and only eight Boers. Many of the dead are buried in the nearby **Ambleside Military Cemetery**, **Chieveley Military Cemetery**, and **Clouston Field of Remembrance.**

Close by, the **Armoured Train Memorial** (between Frere and Chievely on the R103) marks the spot where Winston Churchill, then war correspondent of the *Morning Post*, was captured by the Boers in 1899.

►► Dundee 188B3

200 miles from Durban
Tourist Information, Victoria Street (tel: 034-212 2121,
fax: 034-218 2837, e-mail: info@talana.co.za)
Open: Mon–Fri 9–4:45
Founded by Peter Smith from Dundee in Scotland, this quiet town in the foothills of the Biggarsberg Mountains saw the first true battle of the Anglo-Boer War (see page 206). The **Talana Museum►►** (Vryheid Road, tel: 034-212 2654. *Open* Mon–Fri 8–4:30, Sat–Sun 10–4:30. *Admission: inexpensive.* The museum arranges tours of all the battlefields) is one of the most impressive local museums in South Africa, built around Peter Smith's cottage (used as a dressing station during the battle) and many of the battle's gun emplacements and forts. Displays include the development of Dundee, the local Stone Age site of Nkupe Cave, Zulu history, glass, blacksmithing and carpentry, and early mining. The coach house has wagons, farming, and transportation exhibits. Best of all are some stunningly graphic exhibitions on the Zulu and Anglo-Boer Wars.

The small **MOTHS Museum** (corner of Beaconsfield and Wilson streets, tel: 034-212 1250. *Open* on request, ask at the cottage) has a fascinating collection of military memorabilia from 1879 onward. About 20 miles from Dundee, the **Maria Ratschitz Mission** (tel: 034-212 651 1722. *Open* by arrangement) was built at the base of Hlatikulu Mountain in 1886 by Trappist monks. It is a delightful building with some fine paintings and stained glass.

►► Itala Game Reserve 188B3

Louwsburg, about 40 miles east of Vryheid
(tel: 033-845 1000)
For opening times see panel page 191
Most of this beautiful 73,276-acre park in the Pongola River valley, is made up of rocky kopjes, deep valleys, and bushy thickets but about a quarter of the area is rolling golden grassland. It is well stocked with all the major animals

---

SHOPPING STOPS
Elandskraal, near Dundee, is a country town so in touch with its German roots that it still has an "oompah" band. The very cheap and very basic local trading store is used as a supply base by the local tribespeople, who wander the aisles dressed in traditional beads and blankets. At Wasbank, Tactile Handcrafts (tel: 0346-511 678) sells individually designed and created carpets and tapestries.

202

DRESSING FOR WAR
During the Anglo-Zulu Wars, the British wore single-breasted red tunics, blue trousers, and pith helmets. They carried .45 Martini Henry rifles, capable of firing 55 rounds every three minutes, with a range of 984 yards. Zulu warriors went into battle wearing a loincloth and small headdress (to distinguish regiments). They carried a shield, a short stabbing *assegai* (spear), *knobkerrie* (heavy wooden battle hammer), and throwing spears. By the outbreak of war, they also had an estimated 10,000 obsolete rifles. They picked up 800 modern Martini Henry rifles, with ammunition, after the Battle of Isandlwana.

except lion, and includes a healthy rhino population. There are guided drives, night drives, and game walks. Those who want a real experience of the bushveld should join one of the three-day hiking trails.

▶▶ **Ladysmith** see pages 206–207

▶ **Vryheid**   188B3
214 miles northeast of Durban
Tourist Information, corner of Market and Landrost streets
(tel: 034-982 2133)
In 1884, the Boers in northern Natal helped Dinizulu, son of Cetshwayo, dispatch his rivals and take the throne. In recognition, he granted them land to establish a Boer republic. The pristine market town remains heavily Afrikaner.

There are three interesting museums (*Open* Mon–Fri 7:30–4. *Admission: inexpensive*). The 1884 Cape Dutch revival **Lukas Meijer House** (Mark Street) was the home of the president and is now the main cultural museum, with period furnishings and exhibits on banking, printing, mining, and Zulu crafts. The **Nieuwe Republiek Museum** (Landrost Street) was built in 1885 as the council chambers and government offices of the Volksraad, and tells the story of the short-lived republic; the fort and prison cells were added in 1887. The **Old Carnegie Library** (1906, corner of Mark and Landrost streets) houses the local history collection.

Three of the major battles of the Anglo-Zulu War were fought not far from Vryheid: one at **Ntombe Drift** (March 12, 1879), closely followed by those at **Hlobane** (March 28, 1879) and **Kambula** (March 29, 1879).

THE PRINCE IMPERIAL
In 1879, Prince Napoleon Louis Eugène Jean Joseph, son of Napoleon III and the Empress Eugénie, begged to be allowed to head for South Africa with the British troops. Despite official misgivings, he was eventually allowed to go as an observer, and he set off on June 1 without a suitable escort. His party was attacked by Zulus and, while his retinue managed to escape, he had trouble mounting a frightened horse and was stabbed 17 times. His death marked the end of the Bonaparte pretensions to the throne of France.

203

Red wool and brass buttons—a hot and visible uniform for an African war

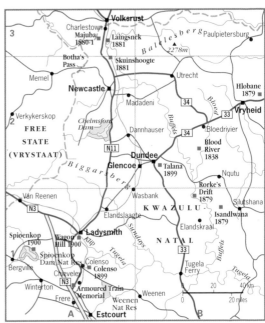

Tour

The Disputed Territory

For over 50 years, the grasslands of northern Natal saw bitter conflict as a result of the territorial ambitions of the Zulus, Boers, and British. The area has South Africa's largest concentration of battlesites; most remain untouched and are intensely evocative of the action and tragedies that once drenched them in blood.

The official Battlefields Route covers 11 towns, over 50 battlefields, and museums, war graves, and memorials. Maps, guides, tapes, and tours are available. Many sites are reached via minor roads and it is impossible to crete a continuous route between them. Instead, they are arranged below chronologically (see also **South Africa Was**, pages 30–39, **Battlefields**, pages 202–203, and **Zululand**, pages 212–213).

Boer-Zulu War (1838)

Blood River (30 miles east of Dundee, tel: 034-632 1695. *Open* daily 8–5). Following the massacre of Piet Retief (see page 33), a Boer commando of 464 men and 64 wagons, led by Andries Pretorius, took a solemn vow of retribution (see page 167). On December 15, they circled the wagons into a D-shaped formation at the confluence of the Ncome River and a *donga* (large ditch). Next morning, they woke to find themselves surrounded by over 10,000 Zulus. Three times the Zulus were driven off by fierce rifle fire, then Pretorius led a mounted charge: the Zulus fled, trapping their own reserve in the river. In all, 3,000 Zulus died, with only three Boers wounded. The river was renamed after the slaughter and December 16 remains a national holiday. Today, 64 bronze wagons mark the battlefield; a small interpretation center and a monument stand nearby.

Anglo-Zulu War (1879)

Isandlwana (50 miles southeast of Dundee, off the R68, tel: 0342-710634. *Open* Mon–Fri 8–4, Sat–Sun 8:30–4. *Admission: inexpensive*) was a tragic mistake. Neither side intended to fight, but at about 11:30 AM on January 22, 1879, a British patrol

Left: Rorke's Drift battlefield, from the Zulu perspective. Above: memorial wagons at Blood River

stumbled over the Zulu army of 20,000 warriors, who were forced into attacking the main British column of 1,774 men. Within two hours, 1,329 British and over 1,000 Zulu soldiers lay dead. Survivors fled across **Fugitive's Drift**, where most were then killed.

Rorke's Drift (26 miles from Dundee, off the R68, tel: 0346-421 687. *Open* daily 8–4. Crafts center open Mon–Fri 8–4; Sat 10–3. *Admission: inexpensive*) is named after James Rorke, a British soldier who set up a trading post here

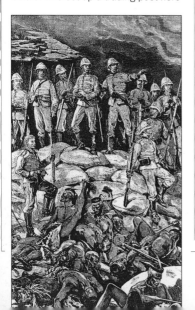

in 1849. In 1878, the farm became a Swedish mission and a British military base. At 3:15 AM on January 22, 1879, two survivors of the battle at Isandlwana raised the alarm at Rorke's Drift, 9 miles from Fugitive's Drift. The tiny garrison of 139 soldiers, 35 of them hospital patients, began to fortify the base using everything from maize sacks to cookie boxes. The attack, by four Zulu regiments (4,000 men) under the command of King Cetshwayo's brother, Dabulamanzi, began at 4:30. Twelve hours later the Zulus finally withdrew, leaving behind nearly 600 dead. Only 17 British soldiers were killed. Eleven Victoria Crosses were awarded to the defenders—more than any other single engagement in history. The rebuilt hospital is now home to an interpretation center.

First Anglo-Boer War (1880–1881)
Majuba (on the N11 between Volksrust and Newcastle. *Admission: inexpensive*). On April 12, 1877, the British annexed the South African Republic; on December 13, 1880, guerrilla resistance blossomed into full-scale war. The governor of Natal, Sir George Colley, marched north, only to lose 150 men at Laingsnek (January 28) and a further 150 at Skhuinshoogte (February 8).

A 19th-century engraving of the battle at Rorke's Drift

On February 27, Sir George assaulted the Boer-held Hill of Doves, Majuba, with a force of 579 men. By morning, 91 British, including Colley, were dead. It was the deciding point in the war. The British signed an armistice on March 6, returning the ZAR to the Boers.

Second Anglo-Boer War (1899–1902)

Talana (Dundee, see also page 202). By the time war was declared on October 9, 1899, 4,000 British troops were stationed in Dundee, ready to protect the local coalfields. On October 20, **Talana Hill** (hiking trail from the Talana Museum) became the scene of the first battle of the Anglo-Boer War when a 14,000-strong Boer army attacked the British camp. In a hard-fought struggle, the British eventually repelled their attackers, leaving 51 British and 145 Boers dead. Two days later, the British retreated. (This was the first time the British abandoned their red coats in favor of practical khaki.)

Ladysmith▶▶ (144 miles from Durban. Tourist Information, Town Hall, Murrchison Street, tel: 036-637 2992, www.ladysmith.co.za. *Open* Mon–Fri 8–4, Sat 8–noon) became a focal point for the Anglo-Boer war following the British rout at Nicholson's Nek on October 30, 1899. From November 2, the little town on the Klip River was besieged by the Boers for 118 days, while 53,000 troops fought a series of bitter and bloody encounters nearby. The siege was eventually lifted by Sir Redvers Buller on February 28, 1900. Like Mafeking, it captured the public imagination, and Ladysmith became a household name across the Empire. It finally proved disastrous for the Boers, who had pinned down too

---

❏ **Life under seige**

At the start of the siege, there were nearly 20,000 people crowded inside the 17-mile perimeter of Ladysmith, 12,500 of them fighting men, many others battle-weary refugees from northern Natal. There were also 4,000 cattle and a good supply of rations. Although regularly shelled by the Boers, surprisingly little damage was done to people or property. As time wore on, however, the effects of poor sanitation and inadequate fresh food meant that about 30 people were dying from disease every day. When Sir Redvers Buller finally arrived, he found 2,800 people sick and wounded, and 3,037 soldiers and 54 civilians dead. ❏

---

many troops in an area with no lasting strategic value.

The **Siege Museum** (Murchison Street, tel: 036-637 2992. *Open* Mon–Fri 9–4; Sat 9–1. *Admission: inexpensive*) has vivid displays and graphic descriptions of events, and will provide a detailed guide to local sites, best appreciated from the high ground on one of the encircling hills. The museum building, originally the local market hall, was used as a rations store during the siege. Next door, the **Town Hall** (1893) acted as a hospital, but was still shelled by the Boers, who did not believe that the Red Cross flag was genuine. You can see the scars on the clock tower. In front stand two British 6.3-inch Howitzer RML guns, Castor and Pollux, and a replica Boer Long Tom field gun.

A British Howitzer gun outside the Town Hall in Ladysmith

Spioenkop, a battle that finally resulted in victory for the Boers

Behind it, the **Cultural Centre** (25 Keate Street, tel: 036-637 2231. *Open* Mon–Fri 8–4, Sat by arrangement . *Admission; inexpensive*) is a showcase for Ladysmith's cultural achievements and local heroes, such as Ladysmith Black Mambazo, and boxer Sugarboy Malinga.

Inside **All Saints Anglican church** (1882), memorial tablets list those who died in the siege and the relief, alongside stained-glass windows and the Regimental Standard, presented to the Natal Carbineers by the Prince of Wales in 1925. In the gardens of the Hindu **Vishnu Temple** is a statue of Mahatma Gandhi, who was a stretcher bearer with the relief column. The Muslim **Sufi mosque** is considered one of the most beautiful in South Africa. The **Blockhouse Museum** (4 miles from Ladysmith, off the Harrismith road, tel: 036-635 4091. *Open* by appointment) is a replica of a British blockhouse, with a collection of Zulu and Boer War artifacts.

Wagon Hill (Platrand, 3 miles south of Ladysmith) was a key British defensive position during the Siege of Ladysmith. On January 6, 1900, Boer commandos stormed the hill, but had to retire after a fierce battle. Various fortifications are visible and there are several memorials. The modern

---

❑ **Long Tom**
The Boers had only four of these famous field guns. Made in France, the 155mm Creusot weapons fired 97-pound shells over a distance of about half a mile. Each gun weighed 7 tons and was pulled by 16 oxen. ❑

Burgher Memorial, with its seven stylized stone hands, commemorates the 781 Natal Boers who died during the war, 310 of whom are buried here.

Spioenkop (off the R600, west of Ladysmith. *Admission: inexpensive*). On January 23, 1900, this small, rocky hill was attacked by 1,700 British troops. The 15 Boers fled, leaving it deserted. In the dark, misty conditions, the British sited their lines wrongly. The next morning 3,600 Boers attacked in earnest. Although the battle lasted all day, the *kopje* was never reinforced from the 25,000 British troops below, command was confused, and a massacre ensued. By the evening, with 243 dead and over 500 wounded, both sides believed they had lost, and withdrew. Several hours later, the astonished Boers found the hill deserted and moved in. The battlefield is now part of the **Spioenkop Dam Nature Reserve** (tel: 036-488 1578. *Open* Oct–Mar, 6 AM–7 PM; Apr–Sep, 6–6).

**DRAKENSBERG
MUSEUMS**
In Estcourt, Fort Durnford
(Tourist Information and
museum, Kemps Road,
tel: 036-352 6253, e-mail:
brta@futurest.co.za. *Open*
Mon–Thu 9–12, 1–4:30,
Fri 8–12, 1–3:45, week-
ends by appointment),
the largest fort in Natal
(1847), is now a military
and social museum.
Winterton Museum (Kerk
Street, tourist information
tel: 036-488 1180;
museum tel: 036-488
1885. *Open* Wed, Fri 1–4;
Sat 9–12. *Admission:
inexpensive*) covers local
geology, flora, fauna, and
history. In Himeville, a
loop-holed fort, is a
museum of rural life
(tel: 033-702 1184. *Open*
Wed, Fri, Sat, Sun 10–12.
Admission: inexpensive).

GUIDED HIKES
The Mountain
Backpackers' Club
(tel: 031-266 3970) runs
regular guided hikes
through the Drakensberg
and can provide informa-
tion for those wishing to
set out on their own. For
other information, contact
KZN Nature Conservation
Services (see page 256).

The Drakensberg

The high Drakensberg, which run for 125 miles along the western border of KwaZulu-Natal, are part of a much longer chain of basalt stretching from the Cape to the Limpopo. They were known to the Zulus as *uKhahlamba* (Barrier of Spears); the Afrikaners named them Dragon Mountains.

With jagged 9,840-foot peaks, flowing fields of red-gold grass, meadows as rich in flowers as a medieval tapestry, San rock paintings, raptors soaring on the thermals, and gushing waterfalls, manmade attractions would seem superfluous. The mountains are preserved as a recreational wilderness, with unsurpassed walking, hiking, and climb-ing. Detailed maps are available at trailheads; permits are needed for most longer hikes. There are also numerous small resorts, cottages, and campsites, with gentle strolls through the lower-lying hills. Activities include superb trout fishing, climbing, bird-watching, riding, and hot-air ballooning. The best months to visit are probably April and May. The frosty winters are too cold, while in midsummer mist and rain may obscure the views.

▶▶▶ Central Drakensberg   188A2

The central section of the Drakensberg has the highest mountains in the country, crowned by Injasuti (11,346 feet). Close behind are Champagne Castle (11,097 feet), Giant's Castle (10,870 feet), and Cathkin Peak (10,329 feet). Cathedral Peak (9,853 feet) is the easiest climb in the Natal range. Below them, the 85,253-acre **Giant's Castle Game Reserve** has splendid herds of eland, while its birds include black eagle and lammergeier. Carcasses are laid out at the **Lammergeier Hide** (May–Sep, Sat–Sun only; tel: 036-352 4617; reservations essential, arrive before 8 AM) to attract the huge, rare, bearded vultures.

The area is also one of the world's richest stores of San art: the **Main Caves** (1¼ miles south of Main Camp. *Open* daily 9–3; ask here for information on other caves in the area. *Admission: moderate*) have over 500 paintings in a single large shelter and a small Bushman Site Museum.

The **Kamberg Nature Reserve** has excellent trout fishing (season Sep 1–Apr 30; permits obtainable from the office), while the 2½-mile **Mooi River Trail** is specifically designed for travelers with disabilities. The **Ardmore Studio** (D275, off Champagne Castle road, tel: 036-468 1314. *Open* daily 9–4:30) is a collective of over 40 superb Zulu and Sotho artists.

▶▶▶ Northern Drakensberg   188A2

The north is dominated by the **Amphitheatre**, a 5-mile crescent flanked by two peaks—the Sentinel (10,381 feet) and the Eastern Buttress (9,994 feet). Between them, the skinny **Tugela Falls** skip over several cascades before plummeting 2,014 feet. With a combined drop of 3,110 feet, these are the second-highest falls in the world (the highest are Angel Falls, Venezuela). Drive to the base of Sentinel Peak, and walk to the waterfall along the rim of the Amphitheatre on reasonably flat ground, or climb the summit of the Sentinel via a hiking trail and chain ladders. The Tugela River is only one of five major rivers, which include the Orange, born on **Mont-aux-Sources**

(10,765 feet). Much of this area comes within the 19,769-acre **Royal Natal National Park**, which has over 200 bird species and several sites with San rock paintings. The road from **Bergville** (Tourist Information, tel: 036-448 1557, fax: 036-448 1088, www.drakensberg.co.za) to Harrismith leads over the breathtaking 6,872-foot **Olivershoek Pass**.

▶▶▶ Southern Drakensberg   188A2

Tourist Information, Main Street, Underberg (tel: 033-701 1471, fax: 033-702 1158, e-mail: sdpa@futurenet.org.za)
Although close to the coast and major cities, this is the most rugged of the three areas, with several small nature reserves and some heavy-duty hiking for those who want a challenge. The **Giant's Cup Trail** (37 miles, five days) runs south from Sani Pass to Bushman's Nek, and is part of the National Hiking Way.

The remote, tortuous, rugged, and spectacularly beautiful **Sani Pass** is the highest in South Africa, climbing from 3,936 to 9,427 feet as it crests the jagged dragon's back. It follows the upper valley of the Mkomazana River and was always the traditional crossing between the Drakensberg and Lesotho. Much of the road runs through protected wilderness areas (a four-wheel-drive vehicle and passport are required).

THE SOUND OF MUSIC
The Drakensberg Boys Choir is magnificent. The school near Winterton educates boys from 9 to 15 years old. The choir has toured in the United States, Europe, Israel, and the Far East. When at home, it holds regular concerts on Wednesdays at 3 PM in term time in the school auditorium (tel: 036-468 1012).

The Amphitheatre is the most dramatic and instantly recognizable rock formation in the Natal Drakensberg

The Colonial Buildings in Pietermaritzburg

MARATHON
In May each year, South Africa's athletes have their day with the running of the Comrades Marathon. It is a staggering 51 miles in length, between Durban and Pietermaritzburg, uphill and downhill in alternate years.

Pietermaritzburg and the Natal Midlands

▶▶▶ Pietermaritzburg 188A2

Pietermaritzburg Publicity Association, 177 Commercial Road (tel: 033-345 1348, fax: 033-394 3535, e-mail: ppa@futurenet.co.za)
Open: Mon–Fri 8–5, Sat 8:30–12:30

Founded by the Voortrekkers in 1838, and set in the fertile Msunduze Valley, Pietermaritzburg was named after two Boer trek leaders killed by the Zulus, Piet Retief and Gerrit Maritz. Since 1845 it has been capital of Kwazulu-Natal (currently sharing the honor with Ulundi).

The streets around **Church Street** reveal a feast of magnificent Victorian and Edwardian architecture, in particular the towering red-brick **City Hall** (1900). Also noteworthy are the 1889 **Old Natal Parliament** (tel: 033-355 7708/26. *Open* Mon–Fri 8–5); **Old Government House** (home of the governors until 1910); and Philip Dudgeon's fine **Standard Bank** (1882). A statue of Mahatma Gandhi by Phil Kolbe stands in front of the old **Colonial Buildings**. Bishop John William Colenso, who established the Church of England in Natal, is buried in the **Cathedral of St. Peter** (1872). **St. George's Garrison Church** (1898) is part of **Fort Napier** (1843). There is also a fine Hindu temple, the **Sri Siva Soobramoniar and Marriamen Temple** (Lower Longmarket Street. *Open* Mon–Sat 7–6, Sun 8–6).

Museums
The **Natal Museum** (237 Loop Street, tel: 033-345 1404. *Open* Mon–Sat 9–4:30, Sun 2–5. *Admission: inexpesive*) covers dinosaurs, bird and marine life, pan-African art, from San rock paintings to Asante wooden pillows, Portuguese shipwrecks, and settler history. The **Macrorie House Museum** (11 Loop Street, tel: 033-394 2161. *Open* Tue–Thu 9–1, Sun 11–4. *Admission: inexpensive*), the atmospheric Victorian home of Bishop Macrorie, is now restored and contains beautiful antiques and costumes. The **Tatham Art Gallery** (corner of Church Street and Commercial Road, tel: 033-342 1804. *Open* Tue–Sun 10–6. *Admission free*) is housed in the **Old Supreme Court** (1871) and displays late 19th- and early 20th-century paintings, porcelain and glass, and an exciting collection of contemporary South African art. The annex shows ethnic arts being made. The **Voortrekker Museum** (Longmarket, tel: 033-394 6834. *Open* Mon–Fri 9–1, 2–4, Sat 8–noon. *Admission free*) is in the gabled **Church of the Vow**, built in 1841 in repayment of the Covenant (see page 167). Next door, **Welverdient House** was the home of Andries Pretorius (see page 162). The **Comrades Marathon Museum** (Connaught Road, Scottsville, tel: 033-394 3511. *Open* Mon–Fri 8:30–4:30, Sat–Sun by arrangement. *Admission free*) is dedicated to the gruelling, annual race (see panel opposite).

Parks and gardens
The **Garden of Remembrance** has a memorial to 13,000 South Africans who died at the Battle of Dellville Wood in World War I, with a Weeping Cross that supposedly oozes sap on its anniversary. The beautiful **Natal National Botanic Gardens** (2 Zwartkop Road, Prestbury, tel: 033-344 3585. *Open* daily, dawn–dusk. *Admission free*) contain plants indigenous to Natal.

▶ The Natal Midlands   *188A2/B2*
Between the Drakensberg and the coastal belt, the **Midlands Meander** (brochures available) leads through rolling, green hills and delightful country towns, visiting artists' studios, tea gardens, and antiques shops. In **Howick** (Information, tel: 033-330 5305), go to the 312-foot **Howick Falls** on the Mgeni River, walk down into the gorge, and visit **Howick Museum** (Fallsview, tel: 033-330 6121, ask for museum. *Open* Tue–Sat 9:30–4:30. *Admission: inexpensive*) for local history and militaria. **Midmar Public Resort and Nature Reserve** (tel: 033-330 2067. *Open* daily 8:30–6. *Admission: moderate*) has small-game viewing and water sports.

GANDHI IN AFRICA
On June 7, 1893, at Pietermaritzburg station, a young high-caste Indian lawyer, Mohandas Karamchand Gandhi, was ejected from first class and told to sit in the luggage wagon. When he protested, he was thrown off the train. The incident was a turning point in his life. For the next 20 years, he fought for the rights of Indians, developing his theories of *satyagraha* (passive resistance) and influencing the course of South African nationalism. He returned to India in 1914, was given the honorific "Mahatma" (Great Soul), and went on to change the course of world history and philosophy.

211

EMBLEMS
Pietermaritzburg's coat of arms, supported by wildebeest, had to be altered in 1908 as the original version showed the animals running in the wrong direction—a symbol of cowardice. The elephant is a Zulu symbol for a great ruler's place, Umgungundhlovu.

The elephant marks Pietermaritzburg's status as a capital

THE BLOODSTAINED KING

In 1828, Dingane (ca1795–ca1843) assassinated his half-brother Shaka and became the Zulu king. In 1838, he met with Piet Retief and a party of 101 Boers to negotiate a treaty. He supposedly signed a land deal, but then killed the Boer party and attacked Boer camps at Bloukrans River and Boesmans River. Afrikaner retribution (see page 204) led to his eventual downfall. In 1840 his half-brother Mpande overthrew him, and he fled to Swaziland.

KWABULAWAYO

Shaka built a *kraal* overlooking the Nkwalini Valley (about 16 miles from Eshowe on the P230). Here he executed all those who had tormented his mother during their struggle, naming it KwaBulawayo ("the place of killing"). Warriors who returned without their spears were punished at Coward's Bush.

Men build the frame of the house, but women do the thatching in Zulu communities

Zululand

▶ Eshowe and environs   *188B2*

Tourist Information, Osborne Road (tel: 035-474 1141, fax: 035-474 4733, e-mail: eshowe@uthungulu.co.za) Open: Mon–Fri 7:30–4, Sat 9–noon.

Eshowe ("the sound of wind in the trees") is a lovely little hill town near the last remnants of the indigenous **Dhlinza Forest** ("a gravelike place of meditation"). Massive, brick-built **Fort Nongqai** (1883) garrisoned the Natal Native Police. It now houses the **Zululand Historical Museum** (Nongqai Road, tel: 035-474 1141. *Open* daily 9–4. *Admission: donation*), with fine collections of furniture, royal *ingxothas*, Zulu household items, St. Lucia ammonite fossils, and a silver beer mug given to King Cetshwayo by Queen Victoria in 1882. The **Vukani Museum** (Osborne Street, tel: 035-474 5274. *Open* Tue, Thu 9–1 or by arrangement. *Admission: inexpensive*) has a wonderful collection of Zulu basketry and pottery. Just out of town, the **Martyr's Cross** (KwaMondi Road) celebrates Eshowe's first Christian martyr (1877) on a hill with superb views.

Cetshwayo's first *kraal* (1860) was at **Gingindlovu** ("swallower of the elephant"), named to commemorate Cetshwayo's victory over his brother, Mbulazi, for the Zulu throne. The king died in 1884 and is buried in **Nkandla Forest** ("place of exhaustion"), 4,003 acres of unspoiled indigenous forest.

Between Eshowe and little colonial Melmoth are several excellent Zulu cultural villages. All have good dance troupes, a living village, a *sangoma* (healer), and traditional food. **Shakaland** (9 miles from Eshowe on the R68, tel: 035-460 0912. *Open* daily, tours at 11, 12:30, or stay overnight) was created as a set for the TV series *Shaka Zulu* in 1985, as the *kraal* of Shaka's father,

Zenzangakhona. It is popular with tourist groups from Durban and puts on a good show. **Simunye** (28½ miles from Eshowe, off the D256, tel: 035-454 7103) combines Zulu heritage with the Voortrekker experience, including ox-wagon rides, in an excellent hideaway camp (overnight guests only). Nearby, **KwaBhekithunga** (Stewart's Farm, off the R34 between Empangeni and Melmoth, tel: 035-460 0644. *Open* for tours by appointment. *Admission: expensive*) has a fine craft center.

▶▶ Hluhluwe-Umfolozi National Park   *188C3*

Established in 1897, this is a 237,226-acre complex of two parks linked by a corridor of land 5 miles wide, with habitats ranging from woodland and forest to savannah and grassland. It shares with St. Lucia the distinction of being the oldest wildlife sanctuary in Africa. In the 1960s, it was the home of Operation Rhino, a conservation program to ensure global survival of the white rhino, and still has the world's largest concentration of black and white rhino. It also has all the other major species, a wide selection of birds, and a small museum of Zulu culture and history.

Impala at a water hole in Hluhluwe-Umfolozi National Park

Dumazulu (6 miles south of Hluhluwe Village, tel: 035-562 0144. *Open* 8:15, 11, 3:15 for tours and dance displays; and at 6 PM including dinner—minimum 20 people. *Admission: expensive*) is probably the best of the many Zulu villages in the country; the name means "thundering Zulu." Situated right out in the bush, it has an authentic feeling of old Africa that is entirely lacking at many of the more polished attractions. Nearby, **Ilala Weavers** (tel: 035-562 0630) is a magnificent crafts shop stocked with art from 1,200 Zulu craftsmen and women.

The private, 42,009-acre **Phinda Resource Reserve** (run by CCAfrica; 18½ miles north of Hluhluwe village, tel: 011-775 1000) includes sand forest, mountain, wetlands, and river valleys. The whole area has been restocked with a wide range of game, including the "Big Five," and has several luxury lodges that offer their guests excellent game watching, bushwalks, canoe safaris, and river cruises.

▶ Mgungundlovu   *188B3*

In 1828, Dingane moved the Zulu capital to Mgungundlovu ("the place of the great elephant") in the Mfolosi Valley. It was here, in 1838, that he murdered Piet Retief and his followers. The city was torched when Dingane abandoned it in 1839, but its core has been accurately rebuilt. There is an obelisk **memorial** to Piet Retief and his followers. Most of the ancestors of the Zulu royal lineage, including Dinizulu (1884–1913) and Senzangakhona (father of three kings: Shaka, Dingane, and Mpande), are buried nearby at **eMakhosini** ("the place of kings").

ADOPTED CHIEF
John Dunn, a friend of Cetshwayo, was the only white man in history to become a Zulu chief. He settled near the Ongoye Forest, married 49 Zulu wives, and fathered 117 children. His furniture is displayed at Fort Nongqai.

213

ROYAL GUESTS
Shakaland, Kwa-Bhekithunga, Simunye, Dumazulu, and Ondini (see page 215) all have moderately priced overnight accommodations in traditionally shaped beehive huts (including features such as electricity and plumbing), with a traditional Zulu dinner and entertainment around the fire.

INTO THE BLUE
There are excellent opportunities for scuba diving all along the Natal coast and down into the Eastern Cape. Remote Sodwana Bay has the most colorful coral reefs, while the Aliwal Shoal, off Umkomaas, provides the most exciting dives. Alternatively, try the Protea Banks, or even No. 1 Fishing Ground, about 2 miles from Durban. Contact: South African Underwater Union (tel: 021-930 6549).

Northern KwaZulu

Traditional homeland of the Tonga and Mabudu peoples, this remote Maputaland region of KwaZulu-Natal, near the Mozambique border, covers 3,475 square miles of hot, flat, sandy, tree-covered terrain, crisscrossed by rivers. It has heavy summer rains, dense populations of hippo and crocodile, and a staggering array of birds. Much of the area is now carved up into magnificent, remote game parks, rich in game and empty of people. Notable are the 85,609-acre **Mkuzi Game Reserve** (about 208 miles northeast of Durban), an area of fever trees and fossils in the foothills of the Lebombo Mountains, and **Sodwana Bay National Park** (about 248 miles from Durban via the Lower Mkuzi road, tel: 035-845 1000), with lakes, coastal dune forest, and both tidal and coral reefs, which make it a magnet for divers.

In the far north, the large inland **Ndumo-Tembe National Park** comprises the 24,711-acre **Ndumo Game Reserve**, often described as a miniature Okavango, teeming with wildlife, fish, and over 400 bird species, and the smaller **Tembe Reserve**, set up to provide a safe haven for Mozambique's elephants. On the coast, **Kosi Bay Nature Reserve** (accessible only by four-wheel-drive vehicles) protects towering dunes, mangrove swamps, and golden sand beaches where leatherback and loggerhead turtles waddle ashore to lay their eggs. Farther south, magnificent coastal forests surround Lake Sibaya, South Africa's largest freshwater lake. Inland is another huge lake, the Pongolapoort Dam, built artificially for irrigation.

▶▶▶ St. Lucia   188C3

Tourist Information, corner of Katonkel and McKenzie streets (tel: 035-590 1143)

The unique 95,587-acre **Greater St. Lucia Wetland Park**, one of the three most important wetlands in Africa, surrounds an ancient 25-square-mile lake, with several distinct ecosystems including coastal dune, wetland, estuarine, bushveld, coastal forest, mangrove swamp, lily pan, and grassland. It is a magnificent bird-watching area, with 450 species including large colonies of pelicans and flamingos, Goliath and other herons, fish eagles, and three species of kingfisher. **False Bay Park** on the northwestern shore of Lake St. Lucia comprises 5,553 acres of dry forest and coral ridges. Hundreds of rare pink-backed pelicans congregate in the trees on the banks of the Hluhluwe River from December to April.

The **Crocodile Centre** (*Open* daily 8–4:30; feeding time Sat 3. *Admission: moderate*) has a small ecology museum and live crocodiles of every species in Africa. An 80-seat launch, the *Santa Lucia* (tel: 035-590 1340. Tours, taking two hours, daily at 8:30, 10:30, 2:30. Reservations essential. *Admission: expensive*), runs regular trips around the lake. You can also rent private boats from Charters Creek and Fanies Island. There is good fishing (except in the Marine Reserve), but swimming and water sports are not a good idea, with about 2,000 crocodiles, 800 hippos, black-fin, and Zambezi River sharks. Deep-sea fishing is available from St. Lucia town. The **Marine Reserve** stretches along the coastline from Sodwana Bay in the north to Cape Vidal in the south and 2 miles out to sea. It contains the southernmost coral reefs in the world.

DUNES
St. Lucia has the highest forested sand dunes in the world, towering mountains of golden sand knitted together by ancient root systems. Unfortunately, the sand contains huge deposits of valuable titanium and zirconium, which is already being mined on unprotected dunes in the Richards Bay area. Environmentalists have finally won a bitter battle with the mining consortiums, who wanted to tap the deposits within the national park. Visits to the Richards Bay mining operation can be arranged (tel: 0351-903 444).

ANIMAL TRAFFIC
Increasing numbers of
South Africa's farmers
and game reserves hold
regular auctions at which
anything from a cheetah
to a dung beetle may be
sold. The inclusion of
species such as rhino is
part of a serious drive to
save them from extinction;
gentler animals, such as
antelope and zebra, may
be bought purely for
domestic use. Many new
hunting or game reserves
are opening for tourists,
and there is a move to
farm game for the table.

*Northern Natal, with its
rich tropical waters,
offers excellent fishing in
the lagoons, lakes, and
open sea*

▶**Ulundi**   *188B3*

*Tourist Information, at the KwaZulu Cultural Museum
(tel: 0358-702050)*

Every Zulu king founded his own new capital, abandon-
ing that of his predecessor, and in 1873 Cetshwayo built
Ulundi. On July 4, 1879, British troops, led by Lord
Chelmsford, defeated 20,000 Zulus at Mahlanathini Flats.
The military power of the Zulus was finally broken: King
Cetshwayo was soon captured and his kingdom annexed
to the British Empire. Ulundi is now joint capital of
KwaZulu-Natal and seat of the **Legislative Assembly**,
where amazing tapestries depict the history of KwaZulu
(viewing by appointment only, tel: 0358-202 101).

Ulundi was succeeded by a new capital at **Ondini**, which
was then destroyed by Swazi invaders. Archeologists have
uncovered the foundations, and the royal *kraal* has been
rebuilt in traditional style, with dome-shaped woven grass
dwellings (*uhlongwa*), as part of the **KwaZulu Cultural
Museum** (King Cetshwayo Highway, tel: 0358-702050.
Open Mon–Fri 8–4, Sat–Sun 9–4. *Admission: inexpensive*).
There is also a kitchen garden and crafts market.

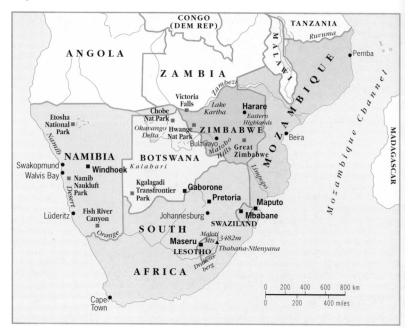

PRACTICALITIES
Check before leaving whether you need a visa to enter any of these other countries. If you need one for South Africa, make sure it is multientry: a quick trip across the border, or even the shortcut through Swaziland, will cancel your initial entry. Namibia, Botswana, Zimbabwe, and Mozambique all have cerebral malaria and you must take prophylactics. Few car rental companies will allow you to take a vehicle over the border, so shop around or arrange for a new vehicle to meet you at the border. The water should be safe in all countries except Mozambique.

Right: Namibia's sand dunes are the highest in the world

South Africa has six neighbors—tiny mountainous **Lesotho**, tucked into the Drakensberg; the gentle kingdom of **Swaziland**, which tumbles off the escarpment between Kruger National Park, Mozambique, and KwaZulu-Natal; poverty-stricken **Mozambique**, only now emerging tentatively from the devastation of war; the vast desert expanse of **Namibia**, famous for its diamonds and the shipwrecks of the Skeleton Coast; triumphant **Botswana**, which has quietly proved a stable democracy in the whirlwind of African politics; and **Zimbabwe**, home to the Victoria Falls, one of the seven natural wonders of the world, and to the Karanga-Rozwi, builders of the magnificent stone city of Great Zimbabwe, center of a mighty kingdom from the 13th century.

South Africa is at present orderly, organized, and—by African standards—sophisticated. Its population is largely urban and increasingly distanced from its heritage and traditions. By contrast, its neighbors were colonized for far shorter periods, with foreigners not taking full possession until the late 19th century, and handing back the reins of power far sooner than in South Africa. With extraordinary luck and political cunning, Lesotho and Swaziland managed to remain independent protectorates throughout the colonial period. The result is that all have the distinct, flamboyant cultures that are hard to find in South Africa itself. There can also be a greater degree of what may seem like chaos, but is all part of the diverse, exciting experience that is Africa. Some have more severe problems, such as Zimbabwe's economic meltdown and the devastating floods in troubled Mozambique, but tourism carries on regardless—you and your hard currency will be very welcome.

Because these countries have far smaller populations than that of South Africa, most have managed to set aside

Beyond South Africa

much larger areas as national parks and reserves. You have a chance to experience nature in the raw from the many small camps dotted across the wide landscapes. Namibia, Botswana, and Zimbabwe all have world-class game parks, with few of the crowds that gather at Kruger. And then there are the spectacles—the biggest waterfalls, highest sand dunes, and second-largest canyon in the world; and the great rivers—the Zambezi, Limpopo, Chobe, and Okavango.

All distance is relative, and in Africa people happily travel hundreds of miles for a weekend. South Africa's neighbors may seem far away, but it is easy to hop on a plane and sample an exciting and different view of Africa.

PRACTICALITIES
There are regular flights from Johannesburg to Maseru, and good connections by car (four-wheel-drive vehicles recommended for some roads). The currency is the *loti* (plural *maloti*). Most E.U. and Commonwealth citizens can enter without a visa; other nationalities should check. For further information, contact the Lesotho Tourist Board, Christie House, Maseru 100 (tel: 266-313 760, fax: 266-310 108). In South Africa tel: 012-467 640; U.K. tel: 020-7373 8581; U.S.A. tel: 202/797 5533.

Lesotho

Lesotho, made up almost entirely of rugged mountains and totally surrounded by South Africa, calls itself the "Kingdom in the Sky." In the 1820s a Sotho chief, Moshoeshoe the Great, fled to the mountains from the Mfecane wars raging across the highveld. Eventually he settled in a natural fortress, Thaba Bosiu (the "Mountain of the Night"), near modern Maseru, where he and some 40,000 followers formed the BaSotho nation. For almost a century, the tiny kingdom battled to survive, against other refugees, Trekboers, and the British. The king skillfully steered a middle course, maintaining his kingdom's independence until his death in 1870. Basutoland eventually became a British colony in 1884 and voted to remain one in 1910 during the Union of South Africa, thus escaping apartheid. In 1966 it became an independent constitutional monarchy.

Above all, Lesotho is for lovers of the great outdoors. It has only one museum, at the **Morija** mission station, while the capital, **Maseru** ("red sandstone"), is a quiet, pleasant but undistinguished place. However, the scenery is stunning, and there are vast mountain vistas, including Thaba-Ntlenyana, the highest peak in southern Africa (11,421 feet). Walkers can ramble on moorland, by rocky streams, and through woodland. Pony trekking and fishing are specialties. You can find fossil-laden cliffs and faint, ancient San paintings in caves and under overhangs. Villages dot the hills and a thriving crafts industry makes fine wool and mohair tapestries, basketry, leather, jewelry, and pottery. And the Katse Dam water development project will provide Lesotho with a base for water sports.

The Sotho are great horsemen

NATIONAL HATS
The national dress of Lesotho is a colorful blanket and a conical straw hat, the *mokorotlo*, a word denoting disagreement. The hat is said to take its shape from the mountain of Qiloane, parting sight of Moshoeshoe's son, who left court because he disagreed with dealings with the British. It became a symbol of nationalism.

Swaziland

Swaziland tumbles off the African plateau between South Africa and Mozambique, with high montane forest in the west and burning savannah lowveld in the east. Founded by King Sobhuza I during the upheavals of the Mfecane in the early 19th century, the country narrowly escaped absorption into South Africa. In the early 20th century, a fund was established to buy back land from the Boers, ensuring legal title for the Swazi people. The country was a British protectorate for 66 years, gained independence in 1968, and is an absolute monarchy under the benign rule of King Mswati III. It is a peaceful, largely agricultural country with a population of about 800,000, and survives on the sugar crop and income from immigrant workers to the South African mines. South African tourists come here for the outdoor activities, but most visitors are passing through en route to Durban or Kruger National Park.

The capital, **Mbabane**, is a pleasant, small, low-rise city. From here, a road leads southeast to Manzini through the **Ezulwini Valley**, the "heavenly place," heart of royal Swaziland. **Lobamba** has the Houses of Parliament, the National Museum, a traditional Swazi village, and several fine crafts workshops. Nearby are the **Mlilwane Wildlife Sanctuary** and **Mantenga Falls**. **Piggs Peak**, in the mountainous northwest, offers spectacular views, walking, and other outdoor activities. There are three further game parks in the eastern section, **Hlane Royal National Park**, **Mbulizi Game Reserve**, and **Mkhaya Game Reserve**.

The country blends ancient traditions and Western culture, with traditional villages and people wearing national dress. Twice a year there are major festivals. In the male **Ncwala**, or First Fruit Ceremony (December/January), the young men bring ocean foam and *lusekwane* (acacia) branches to the king, who dances with his warriors. The female **Umhlanga** (reed) dance (August/September), is in honor of the Queen Mother (see panel).

PRACTICALITIES
There are good road connections and flights from South Africa. The currency is the *lilangeni* (plural *emalangeni*) linked to the SA Rand. Ministry of Tourism, Environment and Communication, P.O. Box 2652, Mbabane (tel: 268-404 4556, e-mail mintour@rednet.co.sz). In South Africa tel: 012-344 1924; in the U.K. tel: 020-7630 6611; in the U.S.A. tel: 202/362 6683.

The Organ Pipe Donga, in the Mkhondvo Valley

PRACTICALITIES

There is a good road north and regular flights and trains to Harare, Bulawayo, and Victoria Falls leave from Johannesburg and Cape Town. There are luxury train safaris up to Victoria Falls from South Africa (see page 235) and a homegrown Zimbabwean Rail Safari, 2c Prospect Avenue, Raylton (P.O. Box 2536) Bulawayo, Zimbabwe (tel: 19-75575; fax 19-42217). The currency is the Zimbabwe dollar.

Zimbabwe Tourist Development Corporation, P.O. Box CY286, Causeway, Harare (tel: 04-758 712, fax: 04-758 828). In the U.K., tel: 020-7836 7755; in the U.S.A., tel: 212/980 5984; in South Africa tel: 012-342 5135.

Zimbabwe, ruinous capital of great priest-emperors, has handed its name on to a new country

Zimbabwe

Due north of South Africa, across Kipling's famous "great, grey, green, greasy Limpopo River, all set about with fever trees," is Zimbabwe, a landlocked country with a turbulent history as the renegade colony of Southern Rhodesia. There are only two cities of any real size: **Harare**, the capital, in the northeast and **Bulawayo** in the southwest. The Nyanga, Vumba, and Chimanimani mountain ranges together form the lush, green **Eastern Highlands**, whose pine forests, coffee farms, and mountain lakes are popular with locals escaping the searing summer heat. There are plenty of activities including golf, riding, trout fishing, and hill walking. In the far southwest, the outer fringes of the Kalahari Desert creep across the border to the magnificent rocky **Matobo Hills**. Most of the country is a high plateau (at around 3,280–4,920 feet), perfect for farming and wildlife.

There are two main tribes, the majority Shona and the Ndebele, an offshoot of the Zulus, whose first leader Mzilikaze fled north to escape Shaka's wrath (see pages 30–31). Shona art has become world famous since the late 1980s, and Zimbabweans are also brilliant musicians, with names like the Bundu Boys, Stella Chieweshi, and Thomas Mapfumo achieving some international and a great deal of African fame. Many people are immensely hospitable and charming, with an infectious sense of humor.

THE VICTORIA FALLS One of the wonders of the natural world, known locally as Mosi Oa Tunya ("the smoke that thunders"), these waterfalls on the massive Zambezi River are the largest on earth. They are 200–345 feet high, 5,537 feet wide, and in full flood some 120 million gallons of water cascade over the brim every minute, sending a jet of rainbow-sparkling spray 1,640 feet into the air. The town has a lot to offer, from elephant and hot-air balloon rides to traditional dancing, but the most popular activities involve the river. Leisurely cruises run upstream from the Falls, while downstream, rafts tumble through 5 miles of twisting gorges tossed in some of the world's wildest white water.

LAKE KARIBA The Kariba Dam across the Zambezi is 413 feet high and contains 1,372,350 cubic yards of concrete and 12,125 tons of steel. Behind it is the fifth-largest manmade lake in the world, 180 miles long, up to 20 miles wide, and up to 394 feet deep. On its shores and waters a booming vacation business has grown, with numerous water sports, sailing, houseboats, angling and game fishing, and beaches and beer for

sunseekers. Away from Kariba town, several small, remote reserves offer excellent game viewing.

HWANGE NATIONAL PARK This vast game park, covering 5,656 square miles in the northwest corner of Zimbabwe, is one of the finest in Africa. It has 107 mammal and 410 bird species, but is renowned above all for its herds of elephant and for the stately sable antelope, national emblem of Zimbabwe. There are several comfortable Parks Board camps and an increasing army of private game lodges offering luxury accommodations, guided drives by day and night, and even bush walking and riding. Only three are actually within the park (operated by Wilderness Safaris).

GREAT ZIMBABWE From the 13th to the mid-16th century, Great Zimbabwe was the capital of a huge empire that stretched halfway across southern Africa and traded for gold and ivory with the Arabs and Portuguese. In its latter years it was ruled by the Mwene Mutapa (a title meaning "Great Plunderer"), an autocratic, semidivine priest-king. The city, the most magnificent of a number of virtually unknown stone-built towns in the region, is thought to have had a population of some 50,000 in its heyday. Today, abandoned to the baboons, it is an atmospheric ruin, one of the largest stone structures in Africa. Although only a short detour from the main Jo'burg–Harare road near Masvingo, it is off the beaten track for most Zambezi tourists.

Victoria Falls, the largest and one of the most beautiful waterfalls in the world

PRACTICALITIES
There are good roads and train services and regular flights from South Africa to Gaborone and Maun. Nationals of most Commonwealth and E.U. nations and the U.S. may enter without a visa. The currency is the *pula*. Botswana Tourist Board, P Bag 0047, Gaborone (tel: 267-353 024, fax: 267-308 675). In South Africa tel: 012-342 4760; in the U.K. tel: 020-7499 0031; in the U.S.A. tel: 202/244 4990 and 212/889 2277.

Canals and reeds in the Okavango Delta

Botswana

Once the British colony of Bechuanaland, Botswana is as large as France or Texas but with a population of only about 1.5 million, mostly of the SeTswana tribal group. With nearly three-quarters of the country covered by uninhabitable Kalahari sand, almost the entire population is clustered in the lush green hills of the southeast corner around the capital, **Gaborone**.

At independence in 1966, Botswana was one of the ten poorest countries in the world; today, it is one of the wealthiest in Africa, thanks to the discovery of huge diamond fields and the successful development of the beef cattle industry. It is peaceful, stable, and democratic.

Nearly 20 percent of the country is national park. In the far south, the huge arid **Kgalagadi Transfrontier Park** crosses the South African border, next to the smaller **Mabuasehube Game Reserve**. The first "peace park" in southern Africa, it covers an area far larger than the Kruger, although the scarcity of water and the scrubby vegetation do not allow the same density of wildlife to survive. There are few roads and facilities in the Botswana section.

In the center of the country is the even larger and more remote **Central Kalahari Game Reserve**, set up originally as a home for the San people. In the far north, near the Zimbabwe border, the **Chobe National Park** is the richest in game and facilities of all Botswana's parks, offering game viewing equal to the great parks of Kenya and Tanzania, and particularly famous for its massive herds of elephant.

Pride of place, however, goes to the **Okavango River**, which heads south and west from Angola toward the sea but never makes it, fanning out instead into the magnificent, 5,019-square-mile inland **Okavango Delta**, with over 350 bird species. It is a fantastic wilderness of reeds and water lilies, much of it only negotiable by canoe. The neighboring **Moremi Game Reserve** has excellent game viewing.

Namibia

Namibia is four times the size of Germany, with a population of a little over 1 million. A German colony known as South West Africa from 1890, it was handed over to South Africa at the start of World War I and remained part of that country until independence in 1990. There is a distinctly Germanic air to the architecture, especially in the little coastal towns of **Luderitz** and **Swakopmund** and in the hilly capital, **Windhoek**. German cakes, sausages, beer, and oompah bands add a slightly surreal quality to local festivals, and there is still one tribe, the Herero, whose married women wear the full heavy skirts of 19th-century German missionaries, adding their own towering cloth headdresses.

Most of Namibia is desert, with the Kalahari merging into the even more forbidding **Namib Desert**. Even the coast is desolate. A huge area in the far south is forbidden territory, left to the diamond diggers, while the northern section is known as the **Skeleton Coast** after the many who died in shipwrecks on its terrifying rocks. Between them is the **Namib Naukluft Park**, an enormous reserve of red-gold sand dunes, including the 1,000-foot-high **Sossusvlei Dunes**, the highest in the world.

Inland is another geological marvel, the **Fish River Canyon**. This giant ravine, second in size only to the Grand Canyon, is 100 miles long, 17 miles wide, and up to 1,800 feet deep. A 15-mile road leads to a number of viewing platforms and a rugged 56-mile, five-day hiking trail runs along the bottom.

In the north, where the desert gives way to acacia savannah, the 8,598-square-mile **Etosha National Park** is centered around a 1,930-square-mile pan. The name means "place of dry water" but there is still enough water to support one of the largest concentrations of wildlife in Africa. Yet more excellent game viewing can be found in the **Caprivi Strip**, the neck of land that stretches out into the Zambezi Valley in the far north.

PRACTICALITIES
There is a good road north and regular flights to Windhoek from Johannesburg and Cape Town. Most E.U. and U.S. citizens can enter without a visa. The currency is the Namib dollar, which has the same value as the SA Rand. Namibia Tourist Board, P.O. Box 13346, Windhoek (tel: 061-284 2111, fax: 061-284 2364, e-mail: tourism@iwwn.com.ina). In South Africa, tel: 011-784 8024 or 021-419 3190, fax: 011-784 8340; in the U.K., tel: 020-7636 2924, fax: 020-7636 2969; in the U.S.A., tel: 212/ 465 0619.

223

The wind whips the Namib Desert into towering pinnacles of red-gold sand

Mozambique landscape

Mozambique

A long, skinny country running north for 1,217 miles up the Indian Ocean coastal plain, Mozambique began as part of the Omani Sultanate, at the southernmost tip of the Arab gold, ivory, and slave trade. It is hot and humid, and the swamp fevers nearly defeated the earliest Portuguese traders, but the promised prizes inland were worth the hardships and it became a Portuguese colony. Best known as a scruffy but charming Mediterranean-style playground for white Rhodesians and South Africans, it used to be a source of good food, wine, and loose women, with some of the finest beaches in Africa.

Independence changed all that. In 1975, the Portuguese withdrew abruptly and some 80 percent of whites departed, decimating the infrastructure. Frelimo, a hardline Marxist organization, took power and instituted extreme socialist government. Almost at once civil war broke out between Frelimo and the anarchic Renamo (Mozambique Resistance Movement), largely funded by Rhodesia and South Africa. When peace was restored after nearly 20 years, the country had become one of the poorest in the world.

Today, Mozambique has renounced its hard-line policies and is trying desperately to reconstruct some sort of life for its citizens. Roads are gradually being opened, power restored, and the land cleared for agriculture so that the hundreds of thousands of refugees can return. The first glimmerings of renewed tourism are also in view. The capital, **Maputo**, has several luxury hotels, including the historic Polana, and you can again stroll the boulevards and eat *peri-peri* prawns, while several small beach resorts have sprung up within day-trip distance. The second city and largest port, **Beira**, is also making great efforts to re-create a vacation environment. However, most tourism is still concentrated on **Vilanculos** and its classy, offshore resort islands of **Santa Carolina** and **Benguela**. For now, the rest of the country is suitable only for those with a good four-wheel drive and a strong sense of adventure.

PRACTICALITIES
All visitors must obtain a visa before arrival. The currency is the *metical*, but many places may ask for payment in US$ or SA Rand. Roads across Mozambique are gradually opening up, but it may be safer to fly and you should always get local advice before traveling. Do not stray beyond clearly marked settlements: there are an estimated 2 million land mines still to be located and defused. Local tourism information is hopeless. Try contacting the commercial Mozambique Travel Centre (tel/fax: 011-659 1766, e-mail: moztrav@mweb.co.za).

Practicalities

Accommodations

The Cellars-Hohenort Hotel, Cape Town

Middle-class South Africans have an exceptionally high standard of living, and even higher expectations, so while the tourist industry murmurs self-deprecatingly about pulling standards up to the international norm, South Africa actually provides excellent accommodations, with service often surpassing European levels.

Luxury If there is a shortfall in the number of beds, it is in the luxury category; few locals can afford five-star prices, and the relatively small number of international business-people have up to now been comfortably accommodated in such classic hotels as the Mount Nelson in Cape Town. This is changing as international chains, including Sheraton, Intercontinental, and Hilton, leap onto the bandwagon.

Meanwhile, South Africa does have some wonderfully luxurious small hotels: the Cellars-Hohenort in Cape Town, the Grande Roche in Paarl, and the Coach House near Tzaneen in the Drakensberg, for example. Scattered throughout the country in historic buildings and stunning settings, with lush gardens, antiques, impeccable service, and wonderful food, most are marketed through organizations like Small Exclusive Hotels of Southern Africa or the Portfolio of Country Places.

Chains For those who cannot afford this sort of luxury there are several chains with cross-country facilities, although here you pay for comfort and convenience, not atmosphere. Holiday Inns are well represented, from the upscale Crowne Plazas to the basic three-star and very affordable Garden Courts. Protea, the largest, have a huge network, but the star ratings, price, and efficiency vary widely from property to property, so check before reserving.

Game lodges A trip to Africa would not be complete without at least a couple of nights' game viewing. If you have the cash, head for one of the exclusive game lodges, such as Sabi Sabi or Mala Mala in Mpumalanga, Phinda or Ndumo in Natal, or Shamwari in the Eastern Cape. Not only are they totally charming, but the game viewing is superb and the knowledge of the rangers encyclopedic. You can also get off the roads, and do walks and night drives, activities still largely taboo in the national parks.

The facilities offered within the national parks are much cheaper. Most have at least one full-service lodge, they all have self-catering chalets, *rondavels* (small, simple circular rooms), camping and trailer facilities, a camp store with basic foods, and a gas station.

226

FURTHER INFORMATION
For central booking numbers and hotel listings, see pages 258–263. Most guesthouses have only two or three rooms available, so few are listed here. SATOUR and the South African AA both publish annual guides to recommended guest-houses, farmhouses, bed-and-breakfast, and self-catering establishments. *Sleep Over* is an annual guide to guesthouses and B&Bs. Fax: 021-790 1055; e-mail: lannice@ifrica.com Alternatively, ask at the local tourist office.

Traditional African architecture receives a starry gloss at many bush lodges

Self-catering If you want to travel cheaply, this is the way to do it. There is an extraordinarily wide choice of self-catering accommodations, and many establishments offer a range to satisfy all tastes and pockets. There are many time-share properties along the Natal coast, most of which can be rented by casual visitors. Cape Town has increasing numbers of apartments to let. Rural retreats offer full service or self-catering in furnished chalets, tents with fitted bathrooms, simple huts, or real bush camping. In most small towns someone has a spare cottage, often charmingly furnished, at a ludicrously low price. The only drawback is that you will have to take cutlery and crockery for picnics and supply yourself with the basic foodstuffs—feasible only if you have your own transportation.

Guesthouses The bed-and-breakfast business is also booming throughout the country. Usually tucked away in residential suburbs, many are delightful historic houses, such as Cape Dutch farms, as well as rambling Victorian mansions with four-poster beds and patchwork quilts. Prices are reasonable and you will get a huge cooked breakfast and charming hospitality from a (probably) middle-aged Afrikaner lady who wants nothing more than to sell the delights of her country to you.

VACATION HOMES

A growing potential market, right along the coast, but clustered around Cape Town and Durban, are the casual short-term rentals of various vacation homes that belong to South Africans, as well as the increasing number of foreigners investing in the property boom. Rates and facilities can be excellent, but the trick is to find what is available. There are only a few small agencies; most are managed by local real estate agents. The best place to look is on the web.

Bed-and-breakfast South African-style is affordable and often delightful

Food and drink

South Africans like meat—lots of meat. It may be beef, lamb, or pork, or a variety of more exotic options from springbok or impala to crocodile and ostrich, but it must come in large quantities. They also have a very sweet tooth. If anything is a South African staple today, it is a vast slab of steak, usually smothered in barbecue sauce.

In the small towns, there is often little choice about where to eat, but the meal you get will be filling and wholesome, and you can request half portions, sauceless steaks, and salads. Along the coast, in the main cities and in the top hotels, the story is very different, with South Africa offering fine and imaginative cuisine, often based on traditional recipes and using the finest of local ingredients.

Cape Dutch food The famous Cape Dutch cuisine grew from several intertwined influences. The newly arrived Dutch brought their traditional thick soups, stews, *frikkadels* (meatballs), and breads, adapting them to available ingredients. Many had Cape Malay servants, and the spices and curries of the East Indies and South India soon crept into the diet. Later arrivals included German settlers who brought their sausage-making skills, and French Huguenots who brought

Menus offer a wide choice in South Africa

Tomato bredie *(left) and* bobotie *(right) are two of the classic mainstays of Cape Dutch cuisine*

konfyt (preserved fruits) and endowed the Cape Winelands with a taste for fine dining that survives to this day.

The Voortrekkers had to survive away from civilization for years on end, in intense heat and very primitive conditions. *Biltong*, strips of meat salted, spiced, and dried, was probably their best way of carrying protein. It can be eaten dry or reconstituted as part of a stew, can be made from beef or game shot en route, and can be easily cured in the sun on a drying rack. *Biltong* is still a universal food in South Africa and is now even creeping into high society, with fine shavings in soups and salads.

The *braaivleis* (literally "roasted meat") is a ritual as central to the white South African lifestyle as the "barbie" to Australians—and for much the same reason. It began with whatever could be shot being grilled over an open fire—tough food for tough men. Today, the central ingredient is still steak, and with it comes *boerewors* (literally "farm sausage"), highly spiced pork, mutton, and beef sausage, flavored with coriander, ginger, mace, cloves, nutmeg, thyme, fennel, rosemary, mint, and red wine or vinegar. Sosaties are kebabs marinated for several days in sweet and sour sauces, based on Indonesian satay. On the side are the salads, roasted mealies (corn on the cob), pot bread (baked in a cast-iron pot), or *roosterkoek* (bread cooked on the coals or ashes)—and plenty of alcohol.

HEALTHY DIET
Traditionally cooked over an open fire, the black African staple is a thick porridge (*pap*) of indigenous sorghum or maize, introduced to the continent by the 15th-century Portuguese sailors. Accompanying this come thin stews of spinach, beans, pumpkin, tomatoes, and onions with added chicken, mutton, or beef on special occasions. Other protein comes from sour milk, mopani worms, grasshoppers, ants, and edible beetles. It is a remarkably healthy diet, with little fat, salt, or excess sugar, but is being compromised by a dependency on sugary soft drinks, bottled beer, and white bread.

229

Stews, known as *bredies* in the Cape and *potjiekos* in the Transvaal, are traditionally fat-tailed mutton or venison cooked very slowly in a three-legged cast-iron cooking pot (a *potjie*—pronounced "poykey") over an open fire. Any available vegetable can be thrown in, but common additions are tomato, pumpkin, butternut squash, beans, onion, potato, and *waterblommetjie* (water lily). The savory stew is often served with something sweet, such as a compote of dried fruit, sweet potatoes glazed in orange caramel, or sugary pumpkin fritters.

Biltong is still a South African staple

Pancakes make a handy snack

Asian cuisine Alongside those dishes that have been adopted and adapted into the white diet, there is still a strong tradition of "Malay" and Indian cuisine; this received a fresh injection of authenticity with the arrival of the Indian cane workers in Natal in the early 20th century. Here are the real curries and rice-based *breyanis* (similar to the Indian biriyani), served with *sambals* (chutneys) and *atjar* (pickles). Most famous of the Malay dishes is *bobotie*, a mild baked curry of minced lamb with dried fruit, topped with an egg custard, which has been designated the South African national dish.

Fish With two oceans and plentiful fresh water inland available, one of the greatest treats in the country is the extraordinary range of fish to choose from. In addition to oysters, mussels, limpets, crayfish, and perlemoen (abalone), there are superb white fish such as kingclip, yellowtail, snoek, and kabeljou. The finest prawns are said to be from Mozambique, served Portuguese style in a marinade of olive oil, lemon juice, garlic, bay leaves, *peri-peri* (chili), and ground cloves. Alternatively, look for Cape Malay pickled fish (Cape salmon, kingclip, yellowtail, or any other firm white fish), served traditionally at funeral feasts. Inland, try the smoked salmon trout or barbel.

Desserts To finish off your typically South African meal, you should leave room for a calorie-laden dessert such as *melktart* (a cinnamon-flavored milk tart of Dutch origin), Cape brandy pudding (a British-style steamed pudding laden with brandy), or *koeksisters* (small braided dough-nuts that have been soaked in honey or a thick syrup of concentrated fruit juices).

ALCOHOL
Maheu, a thick white beer made from sorghum, is the drink of choice for all social occasions in traditional black society. Most South Africans wash down their *braai* (barbecue) with a lager (Castle, Lion, Ohlssons, or Amstel) or some Cape wine (see pages 88–89). Finish your meal with a local liqueur, such as the *naartjie* (tangerine)-based Van der Hum or Amarula Cream (made from the fruit of the wild marula tree). Beware local moonshine firewaters—*mampoer* or *witblitz*—unless you have a head like iron or a death wish.

Shopping

Souvenirs of South Africa are plentiful—some tacky, many expensive, and some exquisitely beautiful. Unfortunately, many of the best—ostrich feathers, huge stone statues, fire-baked pots, helicopters made of wire, 7-foot-tall wooden giraffes—are extremely difficult to transport.

Animal products Ostrich farms sell expensive shoes or handbags, and cheap feather dusters or "blown" ostrich eggs (plain, filled with fruit, painted—usually badly—or carved). Antelope skins are legal if you can face the social comment, but do not buy ivory—you are not allowed to bring it home.

   Few of the more spectacular shells and corals you see are actually South African. Most shells for sale are collected live, an activity that is illegal if carried out in protected areas and is certainly not eco-friendly. Collect your own abandoned shells on the beach; they come free and you will not harm the environment. The rich blue perlemoen shells or jewelry made from them are fine, as the contents are harvested for food.

Baskets, bowls, and beads Many traditional crafts, such as stunningly patterned baskets made by the Sotho and Zulus, and simple hardwood bowls and spoons, are still going strong. Intricate Zulu beadwork is magnificent at its best; look for traditional aprons and veils, or simpler (and cheaper) pen holders.

Jewelry and gemstones Gold and diamonds are both sold in abundant quantities, as are many other gemstones, from emerald earrings to huge slabs of amethyst crystal. For an entertaining half hour, head for the gemstone scratchpatches, found in all the main cities. These contain huge cans filled with tumble-polished semi-precious stones. You can select your favorites and buy by weight at unbelievably low prices.

Food, wine, and flowers Look for estate-bottled wines; dried or glacé fruit, *konfyt* or jams (try more unusual flavors such as prickly pear), and *biltong* (vacuum-packed).

Curios Finally, there are the almost obligatory soapstone heads, wooden hippos, copper ashtrays, and T-shirts, which range from the pleasant to the totally awful.

Pots and baskets in Umgababa Market, near Durban

231

Entertainment

There is surprisingly little entertainment in South Africa. Most socializing is done at home, though people are beginning to eat out more, and most towns of any size have a movie theater with latest-release international films. But outside the cities there are few lively bars and clubs: many people get up with the sun, so dining is early and most nightlife is over by 11 PM.

Traditional music and dance These days tribal dance is almost exclusively a tourist attraction. Several "tribal villages," particularly in Natal, put on dance displays. Go to at least one, as the Zulu and Shangaan dancers are spectacular and it will probably be your only chance to see something of a fast-vanishing lifestyle. The quality of the performances and explanations varies, so choose carefully. Some of the best are found in and around Durban, at Simunye, Dumazulu, Shakaland, and KwaBhekithunga (see pages 201 and 212–213); and in Gauteng, at Gold Reef City, Sibaya, and Lesedi; (see pages 152, 156, and 171).

Township jazz Headed by such luminaries as Miriam Makeba, Ladysmith Black Mambazo, and Hugh Masekela, South Africa's township musicians combined tribal rhythms with jazz and swing to create a unique, thriving heritage of music and dance. Many of its themes, such as the *toyi-toyi* (Struggle dance of the people), the *mapantsula* (township jive), and *isicatamiya* (a choir tradition from the mines and men's hostels) grew out of the Struggle. Music was one of the few relatively safe ways in which to protest against apartheid. For safety reasons, most township shebeens (once illegal pubs), in which the movement has its roots, should be visited only on organized tours; fortunately the musicians are beginning to move into mainstream venues.

CAPE TOWN
The Jazz Café, 41 The Drive, Camps Bay (tel: 021-438 0783). Nightly jazz in a popular complex. Three restaurants: Pacific fusion, Japanese, and seafood.
Dockside Cape Town, Century City, next to Ratanga Junction (tel: 021-552 2030).

DURBAN
The Bat Centre, Maritime Place, off Victoria Embankment (tel: 031-332 0451). Very lively small mall, combining the best of crafts shopping with the traditional **African Zansi Restaurant and Bar**, a café, craft workshops, and regular jazz nights, dance, and classical theater. There are jazz nights at the Hilton Hotel every Thursday and, when in town, **Ladysmith Black Mambazo** play regular Saturday nights at the Beatrice Street Hostel.

232

The costumes of the Gold Reef City dancers are carefully designed not to offend family sensibilities

JOHANNESBURG
Kippies at the Market, Newtown (tel: 011-834 4714) hosts jazz, Afro-jazz, jazz fusion, and blues.

PRETORIA
There are no downtown jazz clubs; for the best go to the shebeens. However, the street musicians in **Hatfield Plaza** (tel: 012-342 2932) give excellent open-air concerts.

The classics The cultural boycott isolated South Africa from the rest of the world, but it also forced the country to rely on its own resources, resulting in flourishing local culture. The Market Theatre in Johannesburg was particularly dynamic, creating a theater of protest that drew rave reviews in London and New York. Today, classical music and theater are under siege, with government funds being diverted to lay drains and build houses, while the outbreak of peace has left many writers temporarily silent.

Each of the main cities has its own symphony orchestra, ballet corps, opera, and theater, although most are likely to have their funding cut unless they become more multicultural. The focus is firmly European, but artists broke the race barrier long before most, and the townships are beginning to produce some highly talented, classically trained black actors, dancers, and singers.

CAPE TOWN
Artscape Theatre Centre, Foreshore (tel: 021-421 7695; box office: 021-421 7839, credit card bookings). Concerts, theater, opera, and ballet.

DURBAN
Natal Playhouse, Smith Street (tel: 031-369 9555). Home of the Natal Philharmonic Orchestra. Four theaters—The Cellar, The Drama, The Loft, and The Studio.

JOHANNESBURG
Civic Theatre, Loveday Street Extension, Braamfontein (tel: 011-403 3408).
Market Theatre, Wolhuter Street, Newtown (tel: 011-832 1641).

PRETORIA
State Theatre, Church Street (tel: 012-322 1665). Six auditoria offering ballet, opera, and music, as well as some of the most dynamic theater being put on in the country.

Sun City is South Africa's answer to the glitter of Las Vegas

233

ENTERTAINMENT INFO
To find out what's on, check the relevant section of local daily newspapers, the national *Weekly Mail & Guardian* (published Fridays), or the regional Metro sections of the *Sunday Times*. In Cape Town, look at *Cape Review*, while Cape Town and Durban both have a monthly *What's On* available free. In Johannesburg, buy *Blakes Guide to Johannesburg and its Environs*, or *Johannesburg Alive!*, published by *The Star*.

Tickets for major venues from Computicket: Cape Town (tel: 021-918 8950); Durban (tel: 031-304 4881); Johannesburg (tel: 011-445 8445); Pretoria (tel: 012-328 4040). *Open* Mon–Fri 9–5, Sat 9–4. Cash or credit card.

Practicalities

Trains

South Africa has a magnificent network of railroad lines. Unfortunately, it has virtually no trains. Half the tracks are derelict, many run only freight, and even major inter-city routes have only one scheduled passenger service a day. Cape Town and Johannesburg have reasonably efficient suburban networks, but sadly these suffer from major security problems.

Main-line Racism and snobbery killed off the passenger services, which were seen as low-class and dangerous. In fact, while second class is not that comfortable for long journeys, first class is cheap, safe, comfortable, and spacious. Trains are slow, but you can stretch out between crisp white sheets for a leisurely night's sleep, after an old-fashioned dinner in the dining car. There are not enough services to make touring by train practical, but they are excellent for cross-country journeys.

The Blue Train is the successor to the original Union Limited, and replaced the venerable steam service in 1939. It is now one of the most famous—and expensive—trains in the world, running regular scheduled services between Pretoria and Cape Town, a sybaritic 24-hour journey; from Gauteng to Nelspruit for Kruger Park; and north to Zimbabwe's Victoria Falls. For details, contact The Blue Train, P.O. Box 2671, Joubert Park 2044 (tel: 011-773 7631).

The Pride of Africa, run by Rovos Rail, Victoria Hotel, P.O. Box 2837, Pretoria 0001 (tel: 012-323 6052), is billed as the "world's most luxurious train." From its home base in Pretoria, the company offers services to Cape Town, along the Garden Route to Knysna, via the Kruger to Maputo in Mozambique, and via Victoria Falls to Dar es Salaam (Tanzania). With vintage locomotives and refurbished original cars, the train is less a mode of transportation than a vacation in itself, with numerous stops and tours to places of interest en route.

International commuters between Zimbabwe and South Africa at the taxi rank beside Messina station

For total historical accuracy try the **Union Limited**, 3 Adderley Street, P.O. Box 4325, Cape Town 8000 (tel: 021-405 4391), whose locomotives and cars are all accurately restored originals. There are 6–15 day-trips a year from Cape Town to the Winelands and other nearby areas, with infrequent 9-, and 15-day safaris to the Garden Route, Mpumalanga, and the Zambezi. Profits go toward preservation work at the Transnet Museum.

The **Shongololo Express**, named after a shiny brown millipede, aims for a high standard of comfort at more affordable prices. It makes a huge loop around South Africa and Namibia, taking in most tourist highlights, from Kruger to the Cape. Contact 9 Rotherfield Avenue, Essexwold, Bedfordview 2007 (tel: 011-435 3821).

Bushveld Train Safaris, P.O. Box 237, Warmbaths 0480 (tel: 014-736 3025) run six 2-day weekend excursions a year and monthly 8- to 10-day excursions from Pretoria. Aimed at the local market and popular with school groups, they are simple and cheap (no restaurant car). There are some restaurant stops, but self-catering will be required, too.

The **Banana Express** (tel: 039-682 4821) is based at Port Shepstone on the Natal South Coast. There are two itineraries: a 90-minute journey through the banana and sugar plantations to Izotsha (weekly), and a three-day trip to Paddock and the Oribi Gorge (daily in season; three days a week out of season; reservations essential). In the Western Cape, the **Outeniqua Choo-Tjoe**, one of the most enjoyable and scenic services in the country, runs through the heart of the Garden Route between George and Knysna (twice daily, Mon–Sat, tel: 044-801 8288/8208).

MAINLINE RESERVATIONS
Reserve first- and second-class tickets at least 24 hours in advance, either at the stations or by phone. Order your bedding at the same time. Cape Town: information 021-449 2991, reservations 021-405 3871; Durban: information 031-361 7098, reservations 031-361 7621; Johannesburg: information 011-773 5878, reservations 011-773 2944; Pretoria: information 012-315 2757, reservations 012-315 2401.

Opposite: (top) the Blue Train and (below) luxurious living on the Pride of Africa

Practicalities

TOP TRAILS – 1
Boland Trail, Hottentots-
Holland Reserve, Western
Cape (25 miles, two- or
three-day options, tel:
021-886 5858);
Cederberg Mountains,
Western Cape
(one–seven-day routes,
tel: 027-482 2817);
Drakensberg Mountains,
Natal (one hour–ten days;
tel: 033-845 1000);
Blyderivierspoort Trail,
Mpumalanga (40 miles,
five days, tel: 013-769
6019); Klipspringer Trail,
Augrabies Falls National
Park, Northern Cape (25
miles, three days, tel:
012-343 1991).

*Up Table Mountain, the
hard way*

Hiking

There is superb hill walking in the Cederberg, KwaZulu-
Natal, and Mpumalanga Drakensberg; coast and forest
paths along the Garden Route; savannah, and even desert
walking in the Northern Cape and Northern Province.
There are over 200 designated long-distance trails and a
multitude of other options, from short strolls to more
arduous day-trips. Most are accessible by anyone of
reasonable fitness, and a few are even laid out for
wheelchair access. Brochures and sketch maps of many
walks are available, and most are clearly route-marked.

Selecting your trail Take note of local terminology. What
South Africans call a "backpacking trail" is actually an
area crossed by trails, usually fairly rugged, where you
can make multiday hikes, choosing your own campsite as
you go. A "hiking trail" is a designated route, marked by
painted footprints or stakes, and usually several days' in
length. There are basic accommodations in huts or
chalets, but you will be expected to pack all your own
supplies. "Day walks" are precisely
what you'd expect, an energetic, self-
guided day out. "Guided wilderness
trails" are usually relatively easy
day-trips in the parks and reserves,
led by a knowledgeable ranger.
"Interpretive trails" are short, well-
cleared, and marked paths with
regular explanatory displays.

Many trails limit the number of
people in any party and on the route,
so reserve a place in advance. You
may also need a permit. The local
tourist office will be able to give you
details, but for longer-range planning, contact the **Hiking Federation
of South Africa**, P.O. Box 1420,
Randburg 2125 (tel: 011-886 6524,
fax: 011-886 6013) and the **National
Hiking Way Board** (tel: 012-310 3839).
Alternatively, buy *Hiking Trails of
Southern Africa* by Willie and Sandra
Olivier (published by Southern Book
Publishers), probably the best of the
current crop of detailed hiking
guides.

On the track Never underestimate
the environment and do not hike on
your own. Ideally, go in a group of at
least three or four. Get a detailed
route map and study it carefully, for
gradient as well as distance. Always
let someone know where and when
you are going and when you expect
to return, so they can raise the alarm
should you fail to show. Keep a safe
distance from all wildlife, big or
small. For more on safety in the
bush, see page 252.

Take the climate into consideration when deciding on the degree of difficulty you are prepared to tackle. South Africa's mountains are not particularly high and you will not have to acclimatize to the altitude, but they do produce some treacherous and very fast-moving weather. Several people are killed each year in the Drakensberg and even on Table Mountain, trying to escape from incoming fog. If the mist comes down, find shelter and sit it out. In winter the mountains can be cold, wet, and slippery, while in bright sunshine the glaring heat and harsh light can damage pale skin and eyes.

The problems of heat are greatly increased in the savannah of the Northern Province or the Kalahari scrub of the Northern Cape, where in midsummer it can be like hiking in the Sahara. Treat the sun with extreme respect, do not try to be too energetic during the midday hours, and make sure you drink far more water than you think you need. Savage thunderstorms may whip across the country on summer afternoons. Keep well clear of trees or prominent rocks in case of lightning, and stay out of riverbeds, however dry they may seem, in case of flash floods. Never start an unprotected fire or throw away a match: the vegetation is often tinder dry and a bush fire can rampage for miles before it burns out or is brought under control.

The Drakensberg is relatively painless hiking territory

TOP TRAILS – 2
Magoebaskloof Trail, Northern Province (two sections—Dokolewa, 22 miles, three days; Grootbosch, 30 miles, three days, tel: 013-764 1058); Otter Trail, Tsitsikamma Coastal National Park, Eastern Cape (25 miles, five days, tel: 012-343 1991); Swartberg Trail, between the Great and Little Karoos, Western Cape (40 miles, five–six days, tel: 044-279 1739).

Game walks offer a quieter and more intimate bush experience

OTHER USEFUL ADDRESSES

Association of Southern African Travel Agents (ASATA), P.O. Box 31742, Braamfontein 2017 (tel: 011-403 2923).

Southern African Tourism Services Association (SATSA), P.O. Box 65924, Benmore 2010, Gauteng (tel: 011-883 9103/4).

Qualitour Tourism Classification, P.O. Box 1295, Wingate Park 0153, Gauteng (tel: 012-663 5080). A private agency classifying standards across the tourism board, from hotels to tour operators.

Tours and safaris

GENERAL TOUR OPERATORS

Abercrombie & Kent Safaris, P.O. Box 782607, Sandton 2146 (tel: 011-781 0740, fax: 011-781 0733, www. abercrom biekent.com. In the U.K., tel: 020-7730 9600; in the U.S., tel: 800/323 7308 toll-free or 708/954 2944). Upscale worldwide tour operator, running organized tours and tailor-made itineraries in South Africa and surrounding countries.

Rennies Travel, Head Office, 10th Floor, Safren House, 19 Ameshoff Street, Braamfontein, P.O. Box 9395, Johannesburg (tel: 011-407 2800, fax: 011-403 3698, www.rennies.travel.co.za. In the U.K., tel: 01733-330 111; in the U.S., tel: 805/855 1572). One of the largest incoming tour operators in South Africa, and the local Thomas Cook representative, with some 70 branches nationwide.

Springbok Atlas, 48 Tulbagh Road, Pomona, P.O. Box 14884, Bredell (tel: 011-396 1053, fax: 011-396 1069, www.springbokatlas.com). One of South Africa's largest operators, with many local offices and tours of most major cities, day-trips and safaris, as well as countrywide coach tours.

Welcome Tours and Safaris, P.O. Box 2191, Illovo 2121 (tel: 011-442 8905, fax: 011-442 8865, www.welcome.co.za). Coach and minibus tours throughout the country.

SOUTH AFRICA BY AIR

African Ramble Air Safaris, P.O. Box 736, Knysna 6570, Western Cape (tel: 044-384 0080, fax: 044-384 0795, e-mail: aframble@cis.co.za). Personalized, fly-in tours to eco-tourist and off-beat destinations throughout southern Africa.

Bill Harrop's "Original" Balloon Safaris, P.O. Box 67, Randburg 2125 (tel: 011-705 3201/2, fax: 011-705 3203). Hot-air balloon rides over the Magalies River valley, Gauteng.

Civair Helicopters, P.O. Box 120, Newlands, Cape Town 7725 (tel: 021-419 5182, fax: 021-419 5183, e-mail: civair@mweb.co.za). Tailor-made and charter helicopter tours of Cape Peninsula and the Winelands, plus whale-spotting.

Court Helicopters, P.O. Box 2546, Cape Town 8000 (tel: 021-425 2966/7, e-mail: courtva@iafrica.com). Helicopter charters, tailor-made tours, and regular sightseeing flights over Cape Pensinula and the Winelands, Mpumalanga, Sun City, and the Natal coast.

Dragonfly Group, P.O. Box 987 Northlands 2166 (tel: 011-884 9911, fax: 011-884 9915/6). Helicopter tours of Sun City, Mpumalanga, Johannesburg, Cape Town, and Durban. Also safaris and day-trips across the country.

SPECIALIST NATIONWIDE OPERATORS

Adventure Safaris & Sports Tours, P.O. Box 32176, Camps Bay, Cape Town 8040 (tel: 021-438 5201, fax: 021-438 4807, e-mail: adventurepic@icon.co.za). Short breaks, mini-safaris, and special interest tours including golf, cycling, diving, hiking, fishing, hunting, river-rafting, game-viewing, whale-watching, wine-tasting, and sailing.

C. Africa Tours, P.O. Box 882, Benoni 1500 (tel: 011-845 1194, fax: 011-421 8550, e-mail: cafrica@icon.co.za). Tailor-made and small group tours for those following Kosher or Hallal customs.

CCAfrica/Afro Ventures, Pinmill Park, Block F, Katherine Street, Sanddown, Private Bag X27, Benmore, 2010, Gauteng (tel: 011-775 0000, e-mail: information@ccafrica.com). Two of Africa's best luxury safari companies have merged to form one of the most influential upscale providers of lodges, tailor-made, and mobile camping safaris in southern Africa.

Dive the Big Five, P.O. Box 2209, White River 1240, Mpumalanga (tel: 013-750 1832, e-mail: divebig5@iafrica.com). Shark, reef, and wreck diving coupled with a safari. Tailor-made or packaged options.

Drifters Adventours, P.O. Box 48434, Roosevelt Park, Johannesburg 2129 (tel: 011-888 1160). Small group, off-beat camping safaris throughout southern Africa.

Felix Unite, P.O. Box 2807, Clareinch 7740, Cape Town (tel: 021-683 6433, fax: 021-683 6486, e-mail: tours@felix.co.za). South Africa's premier adventure tour operator with river trips on the Gariep, Tugela, Doring, Cunene, and Breede rivers, along with mountain-biking and hiking.

Harleyday Tours, P.O. Box 141, Koelenhof 7605 (tel: 021-882 2558, e-mail: anttract@iafrica.com). Harley Davidson tours of the Western Cape, Mpumalanga, and Namibia.

Kokanya Tours, 10 Kwartel Road, Rand Park Ridge, Randburg (tel: 011-793 6017, e-mail: kokanya@lia.co.za). A wide range of special interest tours from adventure and birding, to cultural tours and fishing.

Which Way Adventures, P.O. Box 2600, Somerset West 7129 (tel: 021-845 7400, e-mail: whichway@iafrica.com). 4WD and camping safaris, white-water rafting, canoeing, and rappeling on the Doring, Breede, and Orange rivers.

GOLFING HOLIDAYS
The following companies offer golf, mixed with game-viewing for nongolfers.
Fairway Safaris, P.O. Box 73618, Fairland 2030 (tel: 011-803 8491).
Golf Adventures International, P.O. Box 1641 Rwonda 2128, Gauteng (tel: 011-802 2251).
Golf & Game Safari Company, P.O. Box 543, Pennington 4184, KwaZulu-Natal (tel: 0323-975 3164).
Golf Line, P.O. Box 611, Alberton 1450 (tel: 011-907 1632/3).
South African Golf Safaris, P.O. Box 3051, Paarl 7620, Western Cape (tel: 021-863 8833).

239

Elephants keep a wary eye on passing safaris

Practicalities

Tours and safaris

REGIONAL SPECIALISTS
For day-trips in and around the major cities, see the relevant A–Z listings.

Western Cape
Cape Eco Trails, P.O. Box 313, Noordhoek 7985 (tel: 021-785 5511). Outdoor adventures including 4WD and walking tours of Table Mountain and the peninsula.
The Capevine, P.O. Box 3799, Tygerpark 7536, Cape Town (tel: 021-913 6611). Upscale small group and tailor-made tours of the Western Cape, specializing in wine, gourmet food, culture and heritage, wildlife and gardens.
Ocean Adventures, P.O. Box 1812, Plettenberg Bay 6600 (tel/fax: 044-573 5083). Whale- and dolphin-watching.
Vineyard Ventures, P.O. Box 554, Sea Point, Cape Town 8060 (tel: 021-434 8888). From a half-day to a week touring the Winelands, with tastings and cellar tours.

KwaZulu/Natal
Adventure Unlimited, P.O. Box 22045, Glenashley 2022, KwaZulu-Natal (tel: 031-569 3604). 4WD rental and safaris.
Andy Cobb Eco Diving, P.O. Box 386, Winkelspruit 4145 (tel: 031-916 4239). Diving and game park safaris.
PMB Heritage Tours, P.O. Box 13830, Cascades, Pietermaritzburg 3203 (tel: 331-443 260). Military history tours of the Anglo-Boer War and Zulu wars battlefields.
Dinizulu Safaris, P.O. Box 11, Hluhluwe 3960 (tel: 035-562 0025). Open-topped 4WD game drives in Hluhluwe-Umfolozi National Park, beach tours of Sodwana Bay and Lake Sibaya, and Zulu cultural visits.

Mpumalanga
Lawson's Specialised Tours, P.O. Box 507, Nelspruit 1200 (tel: 013-755 2147). Specialist bird-watching, wildlife, and photographic tours.
Lowveld Environmental Services, P.O. Box 5747, Nelspruit 1200 (tel: 013-744 7636). Kruger safaris with drives in open vehicles.
Safari Services, P.O. Box 1405, Nelspruit 1200 (tel: 013-752 6259). Excellent custom-designed tours of the heart of big game country.

Hikers by the Mac-Mac pools

Northern Province
Equus Horse Safaris, 36 12th Avenue, Parktown North, Johannesburg 2193 (tel: 011-788 3923). Horse-riding and camping in the Lapalala Wilderness Area (Waterbergs).

Northwest Province
Airtrack Adventures, P.O. Box 630, Muldersdrift 1747 (tel: 011-957 2322). Hot-air balloon rides over the Pilanesburg National Park and Crocodile River.

Travel Facts

Arriving

Arriving by air
Of the three major international airports, the biggest is **Johannesburg International**, 15 miles east of Johannesburg, tel: 011-356 1111 (inquiries); airport shuttle (tel: 011-884 3957).
Cape Town International is 14 miles east of Cape Town (tel: 021-934 0407); airport shuttle (tel: 021-934 0802).
Durban International is 12 miles southwest of Durban (tel: 031-408 1066); airport shuttle (tel: 031-267 1548). All have duty-free facilities, bus links with the major hotels, taxis, car rental offices, tourist information, and hotel reservation desks.

There are scheduled flights from all over the world. Destinations of the state airline, **South African Airways (SAA)**, include New York, Miami, Hong Kong, and Sydney, with regular services from London Heathrow to Johannesburg, Cape Town, and Durban. An arrival **tax** is included in the price of an international or domestic ticket. A special tax is

Short-term parking at Cape Town International

collected on arrival at Skukuza (Kruger National Park) airport. The rate is higher if you are visiting a private game reserve than if you are staying in Kruger.

SAA offices abroad:
Australia 9th Floor, 5 Elizabeth Street, Sydney NSW (tel: 02-223 4448)
U.K. St. George's House, 61 Conduit Street, London W1R 0NE (tel: 0171-312 5005; reservations 0870 747 1111)
U.S.A. 515 E. Las Olas Boulevard, Fort Lauderdale, FL 33301 (tel: 1-800-722 9675, www.flysaa.com).

Airline offices in South Africa:
South African Airways (SAA)
Johannesburg International Airport, Kempston Park 1627, Gauteng (tel: 011-978 1111); Cape Town (tel: 021-936 1111)
Air France P.O. Box 41022, 196 Oxford Road, Craighall (tel: 011-880 8040)
British Airways P.O. Box 535, Parklands, 158 Jan Smuts Avenue, Rosebank (tel: 011-441 8600)
KLM Royal Dutch Airlines P.O. Box 8624, Sable Place, 1a Stan Road, Morningside, Sandton (tel: 011-881 9696)

Qantas 2nd Floor, Grosvenor Court, 195 Jan Smuts Avenue, Parkton North, PBI Parklands 2121 (tel: 011-441 8550)
Virgin Atlantic 2nd Floor, South Block, Hyde Park Shopping Centre, Jan Smuts Avenue (tel: 011-340 3400).

Arriving by land
South Africa has borders with Namibia, Botswana, Zimbabwe, Mozambique, Swaziland, and Lesotho. Most crossings are open at least 8 AM–6 PM daily. There are good roads, and bus and train links with Namibia, Botswana, Mozambique, and Zimbabwe. If you intend to take a shortcut through Lesotho and Swaziland ask for a multiple-entry visa, which allows you as many border crossings as you like within a specific time period.

Arriving by sea
Several cruise companies, including CTC Cruise Lines, Cunard P&O Cruises, and Royal Viking Line, stop in South Africa. The RMS *St. Helena* runs four scheduled services a year between the U.K. and Cape Town (tel: South Africa – 021-425 1165; U.K. – 01326-211466; U.S.A. – Traveltips 718-939 2400); several companies provide passenger services on cargo freighters.

Customs regulations
Currency You may only import or export up to R5,000 ($714) in notes, but unlimited foreign currency and travelers' checks may be imported. You may need exchange control receipts to reconvert leftover rand.
Duty-free allowance For visitors over 18 years old, the allowance is 400

The Romans would have been proud of the Free State roads

cigarettes, 250 grams of tobacco and 50 cigars, 1 liter of spirits, 2 liters of wine, 50ml of perfume, and 250ml of toilet water. You may take in gifts worth up to R500 ($72).
Drugs Narcotics and habit-forming drugs are prohibited. If you are using prescription drugs, carry a letter from your doctor.

Travel insurance
Make sure you have travel insurance that covers medical treatment, air ambulance, and repatriation (South Africa has no national health service and treatment can be expensive), loss or theft of luggage, papers, or money, and travel delays or cancellation. If you are planning to take part in any adventure sports, you may have to pay an additional premium.

Documents
Visitors need a full passport, valid for at least six months beyond the intended stay. Citizens of Australia, Canada, Ireland, New Zealand, the United Kingdom, and the United States do not need a visa. You may need a credit card or other proof that you can support yourself and you may be required to show that you have a ticket home, or can buy one.

Your national driver's license is valid if it is written in English and includes your photograph. If not, apply for an international driver's license, valid for up to three years (depending on the type of permit) before leaving home.

Essential facts

Climate

As a whole, South Africa has an average annual rainfall of 18 inches a year and an average of 8½ hours of sunshine a day. Average midwinter (June–July) temperatures range from ±32 degrees F at night to ±68 degrees F at midday. Average midsummer (December–January) temperatures are ±59 degrees F at night to ±95 degrees F at noon.

This means little, however, as there are several distinct climatic zones in the country dependent on longitude, latitude, vegetation, and altitude. It can be cool and gray in temperate Cape Town, hot and sticky in monsoon Durban, crisp and chilly in the high Drakensberg, and hot and dry in the Kruger, all at the same time. It can also go from cool and overcast to blasting sun in the same place in the space of a few minutes. Always check local conditions, and always add sunblock, a hat, an umbrella, and a sweater or jacket when packing.

National holidays

January 1	**New Year's Day**
March 21	**Human Rights Day**
March/April	**Good Friday**
March/April	**Easter Sunday**
March/April	**Easter Monday**
March/April	**Family Day**
April 27	**Freedom Day**
May 1	**Workers' Day**
June 16	**Youth Day**
August 9	**National Women's Day**
September 24	**Heritage Day**
December 16	**Day of Reconciliation**
December 25	**Christmas Day**
December 26	**Day of Goodwill**

Time differences

South African Standard Time is two hours ahead of Greenwich Mean Time (Universal Standard Time), seven hours ahead of U.S. Eastern Standard Time and eight hours behind Australian Eastern Standard Time.

Opening times

Banks: Mon–Fri 9–3:30, Sat 8:30–11. Most have Automatic Teller Machines (ATMs) outside, operational 24 hours a day.
Businesses: Mon–Fri 8–5 , with an hour for lunch between noon and 2. Some are open limited hours on Saturday morning.

244

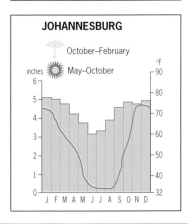

CAPE TOWN (KAAPSTAD)

May–August
October–March

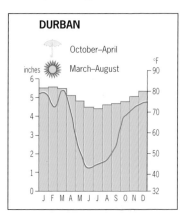

JOHANNESBURG

October–February
May–October

DURBAN

October–April
March–August

Gas stations: most open 7–7 daily; many are open 24 hours a day.
Post offices: Mon–Fri 8:30–4:30, Sat 8–11:30/12:30.
Stores: Mon–Fri 8–5, Sat–Sun 8:30–12:30 (cities only)—although hours are often longer in the main shopping areas and vary from province to province.
Many small towns, still controlled by the Dutch Reformed Church, close down completely on Sunday, so make sure you stock up on gas, food, and other essentials on Saturday.

Money matters

Currency The South African currency is the Rand (R), divided into 100 cents. Bank bills are issued in denominations of R200, R100, R50, R20, and R10.

Exchange facilities Most banks have exchange facilities for major currencies, but it is advisable to carry U.S. dollars or U.K. pounds sterling.The Standard Bank, with 900 branches across the country, is part of the worldwide Cirrus network and you can obtain money from its ATM machines if your national check card or credit card bears the Cirrus logo. Thomas Cook (Rennies) and American Express operate bureaux de change in all major cities. Banks require I.D. for you to change money.

Shelves are piled high in the back street grocery stores

Checks and credit cards Many hotels, stores, and restaurants in tourist and urban areas accept travelers' checks. Most businesses, tour operators, airlines, hotels, and restaurants accept international credit cards including Visa, MasterCard, American Express, and Diners Club. MasterCard holders may use any Thomas Cook Network location to report loss or theft of their card and obtain an emergency card replacement free.
Thomas Cook MasterCard Travellers Cheque Refund Centre (24-hour service—report loss or theft within 24 hours), tel: 0800-998175.

Prices There is a secondary economy, based on the former townships, where prices are a fraction of those in the old white habitat. For most tourists, South Africa is affordable, but not cheap. Upscale hotel prices are on a par with those in the U.S.; car rental is more expensive.

VAT Value Added Tax at 14 percent is levied on most items and services, including accommodations, goods, transportation, and tours. Keep receipts on goods over R250 and claim back the tax when you are leaving the country. Make sure they are accessible as you may have to show them.

Getting around

By car

Car rental Budget, Hertz, Imperial, and Avis have offices throughout the country, including all main airports; you can rent from one office and return at another (for a premium). Local firms offer a cheaper, more limited service. Everything from an economy compact to four-wheel drive, chauffeur-driven limousine, Kombi (Volkswagen minibus), or motor home (RV) is available, all in excellent condition. However, car rental is expensive, with hefty base rates doubled by extras such as Collision Damage Waiver and insurance. Shop around for deals and, with huge distances to cover, always look for unlimited mileage. You should not need 4WD, even in the game parks, but check that your insurance covers you for dirt roads (some policies forbid them, which cuts out serious game viewing). Make sure you have a full set of spares and a jack before setting out.

Car Rental Central Reservation:
Avis (tel: 011-923 3500 or toll-free 0800-021 111 , www.avis.co.za)
Budget Rent a Car (tel: 011-392 3907 or 0860-016 622, fax: 011-392 3015, www.budget.co.za)
Europcar (tel: 011-396 900 or toll-free 0800-011 344; fax: 011-396 1406, www.europcar.co.za)
Hertz (tel: 021-386 1560 or 0800-600 136 toll-free, fax: 021-386 8270)
Imperial Car Rental (tel: 011-453 0005 or toll-free 0800-131 000, fax: 011-453 6278)
Classic Twin Tours (tel: 021-882 2558, fax: 021-882 2287, www.classictwin tours.com. MGB roadster and Harley-Davidson motorbike rental.

Driving tips South Africa has excellent roads. Traffic is light, tempting drivers to go too fast, and the country has an appalling accident record. Concentrate every second—anything from a herd of goats to a child can appear from nowhere. There is a growing number of toll roads; keep some change handy for the tolls, which are reasonable.

Gas stations are plentiful on major routes, infrequent elsewhere. Most service stations will accept local garage cards (which are like store cards), but not credit cards, so carry enough cash. Windshield washing is standard. On long journeys, check the oil, water, and brakes before setting out, take a can of fuel (you can buy cans at larger gas stations), together with spare tires (and jack) and fan belt. Carry water, emergency food supplies, and a blanket in case you get stuck overnight. The AA of South Africa (see below) recommends remaining on national routes where help can be summoned quite easily.

Regulations Driving is on the left. The speed limit is 37 mph in built-up areas, 62 mph on rural roads, and 74 mph on freeways, unless otherwise indicated. There are severe fines for exceeding the designated speed limit. Yield to the right at intersections and traffic circles. Seat belts are compulsory. Always carry your driving license, and do not drive under the influence of alcohol. Traffic laws are strictly enforced and penalties are harsh.

The **Automobile Association of South Africa** (tel: 0800-010101) has reciprocal arrangements with many other driving associations and will give advice and travel information as well as arrange emergency rescues.

By air
Several small airlines together create an excellent network of domestic flights, serving surprisingly small towns and some of the main tourist sights. Fares are not particularly cheap, but there are usually discounts for advance booking. Chartering a small plane may not prove outrageously expensive if several of you can share the cost, and you may even be able to rent your own light aircraft, so take your pilot's license if you have one.
Nationwide Air (tel: 011-327 3000)
British Airways-Comair (tel: 011-921 0222)
SA Express, the domestic wing of SAA (tel: 011-978 5569)
SA Airlink (tel: 011-978 1111).

By train see page 234

By bus

Long-distance buses are a popular form of public transportation, with services around the clock on all inter-city routes. Always reserve in advance.

Greyhound (tel: Johannesburg 011-249 8700, fax: 011-830 1528; Cape Town 021-418 4310, fax: 021-418 4315; Durban 031-309 7830, fax: 031-309 7746)

Intercape (tel: 021-386 4400, fax: 021-386 2488, e-mail: marius@intercape. co.za)

Translux (tel: Johannesburg 011-774 3333, fax: 011-774 3318; Cape Town 021-449 3333, fax: 021-449 2545; Durban 031-308 8111)

The Baz Bus (tel: 021-439 2323, www. bazbus.com). Cheap hop-on-hop-off bus around main tourist attractions.

By minibus taxi

The cheapest (but most uncomfortable) way of getting around is via the growing army of taxis. They are now fanning out to provide a country-wide network of routes. There is no advance booking and no schedule; they simply wait until full (and that can mean 22 people in an eight-seater). Standards of maintenance and driving are sometimes dodgy, with a high accident rate, and the city depots are usually in the former

townships. They are not usually recommended for tourists.

Hitchhiking

Hitchhiking is not recommended anywhere in the country.

City transportation

There is little useful public transportation in South African cities. Durban has a bus service between the city and the surrounding suburbs provided by the **Mynah Shuttle** (tel: 031-309 4126) and **Aqualine** (tel: 031-309 4142). Cape Town and Johannesburg have infrequent and inefficient services, safe only in daylight hours.

Taxis are common, metered, and expensive in major cities, almost nonexistent in smaller towns. You cannot hail them on the street and taxi stands are rare. Most stores and restaurants will call one for you, even if you just walk in off the street.

Cape Town Marine Taxi (tel: 021-434 0434)

Durban Eagle Taxis (tel: 031-332 2911)

Johannesburg Maxi Taxis (tel: 011-648 1212)

Pretoria Rixi Mini Cabs (tel: 012-325 8072).

Durban is the only city in South Africa with a good local bus service

247

Student and youth travel

There is a growing range of good cut-price backpackers' accommodations, and student and youth discounts. Take an International Student Identity Card (ISIC) and join Hostelling International (the Youth Hostel Association) before you leave home.

Hostelling International South Africa (HISA), St. George's Mall, P.O. Box 4402, Cape Town 8000 (tel: 021-424 2511, fax: 021-424 4119, www.hisa. org.za) has youth hostel information and reservations and a budget travel and information service.

South African Student Travel Service (SASTS), P.O. Box 32544, Braamfontein (tel: 011-316 3045, fax: 011-339 7535). Student and youth discount cards, and a full student travel agency.

Communications

Media

Television and radio The South African Broadcasting Corporation operates three television services in 11 languages and 22 radio services in 11 languages. e-TV is a local independent TV channel (English). M-Net is a mainly English-language cable network. CNN and Sky TV are available outside SABC broadcasting hours (including the morning news); BBC World Service TV is available in a limited number of hotels; and satellite TV is also operational. One of the best radio stations is the English-language SAFM.

The press There are five daily and five Sunday national newspapers. The *Sowetan* has the highest circulation, followed by *The Star* and the *Sunday Times*. The *Weekly Mail & Guardian* has international news.

Post

There is a good postal service. For post office hours, see Opening times, page 245. General delivery facilities are available in the main post office in each town; take identification to claim mail.

Cape Town GPO, corner of Parliament and Darling streets (tel: 021-464 1700)

Durban GPO, corner of West and Gardiner streets (tel: 031-305 7521)

Johannesburg GPO, Sandton City (tel: 011-783 6312)

Pretoria Church Square Post Office (tel: 012-339 8000).

Telephones

The telephone system is good, with a reasonable number of public phones in the larger towns. Phonecards for green public phone booths are available in pubs, at newsstands, etc. Cash telephone kiosks operate on a minimum of 20 cents. Standard rates are Mon–Fri 7 AM–5 PM. At other times, including all weekend, Callmore Rates are 70 percent cheaper on local calls (50km radius), and about 50 percent cheaper for calls further afield. Prices for overseas calls are high and the markups in hotels are huge. **MTN** and **Vodacom** have 24-hour desks at all major international airports, offering rental of mobile phones.

- International dialing code for South Africa 27
- Domestic information 1023
- Domestic operator services 0020
- International information and other inquiries 0903
- International operator 0900
- International direct dial 09 + the country code
- International codes:

Australia 61; Botswana 267; Canada

1; Lesotho 266; Namibia 264; New Zealand 64; Swaziland 268; U.K. 44; U.S. 1; Zimbabwe 263.

South Africa is part of the Home Direct scheme and you can use most home telephone charge cards. Calling collect: Australia (tel: 0800-99 0061); Canada (tel: 0800-99 0014); U.K. (tel: 0800-9900 44); U.S. (AT&T) (tel: 0800-990 123).

Fax and e-mail

Most hotels and businesses have fax facilities. Local stationers or "copy shops" have public fax machines. Fax numbers are listed in the local telephone directory. Business hotels can arrange e-mail connections and there are many internet cafés. Multinational servers are present.

Language

There are 11 official languages—English, Afrikaans, Ndebele, Northern Sotho, Southern Sotho, Swazi, Tsonga, Tswana, Venda, Xhosa, and Zulu. The language of government and administration is English. Most people speak at least a smattering of English and Afrikaans.

Multilingual do's and don'ts

Washington D.C. 20008 (tel: 202/232 4400, fax: 202/265 1607).

Foreign embassies in South Africa
Australia
292 Orient Street, Arcadia, Pretoria (tel: 012-342 3740, fax: 012-342 8442)
Canada
1103 Arcadia Street, Hatfield (tel: 012-422 3000, fax: 012-422 3052)
Ireland
Tulbagh Park, 1234 Church Street, Colbyn, Pretoria (tel: 012-342 5062, fax: 012-342 4752)
New Zealand
1110 Arcadia Street, Hatfield (tel: 012-342 8656, fax: 012-342 8640)
U.K.
"Greystoke," 255 Hill Street, Arcadia (tel: 012-483 1200, fax: 012-483 1302)
U.S.A.
877 Pretorius Street, Arcadia (tel: 012-342 1048, fax: 012-342 2244).

Health
Inoculations It is worth taking polio, typhoid, and tetanus boosters and the ten-year hepatitis A vaccination.

Medical help Medical and hospital standards are excellent. Doctors are listed in local telephone directories under "Medical Practitioners." Pharmacies include:
Cape Town
K's Pharmacy, 52 Regent Road, Sea Point (tel: 021-434 9331. *Open* 9–9)
Rustenberg Pharmacy, Fountain Shopping Centre, Main Road, Rondebosch (tel: 021- 685 5998. *Open* 8:30 AM–10 PM)
Durban No 24-hour pharmacies. Medicine Chest Chemist, 155 Berea Road, Berea (tel: 031-305 6151. *Open* daily 8 AM–midnight)
Daynite Pharmacy, 9a Nedband Circle, corner of Point Road and West Street (tel: 031-368 3666. *Open* daily 7:30–11 PM)
Johannesburg
Daelite Pharmacy, Sandton (tel: 011-883 7520. *Open* until 10:30 PM daily)
Pretoria
Unitas Hospital, Clifton Avenue, Lyttleton (tel: 012-664 1100. *Open* 24 hours).

Hazards Aids is endemic with 49 percent of the sexually active population estimated to be HIV positive.

Emergencies

Police
To contact the South African Police (SAP), see listing SA Police Service under Government Departments in local telephone directories.

Emergency telephone numbers
Police, Emergency and Crisis Services (ambulance, fire, mountain rescue, etc): 10111 and ask for the relevant service
AA Breakdowns: tel: 0800-010101 toll free.

Embassies and consulates
South African embassies abroad
Australia
Rhodes Place, State Circle, Yarralumla, Canberra, ACT 2600 (tel: 6-273 2424, fax: 6-273 2669)
Canada
15 Sussex Drive, Ottawa, Ontario K1M 1M8 (tel: 613-744 0330, fax: 613-741 1639)
United Kingdom
Trafalgar Square, London WC2N 5DP (tel: 020-7451 7290, fax: 020-7451 7284)
United States
3051 Massachusetts Avenue, N.W.,

Blood for medical use is carefully screened and tested.

Check with a doctor if you are bitten by a snake, spider, scorpion, or an animal that might be carrying rabies, or if you stand on any creature in the ocean. Treat even minor grazes with caution, as there are parasites and poisonous plants to which you will have no immunity. Clean, disinfect, and cover any wound and see a doctor if it shows signs of going septic.

Malaria is found only in the Northern Province, Mpumalanga, and KwaZulu-Natal. You must take prophylactics if going into these areas or any of the surrounding countries. You must start taking the pills a week before you leave and continue to do so for four weeks after you return home. As the disease can take up to six months to develop, you should check with your doctor if you have flulike symptoms within this period.

Tap water is safe. In bush camps, check before drinking. Do not drink from rivers or lakes without purifying the water, and don't swim or paddle in natural water without checking. In certain areas, the water may be infected with bilharzia—and there is the possibility that crocodiles or hippos are lurking.

Take precautions in the sun. Wear a hat and high-factor sunblock, and stay in the shade during the intense midday heat. If you feel giddy in the sun, go indoors, drink large quantities of cool liquid, and have a cool bath. If you don't feel better, call a doctor, as you may have heatstroke.

If you are hiking in the mountains or in the desert, see **Surviving in the wilds** below.

Survival
The urban jungle Most South African cities have a bad security problem. Central Cape Town and Durban require normal vigilance and precautions in daylight hours, but large segments of Johannesburg are virtual no-go areas.

The first rule is to try not to look rich: don't walk the streets festooned

Guard against pickpockets when in vacation mood

in cameras or wearing jewelry. Use travelers' checks and credit cards wherever possible instead of carrying cash; take only what you need for the day, and always keep your money in several places. Never walk the streets after dark—take a taxi, however short the journey.

If you are mugged, hand over your valuables—do not resist. Wait until your assailant is out of sight before heading for the phone.

Try to make long-distance journeys in daylight and to reach your destination before dark. Keep car doors locked and wind up windows at traffic lights. Do not pick up hitch-hikers or stop to help people: if they seem to be in real trouble, telephone the nearest police station. Always park in well-lit and preferably busy places.

The former townships are generally unsafe for foreigners unless you go with an escorted tour.

251

Surviving in the wilds However cuddly they seem, many wild animals will happily take your hand off. Do not attempt to pet or feed animals, or even get out of the car for a better photo, without an experienced armed ranger.

When bush walking, always tell somebody where you are going and when you plan to be back. Wear desert boots with good treads and ankle support, thick socks, and long trousers to protect your legs against thorns and wildlife.

Take a hat, sunglasses, and high-factor sunblock, a long stick for dealing with unwanted wildlife, a water bottle, and emergency high-energy rations (such as trail mix).

A foil space blanket, some analgesic tablets, water purifiers, antihistamines in case of any allergic reaction (after a bite), insect repellent, and adhesive bandages are useful for emergencies.

If you stumble on a snake, try not to provoke it. If bitten, stay calm, but get immediate help. Keep checking for spiders, scorpions, and ticks; if you are bitten seek immediate medical advice.

When camping, take warm clothes for the evening and wet- and cold-weather gear in the mountains. Shake out your sleeping bag before you get in and hang your shoes upside down to deter creepie-crawlies. Keep food well sealed and out of reach of ants and monkeys.

Be careful about swimming on empty beaches. The African seas are treacherous with dangerous currents and riptides. Never let children swim unattended or go into the surf on rafts. If the beach is packed but nobody is swimming, there is probably a good reason. Many beaches have lifeguards but they are not on duty around the clock.

Other information

Camping
South Africa has a network of pleasant campsites, with shady pitches, and good washing and cooking facilities (including your own *braai*/barbecue and a generous stack of wood). Larger campgrounds may have self-catering cottages, a store, gas station, swimming pool, and restaurant. Travelers

252

Camping is popular and facilities are excellent

with trailers or campers (RVs) are unlikely to find individual hookups for electricity, water, etc. The South African Automobile Association publishes an annual guide to good campsites, available from them (tel: 011-483 3044) or local bookshops.

Camping rough is not a good idea for security reasons.

Camper rental:
Britz (Johannesburg tel: 011-396 1860 or toll-free 0800-117 460, fax: 011-396 1937; Cape Town tel: 021-981 8947, fax: 021-981 8946; Durban tel: 031-729 326, 031-729 239. www.britz.com). South Africa's largest campervan and 4WD rental with offices around the country.
Buffalo Camper and 4x4 Hire (tel: 011-704 1300, fax: 011-462 5266, e-mail: campers@buffalo.co.za)
Campers Corner (Johannesburg tel: 011-787 9105, fax: 011-886 3187; Cape Town tel: 021-905 1503, fax: 021-905 4493. www.campers.co.za)
Camper Vacations (tel/fax: 011-392 1051, e-mail: camvac@iafrica.com)
Holiday Camper Hire (tel: 011-708 2176, fax: 011-708 1464, www.argo-navis.com/campers)
Knysna Camper Hire (tel: 044-382 2444, fax: 044-382 5887, e-mail: knysnacampers@pixie.co.za).

Children
South Africa is probably the most child-friendly country in Africa, with a fine climate, glorious beaches, entertainment, good food and hygiene, and excellent health care. There are plenty of family accommodations options, including some with self-catering and campgrounds, and for fussy eaters pizzas and hamburgers are on tap. Stores are well stocked with all the essentials from diapers to formula and baby food, and finding reliable babysitters is easy. The only drawbacks are the various stinging and biting creatures that lurk in long grass and under water; the ferocity of the midday sun; and the enormous

distances when touring. Take plenty of snacks and entertainments and make sure your children wear sunblock, hats, and shoes when outside. Keep them in view and make sure they are properly supervised by a strong swimmer in the sea. There can be treacherous tides and waves as well as jellyfish, sea urchins, and even the occasional stray shark.

Only children over the age of four are permitted on game-viewing expeditions organized by private safari companies and lodges. If you have your own transportation, they can start younger, but remember that children have a limited attention span and are not disposed to sit quietly while watching the animals. Also, peak game-viewing times are early morning and late afternoon/early evening—which may disrupt schedules for young children. Many upscale hotels will not accept children under 12.

253

Parent-free breaks
Several companies offer parent-free adventure breaks, from one day and upward, for older children (usually seven to nine years and up), with everything on offer from volleyball to rappelling, and canoeing to ecology classes:
The Wilderness Trust of South Africa P.O. Box 577, Bedfordview 2008 (tel: 011-453 7645)

National Environmental Adventure Trust P.O. Box 260, Gilletts 3603 (tel: 031-77 3334).

For a list of other organizations running breaks for children and young people, try the Department of Environmental Affairs and Tourism, tel: 012-310 3707, or regional tourist information offices.

Visitors with disabilities
Many major sights and hotels have ramps and toilets for people who use wheelchairs, but facilities vary. Staff are usually willing to assist those with special requirements.
National Council for the Physically Disabled in South Africa (tel: 011-726 8040, fax: 011-726 5705, e-mail: ncppdsa@cis.co.za)
South African National Council for the Blind (tel: 012-346 1190)
South African National Council for the Deaf (tel: 011-482 1610)
National Accessibility Scheme Satour (tel: 012-482 6200)
Flamingo Adventure Tours/Disabled Ventures, P.O. Box 60554, Flamingo Square 7441, Western Cape (tel/fax: 021-557 4496, www.time2travel.com/ct/flamingo/index. Tours of the Western Cape for travelers with disabilities, with specially adapted vehicles and a registered nurse as tour guide. Also mainstream tours. For information before you travel:
U.K.—RADAR (Royal Association for Disability and Rehabilitation), 12 City Forum, 250 City Road, London EC1V 8AF (tel: 020-7250 3222, fax: 020-7250 1212, minicom: 020-7250 4119).
U.S.A.—SATH (Society for the Advancement of Travel for the Handicapped), 347 Fifth Avenue, Suite 610, New York NY10016 (tel: 212-447-7284, fax: 212-725-8253).

Senior citizens
There are some facilities for senior citizens, but most are for South African nationals only. Keep proof of your age handy and you may be able to get discounts on some national

The Jama Madjid mosque, Durban

parks accommodations, movie and theater tickets, and some restaurants. **The Association for Retired Persons and Pensioners (ARP&P)** (tel: 021-531 1768).

Maps
There is a wide range of free maps of the country, regions, and cities available from SATOUR. Most are as good or better than anything on sale, other than the full A–Z city plans, which are very comprehensive. CNA booksellers are probably the best places to buy commercial maps, while hiking trail maps are available from the national parks shops.

Measurements
South Africa uses the metric system.

Places of worship
You will find Christian churches of every denomination, from Catholic, Anglican and Dutch Reformed to a variety of evangelical sects throughout the country. With large Jewish, Indian, and Malay populations, there are also synagogues, mosques, and Hindu temples. Check the telephone directory.

Electricity
220–240 V A.C. 50 Hertz. Plugs have three round pins. Power is reliable in cities, but you may experience some problems in remote areas, and bush camps may not be equipped with electricity, so take a flashlight. Appliances may need a converter.

Tipping
Tipping is common, but not obligatory. Give waiters and taxi drivers 10 percent and porters R4–R5 per bag. Many hotels run a staff box at the front desk for one lump sum on checkout. Otherwise, give a few rand to the room staff and doorman. Tip tour guides and game rangers at least R20–R25 a head per day.

Toilets
Most tourist venues, service stations, and shopping centers have good public toilets. In nature reserves, parks, and at the seaside they can be primitive but are usually spotless. There may be a small fee.

CONVERSION CHARTS

FROM	TO	MULTIPLY BY
Inches	Centimeters	2.54
Centimeters	Inches	0.3937
Feet	Meters	0.3048
Meters	Feet	3.2810
Yards	Meters	0.9144
Meters	Yards	1.0940
Miles	Kilometers	1.6090
Kilometers	Miles	0.6214
Acres	Hectares	0.4047
Hectares	Acres	2.4710
Gallons	Liters	4.5460
Liters	Gallons	0.2200
Ounces	Grams	28.35
Grams	Ounces	0.0353
Pounds	Grams	453.6
Grams	Pounds	0.0022
Pounds	Kilograms	0.4536
Kilograms	Pounds	2.205
Tons	Tonnes	1.0160
Tonnes	Tons	0.9842

MEN'S SUITS
U.K.	36	38	40	42	44	46	48
Rest of Europe	46	48	50	52	54	56	58
U.S.	36	38	40	42	44	46	48

DRESS SIZES
U.K.	8	10	12	14	16	18
France	36	38	40	42	44	46
Italy	38	40	42	44	46	48
Rest of Europe	34	36	38	40	42	44
U.S.	6	8	10	12	14	16

MEN'S SHIRTS
U.K.	14	14.5	15	15.5	16	16.5	17
Rest of Europe	36	37	38	39/40	41	42	43
U.S.	14	14.5	15	15.5	16	16.5	17

MEN'S SHOES
U.K.	7	7.5	8.5	9.5	10.5	11
Rest of Europe	41	42	43	44	45	46
U.S.	8	8.5	9.5	10.5	11.5	12

WOMEN'S SHOES
U.K.	4.5	5	5.5	6	6.5	7
Rest of Europe	38	38	39	39	40	41
U.S.	6	6.5	7	7.5	8	8.5

255

Tourist services

Tourist services in South Africa
The South African Tourist Board has only one office in South Africa: **SATOUR Head Office**, 442 Rigel Avenue South, Erasmusrand 0181 (Private Bag X164), Pretoria 0001 (tel: 012-347 0600, fax: 012-347 8745, e-mail: satour@icon.co.za). Provincial tourist office addresses are listed at the start of each chapter in the A–Z section of this book. Local details are given in each town listing.

SATOUR abroad
Australia Level 6, 285 Clarence Street, Sydney, NSW 2000 (tel: 02-9261 3424, e-mail: satbysyd@ozemail.com.au)
Benelux: Jozef Israelskade 48, 1072SB Amsterdam (tel: 020-471 4656, fax: 662 9761, e-mail: heldoorn@satour.nl)
U.K. 5 Alt Grove, London SW19 4DZ (tel: 020-8944 8080, fax: 020-8944 6705, e-mail: satour@satbuk.demon. co.uk)
U.S.A. 500 Fifth Avenue, 20th Floor, New York, NY 10017 (tel: 212-730-2929, fax: 212-764 1980, www. satour.org).

National Parks
Most game parks provide accommodations with basic *rondavels* (huts) and camping; larger ones have a lodge with hotel-standard accommodations. All have at least one restaurant, a provisions store, and gas; some have their own post office, fax, and laundry. Opening hours for all parks are from sunrise to sunset (roughly 6–6); reach the gate well before then to allow time to drive to the camp. The self-catering camps are very popular and it is worth reserving in writing well in advance (up to a year), especially in local school and public holidays. For details of individual parks, see the A–Z section. (See also **Surviving in the wilds**, page 252.)
National Parks Board P.O. Box 787, Pretoria 0001 (tel: 012-343 1991, fax: 012-343 0905, www.parks-sa.co.za). Operates 11 of the major parks, including Kruger.
KZN Nature Conservation Services, P.O. Box 13069, Cascades, Pietermaritzburg 3202 (tel: 033-845 1000, fax: 033-845 1299, www.kznncs. org.za). Manages all parks in KwaZulu-Natal.
Many smaller parks and reserves run by local conservation bodies offer walking, hiking, and climbing. For further information:
Cape Nature Conservation P.O. Box X9086, Cape Town (tel: 021-483 4083)
Department of Nature Conservation P.O. Box 517, Bloemfontein, Free State (tel: 051-405 5263)
Transvaal Nature Conservation Private Bag X209, Pretoria 0001 (tel: 012-323 3403).

A self-drive tour in the Kruger

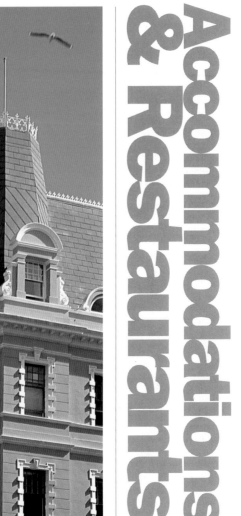

Accommodations & Restaurants

ACCOMMODATIONS

Central Booking

Bed 'n' Breakfast
P.O. Box 91309, Auckland Park 2006
tel: 011-482 2206/7 fax: 011-726 6915
e-mail: reed.res@pixie.co.za
In the U.K. tel: 01787-228 494.
Central headquarters for small guesthouses, bed-and-breakfasts, and self-catering establishments throughout South Africa.

The Cape Collection
P.O. Box 41465, Sea Point 8060 tel: 021-419 1854 fax: 021-425 3861 www.fortesking.co.za
A small but varied collection of hotels around Cape Town, the Winelands, and Garden Route.

CCAfrica ($$$)
Pinmill Park, Block F, Katherine Street, Sanddown, Private Bag X27, Benmore, 2010, Gauteng tel: 011-775 0000 fax: 011-784 7667 www.ccafrica.com
Small, exclusive, and very luxurious lodges on private game reserves.

Holiday Inn
P.O. Box 782553, 2146 Sandton
tel: 011-780 0143 fax: 011-780 0257
bookings, in the U.K. tel: 0800-897 121 (toll-free); in the U.S.A. (toll-free)
tel: 800-421 8905 www.basshotels.com
Large chain of hotels, including the local Holiday Inns in their many incarnations.

Hostelling International South Africa
3rd floor, St. George's House, 73 St. George's Mall (P.O. Box 4402), Cape Town 8001
tel: 021-424 2511 fax: 021-424 4119
www.hisa.org.za
The local youth hostel affiliate.

Jacana Country Homes and Trails
P.O. Box 95212, Waterkloof 0145
tel: 012-346 3550/1/2 fax: 012-346 2499
e-mail: jacana@lia.co.za
Central marketing for a wide range of farm stays and country cottages.

Leading Independent Hotels of Southern Africa
P.O. Box 598, Pennington 4184, KwaZulu-Natal tel: 039-975 1056 fax: 039-975 1057
www.braddens.co.za

National Parks Board
643 Leyds Street, Muckleneuk (PO Box 787, Pretoria 0001 tel: 012-343 1991
fax: 012-343 0905 and 44 Long Street, Cape Town, PO Box 7400, Rogge Bay 8012
tel: 021-422 2810 fax: 021-424 6211
Accommodations in the national parks, from campsites to lodges.

Portfolio Town and Country Retreats
Shop 5E, Mutual Square, Oxford Road, Rosebank, 2196 Johannesburg
tel: 011-880 3414 fax: 011-788 4802
www.portfoliocollection.co.za
Central marketing for a wide range of guesthouses and small hotels throughout South Africa, from the most basic to the most luxurious.

Protea Hotels
5th Floor, Nedbank Foreshore Building, Heerengracht, Cape Town 8000
tel: 021-419 5320 fax: 021-425 2956

www.protea-hotels.co.za
The largest South African chain; most hotels are comfortable and reasonably priced, if lacking in atmosphere.

Relais Hotels
P.O. Box 654, Cape Town 8000
tel: 021-423 1426 or 0800-600 889 (toll-free)
fax: 021-423 1439 www.relais.co.za
Luxury small and suite hotels, most in the Cape.

Small Exclusive Hotels of Southern Africa
5 Orwell Court, 13 Orwell Place, Ipswich, Suffolk IP4 1BD, U.K. tel: 01473-225 844 fax: 01473-226 199).
Atmospheric, well-appointed hotels serving excellent meals.

Sun International
P.O. Box 784487, 2146 Sandton
tel: 011-780 7444 fax: 011-780 7701
In the U.K. tel: 01491-411 222;
in the U.S.A. tel: 954/713 2501
A range of hotels from the very comfortable to the totally luxurious, including Sun City. Most with casinos.

The best cheap accommodations are in small bed-and-breakfasts that have only a couple of rooms and have not been listed here. Ask agencies or local tourist offices for recommendations. The following recommended hotels have been divided into three price categories:
- budget ($)—under $50
- moderate ($$)—$50–$150
- expensive ($$$)—above $150

WESTERN CAPE

Cape Town and the Cape Peninsula

Cape Grace ($$$)
West Quay, V&A Waterfront, Cape Town
tel: 021-410 7100 fax: 021-419 7622
www.capegrace.com
Luxury country-house style hotel right on the V&A Waterfront, with seamless efficiency and comfort and excellent food.

Cape Victoria ($$)
corner of Wigtown and Torbay roads, Greenpoint tel/fax: 021-439 7721
A turn-of-the-century guesthouse on the slopes of Signal Hill, with gardens and views.

Cellars-Hohenort ($$$)
93 Brommersvlei Road, Constantia
tel: 021-794 2137 fax: 021-794 2149
www.cellars-hohenort.com
Magnificent small Cape Dutch hotel with extensive gardens, great views of Table Mountain, and a restaurant with delectable food. Swimming pool, riding.

iKhaya Guest Lodge ($$)
Dunkley Square, Cape Town
tel: 021-461 8880 fax: 021-461 8889
Small African-style lodge in the city center, magnificently designed with carvings and handcrafted furniture. Some self-catering apartments.

Kensington Place ($$)
38 Kensington Crescent, Higgovale
tel: 021-424 4744 fax: 021-424 1810
www.kensingtonplace.co.za

Small, luxurious furnished guesthouse (eight rooms) in a residential suburb at the foot of Table Mountain. Pool.

Mount Nelson ($$$)
76 Orange Street, Cape Town
tel: 021-423 1050 fax: 021-424 7472
www.mountnelson.co.za
An elegant pink hotel in the heart of the city, the "Nellie" is one of the world's greatest historic hotels. It also has three of Cape Town's finest restaurants. Swimming pools.

The Town House ($)
60 Corporation Street tel: 021-465 7050
fax: 021-465 3891 www.townhouse.co.za
Modern, well-designed city center hotel.

Travellers Inn ($)
208 Long Street, Cape Town
tel: 021-424 9272 fax: 021-424 9278
A clean, budget backpackers' B&B in a historic Victorian gingerbread mansion in the city center.

Victoria Junction ($$)
Corner of Somerset and Ebenezer roads,
Gallows Hill, Cape Town tel: 021-428 1234
fax: 021-418 5678 e-mail: vicjunct@icon.co.za
A Protea hotel in the city center, heavy on the chrome, glass-brick, and spotlights.

Vineyard ($$)
Colinton Road, off Protea Road, Newlands
tel: 021-683 3044 fax: 021-683 3365
www.vineyard.co.za
Large Georgian country house hotel, built originally for a local socialite, Lady Anne Barnard. Carefully restored and furnished with antiques. Set in beautiful gardens on the Liesbeeck River, with superb mountain views. Swimming pool and excellent French restaurant.

The Winelands, Breede Valley, and West Coast

L'Auberge du Quartier Français ($$/$$$)
Huguenot Street, Franschhoek
tel: 021-876 2151 fax: 021-876 3105
www.lqf.co.za
Elegant country house hotel, with two superb restaurants: Le Quartier, serving formal French cuisine, and the outdoor Café Français, with Cape Provincial cuisine. Reservations advised.

Bushman's Kloof ($$$)
P.O. Box 53405, Kenilworth 7645, Cape Town,
21 miles from Clanwilliam, off the R364
tel: 021-797 0990 fax: 021-761 5551
www.bushmanskloof.co.za
Luxury manor set in a vast private reserve with 34 species of mammal, over 140 species of bird, and a magnificent collection of San art in some 125 sites. Pool, game drives, art walks, bird-watching, and many other activities.

De Ouwe Werf ($$)
30 Church Street, Stellenbosch
tel: 021-887 4608 fax: 021-887 4626
e-mail: ouwewerf@iafrica.com
B&B in a centrally located house built in 1803. Light lunches, traditional Cape and continental fare, and homemade cakes. Swimming pool.

Diemersfontein Country House ($$)
R303 between Paarl and Wellington
tel: 021-873 2671 fax: 021-864 2095
In the Wellington wine region, this private, friendly

hotel offers traditional Cape hospitality. Swimming pool, riding.

The Farmhouse ($$)
Langebaan tel: 022-772 2060
fax: 022-772 7980
Country house overlooking the Langebaan lagoon. Home-cooked meals. Swimming pool.

Grande Roche ($$$)
5 Plantasie Road, Paarl tel: 021-863 2727
fax: 021-863 2220).
A sumptuous hotel in the heart of the famous Paarl vineyards. Long wine list. Swimming pool.

Kagga Kamma ($$$)
60 miles north of Ceres tel: 021-863 8334
fax: 021-863 8383 www.kaggakamma.co.za
"The Place of the Bushmen" is a private game reserve, with resident San population, in the Cederberg. Accommodations consist of a camp with chalets and the Bushmen Lodge. The (very high) price includes all meals and excursions.

Lanzerac Hotel ($$$)
Jonkershoek Road, Stellenbosch
tel: 021-887 1132 fax: 021-887 2310
e-mail: info@lanzerac.co.za
Hotel in a 150-year-old Cape Dutch homestead on the outskirts of Stellenbosch. The restaurant serves traditional Malay fare.

Marine Protea Hotel ($$)
Voortrekker Street, Lamberts Bay
tel: 027-432 1126 fax: 027-432 1036
Historic hotel in a part of the Cape famous for its crayfish; the restaurant is renowned for its seafood.

Mooikelder Manor House ($$)
Agter–Paarl Road, North Paarl
tel: 021-863 8491 fax: 021-863 8361
Close to Paarl, this lovely Cape Dutch homestead (1835) includes Cecil John Rhodes among its past owners. Friendly, enthusiastic hospitality and antique furnishings. Normally bed-and-breakfast; other meals on request. Pool.

Strassberger's Hotel ($/$$)
Clanwilliam tel: 027-482 1101
fax: 027-482 2678
Relaxing, historic hotel. Swimming pool.

The South Coast, Garden Route, and Karoo

Arniston Hotel ($$)
Arniston tel: 028-445 9000
fax: 028-445 9633
A comfortable hotel in a 200-year-old fishing village. Good seafood restaurant. Swimming pool and water sports. Alternatively, book a self-catering cottage ($) from Arniston Seaside Cottages (tel: 02847-59772).

Belvidere Manor ($$)
Knysna tel: 044-387 1055
fax: 044-387 1059 www.belvidere.co.za
Historic house with Victorian-style cottages, each with a fireplace, next to Knysna lagoon. Excellent restaurant. Swimming pool, boating.

Eight Bells Mountain Inn ($$)
22 miles from Mossel Bay on the Oudtshoorn road tel: 044-631 0000 fax: 044-631 0004
www.eightbells.co.za
Superbly situated for the coast and the Karoo, this is a luxurious little resort with *rondavels* (huts),

Accommodations and Restaurants

Swiss-style chalets, and an excellent country restaurant.

Fancourt Hotel and Country Club ($$)
Montague Street, George tel: 044-870 8282
fax: 044-870 7605 www.fancourt.co.za
Exclusive and luxurious health, golf, and leisure center, now run by Orient Express Hotels. Also has a play center for children.

Hog Hollow ($$)
Askop Road, P.O. Box 503, Plettenberg Bay 6600 tel: 044-534 8879 fax: 044-534 8879
www.hoghollow.co.za.
A friendly, unpretentious 12-room lodge in a private reserve, 11 miles east of Plettenberg Bay, with a wonderful restaurant.

Hunter's Country House ($$)
6 miles from Plettenberg Bay on the N2 to Knysna tel: 044-532 7818
fax: 044-532 7878 www.hunterhotels.com
Exclusive country hotel, with cozy thatched cottages scattered across manicured gardens on the edge of the last remaining indigenous forests. Superb dinner. Swimming pool, riding.

Klippe Rivier Homestead ($)
6 miles west of Swellendam
tel: 028-514 3341 fax: 028-514 3337
A delightful Cape Dutch homestead with antique furnishings, close to historic Swellendam.

Lord Milner Hotel ($/$$)
Logan Road Matjiesfontein 6901
tel: 023-551 3011 fax: 023-551 3020
The tiny village of Matjiesfontein is a national monument, and this hotel harks back to the days when the British aristocracy came to take the Klein-(Little) Karoo air. There is a variety of restaurants (some requiring jacket and tie) as well as a Victorian country pub.

Old Post Office Tree Manor ($$)
Market Street, Mossel Bay
tel: 044-691 3738 fax: 044-691 3104
Comfortable central guesthouse with antique furnishings, in the third-oldest building in town.

The Plettenberg ($$$)
Plettenberg Bay tel: 044-533 2030 fax: 044-533 2074 e-mail: plettenberg@pixie.co.za
Highly comfortable, modern hotel on a rocky headland, with magnificent views and a fine restaurant. Swimming pool.

Rosenhof Country Lodge ($$)
264 Baron van Rheede Street, Oudtshoorn
tel: 044-272 2232 fax: 044-222 3021
Delightful small Victorian hotel with antique furnishings and a fine country restaurant.

Swartberg Hotel ($/$$)
Main Street, Prince Albert tel: 023-541 1332
fax: 023-541 1383
Delightful old Victorian hotel with an interesting history, a friendly laid-back atmosphere, and good country cooking.

EASTERN CAPE

The Cock House ($)
10 Market Street, Grahamstown 6140
tel: 046-636 1295 fax: 046-636 1287
A delightful small guesthouse, built in 1830 and now a National Monument. The food is highly recommended.

Die Tuishuise ($)
36 Market Street, Cradock
tel: 048-881 1322 fax: 048-881 5388
e-mail: tuishuise@eastcape.net
A wonderful hotel with 11 lovingly restored houses, all filled with antiques and each distinctively different. The price of a room gets you a whole house.

Drostdy Hotel ($$)
30 Church Street, Graaff-Reinet
tel: 049-892 2161 fax: 049-892 4582
Designed in 1806 by the noted Cape Dutch architect Louis Thibault, and carefully restored. The rooms are in 1855 slave cabins. Pool.

Hacklewood Hill Country House ($$)
152 Prospect Road, Walmer, Port Elizabeth
tel: 041-581 1300 fax: 041-581 4155
www.pehotels.co.za
This charming, sophisticated Victorian house has been restored and furnished with magnificent antiques. The atmosphere is calm and elegant, the welcome friendly, and the food delicious.

The Halyards Resort Hotel ($$)
Port Alfred 6170 tel: 046-624 2410
fax: 046-624 2466
Resort hotel at the mouth of the Kowie River. Rooms have private balconies overlooking the marina. Water sports, riding.

Settlers Inn ($$)
N2 Highway, below the 1820s Settlers Memorial tel: 046-622 7313 fax: 046-622 4951 email: settlersinn@intekom.co.za
A pleasant modern hotel overlooking Grahamstown, with good food, a pool, and views.

Shamwari Game Reserves ($$$)
45 miles from Port Elizabeth on the banks of the Bushmans River tel: 042-203 1111
fax: 042-235 1224
e-mail: shamwaribooking@global.co.za
Luxury private game reserve, with accommodations in a restored manor house and settler homes. Swimming pools. Game viewing. Expensive, but includes all meals and game drives.

Tsitsikamma Lodge ($$)
on the N2, about 9 miles from the entrance to the Tsitsikamma National Park
tel: 042-750 3802 fax: 042-750 3702
e-mail: tsitsilodge@pixie.co.za
Comfortable log cabins, pretty gardens, a pool, forest walks, and fishing at this early-to-bed resort.

Umngazi River Bungalows ($$)
about 11 miles west of Port St. Johns, Wild Coast tel: 047-564 1115-9
www.epages.net/umngaz
A coastal hideaway with whitewashed thatched cottages and grassy slopes down to the river, dunes, and coastal forest. Fishing, hiking, water sports. Other cheaper Wild Coast hotels include **Trennery's** (tel: 047-498 0004), and the **Kob Inn** (tel/fax: 047-499 0011).

THE FREE STATE, NORTHERN CAPE, AND NORTH-WEST PROVINCE

The Free State
Cranberry Cottage ($)
37 Beeton Street, Ladybrand
tel: 051-924 2290 fax: 051-924 1168
www.cranberrycottage.co.za

A charmingly decorated old sandstone house filled with antiques and fine art in the heart of the Eastern Highlands, with terraces, mature gardens, and real log fires.

De Oude Kraal ($$)
22 miles south of Bloemfontein
tel: 051-564 0636 fax: 051-564 0635
e-mail: deoude@interkom.co.za
Historic country house with pleasant rooms and excellent traditional restaurant.

Franshoek Mountain Lodge ($)
2 miles east of S384/S385 junction,
Ficksburg, Eastern Highlands
tel/fax: 051-933 3938
Small, intimate sandstone and thatch lodge in a valley at the foot of the Witteberg. Good country cooking. Swimming pool, hiking, fishing, climbing, polo.

Northern Cape
Chateau Guesthouse ($)
9 Coetzee Street, Upington
tel/fax: 054-332 6504
Comfortable, art deco-style B&B near the town center.

Egerton House ($)
5 Egerton Road, Belgravia, Kimberley
tel: 053-831 1150 fax: 053-831 1785
e-mail: egerton@kimberley.co.za
A superbly restored and beautifully decorated historic home run by a diamond history enthusiast. Swimming pool and tea garden; lunch and dinner on request.

Gariep Lodge ($$)
Main Street, Okiep, 24 miles east of Upington,
on the Olifantshoek road tel: 027-744 1000
fax: 027-744 1114 e-mail: giulia@cis.co.za
A real Kalahari getaway with small cabins and tents scattered across the dunes in a small private game reserve on the banks of the Orange River. All meals under the stars.

Tswalu ($$)
P.O. Box 420, Kathu 8446, near the Kgalagadi
Transfrontier Park tel: 053-781 9311
fax: 053-781 9316
e-mail: tswalures@kimberley.co.za
The largest private game reserve in South Africa, exclusive Tswalu is made up of a stone and thatch lodge with nine cottages, set in 347 square miles of desertscape, from scrub bush to rolling red-gold sand dunes. There are around 40 species of mammal and 250 species of bird. Activities include game drives, walks, and horseback rides.

North-West Province
Lindbergh Lodge ($$)
P.O. Box 412331, Craighall 2024, on the main
Johannesburg/Kimberley/Cape Town road tel:
011-884 8923/4 fax: 011-884 8925
www.lindberghlodge.co.za
Luxury lodge in 25,000-acre game reserve, close to a water hole with hide. Self-catering cottages, swimming pool, tennis, golf. Game-viewing, walks, mountain bikes, horses.

Madikwe River Lodge ($$)
Derdepoort tel: 014-778 0891
fax: 014-778 0893
e-mail: madikwe@country-escapes.co.za
"Big Five" game viewing at this exclusive game

lodge close to the Botswana border, with luxury chalet overlooking the Marico River. Price includes everything. Swimming pool.

Sun City ($/$$/$$$)
46 miles from Rustenburg; reservations
through Sun International; welcome center
tel: 014-557 3133
South Africa's first and largest casino and entertainment complex, next to the Pilanesberg National Park. Accommodations to suit all pockets: simple family self-catering units at the Cabanas, the comfortable but ordinary Sun City itself, the plusher Cascades, and the ultra-luxurious Palace at the Lost City. Magnificent swimming pools, golf course, water slides, and other sporting activities. See also page 145.

GAUTENG

Johannesburg
The Cottages ($)
30 Gill Street, Observatory tel: 011-487 2829
fax: 011-487 2404
Stylish stone and thatch cottages in large grounds with pool, English gardens, and a hiking trail; dinner on request. Less than 20 minutes from the airport.

Sandton Sun ($$$)
Fifth Street, Sandton tel: 011-780 5000
fax: 011-780 5002
Large and luxurious city hotel, beloved of visiting businessmen and dignitaries.

Thandidille Mountain Lodge ($$)
5 Linda Place, corner of Cliffside Cresent,
Northcliff Ext. 12 tel: 011-476 1887
fax: 011-678 0371
Ten luxurious, individually designed rooms with private patios overlook lush gardens and fine views. Lunch and dinner on request.

The Westcliff ($$$)
67 Jan Smuts Avenue Westcliff 2193
tel: 011-646 2400 fax: 011-646 3500
www.orient-expresshotels.com
Orient Express runs some of the finest hotels and it has achieved its exacting standards with this magnificent salmon-pink place set on a hillside with superb city views. The food is excellent, the service impeccable, and a shuttle bus runs up the steep hill between the rooms and reception.

Pretoria
The Farm Inn ($$)
The Willows, on main road east of Pretoria
tel: 012-809 0266 fax: 012-809 0146
Thatched cottages spread across a working farm with domestic animals, game, and a pool. Children welcome.

Marvol Manor House ($$$)
358 Aries Street, Waterkloof Rodge
tel: 012-346 1774 fax: 012-346 1776
e-mail: mhrelais@satis.co.za
Stately Cape Dutch-style with 11 well-equipped rooms. Facilities include a gym, sauna, two pools, chauffeurs and secretarial service.

Oxnead ($$)
Morreleta Park, Pretoria
tel: 012-984 515 fax: 012-998 9168
This pretty Cape Georgian-style guesthouse serves

superb food and vintage wines in a luxury setting. Swimming pool.

Sheraton Pretoria ($$$)
Corner of Church and Lleyds streets, Arcadia tel: 012-342 4747 fax: 012-342 4741 e-mail: sheraton@iafrica.com
Large modern city hotel next to the Union Buildings, up to the usual Sheraton standards of comfort. Ask for a room with a view.

Elsewhere in Gauteng
Lesedi Cultural Village ($$)
Honeydew, 26 miles from Johannesburg on the R512 tel: 012-205 1394 fax: 012-205 1433 e-mail: lesedi@pixie.co.za
An imaginative development based on Pedi, Sotho, Xhosa, and Zulu traditional culture, with accommodations in traditionally built village houses.

Mount Grace Hotel ($$$)
Magaliesburg tel: 014-577 1350 fax: 014-577 1202
Rustic chic is the keynote at this country house hotel with its thatched cottages and English-style gardens. The food is excellent and there are monthly classical concerts.

262

NORTHERN PROVINCE

The Coach House ($$/$$$)
Agatha, 9 miles from Tzaneen, in the Magoebaskloof Mountains tel: 015-307 3641 fax: 015-307 1466 e-mail: coachhouse@mweb.co.za
This 19th-century coaching inn has delightfully comfortable rooms, panoramic views, and some of the finest food in South Africa. Swimming pool. The same management also runs two other excellent properties locally, the **Magoebaskloof Hotel** ($$) (tel: 015-276 4276, fax: 015-276 4280), and the **Troutwaters Inn** and **Lakeside Chalets** ($) (tel: 015-276 4245).

Elephant Springs Hotel ($)
31 Sutter Road, Warmbaths tel: 014-736 2101 fax: 014-736 3586
Comfortable, antique furnished, colonial hotel within walking distance of the hot springs.

Thornybush Game Reserve ($$$)
Northlands, Hoedspruit tel: 011-883 7918 fax: 011-883 8201 www.thornybush.co.za
Four separate camps range from a bush lodge to a tented camp in this luxury private reserve on the Kruger fringes.

MPUMALANGA

Luxury lodges at Kruger
Most of the lodges scattered through Sabie Sand and Timbavati (see pages 186–187) are similar in style, with a large private game park, and small camps with thatched cottages dotted around a central block. The complex is usually open to the bush with animals, from monkeys to elephant, wandering through at will. All meals are outdoors in good weather, with breakfast and lunch on the terrace, overlooking a water hole or river. Dinner is taken around the bonfire in a boma (open-air enclosure, with fencing against animals and the

wind). All those listed provide the highest quality service, accommodations, food, atmosphere, and game viewing. All have swimming pools. Prices are high, but are usually inclusive (check before booking). You are paying not only for world-class luxury accommodations, but for the upkeep of an expensive private game reserve. If only for a couple of nights, it is worth splashing out ($$$$ means very expensive). The telephone and fax numbers are for reservations.

Inyati ($$$)
Sabie Sand tel: 011-493 0755 and 013-735 5125 fax: 011-493 0837 and 013-735 5032 e-mail: inyatigl@iafrica.com
Small, friendly lodge, with luxuriously appointed thatched chalets, on the Sand River.

Londolozi ($$$$)
Sabie Sand tel: 011-784 7077 fax: 011-784 7667 e-mail: information@conscorp.co.za
Three luxurious camps along the Sand River. The Conservation Corporation also operates tiny **Singita** nearby, and **Ngala**, the only private lodge within the boundaries of the park itself.

Mala Mala ($$$$)
Sabie Sand tel: 011-789 2677/ 013-735 5661 fax: 011-886 4382 www.malamala.co.za
One of the best-known exclusive resorts in South Africa, patronized by the international jet set.

Sabi Sabi ($$$$)
Sabie Sand tel: 011-483 3939/ 013-735 5656 fax: 011-483 3799 www.sabisabi.com in the U.K. tel: 020-8544 0151)
Six miles of river frontage, and three luxurious lodges, including tree and tented camps. The emphasis here is on expert, personalized service. Game-ranger training courses available.

Ulusaba ($$$)
Sabi Sand tel: 011-465 4240/ 013-735 5460 fax: 011-465 6649 www.ulusaba.com
One of the most dramatic of the small reserves; Rock Lodge teeters on the rocks of a large *kopje* (hillock), and Safari Lodge has stilted canopy treehouses.

Hotels outside Kruger Park
Casa do Sol ($$/$$$)
near Hazyview, on R536 to Sabie tel: 013-737 8111 fax: 013-737 8166
Designed like a Spanish village, in the heart of little Ilanga Nature Reserve, with African waiters in French berets and smocks, this hotel appeals strongly to those with a sense of the absurd. It is great fun, very comfortable, and the food is excellent. Swimming pool, riding, walking trails, tennis, golf, fishing.

Cybele Forest Lodge ($$$)
14 miles from Hazyview, off the R40 to White River tel: 013-764 1823 fax: 013-764 1810 www.cybele.co.za
Exclusive, country cottage-style mountain retreat, ideal for rest and relaxation, with beautiful grounds and wonderful meals. Easy access to Kruger Park. Swimming pool, trout fishing, riding.

Hippo Hollow Country Estate ($)
off the R535 near the R40 junction, Hazyview
tel: 013-737 7752 fax: 013-737 7673
Complex of thatched, family-oriented, self-catering chalets surrounding an excellent full-service restaurant. Private verandas with river views.

The Royal Hotel ($$)
Main Street, Pilgrim's Rest
tel: 013-768 1100 fax: 013-768 1188
Beautifully restored and atmospheric Victorian hotel at the center of this little mining town.

KWAZULU-NATAL

Durban and environs
Balmoral Hotel ($)
125 Marine Parade, Durban
tel: 031-368 5940 fax: 031-368 5955
e-mail: balmoral@icon.co.za
This spacious beachfront Edwardian hotel has recently been restored and is excellent value in the city center.

The Country Lodge ($$)
Southbroom, South Coast tel: 039-316 8380
fax: 039-316 8557
Charming, friendly lodge tucked into a cycad forest near the beach. Excellent restaurant.

The Edward ($$$)
Marine Parade, Durban tel: 031-337 3681
fax: 031-332 1692
Large, beautifully refurbished art-deco seafront hotel, with five excellent restaurants.

The Riverside ($$)
P.O. Box 35523, Northway, Durban North
tel: 031-830 600 fax: 031-830 611
A large resort hotel overlooking the Umgeni River and sea, near the beach, with family rooms, kitchenettes, pool, and one of Durban's best restaurants, the Jaipur Palace (see page 265).

The Royal Hotel ($$$)
267 Smith Street, Durban
tel: 031-304 0331 fax: 031-304 5055
e-mail: theroyal@ifrica.com
for U.K. bookings tel: 020-7225 0164)
The Royal has been collecting awards as the city's best hotel and best restaurant for years. Central location, ideal for exploring and shopping. Swimming pool.

Selborne Country Lodge and Golf Resort ($$)
Pennington, South Coast tel: 039-975 1133
fax: 039-975 1811
Elegant country lodge and golf club on a superb 200-acre estate on Natal's south coast, 40 minutes' drive from Durban. Swimming pool.

Battlefields and Zululand
Bushlands Game Lodge ($$)
Hluhluwe tel: 031-337 4222 fax: 031-368 2322 e-mail: lodges@goodersons.co.za
A unique lodge with rooms connected by elevated wooden platforms and walkways. Near the national parks of Hluhluwe/ Umfolozi, St. Lucia, Mkuzi, and Sodwana Bay. Swimming pool. Meals and game drives cost extra.

Fugitive's Drift ($$)
9 miles from Rorke's Drift, near Dundee
tel: 034-642 1843 fax: 034-642 1843
e-mail: fugdrift@dundee.lia.net

Comfortable lodge on a 5,100-acre natural heritage site beside the Buffalo River, overlooking Isandlwana. Extensive library of Africana; the owner is a registered battlefield tour guide and one of the best raconteurs in the region.

Isibindi Eco-Reserve ($$)
6 miles from Rorke's Drift; 33 miles from
Dundee off the R33 to Greytown
tel: 032-947 0538 fax: 032-947 0659
e-mail: isibindi@iafrica.com
Rustic clifftop cabins surrounding a central stone-built lodge. Right in the bush on a small private game reserve, with a traditional Zulu village. River trips.

Ndumo Wilderness Camp ($$$)
Ndumo Game Park tel: 011-807 1800
fax: 011-807 2110 www.wilderness.co.za
Luxury tented camp on stilts next to Banzi Pan, amid South Africa's best bird-watching country.

Phinda Resource Reserve ($$$)
about 18 miles north of Hluhluwe village
(reservations through CCAfrica)
Pristine, private, "Big Five" game reserve between Mkuzi and St. Lucia. Forest Lodge has elegant Japanese-style glass cabins scattered through the woods, while Nyala Lodge has more traditional chalets.

Rocktail Bay Lodge ($$$)
Maputaland Coastal Forest Reserve, south of
Kosi Bay tel: 011-807 1800
fax: 011-807 2110 www.wilderness.co.za
Small, remote lodge with wood and thatch chalets on stilts, next to a deserted turtle beach.

Simunye ($$)
off R68 about 31 miles north of Eshowe
tel: 035-454 7103 fax: 035-450 2534
The best of several Zulu cultural villages in the Eshowe area, with comfortable accommodations in a cliff-face rock lodge or beehive huts, transportation in an ox wagon, on horseback, or in a 4WD, good food, and an excellent cultural program.

Drakensberg and Midlands
Cathedral Peak ($$) 19 miles from Winterton (tel/fax: 036-488 1888); **Champagne Castle** ($$) 20 miles from Winterton (tel: 036-468 1063 fax: 036-468 1306); **Royal Natal National Park Hotel** ($$) Mont-aux-Sources (tel: 036-438 6200 fax: 036-438 6101).
All comfortable, popular, well-run mountain hotels with spectacular scenery and hiking. Swimming pools.

Old Halliwell Country Inn ($$)
Howick tel: 0332-302 602
fax: 0332-303 430
A welcoming inn dating from the 1830s, near the historic hamlet of Curry's Post.

Rawdons ($$)
Nottingham Road tel: 033-263 6044
fax: 033-263 6048 www.rawdons.co.za
Low, thatched country house hotel with charm and elegance.

Sandford Park Lodge ($$)
Bergville
tel: 036-448 1001 fax: 036-448 1047
Delightful country house hotel first opened as a coaching inn in 1850. Good food, lush gardens, and a roaring log fire in winter. Within easy reach of the central Drakensberg area.

263

RESTAURANTS

Outside major cities, restaurant hours are short in the evening, between 7:30 and 9. Many restaurants do not have a liquor license, but you can bring your own drinks; others restrict diners to wine and beer. Call ahead.

In many instances, particularly outside the major cities, the finest restaurants are attached to good hotels. To save space they are not listed twice, so try consulting the hotel list when choosing where to eat.

Food is very reasonably priced. The following recommended restaurants have been divided into three price categories:

- budget ($)—under $10
- moderate ($$)—$10–$20
- expensive ($$$)—over $20

Prices are per person, based on a three-course meal, including taxes but not drinks or tips.

WESTERN CAPE

Cape Town and environs

Aubergine $$$
39 Barnet Street, Gardens tel: 021-465 4909
Elegant town house restaurant with a terrace, chic furnishings, and some of Cape Town's most innovative food, fusing the best of European and Eastern influences. Reservations advised.

Blues ($$)
The Promenade, Victoria Road, Camps Bay tel: 021-438 2040
Highly popular seaside seafood restaurant. Reservations advised.

The Brass Bell ($$)
Kalk Bay Railway Station tel: 021-788 5455
Upstairs sea-food restaurant and downstairs pub overlooking Kalk Bay. Reservations essential.

Constantia Uitsig Restaurant ($$$)
Spaanschematriver Road, Constantia tel: 021-794 4480
One of South Africa's top restaurants, set in a top vineyard, serving a mainly Provençal menu. Reservations essential.

Jonkershuis ($$)
Groot Constantia tel: 021-794 6225
Friendly country-style restaurant at the winery and stately home. Traditional Cape Dutch food with sample plates, while the neighboring **Groot Constantia Tavern** (tel: 021-794 1144) has excellent cold meat and cheese platters.

The Kaapse Tafel ($$)
90 Queen Victoria Street tel: 021-423 1651
Well-established restaurant serving traditional Cape-Dutch and Cape-Malay cuisine.

Leinster Hall ($$$)
7 Weltevreden Street tel: 021-424 1836
South African cuisine from Knysna oysters to Karoo lamb, in a 19th-century Cape house. One of the finest restaurants in South Africa.

The Winelands, Breede Valley, and West Coast

The Africa Café ($/$$)
Heritage Square, corner of Buitengracht and Shortmarket streets tel: 021-422 0221

A wonderful introduction to African food in a friendly, cheerful environment. Historic building with a roof terrace. Dinner only.

Paddagang ($$$)
23 Church Street, Tulbagh tel: 023-230 0242
Traditional Cape specialties, including smoked snoek (barracouta) pâté, *waterblommetjie bredie* (water-lily stew), and *bobotie* (mild curry), on a delightful terrace in the historic heart of Tulbagh. Open daily, breakfast, tea, lunch, and wine tastings. Reservations.

La Petite Ferme ($$)
Pass Road, Franschhoek tel: 021-876 3016
Simply prepared, delicious farm-fresh food, with rainbow trout a specialty. Wonderful views across the Franschhoek valley. Open daily for lunch and tea. Reservations essential.

Rhebokskloof ($$$)
Agter–Paarl Road, Paarl tel: 021-863 8606
Haute cuisine and Cape Dutch food at a charming winery. Try the seven-course, seven-wine *dégustation* menu.

Rheinholds ($)
Main Street, Clanwilliam tel: 027-482 1101
Traditional South African food, with delicious home-baked bread.

Spier ($/$$$)
on the R130 between Cape Town and Stellenbosch tel: 021-809 1100
Thriving Cape Dutch winery with a bar, coffee shop, and more; the Taphuys bar and store can sell fixings for gourmet picnics; the Café Spier serves light lunches, coffee, and afternoon teas; and the Jonkershuis lays out a huge buffet.

Die Strandloper ($$)
On the beach, Langebaan tel: 022-772 2490
Outdoor, literally on the beach, with paper napkins and fingerbowls, this is heaven for those wanting totally delicious seafood in a totally relaxed atmosphere. Reservations essential.

De Volkskombuis ($$$)
Aan de Wagenweg, Stellenbosch tel: 021-887 2121
This fine restaurant on the banks of the Eerste River, whose name and address translate as "the people's kitchen on the wagon road," is housed in a Herbert Baker building. The spectacular menu includes many traditional Cape dishes.

The South Coast, Garden Route, and Karoo

Bientang se Grot ($$)
Marine Drive, Hermanus tel: 0283-23651
Buffet-style seafood restaurant in a cave overlooking the sea.

Copper Pot ($$$)
12 Montague Street, George tel: 044-820 7378
Elegant dining with an emphasis on seafood and impeccable silver service in one of the best restaurants on the Garden Route.

Cranzgots Restaurant ($$)
Cango Wildlife, Cango Caves Road, about 6 miles north of Oudtshoorn tel: 044-382 3629
Large, cheerful restaurant beside the deer park water hole on the crocodile farm. The set menus include crocodile and ostrich fillets—and a tour of the park. Open 9 AM until late.

The Islander ($$)
5 miles from Plettenberg Bay on the N2 to Knysna tel: 044-532 7776
Casual, buffet-style seafood restaurant. Always very busy.

Pink Umbrellas ($$)
14 Kingsway, Leisure Island, Knysna tel: 044-384 0135
Delicious seafood and vegetarian meals and superb afternoon teas and snacks. The pleasant garden is full of pink umbrellas.

EASTERN CAPE

Aviemore ($$$)
12 Whitlock Street, Port Elizabeth tel: 041-585 1125
PE's finest restaurant. Creative versions of traditional South African dishes reveal Pacific "fusion" influences.

Sir Rufane Donkin Rooms ($$/$$$)
5 George Street, Upper Hill, City Centre, Port Elizabeth tel: 041-555 534
One of the region's best restaurants, in a building dating back to 1850. The menu changes every two months, and is full of mouthwatering surprises. Reservations essential.

THE FREE STATE, NORTHERN CAPE, AND NORTH-WEST PROVINCE

Le Must ($$)
11 Schröder Street, Upington tel: 054-332 3971
A popular, pretty restaurant that serves tasty local dishes.

Onze Rust ($$)
just outside Bloemfontein tel: 051-441 8717
South African traditional food, at "Boerekos," former residence of President M. J. Steyn of the Boer Republic. Reservations essential.

Schillaci's ($$)
115 Zastron Street, Bloemfontein tel: 051-447 3829
Atmospheric Italian trattoria and pizzeria with garden dining. Reservations essential.

Star of the West ($$)
Corner of North Circular and Barkly roads, Kimberley tel: 053-832 6463
The food is ordinary, but the atmosphere is great in this authentic 19th-century miners' pub.

GAUTENG

Johannesburg
Anton van Wouw ($$)
111 Sivewright Avenue, Doornfontein tel: 011-402 7916
A full menu of game, *boboties*, *bredies*, and South African desserts. Closed Sunday. Reservations advised.

Carnivore ($$)
Muldersdrift Estate, off D.F. Malan Drive tel: 011-957 2099
Little brother to the famous Nairobi venue, this large, cheerful restaurant cooks all sorts of meat, including game, over an open fire. Also soups,

salads, and vegetarian options.

Gramadoelas at the Market ($/$$)
Market Theatre Precinct, corner of Breë and Wolhuter streets tel: 011-838 6960
A must for all visitors, this is one of the great exponents of African food, from Cape Malay dishes to ostrich omelets and mopani worms. Closed Sunday.

Ile de France ($$$)
Cramerview Centre, 277 Main Road Bryanston tel: 011-706 2837
One of the finest dining establishments in town, serving French provincial cuisine. Lunch Sun–Fri, dinner daily. Reservations essential.

Iyavaya ($$)
69 Oxford Road, Rosebank tel: 011-327 1312
One of the few good places to get traditional African food, with beers and background music from around the continent.

Linger Longer ($$$)
Wierda Road (off Johan), Wierda Valley, Sandton tel: 011-884 0465
Renowned and elegant restaurant with innovative French cuisine.

Randburg Waterfront ($/$$)
tel: 011-789 5052
A popular development with 66 eateries around a small lake with a 1,000-nozzle, 164-foot-high musical fountain. Includes a large number of shops and a flea market.

Pretoria
Chagall's ($$)
924 Park Street, Arcadia tel: 012-342 1200
Fabulous French cuisine in a restored colonial house that has a choice of rooms, from large and cheerful to small and intimate.

Gerard Moerdyk ($$$)
Park Street, Arcadia tel: 012-344 4856
Named after the designer of the Voortrekker Monument. A traditional South African restaurant in a 1920s neo-Cape Dutch house.

La Madeleine ($$$)
Esselen Street, Sunnyside tel: 012-44 6076
This Belgian-run restaurant, serving classic French cuisine, is one of the finest in South Africa.

KWAZULU-NATAL

Durban and environs
Jaipur Palace ($$/$$$)
3 Riverside Hotel Complex, 10 Northway, Durban North tel: 031-563 0287
Curry is almost obligatory in Natal, but this is several cuts above the average, with wonderfully oriental atmosphere and sea views to match some of Durban's finest food.

Langoustine-by-the-Sea ($$)
101 Waterkant Road, Durban North tel: 031-849 768
Excellent seafood with sea views.

Roma Revolving ($$$)
John Ross House, Victoria Embankment, Durban tel: 031-332 6707
Delicious Italian seafood and pasta in a revolving 31st-floor restaurant. Spectacular views. Reservations advised.

1

2

3

Safari Guide

TEEMING WITH LIFE

South Africa has over 130 bird and game sanctuaries, covering nearly 20 million acres. It hosts a staggering 870 bird species; about 160 species of mammal; 115 species of snake, approximately a quarter of which are poisonous; some 5,000 spider and scorpion species; and a vast multitude of other reptiles and insects.

UP BEFORE DAWN

To see the best of the game, go out between dawn and 10 AM, and from 4 PM to dusk. Most animals simply melt into the shade to sit out the heat of day. Wear neutral colors and ideally use a vehicle that gets you above the line of the bushes. In the game parks, animals are used to vehicles and will not be startled as long as there are no loud noises or strange shapes. Talk quietly, don't stand up or wave your arms out of the window, and above all stay in your vehicle.

WATCH THE BIRDIE!

South Africa has six broad bird habitats: *fynbos* (heathland) in the Cape; desert and semidesert in the northwest; thornveld and broad-leaved woodland in the northeast; grasslands in the center; tropical forest along the Natal coast; and the coastal strip itself. Probably the single most satisfying area for bird-watching is northern Natal, where Hluhluwe, Ndumo, and St. Lucia together provide almost the whole range of options.

Bird Life

Out of southern Africa's 870 species of bird, about 500 are either local in distribution, retiring, or classed as vagrants. Consequently, only about 300 can be seen regularly and identified by the nonspecialist, and of these, some—including many of the females—are small, drab "LBJs" (little brown jobs). Keen bird-watchers need a good guide, binoculars, and a great deal of time. Heretical as it may seem to say so, most ordinary tourists simply want to identify those birds which are large or flashy—ideally both.

Savannah dwellers The largest of all, and instantly identifiable, is the huge, flightless **ostrich** (8) which, in the wild, wanders the *vlei* (open savannah grasslands) in company with zebra, antelope, and wildebeest. In practice, you get a far better view of them on farms, in and around Oudtshoorn (see page 80). There are plenty of other options in the grasslands, however. Pride of place goes to the gawky **secretary bird** (7), whose gray wings, black legs, and crest resemble a clerk's jacket, trousers, and quill pen. The **kori bustard** (13), the heaviest bird in the world still capable of sustained flight, strides the veld on long legs, with a tawny back, white underparts, black-spotted upper wings, black-and-white feathering on the neck, and a black crest.

The pure white **cattle egret** (11) follows the herds, whether cattle or rhino, picking up the insects dislodged by their feet, while the little brown **red-billed oxpecker** actually catches a ride on their backs, feeding off their ticks and fleas.

Ungainly **hornbills** are unbalanced by their huge, heavy beaks. The **ground hornbill** (10) is as big as a turkey, black all over except for bald red eyes and throat, and flies clumsily only when pushed; the smaller and more agile **yellow-billed hornbill** has a black-and-white patterned back, white front, and yellow beak. Less commonly seen are **trumpeter**, **grey**, and **red-billed** (9) species.

The **red-eyed dove** (15), **ring-necked Cape turtle dove**, black-faced **Namaqua dove**, and gentle little **laughing dove** (16) in its pastel coat of pinks and blues coo in the dawn from the acacia trees. Game birds scuttle underfoot: the white-spotted **helmeted guinea fowl** (20) with its blue and red head, and the round, sandy **crested francolin** (19). Seen frequently in similar habitats is the pout-chested, pointy-tailed **Namaqua sandgrouse** (17).

Storks are sociable birds, building large, scruffy nests in tenement trees and often forsaking the bush for the rich pickings of the agricultural lands. The **white stork** has a white upper body, black wing tips and tail, and a red bill and legs. **Abdim's stork** (18) is shorter, squatter, and largely black with white underwings. Also found in the region are **saddle-billed**, **African open-billed** (29), and **yellow-billed storks**. With them you will often find the very noisy, curious, and gregarious **Hadada ibis** (12), grayish-brown with a wickedly curved beak.

As dusk draws in, the **nightjars** flutter down to take dust baths and the eyes of the owls blink open. There are numerous species of owl, big and small—**African Scops**, **white-faced Scops** (14), **barn**, **spotted eagle**, **pearl-spotted eagle**, and **Verreaux's eagle owls**.

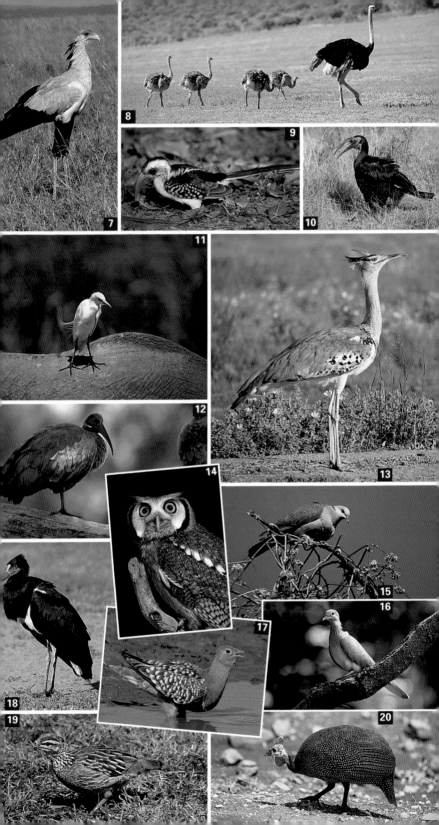

Raptors The great raptors wheel over the veld on the morning thermals. Largest of all is the majestic **lammergeier** (21). The **bateleur** (25) has a dark body with a reddish back patch, pale wings, and scarlet beak and claws, and there are two species of **fork-tailed kites**—the dusty brown black and the black-shoudered, whose markings are similar to those of a gull. The large black-breasted **snake eagle** has a dark brown back and head, white belly and white underwings, banded with black, while the **long-crested eagle** (24) is smaller, dark brown with a distinctive crest, white-feathered legs, and white patches on the wings. Other hunters roaming the skies include several species of **buzzard**, **falcon**, **kestrel**, and **goshawk**, of which the most interesting are probably

the **jackal buzzard**, with dark brown upper body and back and bright chestnut breast, and the pale gray and white **chanting goshawk** (22).

Freshwater fishers Inland waterways and estuaries are bursting with bird life of every shape, size, and color. King of them all, the black-and-white **African fish eagle** (23), plummets from a high dead branch, its raucous shout of triumph still filling the sky as it spears a glistening fish. On lower branches, dark **great** and **reed cormorants** (28) hang their wings out to dry and a **darter** weaves its snakelike neck around in search of food. The elegant **little egret**, white with a black beak and yellow toes, is sometimes mistaken for a heron. The **herons** themselves, **gray**, **black-headed**, and **goliath** (26), stand stock-still, frozen as sculptures in the dappled light. The black-headed **sacred ibis** (30) waits ankle-deep, while an **African spoonbill** (31) sweeps its head from side to side, filtering food with its curiously flattened gray and red bill. A softly gray **blue crane** walks along the shore, proud as a model on a catwalk, trailing its darker tail feathers like a dirty train. In the grass nearby stalks a magnificent **crowned crane** (27), with a charcoal-gray body, gold wingtips, black-and-white face, red chin, and proud crown of golden bristles.

THE THREATENED SEA

Many marine creatures are as endangered as the rhino. Even outside the marine reserves, whales, dolphins, great white sharks, and such organisms as live sea pansies are totally protected, while you need a permit to catch rock lobster, abalone, and linefish. Some coastal dwellers, such as stonefish and several species of sea urchin or jellyfish, should also be left alone, being extremely poisonous. When diving or snorkeling, touch nothing and, above all, do not stand on the fragile coral itself. Never buy coral, coral products, or shells.

Tawny **hamerkops**, **blacksmith** and **crowned plovers**, and **black-winged stilts** wade the shallows in search of frogs and insects, **spur-winged** and **Egyptian geese** gather in noisy crowds, stately parties of **white-faced** and **yellow-billed ducks**, **Cape** (32) and **red-billed teals** float gently by, the **moorhens** scrabbling furiously through the water in an effort to keep up. There is a flash of color in the reeds from a lurking **purple gallinule**, and another from the overhanging branches as a shining turquoise and orange **malachite kingfisher** streaks past, far outstripping even its own pretty cousins, the **woodland**, **brown-hooded** (38), **giant**, **pied**, and **striped kingfishers**.

By the sea To the north, in the Natal dunes, salmon-pink **greater** (3) and **lesser flamingos** stroll the shallow lagoons as heavy flights of **white** and **pink-backed pelicans** (36) zoom overhead. Down on the far south of the Cape coast, colonies of **African penguins** (33) strut the rocks with self-importance. From the skies above, **Cape cormorants** dive-bomb a shoal of sardines. The inshore waters are patrolled by raucous flocks of **terns**, **grey-headed gulls**, and **Cape gannets** (35), with yellowy heads and black-tipped wings. Far out to sea, swooping over the ocean are the massive **black-browed albatross** (34) and smaller **yellow-billed albatross**, the geometrically painted black-and-white **pintado petrel**, the **white-chinned petrel**, and the **sooty shearwater**, the birds of legend and storm.

Great little showoffs What they lack in size, many of South Africa's smaller birds make up for in vivid color. The chestnut head, black-and-white back, and distinctive crest of the **hoopoe** and the orange breast and punklike crest of the **purple-crested lourie** positively pale beside the chestnut back, turquoise, lilac, and black of the **lilac-breasted roller** (40) or the green, yellow, black, and chestnut of various **bee-eaters**. Some starlings are drab, but the incandescent **glossy** and **plum-colored starlings** (43) with their petroleum sheen more than make up for it. Bright yellow **weaver birds** drip-hang neat, round nests from the trees and fluffy little **yellow, blue** (37), and **violet** (41) **waxbills** descend in flocks on new-mown lawns. **Red bishops** (39) parade in black and orange robes; even the **long-tailed widow** makes up for its funereal garb by a dramatically trailing tail. The brightest of them all must be the tiny **sunbirds** that dart through the flower beds like fiery jewels: the all-green **malachite**, the **orange-breasted** with its iridescent blue-green head, the **marico** with green head and back, black belly, and purple and turquoise stripes across the chin, and the lesser **double-collared** (42) with green head, blue back, and scarlet chinstrap.

Scavengers Often treated with contempt, the carrion-eaters perform a valuable service, keeping the bush clean. To track a kill, look for the **Cape** (44), the **lappet-faced**, and **white-backed vultures** (45) circling overhead. Often found at the same sites, or on a garbage dump, the huge **marabou stork** is one of the ugliest birds around, with a heavy hunched body, white front and black back, bald pink head and neck, pink fleshy pouch, and huge yellowish bill.

TOPS AND TAILS

All measurements given for animals are taken as height at the shoulder and, where applicable, length without the tail. Grazers are largely grass-eating, while browsers eat mainly the leaves and young shoots of trees and bushes. Diurnal animals keep daylight hours; nocturnal species come out at night.

Antelope

Blesbok *Damaliscus dorcas phillipsi;* **Bontebok** *Damaliscus dorcas dorcas;* **Tsessebe** (49) *Damaliscus lunatus* Three closely related antelope: the blesbok (37 inches), found only in the north and east, has a rich brown coat with off-white underparts and blaze. The southwestern bontebok (35 inches) from the Cape has a purple-brown coat, white underbelly, rump, socks, and blaze. The tsessebe (47 inches) has a dark red-brown coat, tan underbelly, and a hump. The long, ridged horns splay out and back.

Bushbuck (46) *Tragelaphus scriptus* Nocturnal browsers, bushbuck live alone in well-watered woodland. The rump is higher than the shoulder (31 inches), giving them a hunched appearance. Males have thick, slightly twisted horns, up to 12 inches long. There are over 40 subspecies, whose color varies from gray-brown to chestnut, always with white neck patches and white spots on the flanks.

Duiker The duiker (meaning "diver" in Afrikaans) is one of the smallest of the African antelope. Nervous, nocturnal browsers living alone or in pairs, they are widely distributed from rocky hills to grassland. There are three species in South Africa:

the common gray duiker, *Sylvicapra grimmia* (20 inches), the smaller, rarer red duiker, *Cephalophus natalensis* (17 inches), and the blue duiker, *Cephalophus monticola* (12 inches; actually grayish-brown). All have rounded backs and black marks on the face and top of the tail.

Eland (50) *Taurotragus oryx* The massive eland (7 feet tall; 1 ton in weight) has a light sandy body, faint white stripes across the back, and strips of black hair along spine and belly. Both sexes have long, backward-lying horns with a tight spiral at the base. Timid diurnal browsers, they live in herds in scrubland and semidesert.

Gemsbok (51) *Oryx gazella* The beautiful gemsbok (4 feet) inhabit the semidesert scrub of the Kalahari, where they eat grass, leaves, and tubers and need no additional water. They have a heavy body, a sandy coat with a black tail, black stripe along the flanks and upper thighs, white legs, and black knee patches. The face has black-and-white patches and both sexes have very long, thin, straight horns.

Grysbok These small, nocturnal creatures (20 inches) have a hunched back and chestnut coat sprinkled with white hair. The Cape grysbok, *Raphicerus melanotis*, a grazer, lives only in the far south. Sharpe's grysbok (48), *Raphicerus sharpei*, is a browser and grazer found in the far north. It has a redder coat, a dark band along the muzzle, and whitish belly and inside legs.

Impala (47) *Aepyceros melampus* Largest of the gazelles (3 feet), impala are charmingly pretty and easily seen, living in herds in open grassland. They have a russet back and nose, a white belly, white rings around the eyes, and black stripes on the tail and rump. Males have long, lyre-shaped horns. Both browsers and grazers, they can jump to a height of 10 feet and reach speeds of 60 mph.

Klipspringer, *Oreotragus oreotragus* Little klipspringers (21 inches) browse and graze in small groups on rocky hillsides, bouncing on tiptoe from boulder to boulder on hooves the consistency of hard rubber. Their long, bristly, speckled coat varies from yellow-brown to charcoal gray. Males have short, straight horns.

HARD WORK
Most herd antelope split into male and female groups. The young males are driven out when nearing maturity to join a bachelor herd. The dominant male must remain tireless as he carves out and defends a territory, and guards and services a harem of anything up to 30 females and calves. To establish his own herd, a young male must either defeat him or cut out and kidnap a significant number of females.

RARE SIGHTINGS
Other antelope seen infrequently in South Africa include the huge, magnificent black-and-white sable, *Hippotragus niger;* the heavy strawberry-gray roan, *Hippotragus equinus,* similar to the gemsbok with its black-and-white face; the small beige-and-white oribi, *Ourebia ourebi;* and the tiny red-gold suni, *Neotragus moschatus.*

275

POT BUCK
You are just as likely to find an antelope on your plate as in the bush these days, with many farmers turning their attention to animals that are low-maintenance, perfectly adapted to the environment, resistant to many local diseases, and produce delicious low-cholesterol red meat for the health-conscious. Popular species include eland, kudu, impala, springbok, and gemsbok. Ostrich and crocodile are also widely farmed, while warthog and zebra are sometimes shot for the table, too.

Kudu (56) *Tragelaphus strepsiceros* Found in the north and east, the powerful greater kudu (5 feet) has a sloping back, light grayish-brown coat with faint white stripes, a white crest along the spine, black beard, and white band between the eyes. Males have magnificent horns that curl backward in an open corkscrew. They are browsers, living in small groups in scrubby woodland.

Nyala (55) *Tragelaphus angasii* Similar to the kudu, nyala (4 feet) are found in northern KwaZulu-Natal. They have a dark brown coat with faint white stripes across the back, white-spotted flanks, black mane and beard, white crest along the spine and a white patch on the nose. Males have long, twisting, backward-lying horns. Diurnal browsers, they live in small groups in dense thickets near water.

Red hartebeest (53) *Alcelaphus buselaphus caama* The hartebeest is large (5 feet) with a steeply sloping back, a rich red-tan coat with dark patches along the spine and thighs, and a long, gloomy face. Both sexes have thick, ridged, backward-twisting horns, shaped like a candelabrum. Diurnal grazers, they live in large herds in open grassland.

Reedbuck The Southern Reedbuck (54) *Redunca arundinum* (3 feet) inhabits marshland near water. Usually found in pairs, they are grazers with a dirty yellow to grayish-brown coat with a white throat patch. Smaller Mountain Reedbuck, *Redunca fulvorufula* (28 inches) live in small groups in rocky hills or steep river beds. They have a shaggy grayish coat with white underparts and a reddish-brown head and neck. Both males have short, forward-curving horns.

Grey rhebok *Pelea capreolus* Small, gray, furry antelope (29 inches) with powerful back legs and a hunched back, rhebok are browsers and grazers who live on rocky hills and slopes in groups of 2–20. They have large ears, white rings around the eyes, and a white rim to the tail. Males have thin, straight horns.

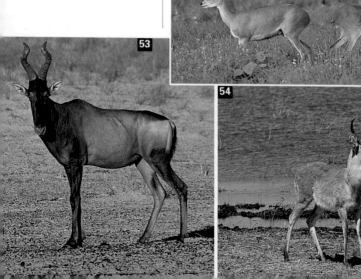

Steenbok (52) *Raphicerus campestris* Similar to the grysbok, the little steenbok (20 inches) often lurks in long grass or a disused burrow for safety. They have a chestnut coat and a white belly. The male has short, straight, very sharp horns. They browse and graze in open land, usually during the day, although they become nocturnal if under threat.

Waterbuck *Kobus ellipsiprymnus* Heavyset waterbuck (5½ feet) graze in small groups in reedbeds and river valleys. They have a shaggy gray-brown coat covered in a musky secretion that not only acts as waterproofing but smells evil and taints the flesh, guarding against most predators. They have a distinctive white circle on the rump. The males have long, ridged horns that curve out and forward.

Wildebeest Technically an antelope, the wildebeest or gnu (5 feet) is said to have been made up of the pieces left over at the end of creation, with "the forequarters of an ox, the hindquarters of an antelope, and the tail of a horse." It also has the long face of a hartebeest, a thick black mane, and the horns of a buffalo. They are gregarious, grazing open grassland in large herds. There are two species in South Africa, the common blue or brindled *Connochaetes taurinus* (57), with a grayish-brown coat and faint black striping, and the rarer black *Connochaetes gnou*, with a darker coat and white muzzle and tail.

NATIONAL SYMBOL
The springbok (6), *Antidorcas marsupialis*, has become South Africa's symbol and given its name to the country's national sports teams. Little could be more different from a rugby player than this dainty little gazelle. The only true gazelle south of the Zambezi, springbok (30 inches) are gregarious browsers and grazers who thrive in large herds in the dry open scrublands on the Kalahari fringe. They have a rich tan back, white underparts, rump, and face, and black stripes along the flanks and tail and beneath the eyes. Males and females have ridged, lyre-shaped horns that curve out and back before hooking in at the top.

277

PRESENT PERFECT
In the 13th century, the king of Malindi (Kenya) sent the emperor of China a present of a giraffe, an oryx, and a zebra. The court was so impressed with the giraffe that the animal became the Chinese emblem of Perfect Virtue, Perfect Government, and Perfect Harmony in the Empire and in the Universe.

FAMILY LIKENESS?
The African elephant differs from the Asian in several key points. It is noticeably larger with bigger ears, has a flat forehead, ringed trunk, concave back, and carries its head higher. In spite of many tall tales, it is no more ferocious and just as capable of domestication as its Asian cousin. Extraordinarily, the elephant's closest relatives are the rock hyrax or dassie (like an overgrown brown guinea pig, about the size of a rabbit) and the marine dugong (said by early sailors to be mermaids).

Plains animals

Buffalo (58) *Syncerus caffer* Deceptively cowlike but irritable and dangerous when roused, buffalo are huge (5–7 feet), with powerful bodies, dark-brown coats, and short, massively heavy horns that clamp the brow like a Viking helmet. They browse and graze, in grassland and forest, live in herds, and wallow in mud for heat regulation.

Elephant (1) *Loxodonta africana* The largest land mammal, the African elephant (10 feet; 13,200 pounds; with tusks up to 11 feet) is a magnificent and surprisingly gentle giant, although swift to anger if alarmed. Sociable and intelligent, they live in matriarchal family groups with a complex social structure. Infants stay with their mother until the age of five, sexual maturity is reached at 15, and life expectancy is 60–70 years. They adapt to a range of habitats, from desert to montane forest, but are happiest in savannah woodland.

Giraffe (62) *Giraffa camelopardalis* Extraordinarily graceful and gentle, the giraffe (16–19 feet tall) has a hide resembling a tan and chestnut crazy quilt, a heavy, sloping body, camel-like face, and small, fleshy horns topped with rounded knobs. There are only seven vertebrae in the immensely long neck and special valves regulate the blood flow to the brain when they bend. Giraffes live in large herds in open woodland and browse on the high leaves of acacia trees. Their only real defense is a powerful kick.

Hippopotamus (61) *Hippopotamus amphibius* Hippos (5 feet tall; 3,300 pounds) have massive barrel bodies, short legs, a tight, shiny gray skin and long, flattened face. They live in colonies of up to 15 and spend their days wallowing in shallow pools, surfacing to breath every five minutes, or lying with nostrils poking out of the water. At night, they walk up to 18 miles in search of good grazing. Totally vegetarian and placid when undisturbed, they kill more humans than almost all other wild animals combined, simply biting people, and even canoes, in half.

Rhinoceros The white rhinoceros, *Ceratotherium simum* (6 feet; 5,000 pounds), gains its name not from its color but from the Afrikaans word *"weit,"* meaning widemouthed. They are grazers, inhabiting grasslands and open scrub. The mouth is square and the front horn considerably longer than the back. The black rhinoceros (2), *Diceros bicornis* (5 feet; 1,900 pounds), is a browser, living in thick bush. A darker charcoal-gray than the white, it has a pointy hooklip, the horns are more even in length, and it is smaller and more aggressive. Both species nearly died out through poaching, but a successful breeding and relocation program has increased the number of whites. The black is still very rare.

Warthog (60) *Phacochoerus aethiopicus* Large, brown, hairy pigs (27 inches), with dark mane, small wide-set eyes, knobbly face, and short, sideways curving tusks, these prodigious diggers live in underground burrows and eat tubers and grass. Usually seen as a family of male, female, and two to three infants, they run in a line, tails straight up in the air. Their nocturnal relative, the bushpig, *Potamochoerus porcus* (25 inches), has a smoother face and squarer muzzle, has larger litters, and keeps its tail down when running.

Zebra These sociable grazers live in large herds on open grassland. The irregular stripes act as camouflage and a system of identification as unique as fingerprints. The common Burchell's zebra (59), *Equus burchelli* (4¼ feet), has brown shadow stripes on the white sections. The rare Cape mountain zebra, *Equus zebra zebra* (4 feet), is slightly smaller, with longer pointed ears, narrower stripes with no shadow, and a plain white belly.

THE BIG FIVE

To see the "Big Five" is considered to be the goal of any successful safari. The definition of the five—lion, elephant, rhino, buffalo, and leopard—came not from their rarity value or even their beauty, but from the early hunters. These were considered to be the most difficult and dangerous animals to shoot, and therefore the finest trophies. Lion, elephant, and buffalo are relatively easy to find, while there are more rhinos in South Africa than anywhere else on the continent. Leopard are widespread but virtually impossible to see.

280

Predators

Cheetah (63) *Acinonyx jubatus* Long (6½ feet), lithe, and built for speed, cheetahs have gold coats with black spots and neat triangular heads. A few genetically aberrant so-called king cheetahs, with larger black splotches, are found in the far north. The fastest animals on earth, clocking up speeds of 70 mph over short distances, cheetahs live in family groups and hunt in the early morning and evening.

Foxes The bat-eared fox, *Otocyon megalotis* (31 inches long), has a speckled gray-brown coat, darker bushy tail, small triangular face, and huge round ears. It lives in semi-arid grass and scrub, in burrows. The unrelated Cape fox (64), *Vulpes chama* (35 inches), has a shiny golden-gray coat and a dark tail, and lives in semidesert scrub and mountain *fynbos*. Often shot as pests, both are harmless and even beneficial, eating mice, small reptiles, and insects.

Hyena The common spotted hyena (67), *Crocuta crocuta* (33 inches), roams the open savannah and woodland in the north and east, while the smaller, rarer brown hyena (66), *Hyaena brunnea* (30 inches), inhabits the Kalahari region. Both have powerful shoulders, weak back legs, and a sloping back. The spotted has a gold coat with black spots, a small, neat head, and rounded ears; the brown has a dark brown coat, stripy legs, and pointed ears. They are mainly nocturnal scavengers, but also prey on young, old, and sick animals. They live alone or in pairs, gathering in groups during the mating season. The spotted has an eerie cry, ranging from a yap to piercing howls and manic laughter.

Jackal Regarded as scavengers, jackals (length 3¾ feet) are about the size and shape of a European fox and behave in a similar fashion. They do hang around kills, farmyards, and garbage cans, but they are also efficient hunters of small animals, and even eat fruit and vegetables. There are two

63

64

65

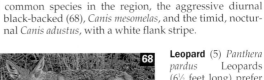

69

281

common species in the region, the aggressive diurnal black-backed (68), *Canis mesomelas*, and the timid, nocturnal *Canis adustus*, with a white flank stripe.

Leopard (5) *Panthera pardus* Leopards (6½ feet long) prefer wooded hills, but accept a wide range of terrain. They are solitary, nocturnal, and extremely difficult to see. Their low-slung bodies have a red-gold coat with clusters of black spots. They hunt anything from mice to antelope, hauling carcasses into trees away from scavengers.

68

67

Lion *Panthera leo* The lion (35 inches tall; 8½ feet long) is the largest cat in the world. The young (69) have spots, but adults are a uniform gold; males have a mane that can range from light colored to almost black. They live in prides of up to 20 or 30 beasts. The females (smaller than males) do almost all the hunting, usually at night or dawn. Not particularly speedy, they rely on stealth, breaking the victim's neck with a blow from a paw or clamping the throat and suffocating it.

Wild dog (65) *Lycaon pictus* Wild, or Cape, hunting dogs have been feared and hunted by man and are now one of the rarest animals in Africa. About 26 inches tall, they have long, skinny legs, powerful jaws, and huge ears. Their coat is brindled black, dark brown, yellow, and white, the patterning on each dog unique. Strictly diurnal, they once lived and hunted in packs of up to 40 members.

RUN RABBIT RUN
There are several species of rabbit in South Africa, but those you see are most likely to be escaped European domestic rabbits. There are two common species of hare, the Cape hare, *Lepus capensis*, and the scrub hare, *Lepus saxatilis*. The spring hare, *Pedetes capensis*, is not a hare, but a marsupial, with powerful back legs and tiny forelegs, rather like a small kangaroo.

282

Primates

Bushbaby Small, tree-dwelling primates with huge eyes, bushy tails, and a piercing cry uncannily like the wail of a hungry baby, bushbabies are closely related to lemurs. They live in colonies, feeding at night on small birds, reptiles and insects, eggs, fruit, and leaves. There are two species in South Africa, the thick-tailed, *Otolemur crassicaudatus* (19–23 inches long), and lesser, *Galago moholi* (14 inches long).

Chacma baboon (71) *Papio ursinus* Chacma baboons are large (4 feet long), with thick yellowy-gray coats, a long black muzzle, and kinked tail. Highly organized socially, they live in troops of up to 50 in rocky, wooded hills. Omnivorous team players, they work together smoothly to hunt or defend, using formidable teeth as weapons. Their call is a sharp coughlike bark.

Monkeys South Africa's two species of monkey are both diurnal and gregarious, living in troops of up to 30, led by a dominant male. The vervet (70) *Cercopithecus pygerythrus* (3½ feet long) has a gray-brown back, pale stomach, and black face ringed by a white ruff. The male has a bright blue scrotum. They prefer open savannah woodland, but range widely, are fearless, and are highly curious. The elusive samango, *Cercopithecus albogularis* (4½ feet), is larger and darker with tufty side whiskers and a dark brown face. They live in the upper reaches of dense montane forest.

Small mammals

Anteaters Africa's vast army of termites supports several species of anteater, all solitary, nocturnal, and rarely seen. The pangolin, *Manis temminckii* (31 inches long), has a heavy scaled, rounded body, flat tail, tiny legs, small triangular snout, formidable claws, and a long, sticky tongue. It is covered with heavy, scaled armor and when threatened it curls up and exudes a foul smell. The aardvark or antbear, *Orycteropus afer* (23 inches), is low-slung, with a heavy body, short legs, and pointy face. It has pale gold fur, a thin almost bald tail, long sharp ears, and piglike snout. Great burrowers, they create vast underground networks of tunnels. The aardwolf, *Proteles cristatus* (35 inches long), resembles a hyena, with a rounded back, long streaked black-and-tan fur, a black muzzle, and pointed ears.

Cats There are four local species of small cat, all nocturnal and rarely seen, hunting small creatures, birds, and reptiles. The caracal, *Felis caracal* (3½ feet long), has a red-gold coat, small head, and large, pointed ears, tufted with black fur. The serval, *Felis serval* (3½ feet long), has a tan body and black spots and stripes on neck and tail. The African wild cat, *Felis lybica* (35 inches long), looks like a domestic tabby, but with a sharper face and longer ears. Even more like a tabby, the small spotted cat, *Felis nigripes* (19–23 inches long), has a tan coat, black spots and stripes, and a rounded face.

Honey badger *Mellivora capensis* Also known as a ratel, the honey badger (37 inches) has a light gray back and a white stripe along the flank, while the head and underparts are a deep brown. They are nocturnal, largely carnivorous, and regarded as pests because of their fondness for both chickens and eggs. Although small, they are aggressive.

Mongoose There are 11 species of mongoose in South Africa, of which six are common: the yellow, *Cynictis penicillata;* slender, *Galerella sanguinea;* white-tailed, *Ichneumia albicauda;* water (marsh), *Atilax paludinosus;* banded, *Mungos mungo;* and dwarf, *Helogale parvula.* All eat a varied diet of insects, small animals, and eggs, and between the species they cover the full range of habitats. Closely related is the scrawny suricate or meerkat (72), *Suricata suricata,* a highly gregarious desert dweller.

Porcupine (74) *Hystrix africaeaustralis* Solitary, nocturnal, and vegetarian, this extraordinary rodent (29 inches long) has a dark face, white bristly mane, and coat of hard, pointed black-and-white banded quills, which puff up to double their size and rattle when the animal is alarmed or angry.

FALSE CATS
Often described as cats because of their appearance, genets and civets are actually related to the mongoose family. With stretched bodies, short legs, and black-and-tan stripes and spots, they are nocturnal omnivores, the genets nesting in trees or underground burrows while the largest of them, the civet, *Civettictis civetta* (4 feet long), is strictly terrestrial. The small-spotted genet, *Genetta genetta* (37 inches long), has a white-tipped tail; the large-spotted (73), *Genetta tigrina* (3 feet), a black tip.

75

76

Reptiles

Of all South Africa's reptiles,
the Nile crocodile (75), *Croco-
dylus niloticus*, is king.

Smaller, but still dramati-
cally big, is the largest of the lizards, the water leguaan or
monitor, *Varanus niloticus* (up to 5 feet long). Many other
lizards, skinks, and ten species of agama thrive in hot
sand and rocky crevices. Some, such as the blue-headed
southern rock agama, *Agama atra*, or the red, green, and
blue common flat lizard, *Platysaurus intermedius*, are as
brightly colored as a rainbow. Pale pinky-brown geckos
lurk on bedroom ceilings and there are at least 20 species
of slow-moving, rainbow-changing chameleon (4). Other
reptiles include tortoises, terrapins, and sea turtles; green,
loggerhead (76), leatherback, and hawksbill turtles all
breed on the beaches of northern Natal.

Snakes have poor eyesight, but a keen sense of smell and
excellent hearing; they prefer to stay out of the way. The
great exception is the short, fat, black-and-tan patterned
puff adder, *Bitis arietans*, which likes sunbathing on open
ground, relies on camouflage, and is all too easily trodden
on. Other poisonous snakes to watch out for are the
bright-green, tree-dwelling boomslang, *Dispholidus typus*
(77); the Cape cobra, *Naja nivea;* the rinkhals or spitting
cobra (78), *Hemachatus haemachatus;* the black mamba,
Dendroaspis polylepis; and green mamba, *Dendroaspis
angusticeps*. The largest snake in South Africa is the
common African python, *Python sebae* (10–16 feet long). It
is not poisonous, killing by squeezing or constriction.
Pythons are a protected species.

77

78

285

Index

Index/Acknowledgments

288

Author's Acknowledgments

Melissa Shales would like to thank the following people for their time, knowledge, and hospitality: Jack Barker, Paul Duncan, Mary Duncan, Carol Sykes, Stephen Fowler, and Steve Lunderstedt of SHL Tours for their help in compiling information; South African Airways, Orient Express Hotels; Sheraton Hotels; Three Cities Hotels; African Ethos, Budget Rent-a-Car, Small Exclusive Hotels of Southern Africa; Sun International, Holiday Inns; and the many tour guides and tourist offices throughout South Africa who went the extra mile to arrange tours and answer awkward queries.

Photographer's Acknowledgments

Clive Sawyer, photographer, would like to thank the following: Hans van den Berg, Durban Graham Stewart of Dumazulu fame; the Manager and staff of the Shamwari Game Reserve; Mr. and Mrs. Uys, Bloubergstrand, Cape Town; the manager and staff at the Drosdty Hotel, Graaff-Reinet

Publishers' Acknowledgments

The Automobile Association wishes to thank the following photographers and libraries for their assistance in the preparation of this book. ALLSPORT UK LTD 199a (S. Botterill); ART DIRECTORS & TRIP PHOTO LIBRARY 159; DE BEERS 140a, 140c, 141a, 141b; BRUCE COLEMAN COLLECTION 131 (J. Burton); MARY EVANS PICTURE LIBRARY 23, 26b, 27b, 28b, 30, 31, 38, 144, 160b, 207; JOHN HOWARD 72; HULTON GETTY 40a (Keystone), 40b, 42c; HUMAN AND ROUSSEAU (PTY) LTD 228b, 228c; KATZ PICTURES (D. Stewart Smith) front cover; THE MANSELL COLLECTION 27a, 28a, 28b, 29a, 29b, 33b, 34b, 35a, 35b, 36/7, 36a, 37, 38/9, 39, 140b, 205b; NATURAL HISTORY MUSEUM 24a, 25; NATURE PHOTOGRAPHERS LTD B. Burbidge 125, Baron Hugo Van Lawick 266 (2), 281 (65), (67), 283 (75); R. Daniel 266 (3), 267 (4), 269 (7), 270 (21), 272 (34) K. J. Carlson, 267 (5), H. Miles 269 (7), P. R. Sterry, 269 (9), 269 (11), (12), (15) (16), 271 (27), (32), 272 (34), 273(45), 274 (46), (48); R. Tidman, 269 (10); 270 (21), 272 (34), 272 (35), 280 (63); E. Jones, 269 (15), 283 (73);P. Craig-Cooper, 269 (13), (17), (18), 270 (25), 271 (26), (28), (29), (30), (31), (32), 272 (36), 273 (37), (38), (39), (41), (42), (43), (44), (45), 274 (48), (49), (52), (53), (54), 277 (55), (56), 279 (60), 280 (64), 281(66), (68), J. Karmali, 269 (19);J. Reynolds, 270 (21), 273 (40); M. Harris 272 (35); E. Jones, 277 (56), 283 (73); M. Gore, 283 (74); J. Sutherland, 284 (77); S. Bisserot, 284 (78), (79); NIC WHEELER cover silhouette; PICTURES COLOUR LIBRARY LTD 141, 160a, 161a, 221, 222b; REX FEATURES LTD 16b (PH Nils Jorgensen), 22a (I. McIlgorm), 41a (M. Peters), 41b 42a 43a (J. Kuus), 42b (S. Bilco), 43b (M. Peters), 44a (Facelly), 111 (J. Witt); MELISSA SHALES 30/1, 198, 212, 239; SOUTH AFRICAN AIRWAYS 242; SOUTH AFRICAN MUSEUM 132a; SPECTRUM COLOUR LIBRARY 74/5,100/1, 129, 136a, 136b, 161b, 209, 217, 219, 220, 222a, 223; ZEFA PICTURES LTD 224, 234a, 234b. The remaining photographs are held in the Association's own library (AA PHOTO LIBRARY) and were taken by CLIVE SAWYER with the exception of pages 15, 49, 153b, 156 which were taken by Malc Birkitt and the back cover (b) and pages 2, 4, 5a, 6, 11c, 16a, 32b, 45, 58, 59, 62, 66, 68, 69, 71, 73, 75, 80a, 80b, 81, 84, 93, 95b, 98, 108, 113, 114b, 115a, 115b, 120/1, 120a, 128, 151, 189, 200, 206, 215, 218a, 218b, 225, 227a, 227b, 231a, 231b, 232, 233, 237a, 241, 257, 270 (23), 274 (50), 279 (62), 284 (76) taken by Paul Kenward.

Contributors

Designer: Alan Gooch **Revision verifier:** Melissa Shales
Revision copy editors Rebecca Snelling, Sarah Hudson, Donna Dailey